Deleuze and Ricoeur

Disavowed Affinities and the Narrative Self

Declan Sheerin

continuum

Continuum International Publishing Group

The Tower Building
11 York Road
London SE1 7NX

80 Maiden Lane
Suite 704
New York NY 10038

www.continuumbooks.com

British Library Cataloguing-in-Publication Data
A catalogue record for this book is available from the British Library.

ISBN: PB: 978-1-4411-1690-1

Library of Congress Cataloging-in-Publication Data
Sheerin, Declan.
Deleuze and Ricoeur: disavowed affinities and the narrative self/Declan Sheerin.
   p. cm.
Includes bibliographical references and index.
ISBN-13: 978-1-4411-1690-1 (PB: alk. paper)
1. Deleuze, Gilles, 1925-1995. 2. Self
(Philosophy) 3. Ricoeur, Paul. I. Title.

B2430.D454S54 2009
126.092'2–dc22

2008056033

Typeset by Newgen Imaging Systems Pvt Ltd, Chennai, India
Printed and bound in Great Britain by the MPG Books Group

Deleuze and Ricoeur

Continuum Studies in Continental Philosophy
Series Editor: James Fieser, University of Tennessee at Martin, the United States

Continuum Studies in Continental Philosophy is a major monograph series from Continuum. The series features first-class scholarly research monographs across the field of Continental philosophy. Each work makes a major contribution to the field of philosophical research.

For Anna, Barbara and Rona

Contents

Preface

My intention in the work ahead is to place the narrative self in question. To do so is to situate it within a fundamental assumption: like any philosophical or psychological construction, it is a solution to a problem. This assumption inevitably invites the following question – 'To what problem are you the solution?' This question of course spawns a multitude of other questions, somewhat like the multiplying brooms of the sorcerer's apprentice. Soon we find the self confronted by demands from without and within – that it deliver answers, that it bear witness to itself – that it testify. Yet perhaps in its attempts to provide such testimony under cross-examination it must be accorded a privilege unheard of in our courts. It must be allowed to shed identity in the provision of its truth, to drop its capitalization and unhinge itself of the attestation of the utterer as soon as it delivers its testimony. 'Yes, that statement came from here a moment ago but it did not come from me – I changed the moment you asked me the question.' This is the self in question to which I devote this book – the self in lowercase.

For many years I have worked with children and their families as a psychiatrist and psychotherapist. Before that however, I worked in the psychiatry of adulthood where the core disorder upon which the chronic hospital wards were established was schizophrenia. It was 'first philosophy' in psychiatry. Beneath its multifarious and often alarming presentations a central feature was though to inhere – a disturbance of the sense of self. Somehow, the self of the schizophrenic had become fragmented, porous and permeable to the selves of others, its secret thoughts available to the mind-reading abilities of the neighbours and its bony vault a useless barrier to the infestation of other people's thoughts. Indeed, the antipsychotic medications used in those days were rather scurrilously referred to as 'ego-glue' by some practitioners, insofar as they stuck the self together again or built up the boundary between oneself and another. Nowadays we are less vulgar with our terminology, but the self remains a critical venture for psychiatrists, psychologists and psychotherapists.

In child mental health services, therapies teem with self-practices – self-awareness groups, self-esteem groups, self-actualization groups; one-week training programmes entitled 'Construct a New Self' allegedly offer practitioners the requisite skills in enabling the disoriented patient to become someone else.

This self that is so much part of the parlance of the mental health services has become over the years something of a fascination to me. We appear to speak of it with the presumption of knowing it, treat it with the presumption of understanding its inner processes and create it when required for those who wish for a new model of the self with the presumption that we have its essence in a manual for therapy. We seem to know this self without in fact knowing it at all. Mental health practitioners have repeatedly failed to ask themselves what is this self that we so precipitously operate upon; what is its form, its matter, its essence. Is it one, is it two, is it several or is it nothing? Is it genetically preformed or an epiphenomenon of cerebral action potentials, or is it simply a cultural product of language and the implantation of memes? Indeed, these health professionals might be astonished, even amused, were they to listen to a group of philosophers discuss the self. What is all the fuss, one of them might ask; I will tell you what the self is – it is me! And therein lies the problem.

I began to question the nature of the self several years ago when I read Charles Rycroft's *A Critical Dictionary of Psychoanalysis*, a little book of only 198 pages. Like Laplanche and Pontalis' *The Language of Psychoanalysis*, it is an introduction to psychoanalytic theory in dictionary form. The layout is simple: after a brief introduction, the body of the text begins with A for 'ABREACTION' as follows:

> ABREACTION The DISCHARGE of EMOTION attaching to a previously repressed experience (see REPRESSION). In the early days of psychoanalysis, abreaction was held to be in itself therapeutic, regardless of whether the patient understood the significance of the repressed experience. See Freud (1895). See INSIGHT.

The text ends with Z for 'ZOOPHILIA' as follows:

> ZOOPHILIA Bestiality. Excessive love of animals.

Almost all entries contain within them words in uppercase. Naturally, this book can be read linearly, simply by moving from ABREACTION to ABSTINENCE to ACTING OUT and so on through the alphabet, advancing as one does traditionally with a book. This is reading by convention, the standard narrative strategy that ensures every word in the book has been read. It is part of what Ricoeur refers to as the operatives of that opaque ideological process that, at its deepest level, integrates our shared world by way of 'symbolic systems immanent in action' and acts in this manner as the guarantor of identity in the face of factors that would sunder the organic relations between the whole and the parts of that identity.[1]

There are however alternative approaches to reading *A Critical Dictionary of Psychoanalysis* that would ensure the same coverage. For instance, one could read the first entry under every letter of the alphabet from A–Z (i.e. ABREAC-TION BAD CASTRATING DEAGGRESSIFICATION) and then return to A and read the second entry under each letter. You would then finish under the letter with the most entries, which is P. Again, we have ensured that the book has been read from cover to cover, but yet again we have entirely missed the point of a dictionary such as this, for this dictionary contains cross-references or transversals throughout the text. ABREACTION has four. ZOOPHILIA has none. Which of ABREACTION's cross-references do you take: DISCHARGE, EMOTION, REPRESSION or INSIGHT? If you cross-reference DISCHARGE you are provided with a further nine words in uppercase. If you follow each of these you will have accumulated a staggering eighty-nine cross-references, some of which return you to ABREACTION. Very soon you are truly lost in the book. If you read it this way there is no beginning and no end, for you can never be sure that you have covered ever single entry. No reading will be the same; each one rearranges the book in its unique connections with the reader. Reader and book become a burgeoning multiplicity and the reading becomes a 'rhizome'[2] – to use a Deleuzian term. The text divides up through the read-ing, becoming fragmented and re-fragmented. New syntactical series are taken up in the reading and the conscious or unconscious decisions to follow one uppercase rather than another each form further conjunctions with the reader, further roots and radicles. Were you to depict the course taken in this reading, it would not describe a two-dimensional line in a Euclidean space but a three-dimensional tangle, a Brownian movement in a curved Reimannian space.

After never quite finishing *A Critical Dictionary* I wondered why a good writer had not created a literary work in just such a manner, a novel about a world or a person presented as a Brownian dictionary in which entries were alphabetized and cross-referenced. Imagine the experience of reading such a book, of never knowing if everything you needed to know in order to understand a certain part of the book were present to mind. The reader is immersed in a circular process, whether controlled, random or chaotic, that falls under what might faithfully be termed a 'cybernetics of reading', where the elements of the sys-tem, in this case the narrative, 'are reciprocally contingent and influence each other's behaviour in a complex manner'.[3]

In fact, such a book exists – or partly. In *See Under: Love,*[4] David Grossman recounts the extraordinary tale of Momik, a child haunted by the Holocaust past of his parents. Grossman interrupts his linear narrative when he attempts to present 'the events in the life of a single individual', that of Kazik, an ancil-lary character. In chapter four entitled 'The Complete Encyclopaedia of Kazik's Life – First Edition', the narrator orders his entries regarding the life of Kazik according to the Hebrew alphabet. Furthermore, he invites the reader to 'feel free to read the encyclopaedia entries in any sequence he chooses, skipping forward and backward at will'. Might not the self be similarly structured, similarly read?

This is one of the central questions of this book. However, in addressing this through the philosophies of Gilles Deleuze and Paul Ricoeur I was tempted to present this book in dictionary or encyclopaedic format. It could be argued that it is insufficient to the task at hand to organize it solely as a linear argument. It appeared to need more than this, for otherwise one risked throwing the self out with the bad argument. I considered an additional structural model – and I was not without precedents from the protagonists themselves. Ricoeur, in *Oneself as Another*, invites us to enter his book 'at any point', given that each study (he emphasizes that these are not chapters) constitutes a total part. He does this to challenge 'the indecomposable simplicity of the cogito'. It is a strategy also employed by Deleuze and Guattari in *A Thousand Plateaus*, a book 'composed not of chapters but of "plateaus" . . . [which] . . . may be read independently of one another, except the conclusion which should be read at the end'.[5] This approach is also taken by at least one literary writer, J. G. Ballard in his book, *The Atrocity Exhibition*. In an author's note to the 2001 edition, Ballard suggests to his readers the following strategy:

> Rather than start at the beginning of each chapter, as in a conventional novel, simply turn the pages until a paragraph catches your eye. If the ideas or images seem interesting, scan the nearby paragraphs for anything that resonates in an intriguing way. Fairly soon, I hope, the fog will clear, and *the underlying narrative will reveal itself*.[6]

I decided however to resist the temptation of departing radically from a linear model of narrative – at least for the bulk of this book. Why? To a large degree I was influenced by Jacques Lacan's distinction between the four fundamental discourses; to forego the 'University Discourse' for something else would almost inevitably invite to the surface one of the other discourses, and given my professional background, this would more than likely be that of the 'Analyst' or even the 'Hysteric'.[7] To combine discourses would also have been problematic since there would be no basis for making any truth claims within a given discourse, given that what might be true in one philosophical position or discourse could well be false in the other. Besides, it would never be clear in any case from which discourse one was speaking.

Yet, a philosophical work should reflect a creative process if that creative process is its prey. Translating the Deleuzian world into a linear narrative of the self will only work under certain conditions and it will be at its most vulnerable when we attempt to place it within narrative itself. It is in the ontogenesis of the narrative self that one needs to be most alert to non-narrative, to non-linearity, to rhizomatic elements. If in creating transversal conjunctions that appear like flight paths out of the text we disrupt cogent argument, it is solely with a view to supporting that very argument by way of demonstrating that there is no other way of demonstrating a non-narrative underbelly to the narrative self, or a *Sea Under: The Self*.

Ricoeur was alert to this, asking what the nature of those events that subtend our self-narratives is when 'purged of every narrative connection?'.[8] Indeed, this event-world beneath the narrative self that eludes capture by language and is, in many respects, unnameable, may only reveal itself through narrative disruption or through a rhizomatic structure, somewhat like Kafka's *The Trial* or *The Castle*. To paraphrase J. G. Ballard – when the fog clears, the underlying unnameable will reveal itself.

Acknowledgements

My thanks go to Richard Kearney and Timothy Mooney.

List of Abbreviations

The following abbreviations refer to the key texts by Deleuze and Ricoeur cited in this work. Citations include page numbers in the English translation followed in italics by the page numbers of the corresponding passages of the original French edition.

Key Works by Paul Ricoeur

FM   *L'Homme faillible* (Paris: Aubier, 1960). Trans. Kelbley, C., *Fallible Man* (New York: Fordham University Press, 1986).

FP   *De l'interprétation. Essai sur Freud* (Paris: Seuil, 1965). Trans. Savage, D., *Freud and Philosophy: An Essay on Interpretation* (New Haven, CT and London: Yale University Press, 1970).

MHF   *La mémoire, l'histoire, l'oubli* (Paris: Seuil, 2000). Trans. Blamey, K. and Pellauer, D., *Memory, History, Forgetting* (London: University of Chicago Press, 2004).

OA   *Soi-même comme un autre* (Paris: Seuil, 1990). Trans. Blamey, K., *Oneself as Another* (Chicago and London: University of Chicago Press, 1992).

RM   *La métaphore vive* (Paris: Seuil, 1975). Trans. Czerny, R. with McLaughlin, K. and Costello, J., *The Rule of Metaphor* (Toronto and Buffalo, NY: University of Toronto Press, 1977).

TN1   *Temps et récit. Tome 1* (Paris: Seuil, 1983). Trans. McLaughlin, K. and Pellauer, D., *Time and Narrative, Vol. 1* (Chicago: University of Chicago Press, 1984).

TN2   *Temps et récit. Tome 2* (Paris: Seuil, 1984). Trans. McLaughlin, K. and Pellauer, D., *Time and Narrative, Vol. 2* (Chicago: University of Chicago Press, 1985).

TN3   *Temps et récit. Tome 3* (Paris: Seuil, 1985). Trans. Blamey, K. and Pellauer, D., *Time and Narrative, Vol. 3* (Chicago: University of Chicago Press, 1988).

Key Works by Gilles Deleuze

B   *Le Bergsonisme* (Paris: Presses Universitaires de France, 1966). Trans. Tomlinson, H. and Habberjam, B., *Bergsonism* (New York: Zone Books, 1991).

C1   *Cinema 1, L'image-mouvement* (Paris, Minuit, 1983). Trans. Tomlinson, H. and Habberjam, B., *Cinema 1: The Movement Image* (London: Continuum, 2005).

C2   *Cinema 2, L'image-temps* (Paris, Minuit, 1985). Trans. Tomlinson, H. and Galeta, R., *Cinema 2: The Time Image* (London: Continuum, 2005).

CC   *Critique et clinique* (Paris, Minuit, 1993). Trans. Smith, D. W. and Greco, M. A., *Essays Critical and Clinical* (London: Verso, 1998).

DG   *Dialogues* (Paris: Flammarion, 1977). With Claire Parnet. Trans. Tomlinson, H. and Habberjam, B., *Dialogues II* (London: Continuum, 2006).

DR   *Différence et répétition* (Paris: Presses Universitaires de France, 1968). Trans. Patton, P., *Difference and Repetition* (London: Continuum, 2004).

ES   *Spinoza et le problème de l'expression* (Paris, Minuit, 1968). Trans. Joughin, M., *Expressionism in Philosophy: Spinoza* (New York: Zone Books, 1992).

ID   *L'île déserte: Textes et entretiens 1953–1974* (Paris: Minuit, 2002). Trans. Taormina, M., ed. Lapoujade, D., *Desert Islands and Other Texts (1953–1974)* (Los Angeles: Semiotext(e), 2004).

KCP   *La philosophie critique de Kant*, 3rd edn (Paris: Presses Universitaires de France, 1963). Trans. Tomlinson, H. and Habberjam, B., *Kant's Critical Philosophy: The Doctrine of the Faculties* (London: Athlone, 1984).

LS   *Logique du sens* (Paris: Minuit, 1969). Trans. Lester, M. with Stivale, C., ed. Boundas, C. V., *The Logic of Sense* (London: Continuum, 2001).

NG   *Pourparlers* (Paris: Minuit, 1990). Trans. Joughin, M., *Negotiations* (New York: Columbia University Press, 1995).

NP   *Nietzsche et la philosophie* (Paris: Presses Universitaires de France, 1962). Trans. Tomlinson, H., *Nietzsche and Philosophy* (New York: Columbia University Press, 1983).

PS   *Proust et les signes*, 3rd edn (Paris: Presses Universitaires de France, 1976). Trans. Howard, R., *Proust and Signs* (London: Athlone Press, 2000).

Key Works by Gilles Deleuze and Félix Guattari

AO   *L'Anti-Oedipe* (Paris: Minuit, 1972). Trans. Hurley, R., Seem, M. and Lane, H., *Anti-Oedipus* (London: Continuum, 2004).

TP   *Capitalisme et schizophrenie Tome 2: Mille plateaux* (Paris: Éditions de Minuit, 1980). Trans. Massumi, B., *A Thousand Plateaus: Capitalism and Schizophrenia* (London and New York: Continuum, 2003).

WP   *Qu'est-ce que la philosophie?* (Paris: Minuit, 1991). Trans. Burchell, G. and Tomlinson, H., *What Is Philosophy?* (London: Verso, 1994).

Chapter 1

Introduction to an Enigma

[We] Westerners are accustomed to . . . confronting ourselves with a still coded meaning, often forgetting the poietic, rhythmic, melodic, more generally carnal requirements which ought to take part in the elaboration and the passing on of the sense. In order to talk to the other, to listen to the other, to hold a dialogue between us, we have to . . . find an artistic, musical . . . way of speaking or saying and of listening.[1]

Introduction

The self has had a long and distinguished career in philosophy. Undergoing many definitions and deformations, it has seen itself coronated by Descartes one day only to be peremptorily dethroned by Nietzsche the next; dumped in the poststructuralist bin when it was out of fashion in the sixties it was resurrected by the neurophilosophers as a physiochemical triumvirate a few years later.[2] Yet through it all the self has remained recalcitrant to revelation, resistant to all attempts to drag it out into the open and in the glare of the sun, strip it bare. Today, it remains an alluring enigma, demanding our attention and our analyses but always skilfully avoiding our grasp. This book sits in the long line of attempts, some more successful than others, some doomed to failure from the first address, to rise to the challenge of knowing the self at the least somewhat better than before and in a manner respectful of personhood.

We take as our starting point what we consider to be the acme of philosophies of the self, that is, Paul Ricoeur's hermeneutic philosophy of the narrative self (best explicated in his 1990 book, *Oneself as Another*) but we will subject it to critique, both from its own genetic origins (in the three-volume *Time and Narrative* where it is first posited) and from its progeny (specifically the late work of Ricoeur, *Memory, History, Forgetting*). Central to this work is one abiding question related to the ontological status of the narrative self, one to which Ricoeur made some exploratory addresses: 'what sort of being is the self?'[3] It is to the face of this question that we will return again and again in orientating the reader to the purpose of the arguments herein and to the justification of whatever materials are brought to these arguments thereafter.

In this chapter we set the scenography for this book by addressing three over-arching elements set in the form of questions: (1) Why draw Deleuze together with Ricoeur on the subject of the narrative self? (2) What possible or putative connectors are envisaged between the two? (3) What investigative strategies are available in moving from one world (Ricoeur's) to what appears to be an alien other world (Deleuze's)? Once this scenography has been set, we will provide a chapter outline of an itinerary which aims to reach the goal of the cohesion of a life (the self as such) through narrative and non-narrative means.

Why Deleuze and Ricoeur?

We need to explain to the reader, at a provisional and necessarily sketchy level, why we have made the seemingly bizarre decision to turn to the philosophy of Gilles Deleuze in attempting to answer the question of the being of the narrative self. Have the anticipated benefits of Deleuze to this enterprise been seriously recognized in advance or just vaguely intuited? It is a reasonable demand to set out from the beginning one's initial thoughts on this matter. The endeavour to bring Deleuze and Ricoeur close together carries with it all the dangers of inventing imaginary animals or mythological creatures; will we create a gryphon whose eagle's head will be blown away by the power of the beating heart of the lion? Or will we render a life-form sustainable, even if monstrous? In beginning this orientation, we offer some provisional considerations that prompted this engagement between Deleuze and Ricoeur. We hope to show that this is a marriage of two minds that admits impediments.

We are led forward by some initial questions addressed to that primal scene where the modern self is born and seemingly instantaneously divided. Did Kant (in his *1st* and *2nd Critiques*) have the last word on the structural nature of the self that would define its shape into the future? Or did Fichte and Schelling, having glimpsed an opening to the outside in Kant's *3rd Critique*? Is the self a self-affection yet almost impossible to grasp, as it is for Kant, or boundless and one with nature, as it is for Schelling? How far has this Kantian image of the self travelled from Descartes before it where the cogito lay housed in an impregnable lighthouse with doubt banished to the waves outside? Was it only superficially bloodied on the shards of broken glass that surround the shattered self of Nietzsche or is it truly in pieces today, no more shattered lighthouse than linguistic illusion, simulacrum of the internet age? Have we as selves become increasingly bits and pieces of figures from fairy tales, childhood comics and television stars, the juncture-point of a multitude of forces and intensities, of fashions and modern myths, of film stars and wizards, brand logos and saturated pop music? Or must we still convince ourselves, like Rousseau, that the self can never be tainted, that it is still, above all these things, irrefrangible?[4]

There is of course no easy answer to any of these questions. Popular opinion would draw us one way or the other, either towards the arrogant self of Descartes that is the pabulum of reality TV or towards the nihilistic remains of Nietzsche in which the postmodern novel gestates and seduces; there seems to be no middle path that does not immediately desiccate the lofty arrogance or the humble rubble of our outlying selves. Should we not just leave the self to itself, accept its existence in conundrum and get on with its meaning in ordinary language? We do after all know what we are talking about when we say, 'Let me tell you about myself' or 'I can do that myself' – the first is an invitation to recount a story, the second a statement of capability and a certification of a boundary that separates the one from the other. The self appears to have different meanings in different contexts. This is not at all surprising. The meanings of words change in context and over time – to be 'Irish' means something different in New York than in Dublin and it means something different now than in the 1920s.

Can this not be the same with the self? Why not just leave it be – its meaning is multifarious. Put another way, why attempt to re-problematize the self? Why draw Ricoeur and Deleuze into a plot to behead the self of itself (the threat to Ricoeur) or freeze a self already lost in the entropy of its own solution (the threat to Deleuze)? Is there anything more to say? The self is either a narrative (the Ricoeurian view), a story we tell about ourselves *or* it is a convenient and functional representation but nonetheless a mischievous one, orchestrating the suppression of the mutinous larval selves and condemning them to a life beneath the floorboards (the Deleuzian view). It cannot be both. Or can it? Does the self need a radical redefinition accommodated by an enlarged conceptualization of Aristotelian and perhaps even patriarchal *muthos* (that we will argue is present already in larval form in Ricoeur) in consort with the mature larvae of Deleuze? An epistemology and ontology of the self requires a greater clarity of the medium in which it is to be understood or in other words, a greater clarity of what the self(s) is and what its fundamental presuppositions are.

The lure in bringing Deleuze and Ricoeur to an approximation is certainly enticing; it presents not a dialogue between two theories but 'something quite different: an attempt to trace the contours of an *encounter* between two incompatible fields . . . What resonates in it, over and above the symbolic exchange, is the echo of a traumatic impact.'[5] Such an encounter is indeed enticing but is it important? We must wait to see – its importance will depend upon its outcome. However, enacting such an encounter is driven by what we maintain to be the importance of resurrecting the debate on the self (above and beyond the acquiescence to ordinary language arguments), particularly within the human sciences where treatments and interventions in the fields of psychology and psychiatry are based on an ill-determined concept of this selfsame self.

Can we manipulate something we simply pretend to know? Which contextual and temporal meaning of 'self' is under the scalpel? Psychoanalysis treats the fatally wounded Cartesian cogito[6]; constructivists and cognitive therapists treat the self as though it were a programmed object of a Socratic encounter requiring a therapy of dialectics,[7] while the systemic therapists treat it as an imaginary postmodern construction, an object of social hegemony and often patriarchal control. The presumptions in all these therapies are enormous and are seldom made explicit. Only the narrative therapists (in particular, Michael White and David Epston), who treat the self as an emplotted story open to retelling, have an explicit philosophical basis to their treatment approach. Yet the surprise is that the philosopher they turn to is not Ricoeur but Foucault.[8]

The confusion that surrounds the practices on the self (some of which are malpractices) and the manner in which theory constructs a self that then becomes the object of its own intervention are cause for some alarm; we need only look at some glossy advertisements for therapeutic training courses (the aforementioned 'Construct a New Self' programme) to grasp the potentially unethical position being taken towards *selfhood* insofar as the self is reduced to the status of a theoretically constructed and impersonal personhood, the now vulnerable object of therapeutic manipulative practices. This then is our avowed ethical position from which the call to explore between the self as narrative and the self as larval and dissolved emanates – this is where this narrative begins.

Fields for Potential and Possible Connectors

In a recent interview, Ricoeur was asked how he coped with his fame as a philosopher. He replied that he was comfortable with not being deemed the 'equal of Deleuze and Foucault, the two thinkers that . . . I have admired the most.'[9] Yet in spite of this remarkable acknowledgement Deleuze and Ricoeur are seldom mentioned in the same breath, even if they do on occasion refer to each other.[10] The importance of such cross-referencing to our philosophical work is worth noting: Ricoeur acknowledges the quality of Deleuze's analysis of Nietzsche and the differential forces at the heart of the human, and he utilizes Deleuze's reading of Bergson for an address to memory and history; Deleuze praises Ricoeur's notion of the 'aborted cogito' in relation to his own construction of the 'fractured "I"'.[11] Yet when we look in more detail the links between them seem to evaporate the moment one tries to accommodate a bolder engagement. There is too much outstanding dissimilarity; there are too many discrepancies. But are these really obstacles to what Ricoeur describes as a 'synthesis of the heterogeneous' or are they in fact essential elements of the 'demand for concordance and the admission of discordance'[12] that are part and parcel of a configuration, a plot?

To engender this encounter, an investigative and largely unpresumptuous style of approach will be crucial. We need to explain this. In order to extract a heterogeneous skeleton from seemingly dissimilar philosophies, a skeleton upon which hangs the different incarnations of Ricoeur's hermeneutical phenomenology and Deleuze's philosophy of pure difference, we must sift through the different styles, the different beliefs and emotional attachments, the panoply of dissertations on each writer by the hordes of academics (and those not so academic) who have sought to utilize their philosophies for their own ends and we must discard all of this and indeed such distracting yet alluring questions as: What difference separates these two great French philosophers? Why have they not been linked together in the way that Ricoeur has been with that other great philosopher of difference, Jacques Derrida?[13]

Instead we must reformulate the questions in a more appropriate manner, for example: What important subjects of discourse do they both address? How do they approach these and how well do they pose their problems? What conclusions do they arrive at? Can we gather their different discourses on particular topics (for instance, the self) and bring them to an approximation so that the results of such an approach will be either additive (Ricoeur and Deleuze = 'Ricoeur + Deleuze') or multiplicative (Ricoeur and Deleuze = 'RicoeurDeleuze')? Upon what similar terrains do their respective philosophical telescopes train their optics? This is not a difficult question to comprehend; yet it presents a substantially difficult problem to tackle.

This is because the surface differences between the two writers are very stark. For instance, Ricoeur acknowledges the importance of metaphor, while Deleuze exhorts us to 'kill metaphor'. Ricoeur's philosophy breathes through with his Christian beliefs, while Deleuze remains largely immured within an atheistic sensibility. Ricoeur is a reluctant philosopher of representation, while Deleuze undercuts this with his version of the Nietzschean philosophy of affirmation and difference. Yet beneath these variations there are sufficient and indeed sometimes startling similarities in key moments of their writings that demand a *rapprochement* or a narrative process that enables Ricoeur and Deleuze to become participants in the 'unstable structure of discordant concordance characteristic of the plot itself'.[14]

This book therefore presents an emplotment of Ricoeur and Deleuze where the bones of their respective philosophic skeletons cross over: the self, difference, the fault line, the virtual, memory, cinema and literature. At the heart of this work is the struggle to find a ground for the narrative self in what we might loosely term a 'Deleuzian world'; if this self needs to be deformed to get it there (by taking it through Spinoza and Bergson), then the Deleuzian world, we will argue, needs to face it with a somewhat altered mien, with the unlikely shadow of Aristotle falling upon it.

Both writers situate their philosophies of the self in their critiques of Kant; both argue for a non-identity in man, a fracture or *fêlure* in the soul (a disproportion for Ricoeur, a difference-in-itself for Deleuze). While Ricoeur presents only a tentative ontology of the narrative self in *Oneself as Another*, Deleuze presents a complete if questionable one in *Difference and Repetition*; yet it is within the mechanisms Deleuze proposes for his ontology that we will attempt to locate a correspondence between him and Ricoeur and a heretofore unexplored

Ricoeurian virtual. The project may or may not succeed insofar as the narrative self is challenged to retain coherence in the face of progressive dissolution. In this sense, the self is up for auction or execution, metaphorization or meta-morphosis, consolidation or dehiscence, rehabilitation or terminal desuetude. With these uncertainties in mind, we must add to the list of possible outcomes of the approximation of the self of Ricoeur with the selves of Deleuze: to 'Ricoeur + Deleuze' and 'RicoeurDeleuze' must be added the subtractive and the divisive – that the self will be less than it was or that it will be shattered either into small fragments or divided to nothing.

This problem of bringing the dissolved and narrative selves together is indeed fraught with difficulties and the anticipated divisiveness of the encounter is very real. We can look at this by analogy. Even if we can argue convincingly for a *descent* from the narrative self to a Deleuzian virtual (through Spinoza, Bergson and Aristotle) it could still be contended that no sustainable life-form for nar-rative identity could possibly emerge from the ruins of representation. In other words, like the impossible mythological gryphon we mentioned earlier, do we not face a similar problem with fusing the selves of Deleuze to Ricoeur – we have no metal helmet for the gryphon's head, no argument to contain the *ascent* from the larval selves of the virtual to the narrative self?

This is a problem we will attempt to overcome. By analogy, it is somewhat like creating a third organ for the gryphon which will siphon off the pressures of the lion's heart, divert them, sublimate them or manage them for the eagle's head. This third organ for the self, we will argue, is the imagination, a primary pro-ductive and poetic imagination at the heart of the narrative self and in the land of the larval selves that can function as this third organ. This will permit an ontogenesis of the narrative self, sprung from difference. Such an ontogenesis, defined as 'the history of the individual development of an organised being',[15] is not just a being but unavoidably a *being-with*. In developing this ontogenesis of the narrative self that bridges Deleuze and Ricoeur and corresponds to our posited ontology, we will argue for the need to work within the terrain of the post-psychoanalytic theories of attachment and love relationships based upon Freud's late studies of separation and loss. Here a constraint on narrative will emerge that will raise questions on what creative potential the narrative self really has.

If the narrative self still faces substantial ontogenetic constraints (at least as narrative) then we may justifiably need to return to what is pre-narrative in order to rehabilitate this self seemingly doomed to dead metaphors and ano-dyne stories. Perhaps we will discover that the problem is badly stated and the narrative self ill-conceived? Perhaps we must return to that fundamental problem at the origins of the narrative self – the *fêlure* in the soul. We will argue for the presence of an Aristotelian power or potency at this fracture in our being, but with its degree of abstraction transformed into something commen-surate with narrative or more precisely with the forces of pre-nominalism or pre-narrative, so that these forces become paradoxically non-narrative elements of the narrative self. In so doing, we will attempt to set up a bridge between the Alice-in-Wonderland language of *délire* and that of a narrative that is the end-point of a poetics of the self.

Investigative Strategies

We should not be disarmed by the seeming opposition between Deleuze and Ricoeur. Even if their approximation turns out to be subtractive or divisive it will not be so without a certain friction, a space in which sparks fly. But how do we foresee working within a space of difference, a space that includes a difference in the very language of Deleuze and Ricoeur? In principle, the explicit intention is to configure a narrative that gathers together parallel elements from both philosophers in addition to the differences between them, differences which can be *bridged* in a manner not radically different from either Ricoeur's synthesis of the heterogeneous or Deleuze's transversal thinking. In other words, what is different or divergent between the two is on the surface, in the language chosen to delineate their respective philosophies; what is convergent is in the depths, in the movements therein, in that which struggles in each philosophy to find expression. We might call this the 'Unthought' or the 'Unsaid'.

But how do we give voice to the 'Unthought', to that which does not speak? Should we invent a device that can explicate the point of chiasmic crossover of the narrative and the larval, a device that can withstand the pressures and yet speak? After all, we construct a bathyscaphe or bathyscope to investigate those regions of the ocean where humans cannot withstand the deforming pressures. What sort of bathyscopic procedure is available to us here? The problem for us is principally a Deleuzian one. His writings are notoriously difficult to understand insofar as his analyses of what is before representation, the ineffable and virtual, are often pitched high into the abstract and cast in the specialized languages of mathematics, systems theory and obscure biology. We do not have a 'Deleuze–Ricoeur Dictionary' where we can look up a word in Deleuzian and find its translation in Ricoeurian or vice-versa. How does one draw out and make accessible what is unsayable? We will employ two approaches as follows:

(1) The first is a structural one whereby we draw the narrative self into this empty space between the two languages; indeed, it is into this empty space that Ricoeur argues the narrative self must revert in order to truly change. It is the locus of the empty square (*la case vide*) of Lévi-Strauss.[16] If we accept that metaphor stands between narrative on the one hand and the unsayable on the other, then by drawing narrative into this empty space it will be by way of 'the rule of metaphor' (a rhetorical device objectionable to Deleuze)

that we translate the language of Deleuze into the language of Ricoeur. It is a means to an end – that of placing within the metaphoric-friendly world of Ricoeur the metaphoric-resistant world of Deleuze. We will return in more detail to this strategy in our chapters on Deleuze.

(2) Our second strategy emerges from the Deleuzian side and this is to place a speaker within the bathyscope, so to speak. Put another way, we will argue that in order to bring the narrative self into the terrain of discordance that characterizes the depths of narrative, specifically the Deleuzian depths, and to accommodate a 'dialogue' between the narrative and the larval or dissolved selves, we must place within this system a 'conceptual persona' that can speak from within. This will constitute the voice of another discourse, perhaps that of the becoming-hysteric or the hysteric-becoming-analyst. Our preliminary thinking in this respect comes from Deleuze and Guattari's *What Is Philosophy?* In the same manner that Nietzsche speaks his philosophy through particular personae (Zarathustra, the Antichrist, Dionysus) or Plato speaks his in part through Socrates, and in the use of these personae to map out a terrain of thought or a procedure for thinking in a certain way, we will argue that the legendary Mad/King Sweeney of Irish mythology functions precisely as such a conceptual persona for the narrative-dissolved self – or as a *narrative persona*. Invoking the crowned and anarchic Sweeney to speak from the immanence of the self is of course a gamble and he may well fail us; but if we have chosen well the results will, to put it crudely but aptly, speak for themselves.

By way of these two strategies (the poetic and the mythological–legendary) we wager that a translation from the virtual and the unsayable to narrative is both sanctioned and potentially exemplified. However, the reader must be forewarned for *as we move between investigations into the virtual and into the actual, both within and between chapters, a stylistic change is almost unavoidable*. It will be as though we moved from the Deleuzian to the Ricoeurian half of the imaginary dictionary and back again. We will attempt to keep the turbulence between these transitions to a minimum.

Towards the Cohesion of a Life: Chapter Outline

Our itinerary will be as follows. We will begin by situating the narrative self between two extremes – its dissolution into non-narrative on the one hand and its rigidification into dead narrative on the other (Chapter 2 titled 'Problematizing the Field of the Self'). These are the poles between which our dialectic will evolve, a dialectic that will define an in-between towards which it will return. Following this, we will briefly outline the self constructed by Descartes (and through to Kant in the following chapter), arguing that this lineage is central to both Deleuze and Ricoeur's varieties of the self. We take this ancestral self as both a problem (in that it has forever changed shape) and as a solution to a problem (the nature of which remains obscure). We will embellish this chapter with examples of how the self constructed in this ancestral lineage presents to us today still many of its problematic elements. In addition, we will posit the case for the legendary Mad/King Sweeney as paradigmatic exemplar of a dissolved/narrative self.

In Chapter 3 ('Critique on the Kantian Self') we will study the self in Kant but placed within the problematic field we set up in Chapter 2. The Kantian self is the cornerstone for the selves of Ricoeur and Deleuze (though it carries with it the baggage of its forebears) and the foundational self of our modern times. Does the self in Kant negotiate the polar difficulties more successfully than the Cartesian cogito or do these problems remain, perhaps in some clandestine form?

The construction of the narrative self as outlined by Ricoeur will be addressed in Chapter 4 ('The Narrative Self'). In explicating the narrative self we will be mindful of the question of style – the style of the self that is covered over in the address to narrative. If the narrative self is a story of sorts then it must be delivered in a style; yet this style may not be adequately captured by the term 'genre'; if this is so, what will be the components of style that encourage us not to forget 'the poietic, rhythmic, melodic [and] more generally carnal requirements'[17] of narrative identity that Irigaray entreats us to respect. Indeed, the lengthy quote by Irigaray that opened this chapter should be seen as a guiding criteriology for the style and manner by which we conduct this quest for the self. In every chapter we will retain this question, this warning of exegetical style.

Under the shadow of a new scenography, the narrative self of Ricoeur will come under attack from its own origins in *Time and Narrative* (Chapter 5 titled 'Questioning the Narrative Self through its Progenitors'). We will deal in detail with the historical development of this self from *Time and Narrative 1* (1983) through to *Oneself as Another* (1992). Among many questions we will raise regarding the integrity of the narrative self, a particular one will represent a sort of foundational problematic: does Ricoeur in spite of professing that narrative identity cannot be 'a stable and seamless identity'[18] nevertheless restrict the narrative-self to one narrative voice, presupposing in so doing a unity, a singularity to the self? Does he reduce difference to identity?

Between Chapters 5 and 7 we will insert an interlude (Chapter 6 titled 'Interlude') by way of connecting Ricoeur's narrative self to Deleuze's dissolved self through Proust. Such an interlude serves the purpose of inaugurating into this book a transversality between Deleuze and Ricoeur, an acknowledgement that some suturing of gaps may need to occur not just in a straight line (the traditional suture) but by purl and cross-stitch.

In Chapter 7 ('In the Land of the Larval Selves'), we will leave the narrative self (wounded but by no means enfeebled) and proceed to clarify the philosophic principles that underpin Deleuze's larval selves, selves borne on a sea of difference where non-narrative components proliferate. This is by no means an easy task as it requires a substantial orientation to his philosophy. Metaphor will be our bathyscope. Central to the argument of this chapter is the placing of Deleuze's philosophy in the line of descent from Schelling, and, therefore, from Kant's *3rd Critique*.

With the ground prepared, we can develop the sense of the self that dissolves into larvae in Deleuze's philosophy (Chapter 8 titled 'Dis/solving the Narrative Self'). Deleuze gives us a frog's spawn of a dissolved self, but where or what is the connection between these larval selves that populate an intensive space and actualized self-narratives? His description of the self is one that would better find representation in Virginia Woolf's *The Waves* than in *Oneself as Another*. This chapter will begin with a response to the question, 'Can the self be a work of art?' or can the 'poetic imagination' ('where all is permitted') usurp an 'ethical imagination' (an imagination 'answerable to the suffering and action of real human beings')[19] in the narrating of the self without endangering the pretensions of the narrative self to coherence? Can such an 'artified' self in a new scenography cohabit with a narrative identity, with an ipse-self, especially when Ricoeur claims that *The Waves* is not literary fiction? At the end of this chapter we will return to the case for Mad Sweeney as paradigmatic exemplar of just such a dissolved/narrative self, now cohabiting in the coherence of a life and functioning in this sense as a voice from within the virtual, as a narrative persona of the self at the between-point of the polar opposites of narrative rigidification and narrative 'dehiscence'.[20]

We will now approach our central concern, that is, the being/becoming of the narrative self, in two ways and in two separate chapters (Chapters 9 and 11): one as an ontological study of the being of the narrative self and the other as a speculative ontogenetic study, a study of the becoming of the self in the genesis of its actions. The former is one that moves from debt to excess, the latter seemingly from excess to debt.[21] In Chapter 9 ('From Debt to Excess') we will address the being of the narrative self by first interweaving Ricoeur and Deleuze with respect to the self and locating the significant sutures and common ground of their respective works on the self/selves. In so doing, we will attempt to achieve our principle goal, that is, to analyse the being of the narrative self and place it within an ontological and epistemological framework that is not antithetical to Deleuze. Essentially, we seek a coalescence of the narrative and the dissolved. While the sutures will be Bergsonian and Spinozist, the postulated ground that will rise up to meet the progressively denarrativized self will be Deleuzian but only insofar as a virtual Aristotle lies in the shadows.

Here we reach a turning point or a reversal of course – like an old steam engine on a turntable. Having travelled from Ricoeur to Deleuze and to first philosophy, we reverse course and move outwards, carrying with us the task of an ontogenesis of the self. Is this indeed a path from excess to debt or is it one from one excess to another? Chapter 10 ('Interzone') represents a moment of reflection, a pause in strategy in order to decide whether we return using the thread of Ariadne that has served us in descent or whether we should choose another thread. How does one map out an itinerary through a territory (an ontogenesis of the self) with only the destination in sight (the narrative self)? In this chapter we will argue for an approach that returns us to the questions raised in the Preface, that is, that we require some creative procedures if we are to develop a self (from Deleuze to Ricoeur) that has the requisite organs to survive and indeed supersede the constraints of narrative identity, and that meet the new requirements we will set down for it: a self founded on *Mitsein*, born into love, but carrying in its depths a fractured soul and a multiplicity at the heart of its narrative parts.

In Chapter 11 ('From Excess to Debt – Evolving Constraints on Narrative Productivity') we will develop these 'new requirements' according to the structure inaugurated in the preceding chapter. We will return to a question posed by Ricoeur himself when he requests a 'systematic investigation of autobiography and self-portraiture [to] verify this instability in principle of narrative identity'.[22] We will take on this challenge with an interrogation of Ricoeur's theoretical narrative self by a narrative self in real-time. This will inform us of some of the constraints the past imposes on self-narratives.

In Chapter 12 ('The Poetic Imagination within the Evolving Constraints of Narrative Productivity') we will introduce the deferred questioning of the narrative self though its own offspring, that is, through Ricoeur's *Memory, History, Forgetting*. This delay is justified because this late work raises further, evolving constraints on narrative identity, principal among them being the problem of our historicality and our mortality. This dual approach will help us in address the following questions: What 'imaginative variations'[23] are truly available to narrative-identity making? What constraints pertain? Where does narrative identity meet its limit point? Where must it connect with 'nonnarrative components in the formation of an acting subject'?[24] A helical structure in the medium of a linguistic multiplicity will be suggested as a structure for the virtual/actual self. In addition, the deployment of a structural element from Lévi-Strauss (the empty square) will act as a conjunction between Ricoeur and Deleuze in this regard, providing us with a self open to the synthesis of the heterogeneous by way of the productive imagination. Finally, we will ask if our being-with acts to unravel our liberties to narrate and to obstruct the poetic imagination. And if we have such liberties why then do we not take them? We will propose that our liberties are enchained by our very historicity and our being-in-the-balance between an against-death and a for-life.

Finally, in Chapter 13 ('Conclusion'), we will summarize the components for a narrative self that places Deleuze at the heart of Ricoeur and Ricoeur on the outside of the inside of Deleuze. Our final position will be in the form of a plea for non-narrative elements for the self and for the very restructuring of the scenography of the narrative self itself.

Chapter 2

Problematizing the Field of the Self

[It] was seldom that his feet would touch the ground because of the swiftness of his course . . . He halted not from that headlong course until he left neither plain, nor field, nor bare mountain, nor bog, nor thicket, nor marsh, nor hill, nor hollow . . . that he did not travel that day.[1]

Introduction

No structure of the self can emerge *de novo*. Like art movements, philosophies of the self develop either as embellishments of former theories, reactions to tradition in the form of new genres of thought or as negations of current creeds by way of an overturning or an inversion of structure. No new species of the self appears from the humus of what has gone before – only variations, reformulations, oppositions and rebellions. All have a history. None is completely original. All have a lineage – a parent, a grandparent, a rejected stepmother.

The overarching purpose of this chapter is to problematize the field of the narrative self. We need to place this narrative self (as Ricoeur describes it) within a lineage and trace it back to what may be described as its own original problematics. But why do this? Indeed, why do this now? Because we will argue that these are precisely the difficulties or problematics that continue today to haunt narrative identity in the form of the self. They have not gone away. They were the problems of Descartes and they remain the outlying problems for the narrative self of our contemporary times.

With this in mind, our strategy in this chapter will be twofold – and indeed we can anticipate a gap, a fault-line between these two strategic parts: (1) a modern contextual threat traced backwards and (2) an old conceptual ancestry traced forwards. First, we must place the modern narrative self between its own polar extremes in order to identify and analyse what precisely are the threats to its coherence at its very margins. This demarcates the liveable spectrum of cohesion for the self-as-narrative and forms the backdrop for the rest of the chapter. We will give examples of these outlying threats in order to demonstrate the real and not merely imagined or postulated dangers posed to a self constructed purely upon narrative elements. Then we must present a brief developmental lineage for the narrative self, that is, a philosophical ancestry and heritage before Kant. Descartes is the distant relative here (in a later chapter we will replay this lineage with respect to the dissolved self). Our purpose in this two-fold strategy is precisely to locate those polar threats, those ghostly problematics in the Cartesian cogito and to argue that they did not go away in Kant and indeed have still not gone away.

However, this particular procedure (the family tree and its ghosts) must ultimately be situated within a higher order of investigation (the work of later chapters), that is, of the nature of a 'genetic phenomenology' or a working back through the development of each writer's thinking on the subject of the self, by which we aim to find common origins and presuppositions and common pre-narrative structures that permit us to establish epistemological and ontological links between the two selves. We will argue that such linkages allow us to retain the ghosts but resist their alluring dangers. And we will introduce, in line with our above strategy that always pulls the self either to dehiscence or to rigidification, to the whirlpool or the rocks, a median line from where the narrative-becoming-dissolved self may speak and be represented.

Between Rigidification and Dehiscence: Context and Counter-context

In *Oneself as Another* Ricoeur sets up his analysis of the question of selfhood between the antipodean extremes of Descartes' *I exist thinking but surrounded by a perpetual crisis of the cogito that takes the form of doubt* and Nietzsche's *anticogito* – not the inverse of the Cartesian cogito but the waves of doubt themselves that destroy the very question to which 'the cogito was held to give an absolute answer'.[2] We use a similar strategy here. By placing the narrative self (not the cogito) between its own potential, even imagined antipodes, we obtain on the one hand the extreme of narrative that is the equivalent of dead metaphor (its relative in literature would be the 'tired and exhausted' in the form of popular fiction) and on the other the dissipation of narrative in the form of schizophrenic thought disorder or multiple and incompatible narratives each of which subverts the traditional structures of narrative (as in some of the writings of Beckett – which may also be termed the 'exhausted' but in another sense).[3] On the one hand, we have replicants; on the other, Alice in Wonderland.

Narrative identity sits precariously in the middle. The figure of Lewis Carroll's Alice presents the fragmentation of the self that she undergoes when the signifiers of ordinary language no longer cooperate in aiming towards a unitary identity. The problematics of stable identity that beset Alice we place in contradistinction with what is effectively her 'Other', in the form of a more

specifically contemporary concern regarding personal identity and the repli-
cation of it. These two problems (the contestation of personal identity in the
deployment of narrative and the uncertain identity of the identical) place the
rest of this book in the context of a dialectic between these two poles: Alice at
the extreme of excess where the self is dissolved into larval selves and in which
life would seem impossible to live, and the replicants at the extreme of a debt
which seems to make of the self a soulless simulation or a dead narrative (itself
the extreme of a dead metaphor). Deleuze's philosophy risks descending into
the claws of the former and Ricoeur's into those of the latter. And these are
not spurious concerns if we remember that Descartes' very preoccupation in
expurgating the cogito of doubt was to ward off these very replicants maraud-
ing outside his window[4] and it was Kant's to circumvent having 'as many-
coloured and various a self as are the representations of which I am conscious'.[5]
We will discuss this in more detail later.

Alice: Becoming-mad

Deleuze refers to a 'becoming-mad' (*devenir-fou*) in *Logic of Sense* in reference to
Alice, who he argues is at the intersection of two elements of Plato's fourfold
ontological classification of all existents: *peras* and *apeiron*, limit and the unlimited.[6] In *Alice in Wonderland* it is Alice who in becoming larger (limit) at the
same moment becomes larger than she was and smaller than she becomes
(unlimited). It is, notes Deleuze, in the 'essence of becoming to move and pull
in both directions at once: Alice does not grow without shrinking and vice
versa'.[7] It is this eluding of the present in a muddle of before and after that
confers the element of paradox and affirms 'both senses and directions at the
same time'. Deleuze describes this 'mad element' that subsists beneath the surface of things as an unlimited in language that if not held in check by the limit
of the referent would become a 'wild discourse incessantly sliding over the referent, without ever stopping'.[8] It is what Jean-Jacques Lecercle calls *délire*.[9]
Indeed, Deleuze questions whether there are not two languages, 'one designating the pauses and rests which receive the action of the Idea, the other expressing the movements or rebel becomings',[10] or in other words, a becoming-délire
of untamed meanings beneath a becoming-narrative. This paradoxical, concealed element of language, the unlimited becoming subsisting under the limit
of reference equips Alice's narrative identity with a becoming that has the
inherent 'capacity to elude the present' and to generate 'infinite identity'.[11]
Becoming larger, becoming smaller, jam tomorrow, jam yesterday but never jam
today, all these reversals have the same consequences: 'the contesting of Alice's
personal identity' through the unsheathing and unearthing of a language concealed.[12] Concealed in this language Alice is multiple, scattered and larval,
although on the surface she is, of course, still narratively Alice.

Parfit and Rachael: Becoming-replicant

If the outside of communicative language (délire or what Lacan refers to as *lalangue*[13]) places narrative identity in contestation (as Alice shows), then communicative language (in the form of a centripetal force that reduces polysemy to unitary reference and language to repetition) engenders a second danger: the evacuation of a unique, ipseity selfhood from personal identity. Ricoeur raises this with respect to that 'most formidable adversary' to his thesis of narrative identity, Derek Parfit. Briefly, Parfit's Reductionist thesis, laid out in *Reasons and Persons* (1986), attacks the very notion of 'a core of permanence'[14] that holds some sort of separate existence for the person, and he supplements this by a series of 'puzzling cases' that includes one in which an imaginary replicator machine makes an exact copy of someone's brain, that is, exact in its organization and in the 'sequence of states of affairs and events'.[15] If the original person dies does he or she nevertheless survive in the replica? Is the self replicable if we take from it a soul (or what Deleuze would refer to as the virtual) and give it instead a programme of narrative construction?

The questions raised by Parfit and that multiply the crisis to narrative selfhood which we are establishing are perhaps more dramatically revealed in Ridley Scott's 1982 science fiction masterpiece *Blade Runner*. Not only does this film pre-empt Parfit's arguments but it also dramatizes a further problematic regarding personal identity that Ricoeur does not raise in *Oneself as Another* but which will be of central importance to us – the question of the relationship of memory to the narrative self.[16] In *Blade Runner*, Rick Deckard is a weary, bounty hunter reluctantly dispatched by the state to search for four android 'replicants' that have escaped from enslaving conditions on an Off-World outer planet. These genetically engineered renegades were created with limited life spans so that their increasing adaptability and humanity would not become a threat to the human race, or rather, the 'humanism' of being human. Driven by fear, they return to Earth to locate their creator and force him to prolong their short lives.

The film's theme is the quest for immortality and the meaning of being human and having selfhood. It is a theme supplemented by an ever-present eye motif. Memories are implanted into replicants which then appear to be the true property of their bearers. In one central scene, Deckard interrogates Rachael, using a device that notes changes in the papillary response to questions, to discover whether she is a replicant or not. He asks her whether she remembers when she was a child the spider that lived outside her window with an orange body and green legs. He reminds her that she had watched it all summer long build a web and then one day she saw a big egg in it and it hatched. Yes, she remembers this, and the details come back to her – how hundreds of baby spiders hatched out of the egg and ate the mother spider. Deckard tells her that these are all implants, not her memories but those of her creator's niece.

A fleeting moment of incomprehension flickers across Rachael's face and Deckard feels sorry for her. He apologizes, telling her that he was only joking and that she is not of course a replicant – even though she is.

The problems raised in this dialogue are substantial: the ownership of memories, the otherness in their source and the empathy of the human for the replicant that believes she is human. The film echoes Descartes' human machines and poses questions beyond those raised by Parfit. For our purposes the questions that span the expanse between Alice and Rachael must be seen as an encasing problematic field within which the arguments of this book will unfold and towards which we will perpetually turn. We should note however that the thesis of narrative identity can neither dispatch Parfit's quasi-Buddhism nor be dispatched by it; either way there are two important points that we should take with us on our itinerary through the mire of self identity: (1) the apparent contradictory nature of imagination that on the one hand configures narrative identity in its difference and on the other leads to a crisis of selfhood through its imaginative variations on personal identity[17]; and (2) the legitimacy or illegitimacy of leaving the body behind – and the Earth for that matter – in constructing enterprises of alternative selfhood and non-selfhood.

Ancestry for the Self in a Problematic Field

The philosophical ancestry of the narrative and dissolved selves, beginning with Descartes, must be set against the polar backdrop articulated above, that is, we must place it in the shadow of these dual, overarching dilemmas (the paradox of infinite identity and the crisis of both embodied and disembodied selfhood).

It is worth noting that the concept of the self has for many centuries been inscribed with ocular metaphors; yet these metaphors carry sheathed within them a multitude of associations which confer upon the self an element of the unlimited and of omnipotence. Although the effects of symbolic and rhetorical mediation are unavoidable, we can try to indicate what precisely is the surplus value that ideology 'adds to the belief' and therefore to account for the effect of this distortion.[18] In the case of the eye-self it is a matter of removing mirrors and banishing smoke. This is our task. Only then can we articulate the naked fears and anxieties that have beset this self for centuries and that encouraged it to retreat to its lighthouse in the first place.

Black vapours: Questioning Descartes' cogito

The eye is the first circle; the horizon which it forms is the second; and throughout nature this primary figure is repeated without end.[19]

Our family tree begins when the gaze of the philosopher (that had seemed from Plato to Rousseau blessed with the unnatural gift of a clarity of reason) became unaccountably sullied. As David Levin puts it, this crystal reason was able to unearth all forms of knowledge clinically detached from the unpleasant deceptions of images and simulacra, dirty shadows, sophisms and cracked reflections. Throughout this long period the ego stood dazzling upon its inner stage, shining light upon the horizon and illuminating the darkest recesses of the known world. The 'I', this first circle, saw all. But when this 'I' was finally placed in the head of René Descartes it saw something much different, something very disturbing indeed. In his *Discourse* of 1637, Descartes compared his rationality with that of people 'he assumes to be unquestionably mad'.[20]

How could I deny that these hands and this body belong to me, unless perhaps I were to assimilate myself to those insane persons whose minds are so troubled and clouded by the black vapours of the bile.[21]

Affronted by these external horrors and threatened with the stain of black bile, Cartesian rationality had to define itself in terms of the inferior other. As Michel Foucault notes in *Madness and Civilization*, Reason is defined by the excluded Unreason and Rationality by the excluded Irrationality.[22] But Descartes' retreat from the eye to the cogito (drawing the attributes of the eye with him) was prompted by the view from his window of men passing by in the street, a view that forced him to wonder whether these men may not have been just 'hats and coats which can cover ghosts or dummies who move only by means of strings?'.[23] But this, as Levin notes, was an ambiguous retreat, for in turning away from madness (the black bile, the insane minds, the harbingers of the replicants of *Blade Runner*), Descartes moved into its proximity. Reason took on the features of the replicants – 'dispassionate, detached, affectively neutralized . . . radically dehumanised'.[24] The insulted eye now provides the substance of Reason and the cogito recapitulates the 'oculo'. This is the theatre of the cogito, the inner circle, the inside of the 'I'. God, though posterior to the cogito, will somehow ground the cogito in its certainty. But the cogito must remain forever surrounded by the rabble (the outside of the inside of the cogito) with their twisted minds and repugnant livers, a rabble it will always have to turn to in order to have acknowledged to itself its ownmost rationality. This is its own entrapment, the price it pays for the lustre of its limpidity.

Naked fears of madness and unreason beset the Cartesian self and it takes refuge in its pellucid retreat. Such fears generate an ideology that establishes a distortion. Are they the same fears that still threaten to upend narrative identity? How would we know? If we look into the cogito itself, into the glare and ask of it those familiar questions Ricoeur repeatedly poses to the self (Who is it that speaks or acts or tells his or her story – who is responsible for it?[25]), then this cogito will not be able to reply precisely because it has no history and therefore no story to tell.

But that should not deter us from asking them of Descartes himself. As a thought experiment we can imagine ourselves able to address him directly, as though from within the Cartesian theatre, just as an audience turns on the play-wright and interrogates his play. To do so results in carving a fissure in the cogito's omnipotence, a fissure that both Deleuze and Ricoeur will recognize as fundamental to their respective selves. The Cartesian cogito, through Descartes, is thus addressed. Who are you to tell a story devoid of doubt and suspicion? Who – if not you – is responsible for those replicants roaming around the streets in the first place? Who imagined them – if not you? Who begets the cogito, delivering it from the unthought and giving it definition? Or, if this self were a modern philosopher, we could ask more astringent questions. What 'pre-narrative elements' prefigure how you have defined yourself? Who lays out your specific plane of thought (with its tapestry of subjective presuppositions) in such a way that you are thought of or configured in this manner and this form?

Now of course this is unfair to Descartes – but our purpose in posing these questions is to make the simple distinction between the Cartesian cogito and the self that signs its name and answers to the question 'Who are you?'. This is because the cogito cannot do such a thing since it is born of lack. Ricoeur is clear on this: the subject of the Cartesian *cogito* is not – by any stretch of the imagination – a *self* but 'an exemplary ego' defined not at all by memory or the ability to give an account of oneself but by its very 'burst[ing] forth in the light-ning flash of an instant'.[26] This cogito was never an infant, a child or a grown up. There is no story to it.

But what then is lacking in this cogito besides its developmental history and the clash of clouds that produced the lightning flash? Precisely the polar extremes of the narrative self that we earlier identified. We have on the one hand the thought disorder of mad minds poisoned by black bile (Alice), and we have on the other the replicants carousing outside his window (Rachael). And the culprit in it all? Descartes' imagination. In other words, we can see that what threatened Descartes' sense of self were the products of his own fertile imagination (cast out upon a sea of doubt) that reached into the horizons of the self and did not like what it saw. Thus was born the Cogito, ill son of Poverty and Contrivance. Meanwhile banished to the wings lie mad Alice and the replicants. (We will see in the next chapter how Kant attempts to rehabi-litate the self by returning the imagination to the stage – and indeed briefly to the very centre of that stage.)

Now we should not assume that the narrative self is going to provide answers either to the questions posed above. How for instance could the narrative self answer the question, 'Who delivers you from the unthought?'. If the answer is 'I do', then this 'I' has become separated from the self, an impersonal magnet internal to the person but external to the self, coaxing it out of the unspoken and the indeclinable. And if the answer is 'Others', then we would need to ask why they would be required in the first place and why indeed they could or should be regarded as separate from the self. What is it about others that inveigles the narrative self to develop from the unthought? Is it love and desire, is it food and sex? Or is it something monumental, like language and the Law of the Father? The difficulty here is that no matter what we propose, an unbridgeable gap remains between these two worlds – that of the unthought which cannot speak and that of the becoming-self that the other lures to a narrative apotheosis. How do we begin to bridge the unbridgeable between the world of Alice and the world of Rachael? How do we think and speak between the two parts of a bilingual dictionary of these worlds, neither in one language nor the other but somehow in both? Ricoeur offers one tantalizing suggestion: we bridge the abyss between these worlds by 'the method of immanence characteristic of anti-poetics (*la poétique anti-référentielle*)'.[27]

Conceptual Personae and the Self

What we contend here is that something is being asked of that space in-between the cogito and the self, in-between lightning flash and narrative. In so contending, we ask into this empty space and in so asking we place an inhabitant there. This is the beginning of our antipoetics. We begin this manoeuvre now rather than after an exploration of the self in Kant, principally so that we may place ourselves in advance of that study in its outside, so to speak, or in the abyss that is outside the traditional hunting grounds of the self, the abyss from which, as we shall see, Kant will demur.

We can put our question another way. Is it possible to insert a set of dividers between the lightning flash and the narrative self and prise this gap open?[28] Deleuze and Guattari provide an answer of sorts in the form of a strategy in *What is Philosophy?*. Or rather, they attempt to populate this space with something pre-individual, something that is a sort of unseen dramaturgist who writes not in spoken language but perhaps in maths or geometry.[29] It is this vague and elusive pre-scriptwriter that 'says "I" and sets up the cogito'.[30] In the case of Descartes, Deleuze and Guattari name this will-o'-the-wisp 'the Idiot'; however it is not an individualized person as such but what they term a 'conceptual persona' that lies between the plane of pre-conceptual thought where the lightning flash is and concepts themselves where narrative is deployed – that is, between the virtual and the actual.

In effect, 'the Idiot' sets up Descartes' subjective predisposition to think in a particular way, perhaps even to think against the movements of thought blown by the winds of the imagination. The conceptual persona reveals a form of mannerism of thought or a geometry behind thought, like the 'anti-narrative' plane of dead imagination 'where action is reduced to the technical repetition of an algebraic formula (a, b, c, d)'[31] or to semicircular patterns[32] but with substantially more vigour in it than Beckett's undying imagination reveals.

The 'Idiot' beneath Descartes is this pre-conceptual thinker who wants the reassurance of truth at all costs (minus the powers of the poetic imagination). Now this concept of a pre-conceptual thinker may seem fanciful, but it is by no means idiotic. It does not always have a name according to Deleuze and Guattari, but it is that 'unseen dramaturgist' that operates before what is thought in order to fashion thought itself, whether through subjective and unacknowledged predispositions to think this way or that or through neuro-physiological systems that organize thought and its relationship to memory according to genotypic constraints, whether universal or particular. This 'Idiot', Deleuze and Guattari note, will return in a Russian context centuries later, a new idiot 'that has no wish for indubitable truths' but wants instead 'to turn the absurd into the highest power of thought – in other words, to create'.[33] This conceptual persona will colonize the works of Beckett (generating the thoughts of the absurd, isolated self in his trilogy), in Ionesco (where the absurd image of thought has spread to the social self in *Rhinoceros*) and in Adamov (where the 'Idiot' has established a complete aesthetic of the absurd and denounced 'the degenerated concepts, the dried-up abstractions that have usurped . . . the dead remnants of the old sacred names'[34]).

We have introduced this concept of the conceptual persona into our work to convey a point raised earlier. If we are to explore beneath the surface of concepts like the self, in the 'pre-individual, non-personal, and a-conceptual' intensive space from where concepts are established,[35] and if we understand concepts (including the self-concept) as our solutions to problems that exist as thought-events in the virtual, then we must 'break with the long habit of thought which forces us to consider the problematic as a subjective category of our knowledge'[36] and invent instead a conceptual persona like the Idiot or Zarathustra to capture these thought-events, a persona who 'lives intensely within the thinker and forces him to think'.[37] In other words, can we generate a conceptual persona for our becoming-narrative self?

The story of the self may be impossible without a narrative in which to situate it, a narrator to tell it and a reader to recreate it. However we are contending that this story is not only enacted by dramatis personae but preconceived by conceptual personae who themselves, 'must always be reconstituted by the reader'[38] alongside or underneath the (re)configuration of what Ricoeur refers to as 'the implied author'.[39] To account for the self without personae, to have it told as an unpopulated argument, to display it in transcendental dialectic or paint it in the metaphors of nature without characters (whatever virtual or real status they obtain) would be like performing the *Oresteia* without Agamemnon, Clytemnestra, Cassandra or Aegisthus on stage but only the chorus chanting and dancing in strophe and antistrophe. This would be the self as 'monstrous fact' and not 'fictitious parable'.[40] For our purposes, we need to hold these two ideas of the self in mind as we traverse the space between Deleuze and Ricoeur, that is, between the lightning flash and the narrative self. Indeed, it is in the glare of the Cartesian Idiot that we trace the developmental conceptualization of the self and we will argue towards the end of this tracing that this self, while sometimes monstrous fact and sometimes fictitious parable, cannot only be subjected to these two determinants but must become also and necessarily monstrous parable and fictitious fact to escape them.

Aporia of the Inscrutability of the Self

What determines our search for the truth of the self? What presuppositions do we lay out before us as we search for the self? If our conceptual persona is the Idiot we can approach the truth of the self in two different ways: via the early one (who wills that $2 + 2 = 4$) or the later Beckettsian one (who wills that $2 + 2 = 5$).[41] Does this not suggest to us that the self may correspond both to $2 + 2 = 4$ and to $2 + 2 = 5$ depending on what presuppositions, what maths of thought we adopt? In other words, the problem of knowing the truth of the self is that it is the self itself that investigates itself – somewhat like an internal enquiry of MI5 or the Stasi that nobody could rightfully trust. It seeks what it is determined to find and in so doing determines what it finds; therefore, it can hardly go wrong since its errors will necessarily define it. We must, therefore, gamble on a search that places the self outside the traditional hunting grounds of the Idiots.

In searching (Aristotelian *zētēsis*) for the self we will take our bearings from Aristotle's warning that 'those who search without first engaging with *aporiai* are like people who don't know where they need to be going'.[42] The self's elusiveness is its very definition, its aporetic nature (lightning flash/narrative helix) determining the search to be something like Alice's search for the object on the shelf in the Sheep's shop in *Through the Looking-Glass*. While the Sheep knits (a beautiful image of narrative synthesis),[43] the object Alice searches for 'is never where she looks, but always on the shelf above or below. It is an empty space lacking its own place, an unfixable element from which determinate elements arise'.[44] This search into an aporia-pocked landscape would also correspond to Carroll's other great search, that for the Snark.

> They sought it with thimbles, they sought it with care;
> They pursued it with forks and hope;
> They threatened its life with a railway-share;
> They charmed it with smiles and soap.[45]

This portmanteau Snark is sought along both a series of real bodies (thimbles, forks) and a series of virtual incorporeals (care, hope); it joins these two series from point to point but 'is never at any single point at a given moment'.[46] It is an aleatory point, a piece of non-sense that is nevertheless 'the differential element from which sense (the two series) derives'.[47] It is an inhabitant of *délire*, of Lacanian *lalangue*. By way of it the real and the virtual are drawn into a relationship via the movements of this empty space through *délire*. Were the Snark to be actualized it would surely be a terrifying creature – half-snake, half-shark.

Is the Self not also aleatory, a movement between the two series (virtual, actual) and not in-itself a thing but rather a differential element? (We will return to this in Chapter 10). Were the Self to be actualized, of what would its component parts comprise? The Sea and an Elf? A mischievous imaginary being that tells stories and bewitches us, and a Sea that is the interminable foldings of a multiplicity of self-molecules? Virginia Woolf's *The Waves* constitutes precisely this multiplicity of self-molecules that is in contrast to an Aristotelian-based narrative.[48]

But why is this important? Carroll explicates a problem that will besiege our search and prepare us for the capture of the uncapturable. Indeterminateness resides at the very core of the self. Where is the Snark? Where is the Self? Indeed, we may call this the aporia of the inscrutability of the self. Yet the nature of this inscrutability of the Self (and of the Snark and the object in the Sheep's shop) will determine, towards the end of this book, how the dissolved and the narrative selves can correspond and how sense can emerge between them through the movements of this putative empty space (and our putative Self). However, it cannot be dismissed that this search may in-itself be as much a constituting and minimal element in the structure of the Self as are the Sea (as chaos and virtuality) and the Elf (as the synthesizer of the heterogeneous).

In acknowledging an indeterminateness and an aporetics inherent in the self (so that we have to resort to unusual methods to try to capture it in our minds), we must be cautious of any critique that argues against a structure of the self (for instance the Kantian one) as incoherent – whether it is or not. The self, we can assume, will have incoherence written into it, an incoherence that is the face of its inscrutability and that multiplies in the same way that the aporias of time multiply once we try to articulate 'the lived experience of time in its immediacy'.[49] With this in mind, we will risk further incoherence by generating a narrative persona for the self that aims to add coherence to the competing demands of the narrative and the dissolved.

Sweeney: Philosophical Bathyscope

Does the tragic king, Suibne Geilt (Mad Sweeney), of the medieval Irish text *Buile Suibhne* (The Frenzy of Sweeney), not conjure up a fitting Snark for the Self?[50] Sweeney, rendered insane by the horrific sights of battle and turned into a bird by the curse of the cleric Ronan, wanders the countryside by way of superhuman leapings from valley to valley, condemned to spend his days eating watercress and his nights sleeping in yew trees.[51] But in this mad state which he describes as feeling like the multiplicity of points on a many-tined antler – 'If I were on each little point/there would be a pointlet on every point'[52] – he composes the most beautiful poetry as testament to his suffering. Ronan's curse is in direct response to Sweeney's throwing of the cleric's psalter into the lake, an explicit rejection of narrative and the word.[53] As Joseph Nagy correctly notes, Sweeney's 'frenzy' (*buile*) is both a becoming-*geilt* and a becoming-poet – a force that 'dislodge[s] the occupants of the roles of "subject" and "object" in the poetic utterance'.[54] Sweeney's tragedy is the loss of self-identity in the metamorphosis to a bird; self-identity is forsaken for the freedom of becoming and the pleasures of 'the warbling of the blackbirds' in contrast to 'the merry prattle that men and women make'.[55] In the end Sweeney returns to himself, but not as a revocation of the same Sweeney, the king of Dal Arie, but as a profound poet (exquisitely balanced between narrative and non-narrative) emerging from the wilderness to confide in the other and share respective life stories.[56] Sweeney represents the disintegration of the narrative or 'molar' self and the line of flight of the larval or 'molecular' selves (the points on the antlers) in a becoming-mad. The narrative self in *Buile Suibhne* thus emerges from the virtual (the wilderness, the unconscious, Schelling's Absolute) rather than being drawn from it by a specified synthesizer of the heterogeneous. Yet in the story of Sweeney is not something drawn out in reverse, at least insofar as Ronan resurrects the unlimited, elevating it to the surface in the maddening of Sweeney?[57] And is not Sweeney's final goal that of telling his story in the face of death while remaining in the clasp of délire?

By inserting Mad Sweeney in the space of the empty square (the in-between) we bridge the gap between Alice and the replicants, and he becomes the differential element that forges sense between the lightning flash and narrative. This is not a rhetorical manoeuvre. The Sweeney persona meets the requirements both of the narrative and the dissolved selves, and presents us with an artistic and mythological figure that we later argue fits the criteria for a 'conceptual persona' of the self that can speak from within, that can be a voice from the Alice-in-Wonderland world where selves take shape. It is a speaking from délire as such, a theft of language. In addition to this role, Mad Sweeney contests the very nature of narrative identity (and indeed gender identity[58]) while at the same time deploying it. It is our task to persuade that Sweeney is our story, our Snark for the Self. Put more simply, can we call upon mythological Sweeney to represent to us the twin series (virtual/actual) of the self in the same manner that other great mythological figures, like Eros and Thanatos, have been summoned?

Chapter 3

Critique on the Kantian Self

[Only because] . . . I can comprehend the variety of my representations in one conscious-ness, do I call them my representations, for otherwise I would have as many-coloured and various a self as are the representations of which I am conscious.[1]

Introduction

In the last chapter we placed the narrative self within a problematic field and showed how the outlying problems of that field were precisely those which threatened Descartes' sense of self and precipitated the birth of a powerful, all-seeing, transcendental, timeless, universal and 'arrogant' self or ego. We also argued that these outliers, though banished from the cogito, need now to become formative elements of the self, need to be reclaimed. But how? How does one draw in such danger without dissipation or rigidification of the self, without becoming-mad as Alice or becoming-replicant as Rachael? The latter, product of the imagination, is something that can be countered by incorporat-ing the imagination into the self (without disguising its machinations). The former, the becoming-mad, is something Kant hopes to expunge in his tran-scendental dialectic. But does he achieve these goals?

The purpose of this chapter is to argue that Kant's attempt to counter both threats, while substantially more successful than Descartes', ultimately fails. But he does leave us both with a divided self, the forerunner supreme of the selves of Deleuze and Ricoeur, and with the possibility of a maddening of the self, though disavowed.

We will limit our Kantian study primarily to his construction of the self in *The Critique of Pure Reason*. Central to the *1st Critique* is what Solomon describes as 'an enormous expansion in the concept of the self, its scope, its power, and richness'.[2] This self becomes an active agent, imposing an immutable common order on nature rather than passively responding to it. But what precisely is this Kantian 'self'? What structure of the self is asserted by Kant and in what manner does the Kantian self set the foundation stone for the narrative self of Ricoeur and the dissolved selves of Deleuze? This question is important given that both

Ricoeur and Deleuze will take Kant as their foundational point of departure.[3] With this in mind, we will extract from the *1st Critique* Kant's presentation of the self, its structure and its pretensions, its determinations and presuppositions. We will also address the question of the productive imagination, so central to Ricoeur's 'synthesis of the heterogeneous' in the construction of narrative. Kant's retreat from an earlier version of the productive imagination, we will argue, vouchsafes a self than remains monochrome rather than 'many-coloured'. Also, we will show how Kant, in moving away from the Cartesian cogito inadvertently returns to a self similar to that of Rousseau and in so doing, the phenomenal world becomes unknowable and the status of the replicants and the real undecidable.

Pretensions of the Kantian Self

Although it is with Descartes that 'the modern philosophical obsession with the self as the locus and arbiter of knowledge' begins,[4] it is through Kant that the self becomes not just a 'focus of attention but the entire subject-matter of philosophy' itself.[5] As Solomon puts it:

> It is with Kant that . . . the self . . . creates the world, and the reflecting self does not just know itself, but in knowing itself knows all selves, and the structure of any and every possible self. The ramifications of this view constitute the transcendental pretence. The underlying presumption is that in all essential matters everyone, everywhere, is the same.[6]

Such presumptions rule out alternative structures of the self or indeed the very mode of existence of the self. The transcendental pretence instead provides the *a priori* assertion that the structures of the mind, of culture and personality 'are in some sense necessary and universal for all humankind, perhaps even "for all rational creatures"'.[7]

Yet the concept of the self that Kant presents in his *1st Critique* is 'notoriously difficult and obscure'.[8] For Kant, the mind transforms the raw data given by our senses through a mediating synthesis by the imagination of this manifold and through the judgements of the understanding by way of its concepts; in this manner what is given to us by sensibility can be thought through the understanding. However, this unity of experience must imply, for Kant, a unity of the self and a common sense for without this there could be no knowledge of experience. But how is this self aware of itself or self-aware? Is there not a contradiction in the self becoming an object of itself as subject, or as Michael Kelly notes, is not the subject as object 'no subject at all'?[9]

To resolve this, Kant divides the self in two, producing an empirical and a transcendental self, one knowable in part, the other barely at all. In this way the faculties are divided in both structure and function; for instance, images are formed as 'a product of the empirical faculty of the productive imagination', while the schemas of sensible concepts (for instance, the ideal triangle that 'can exist nowhere else than in thought') are 'a product . . . of the pure imagination a priori, whereby and according to which images first become possible'.[10] The schemas are therefore 'transcendental products of the imagination'.[11] A further division occurs between pure reason and the understanding insofar as pure reason 'leaves to the understanding everything that immediately relates to the object of intuition or rather their synthesis in imagination'.[12] Thus, the 'objective employment of the pure concepts of reason' or *transcendental ideas* 'is always transcendental, while that of the pure concepts of the understanding must, according to their nature, be always immanent, inasmuch as they are limited to possible experience'.[13]

Within this division of the faculties, the self forms at the edge of the empirical and the transcendental as a two-sided structure, one face to sensibility and one face to transcendental reason. But how does knowledge of this self occur, given its seemingly precarious position and its structural lacerations? For Kant, knowledge of 'myself' is not by way of 'being conscious of myself as thinking, but only when I am conscious of the intuition of myself as determined in relation to the function of thought'.[14] Now, given that time for Kant is the formal condition of inner sense ('time, the form of inner intuition, serves as basis'[15]) and therefore demands a synthesis or a 'running thought . . . a holding together'[16] of the given manifold, then 'we intuit ourselves only insofar as we are affected by ourselves . . . [and] we know the self as determined by the act of synthesis, not as determining in the act of synthesis'.[17] Kant is very clear that I 'cannot present myself as an object'.[18] The object that can be presented is not therefore consciousness of the determining self but only 'that of the determinable self, that is, of my internal intuition (insofar as the manifold contained in it can be connected comfortably with the general condition of the unity of apperception in thought)'.[19]

Thus, the idea that consciousness is in time is the idea of the self as determined and the idea of time being in consciousness is the idea of the self as determining; each captures from a different direction the same idea of 'self-affection'. A further point to note here is that for Kant this self that constitutes 'the unity of apperception' is '*singular* and cannot be resolved into a plurality of subjects'.[20] This is the self of pure apperception, the *I think* of which 'nothing more is represented than a transcendental subject of thought = x, which is known only by means of the thoughts that are its predicates'.[21] It is unknowable, 'in-itself' and despite being intuited through time is not itself 'located in time'.[22] This Kantian pure self is to be understood 'in a problematical sense, not in so far as it contains a perception of an existence . . . but in regard to its mere possibility'.[23] On the other hand, the empirical self is knowable and located in time.[24]

Thus, Kant distinguishes between the 'empirical self' that contains individualized data and the 'transcendental self' that operates in the medium of the *a priori* principles. But how can these two selves interact in such radically differing domains of being?[25] Henry Allison has noted that the self of the *1st Critique* cannot be meaningfully reconstructed because it contains an internally incoherent position that leads us to the 'absurd doctrine that the empirical self both *appears to* and *is an appearance of* the "real," supersensible self'[26] – the absurdity emerging from identifying an atemporal, noumenal self with a temporally determined phenomenal self.[27] This atemporality of the noumenal self creates profound difficulties. For instance, in the 'Transcendental Dialectic', Kant dismantles the notion of Descartes' self as a substantial entity and argues that the transcendental self could not be the object of any possible experience. The self 'as source of the categories . . . cannot be known by the categories'.[28] But this leads to several intriguing questions, as Solomon notes:

> We have noted Kant's conscientious ambiguity about the self, which leaves open such questions as 'who has one?' and 'how many might there be?' But because these are questions that fall under the categories, there can be no appropriate response in the case of the ego itself. So to the question 'who has the self?' we can only answer 'everyone', without being able to say what would seem obvious – that everyone has *one*.[29]

Whether this is as obvious as Solomon suggests is open to question. Nevertheless, this uncertain status of the transcendental self (that it cannot be the object of any possible experience, that it is atemporal and that its relationship is with 'consciousness in general' rather than my consciousness) confers upon each possessor of a self a *cosmic potential* to being, inasmuch as their self is ultimately not theirs but is everything and everyone's and through all time. If one foundational component of the self – indeed, if the 'substratum' that underlies the thinking 'I'[30] – is outside time, how then can the self come into being, begin, persist through time and finally expire? Have we only recourse to Heidegger's Dasein to address this problem? For if that is so, then the narrative self (which we will argue later is located somewhere between Heideggerian historicity and within-time-ness)[31] must then be understood as essentially inauthentic, as second hand and inferior, indeed as suffering 'a progressive loss of ontological density' to the degree that it gains increasingly an epistemological determination.[32]

In Kant's *2nd Critique* there is a change of emphasis, or as Deleuze puts it, a change of chairmanship among the three faculties of reason, the understanding and imagination ('in each Critique understanding, reason and imagination enter into various relationships under the chairmanship of one of these faculties.'[33]) Thus, to be human in the practical sense is to act alongside knowing, to be agents as well as observers and thinkers. In this sense, we can change the world in addition to categorizing sensory experience. In the *2nd Critique*,

the phenomenon (as it is constituted and experienced by us) and the nou-
menon (the world as it is 'in itself') are brought together in the self as an acting
self, as a 'self in itself'. However, what the relationship between the transcendental ego, the acting self and the empirical self is remains entirely unclear.
Nevertheless, it is essential for Kant that the human is an agent of action and
that what defines our actions is morality as a function of reason and therefore
founded upon a set of universal laws that define duty. It is from this acting
self that Ricoeur will take his point of departure when constructing the narrative self.

Divided Self Still Surrounded by the Mad and the Replicant

Solomon acknowledges the indebtedness of Kant to Rousseau. Rousseau's
'inner self' becomes Kant's noumenal self, both hoisted upon a transcendental
pretence that can circumvent 'the conventions and interactions of society' in
order to present 'a spectacularly self-centred image of the moral world'.[34] In
essence, Kant removes the audience from the theatre of the self. The inner
stage is now a self-encased, self-cleaning enclosure; a script lies on the floor but
there are no performers, no author, no stage direction. Only those in the gods
know what is going on. Outside, the audience queue, they bang on the door,
they defile the posters on the walls, they shout imprecations at the gatekeeper
and they hurl abuse at the imagined goings-on inside – but all to no avail. For
they have become the unknowable (replicant? real?) who can never again corrupt
the transcendental ego or drag it through the mire. The imagination appears
to have been contained, the threat of the absurd diverted. This is the theatre of
$1 + 1 + 1 = 1$ (i.e. transcendental + noumenal + empirical = one) based on the
mathematics of $2 + 2 = 4$.

   But is this in fact the case? What has happened to Alice and the biliously
mad? Is there not something of the $2 + 2 = 5$ in Kant's self, something of a seep-
age of the absurd? Despite his vouchsafing the self's unity against the impossibility of a consciousness that 'would be fragmented and would not belong to my
single consciousness',[35] the division of the self into empirical and transcendental forms represents a hierarchical fragmentation nonetheless – even if it has
been collapsed into a nesting of consciousnesses. Indeed, Ricoeur refers to this
division of the self into transcendental/noumenal/empirical as a 'shattering of
the problematic of the subject'.[36] This hardly achieves the determined avoidance of the many-coloured and varied self that Kant sought. However, this man-
ufacture of an unknowable 'out-there' (real? imaginary?) and an irrefrangible
'in-here' (nested and disguised polychromes of the self) are precariously stabi-
lized within the Kantian system by one central buttress that prevents everything
from collapsing in upon itself. It is the faculty of the imagination, or at least,

Kant's second and more effete version, a version contained. In the second edition of *Critique of Pure Reason* the synthesis of the imagination is described as follows:

> An act of spontaneity, which is determinative, and not, like sense, merely determinable, and which is consequently able to determine sense a priori . . . and its synthesis of intuitions according to the categories must be the transcendental synthesis of the imagination.[37]

And a productive imagination is distinguished from a merely reproductive one with the role of the former abiding in the 'unity of apperception'.[38] This is an impressive role but it is not what it was in the *1st Critique*, where we are 'in possession of pure imagination, which is a fundamental capacity of the human soul and which lies *a priori* at the basis of all knowledge'.[39] As Kearney notes in his summary of Heidegger's analysis of the Kantian imagination in *Kant and the Problem of Metaphysics*, this role given to the imagination in the *1st Critique* is as a 'formative centre', a centre '*presupposed* by sensation and understanding rather than as a derived intermediary function which comes *after* them'.[40] But with sensibility and understanding rooted in the transcendental imagination, does not imagination here 'enjoy a certain creative autonomy'[41] or have the potential to run away with itself, to overwhelm the categories and their contents and produce the fantastical? And if our 'pure intuition of time . . . is now identified with pure imagination'[42] as Heidegger reads Kant, then does not our permanence through time depend upon that which synthesizes us as abiding presence – productive imagination? In other words, the transcendental ego only secures its sense of oneness 'insofar as the imagination first proposes an horizon of identity and permanence'.[43] But do we not here depend upon a good imagination, a productive imagination with common sense or with the sense to work with the other faculties to a common accord, that is, to will for the monochrome and the single against the 'many-coloured and various'? What would the Kantian self of the *1st Critique* be with an autonomous imagination at its formative centre bent on the absurd, the fantastical and the evil?

Let us summarize the problems we appear to have identified in Kant's construction of the self. To the empirical self that is knowable he adds as a necessary condition the transcendental self that is unknowable and an outside world of things-in-themselves, of other people, that is also and terrifyingly unknowable. ('I cannot obtain the least representation of a thinking being by means of external experience.'[44]) How do these three delimitations or zones of consciousness communicate or relate to one another and form a sense of self – and across what dimensions of time? Are we born to this division or is it achieved as a mark of a *rites de passage*? Is the Other not indeed the necessary condition of the self first and foremost? If so, then somehow we come paradoxically to know ourselves through the unknowable.

The distinction or cleavage that Kant generates between the empirical and the transcendental or pure self marks a crisis point in self-identity. Now even though this hierarchical construction of Kant may have collapsed over time (as philosophy and psychology coalesced and progressed in their understanding of the self), yet still it is the faculties of judgement and imagination that become the principle players in the narrative self-integument that Ricoeur weaves, an integument that we will argue is wrapped around an abyssal, formative Deleuzian core whose Kantian faculties, especially that of the imagination, undergo a series of crazy disjunctions. Indeed, it is the faculty of the imagination that will interest us most, particularly Kant's first edition of it that Heidegger believed led Kant 'to the abyss' or to the looking-glass world of an unlimited Alice where for a moment Kant sensed that 2 + 2 might begin to equal more than just 4. The transcendental power of this imagination 'frightened' him, claims Heidegger. Staring into the abyss he saw 'the unknown . . . [and] . . . had to shrink back'.[45]

It will be our determination to return to this abyss, to this unknown, the terrain of Deleuze but by way of signposts erected by Ricoeur. The form in which we can draw from this abyss is however uncertain. A hermeneutics or a poetics is proposed – even a poetic hermeneutics.

Chapter 4

The Narrative Self

The thought experiments we conduct in the great laboratory of the imaginary are also explorations in the realm of good and evil.[1]

Introduction

Our search for the self(s) is somewhat clarified by the removal of the smoke and mirrors that made the self of old something like the Wizard of Oz. Without the lighthouse glare that blanched the diseases of the imagination in Descartes' cogito and without the pretence of the Kantian model (Is the pretence simply that the cracks are so obvious we don't see them?) we are left with an uncharted desert beyond the old eye-self, a gloom that nevertheless belongs to the old self, though cut off, disowned, forgotten, unnourished and unharvested. This is what Ricoeur is referring to when he says:

> I must recover something which has first been lost; I make 'proper to me' what has ceased being mine. I make 'mine' what I am separated from by space or time, by distraction or 'diversion', or because of some culpable 'forgetfulness'. I am lost, 'led astray' among objects and separated from the centre of my existence . . . Whatever the secret of this 'diaspora', of this separation, it signifies that I do not at first possess what I am. The truth that Fichte called the thetic judgement posits itself *in a desert wherein I am absent to myself.*[2]

Without the certainties of the eye-self, we are suddenly confronted by a whole series of questions about the nature of a self laid out on a desert that extends far beyond the self-affection that Kant established. Bearing this in mind, we will attempt to establish the following key goals in this brief chapter. First, we must generate an orienting series of questions that can act as a 'culture medium' for our forthcoming analyses of the narrative and the dissolved selves; in other words, our attempt here is to cultivate questions from the problematic field that we set up in the last two chapters. Once we have established this then, secondly, we can engage in a full description of the developmental trajectory of Ricoeur's narrative self as it materializes out of the shattered though disavowed dogmatism of the Kantian self, stands on its own two feet by the end of *Time and Narrative, Vol. 3* and proudly walks out of *Oneself as Another*. We will note its origins in a response to John Locke, its roots in the Kantian faculties of judgement and imagination, its relationship with the Freudian ego and its fundamentally embodied nature in the form of action and work. Finally, informed by our culture medium of questioning, we will identify the key problematical elements that emerge in Ricoeur's narrative self and that will need a fuller exploration in the following chapter.

Oneself as Another or X^Nselves as Myself

If the self is not one, then is it two, is it many, is it multiple? Is it integrated or fragmentary, organized hierarchically or horizontally, laid out on a plane with its components moving through time in parallel or at cross-purposes?[3] Do parts of the self (for instance, old long-untold stories and forgotten memories) exist in the time of Achronos or suspended time or in the extended time of Aion, while other parts or fragments (i.e. those lively and fresh accounts we are in the midst of telling) exist in Chronos, in clock and calendar time, in the present? And what of our as-yet-untold stories? Are they not also part of the self, given that Augustinian time (a time popular with both Ricoeur and Deleuze) includes a present of the future? Is this the present of the self-to-come in another virtuality? And if we remember that Chronos is 'the first bridge constructed by historical practice between lived time and universal time', we must then acknowledge that the narrative self may also exist within a much greater time – 'mythic time'.[4] Mythic time, the time of Sweeney, takes us back to before the division between the universal and the epic on the one hand, and the human and the historical on the other, providing us with an overall 'scansion of time' that orders in terms of one another the differing cycles of duration (celestial, biological and social rhythms).[5] Might we hypothesize that it is in mythic time that the fragments of the self (each to their own duration) are provided with a grounding, a commonality that melts them together into a sense of oneness without unity? And finally, can we find a bridge between Ricoeur's 'mythic time' and Deleuze's 'complicated time', a term borrowed from the Neoplatonists?[6]

These questions are all linked around a more central and fundamental problem which may be stated as follows: is the self a closed or an open system, both in terms of its temporality (oneself in lived time/oneself in cosmic time/oneself in mythic time) and of its spatiality (oneself as myself/oneself as another/oneself as many others/x^Nselves as myself) or something 'between the closed and the open'?[7] These questions should be seen as emerging from the backdrop we have already described, that is, the problematic on the spectrum that extends from Alice to Rachael.

The Narrative Self: Origins in Kant

It is fair to see Ricoeur's narrative self as a response to chapter 27 of Book 2 of John Locke's *An Essay Concerning Human Understanding* ('Of Identity and Diversity') insofar as Ricoeur sees Locke as the inventor not just of the three concepts of identity, consciousness and self and their sequential relationship[8] but also of the intransigence of 'a philosophy of "sameness"'[9]. Ricoeur's narrative self, a response to this intransigence, is indebted to the Kantian self on two accounts: (1) the distinction between productive and reproductive imagination; and (2) the Kantian operation of judgement. For Kant the synthesis of the imagination is as follows:

> An act of spontaneity, which is determinative, and not, like sense, merely determinable, and which is consequently able to determine sense a priori . . . and its synthesis of intuitions according to the categories must be the transcendental synthesis of the imagination.[10]

Furthermore, this is a *productive* imagination, to be distinguished from a merely *reproductive* one that is entirely subject to empirical laws. When Ricoeur establishes the means of production of narrative, he notes that the production of the configurational act can be compared to the productive imagination of Kant.[11] Ricoeur advises us as follows:

> Bracket this *non-verbal* kernel of imagination, that is, imagery understood in the quasi-visual, quasi-auditory, quasi-tactile, quasi-olfactory sense. The only way to approach the problem of the imagination from the perspective of a semantic theory, that is to say on a verbal plane, is to begin with productive imagination in the Kantian sense, and to put off reproductive imagination or imagery as long as possible.[12]

The productive imagination is crucially important for narrative identity, because narrative employs the imagination more so than the will.[13] Indeed, with respect to the succession of generations in which the individual will situate his or her story, he or she will need to 'move back in time by extending this regressive movement through imagination'.[14] Although the production of the configurational act is compared to the imagination in Kant, the configurational act itself is compared to the Kantian operation of judging. The imagination, for Ricoeur, is the gatherer of narrative events, the synthesizer of the heterogeneous;

judgement is the gathering itself. It is this 'grasping together' of the configurational act that is akin to what Kant say of the operation of judgement.[15]

Appearance and Exposition of the Narrative Self

The fundamental structure of the narrative self makes its first appearance in *Time and Narrative, Vol. 1* when Ricoeur discusses the notion of deviation with respect to plot. Indeed, one might say that this appearance is one in disguise, a larval structure of the narrative self whose nature goes unrecognized. Of course, Ricoeur has not at this point reached a formulation of narrative identity, but the form of his statement is echoed precisely, seven years later, in *Oneself as Another*. Emplotment, he says, 'oscillates' between conformity on the one hand and rebellion to narrative tradition and its paradigms on the other. Between the two extremes 'lies the entire range of combinations involving sedimentation and invention'.[16]

By the end of *Time and Narrative, Vol. 3*, Ricoeur summarizes his central hypothesis regarding temporality which is that it cannot be spoken of 'in the direct discourse of phenomenology' but only by way of 'the indirect discourse of narration'.[17] Narrative effectively becomes 'the guardian of time'. As Ricoeur pursues time through narrative, the aporias or puzzles of time multiply. In the end, Ricoeur is left with three major aporias: the aporia of the inscrutability of time and the limits of narrative; the aporia of totality and totalization; and the aporia of the dual perspective on time – the phenomenological and the cosmological and their mutual occultation, an occultation that reaches its most 'virulent' level in Heidegger.[18]

It is this last aporia that takes centre stage for the narrative self, for it is upon this split which separates the two perspectives on time that Ricoeur builds a third time in the form of a series of connectors that function to bridge the 'fracture'. This third time cannot be assigned either to history or to fiction but rather to the 'interweaving' or 'criss-crossing' of their respective referential intentions. This dialectic of interweaving that fosters 'a fictionalization of history and a historization of fiction'[19] would be a somewhat inadequate application of poetics to aporetics were it not for what Ricoeur calls 'an offshoot' born of the mutual fruitfulness of fiction and history: this 'fragile offshoot' is narrative identity. Punctuating the even flow of cosmological time with the variable intensity of human events, this offshoot that issues from the chiasmus of history and fiction assigns to the individual 'a specific identity that we call their narrative identity'.[20]

This narrative identity rises above the antinomy of the subject identical to itself versus the 'pure manifold of cognitions, emotions, and volitions' that Hume and Nietzsche propose, an antinomy to which there is no solution.[21] For Ricoeur, self-identity must be seen as two-fold: (1) formal or substantial identity understood 'in the sense of being the same (*idem*)'; and (2) narrative identity understood 'in the sense of oneself as self-same [*soi-même*] (*ipse*)'.[22] This self-same identity is wedded to a temporal structure 'that conforms to the model of dynamic identity arising from the poetic composition of a narrative text'.[23] The subject's narrative identity is thus characterized by change and mutability; in this process of change the narrative self can be understood to be 'refigured by the reflective application of such narrative configurations'.[24] In other words, the subject 'appears both as a reader and a writer of its own life', a life that is 'a cloth woven of stories'.[25] Ricoeur is very careful with his choice of words. In rejecting the Cartesian egotistical cogito in favour of a self of self-knowledge, Ricoeur provides us with a narrative self that is 'the fruit of an examined life', an examined life 'purged [and] clarified by the cathartic effects' of our own historical or fictional narratives and of our cultures. In this way, self-constancy now implies a self 'instructed by the works of a culture that it has applied to itself'.[26] The self of knowledge as the fruit of an examined life is a tightly articulated self, notwithstanding the array of cultural avenues and textual worlds through which this self can refigure itself.

As an example of this self of knowledge in the sphere of individual subjectivity, Ricoeur turns to Freud and the process of 'working through' in psychoanalysis.[27] Ricoeur identifies a two-fold process at work in Freudian psychoanalysis. The first stage is that of *dispossession*, a regressive path that moves from the pretension of consciousness to be self-evident back to the source of meaning in desire, before the division into subject and object – the stage operates at the theoretical level; the second stage is that of *reappropriation*, done in the work of analysis, where meaning is wrested from the ruins of self-delusion through the activity of interpretation – this is at the level of practice.[28] This theoretical–practical process thus establishes the grounds for meaning to be 'the product of an intersubjective process, involving self and other, self as other'.[29] The importance of Freud's 'working-through' (*Durcharbeitung*) or reappropriation for Ricoeur cannot be overstressed. In becoming an object of consciousness through psychoanalysis, Freud has dispensed with the traditional metaphors of the gaze and of contemplation and exchanged them for 'metaphors of exertion, of overcoming obstacles and hidden forces'.[30] The *I am* becomes an *I can* if we understand that 'the concrete and active sense' of the process of reappropriation is that of 'making one's own what is first encountered as alien'. This process of reappropriation 'cannot take place in abstraction . . . The subject of self-reflection is not a given but a task.'[31]

Through the 'thoroughgoing individual subjectivity'[32] of psychoanalysis, Ricoeur can comfortably abandon the ego's position as a master of consciousness projecting its sovereign gaze and engage instead in the 'concrete sphere of the "I can" . . . [where] . . . the ego is re-inscribed within the problematic of action as a field of potentialities'.[33]

The advantage to Ricoeur of this approach is that this 'I', the subject of utterance of the 'I can', immediately places us within the field of language, by referring to a locutor or the utterer in the utterance.[34] From the outset this is intersubjective. 'I' as personal pronoun is also part of a complex that contains 'you', 'he/she', 'us' and 'they'. 'I' acts here as a linguistic 'shifter', an indicator that, unlike proper nouns and definite descriptions which remain within the field of semantics, functions within 'the gravitational sphere of pragmatics'.[35] Husserl, as Ricoeur informs us, had already noted the necessarily ambiguous nature of the expression 'I'. On the one hand, 'I' is an empty, migrating term that 'designates in each instance a different person for each new use', a person who 'in assuming the word, takes charge of language as a whole'[36]; on the other hand, in so designating one particular speaker, we immediately move from the paradigmatic viewpoint where the 'I' is *un terme voyageur*, available to several virtual utterers, to the syntagmatic viewpoint where the 'I' designates in each case 'one person to the exclusion of any other, the one who is speaking here and now'.[37] It is like the conch in William Golding's *Lord of the Flies*, the shell that moves around the group of boys and designates who has the right to speak.[38]

This two-fold function of the 'I', like that of time, requires connectors. The correlation of this 'I' with a proper name serves to anchor the subject 'to a unique centre of perspective on the world', for example by *inscribing* the iden-tity of this subject within a birth certificate as a triple inscription: 'a proper name conforming to the rule of naming . . . a date in accordance with the usage of the calendar, a birthplace conforming to the rules of localization in public space'.[39] The anchoring of the 'I' to the physical body ('what is mine') in cos-mological time places it firmly in the 'now' and the 'here' – this is the 'I' as 'myself', the 'I' that acts and utters.

Ricoeur now moves this further forward by asking the question: *Who* says I? *Who* is the author, the agent of action? By designating someone with a proper name through the registry of births, what justifies our taking the subject of action over a lifetime as the same throughout? The answer, says Ricoeur, is nar-rative. To answer the question 'Who?' is to tell the story of a life. Therefore the identity of the 'Who' that tells the story must of itself be a narrative identity.[40] Narrative identity, therefore, is not the inflexible and static identity of things (*idem-identity*) but must instead be understood in the sense of this self-sameness or self-constancy (selfhood or *ipse-identity*), an identity that is the result of a diachronic process of construction.[41] It is a working through narrative, a work-ing-through in narrative and a working-out of narrative.

Working through Narrative

This construction over time can take place between the self and an attachment figure, between the self and an analyst, between the self and a community, a cultural event, a work of fiction, a film, a play, a poem, even a song – so long as this other is structured according to the rules of narrative. This other must be a text to be read if narrative identity is to be refigured at the *chiasmus* of self and other. It is this 'interfiguration' of the self that begins to takes shape in Ricoeur's analysis that makes of it a dynamic construction and not a substantial identity, one that is the result of change and conflict.[42] Individuals will, according to Ricoeur, recast or refigure their experiences, ascribing new meaning to events, 'after the model of the narratives that constitute their cultural heritage'.[43] Indeed, it is through narrative, that simple and familiar act of storytelling, that we are permitted 'a privileged mode of access to human time'[44]; and it is in the narratives of a personal history that we can see how the story of a life is 'constituted through a series of rectifications applied to previous narratives'.[45]

We as humans recognize ourselves in the stories we tell about ourselves and we recognize others as like us in the stories they tell about themselves. We are held together in the stories we tell of ourselves and in the stories others tell of us; however, insofar as narrative identity cedes neither to the dispersive force of scattered events in time nor to the prison of a substantial and formal unity, it cannot encompass the inflexible and static identity of the same (*idem*), of the sedimented and the habit-laden. Narrative identity is *ipseity*, dynamic not formal, the result of 'a diachronic process of construction'.[46]

This strategy of opposing sameness of character to self-constancy creates between the two an '*interval of sense*' which must be filled in.[47] We will return to this break or *fêlure* later in this work; however, it is worth noting that this fault line is nothing new in Ricoeur. While in *The Voluntary and the Involuntary* Ricoeur speaks 'about the reciprocity of the voluntary and the involuntary in the nature of human beings',[48] in *Fallible Man*, he notes the disproportion between human finitude and infinitude, or with respect to a moral human being, the disproportion between his or her character and happiness. In the ground between these terms, for Ricoeur, lies a third term: human fragility. This fêlure or fragility remains an inchoate and subliminal presence in the narrative self of *Oneself as Another*.

Towards an Interrogation of the Narrative Self

We will not take the description of narrative identity any further at the moment. We have recounted its essential structure and the context within which this structure has emerged. That it has an even more complex structure or that its nature is that of a multiplicity will arise when we subject narrative identity to a series of further questions in the next chapter. For the time being, we will leave it to Ricoeur to raise the key tasks that he foresaw ahead of him when he first formulated narrative identity. We quote this paragraph at length as it contains within it almost every problem that this book seeks to address:

> Narrative identity is not a stable and seamless identity. Just as it is possible to compose several plots on the subject of the same incidents . . . so it is always possible to weave different, even opposed, plots about our lives. . . . [In] the

exchange of roles between history and fiction, the historical component of a narrative about oneself draws this narrative toward the side of a chronicle submitted to the same documentary verifications as any other historical narration, while the fictional component draws it toward those imaginative variations that destabilize narrative identity. In this sense, narrative identity continues to make and unmake itself. . . . *Narrative identity thus becomes the name of a problem at least as much as it is that of a solution.* A systematic investigation of autobiography and self-portraiture would no doubt verify this instability in principle of narrative identity.[49]

We can pose these questions somewhat differently. What is the relationship between the stable idem and the unstable ipse? If ipse-identity can be woven differently, even become its own opposite, what impact does this have on idem-identity? Even if we assume that they are somehow separate though wrapped around each other like the two ribonucleic strands of DNA, surely change to one will disrupt the bonds between the strands that hold them in place, that force their union? Furthermore, what is the self at the moment of being 'unmade'? Is it a 'non-self' or a 'dissolved-self'? In other words, does it move to the pole of the shattered self of Nietzsche, a self that Ricoeur explicitly rejects?[50] The quixotic remark that '*narrative identity thus becomes the name of a problem at least as much as it is that of a solution*' draws us seamlessly into a Deleuzian ontology of difference-in-itself where the virtual is constituted by the differential nature of ideas as problems. Finally, and somewhat intriguingly, Ricoeur calls for a systematic investigation into autobiography and self-portraiture in support of his argument. Such systematic investigation does in fact exist, and we will supply this towards the end of the book by drawing into the debate on narrative identity the ethological theories of John Bowlby on mother–infant attachment and how variations in this primary relationship can alter and disfigure the future narratives we generate regarding the self.

Chapter 5

Questioning the Narrative Self through its Progenitors

[A] book is a huge cemetery in which on the majority of the tombs the names are effaced and can no longer be read.[1]

Introduction

In this chapter we will address in detail the problematics of narrative identity and the narrative self that arose at the end of Chapter 4. One additional problem we must acknowledge is that, taken on its own or out of context, *Oneself as Another* is a minor work insofar as it is an incomplete one. Ricoeur accepts this when he refers to his Tenth study as an 'exploratory' investigation of the ontological status of the narrative self, an investigation that essentially asks, 'What mode of being . . . belongs to the self, what sort of being or entity is it?'[2] We should note here that some of the crucially important statements in this Tenth study suggest potentially different conclusions or at the very least a supplement to the conclusions Ricoeur arrives at. We will address these in Chapter 8.

Oneself as Another is a minor work for another, though clearly relativist reason: it is situated between two monumental texts that utterly dwarf it, both in size and in the richness of Ricoeur's encounter with his topic. It is like a thin slice of meat between two thick chunks of bread. The narrative self of *Oneself as Another* reads as though divorced from its origins and from the work in which it gestated. Bearing none of the marks of the arguments that emerged in the theoretical quagmire of *Time and Narrative* out of which it was delivered, *Oneself as Another*'s detachment from its ancestors and indeed its descendant (*Memory, History, Forgetting*) is such that it must be compared to them – must be placed between them so that it engages in a dialectic with their procedures and their thoughts to be more fully complete. Put more graphically, the self in *Oneself as Another* appears in its final solution as two-dimensional, stretched between Descartes and Nietzsche to the point of attenuation and loss – loss of the arrogance of the cogito and the elusiveness and intensity of the shattered ego.

It is a 'self, stripped bare'[3] – pinned between two poles, it hangs precariously like a thread made up of entangled words, sentences, speech acts and a plot (*'aiming at the "good life" with and for others, in just institutions'*[4]). It is a self whose life is in the balance.

With this in mind, we will pursue the problematics of narrative identity through a process close to that which Ricoeur employs in *Time and Narrative*, a process called 'working back', one based on Husserl's 'genetic phenomenology'. A full account of this procedure follows. Our intention is that by the end of this chapter we will have interrogated fully the narrative self by way of its own origins or the thoughts that set it up in the first place. In so doing we are wagering that the narrative self will suffer substantial wounds to its integrity but that these wounds will in themselves inaugurate a series of questions which will determine the problems of the self towards which an encounter with Deleuze can be structured and within which some amelioration or mediating *physic* can be sought. This series of questions (Q1–Q13) will be readily identifiable within the text. Essentially this procedure forms an interrogation of the narrative self in retrospect; we will postpone the narrative self in prospect (i.e. its encounter with *Memory, History, Forgetting*) until Chapter 10.

Methodology: Questioning Back

At a crucial point in *Time and Narrative, Vol. 1*, Ricoeur identifies a triple epistemological break that unfolds between history and narrative. This break occurs on the following three levels: (1) procedures – the explanatory processes of history based on authentication and justification take their leave from the explanatory capabilities inherent in narrative and immanent to emplotment; (2) entities – the objects of history (nations, states, civilizations, etc.) are anonymous entities in contrast to the subjects of action (which are characters though not necessarily human ones); and (3) temporality – the epistemological status of historical time which 'either resolves itself into a succession of *homogeneous intervals . . .* or is scattered into a *multiplicity of times*'[5] appears to bear no resemblance to that of narrative time, the time of action, of individual agents and of memory and expectation. To maintain the narrativist model within the orbit of historical explanation and prevent it from completely disintegrating Ricoeur introduces a sublime strategy, which is that of 'questioning back', borrowed and reshaped from what Husserl called his 'genetic phenomenology' as applied in *Die Krisis*. Ricoeur explains that this does not refer to a psychological genesis but to an investigation into a genesis that concerns meaning.[6] Ricoeur believes he will have success with this method (or rather, more success than he believes Husserl had with his questioning back of the life world[7]) because he will be referring to a cultural world whose structures are already in place and where action has already been configured through narrative activity.

Taking a lead from Ricoeur's use of Husserl's genetic phenomenology, it is our anticipation that if we thread the narrative self of *Oneself as Another* through *Time and Narrative, Vols. 1–3* we will discover a much richer weave to narrative identity or a self configured of more complex material. For instance, threading it through *Time and Narrative, Vol. 2* will force an encounter with the difficulties of narrative ending and therefore of the relationship between ending stories of the self and beginning anew. In what sense are all these emplotted stories that are said, themselves emplotted? If we tell a series of self-narratives, each inter-linking, each a fresh story and each a development, a next draft, and if each narrative provides 'discordant concordance' then what is the relation between one self narrative and the next, one draft and the next; does each subsequent discordantly concordant narrative become discordant or concordant with its predecessor? If so, does it then require a meta-narrative to maintain concord-ance, a process that invites an infinite regress? And how will the ipse self survive an interrogation with Ricoeur's reading of Louis O. Mink, a reading which might well reduce the narrative self to an impossibility when, for Mink, history only appears 'once the game is over'?[8]

At the end of this section we will summarize the work so far; in particular we will argue that the self for Ricoeur is best viewed as an attempted solution to a problem – but what is the problem for which the self is an attempted solution? What methods and what discourses have been available in which to express this solution? Working through the semiotic constraints on narrativity and the 'games with time' identified in *Time and Narrative, Vol. 2* – in particular Ricoeur's reading of Boris Uspensky's 'poetics of composition' – we will close our cri-tique on narrative identity by attempting to clarify what are 'the remainders' (Ricoeur's term) that cannot be accounted for by the theory of the self as nar-rative. Outstanding among these remainders in literature will be Virginia Woolf's *The Waves*, a book no longer a work of narrative fiction, according to Ricoeur, but an 'oratorio', a polyphonic work that has passed over the thresh-old marked out by the carnivalistic genre (that generates 'a matrix of plots') and into a plotless 'presentation of consciousness'.[9] By way of this, we must ask a final question: is Ricoeur correct to define and so confine the self within a criteriology that is wedded to emplotment and to traditional genres of narra-tive? Or is this a presupposition that goes unquestioned?

The Narrative Self in Retrospect

Ricoeur introduced the notion of 'Narrative Identity' late in *Time and Narrative, Vol. 3* – largely as an afterthought.[10] So what had he achieved up to this point and how did something so important emerge on revision of the text? *Time and Narrative* is divided into three volumes though it is better understood in its four parts: (1) the circle of narrative and temporality; (2) history and narrative;

(3) the configuration of time in fictional narrative; and (4) narrated time.[11] It is a vast and complex work of just over eight hundred pages, presented in a style that some would argue borders on verbosity.[12] And it does not stop there. The three volumes were conceived as part of a more extensive work that began with *The Rule of Metaphor* and indeed one might say continued through *Oneself as Another* and into *Memory, History, Forgetting*.

Our principle interest in 'retrospecting' (or retro-prospecting) through *Time and Narrative* is to draw out the questions that arise through this reverse interrogation. Most of these questions lie within Part I and Part IV (Section 2); however, we will not ignore what occurs in-between where it is relevant to the narrative self. The questions that arise are however somewhat exhaustive and we will need to gather together a subset of these that best represents the array of concerns that the two slices of bread raise with the meat.[13]

Semantic innovation is what brings together metaphor (as part of the theory of tropes) and narrative (as part of the theory of literary genres) and it is what makes them comparable at the level of acts of language. Whereas with metaphor the innovative exists in the production of 'a new semantic pertinence by means of an impertinent attribution',[14] with narrative, the synthetic work of semantic innovation is by way of the plot. Through this emplotment, multifarious goals, causes and the necessity of chance are united as part of the 'temporal unity of a whole and complete action'.[15] This is what Ricoeur refers to as the *synthesis of the heterogeneous*. Behind both metaphor and narrative lie the productive imagination and the schematism that is its 'signifying matrix'.[16] It is the productive imagination that unfolds the 'vast poetic sphere' of metaphorical utterance and narrative discourse.[17] This is all stated in the first three pages of the 'Preface' yet it is a clear indication that the looming shadow of Kant is not far from Ricoeur's thinking and that Kant's productive imagination will emerge from the three volumes of *Time and Narrative* as a central agency for narrative, metaphor and the 'synthesis of the heterogeneous'.

Let us briefly go through the four parts of *Time and Narrative* with the intention of explicating how Ricoeur arrives at the narrative self at the end of Part IV. In doing so we aim to discover what central hurdles are crossed, what new aporias burst forth in the stitching of old ones and, finally, what problems lie exposed at the end of 'Narrated Time' for which 'Narrative Identity' appears to provide some form of solution? In doing so, we fully expect to discover instances where narrative identity lays some quite significant and secret problems for itself.

Aristotelian plot and Augustinian time

The central presupposition of Part I is that time becomes human time only insofar as it is organized 'after the manner of a narrative'; but narrative is only meaningful to us if it 'portrays the features of temporal experience'.[18] Although this is circular, Ricoeur will show that it is not a vicious but a healthy circle and harmonizes with a hermeneutical assertion. He will do this by recourse to the theory of time in Augustine (Book 11 of the *Confessions*) and the theory of plot in Aristotle's *Poetics* and he will demonstrate how these two halves of the circle reinforce each other. Ricoeur's choice of these two authors is explicitly stated: the analysis of time in the *Confessions* represents the reign of discordance over concordance; the analysis of the configuration of the plot in the *Poetics* establishes the opposite – the dominance of concordance over discordance. At the end of Part I, Ricoeur will bring these two together in what he will call a discordant concordance or more simply, he will demonstrate that in order to resolve the problem of the relation of time and narrative he must establish a mediating role for emplotment between 'a stage of practical experience that precedes it and a stage that succeeds it'.[19]

This is the time of Augustine entwined with the narrative of Aristotle. It is in answer to the aporia of how time can exist if the past is no more, the present evanescent and the future yet to happen that Augustine develops the threefold present (the present of past things in the memory, the present of present things in perception and the present of future things in expectation) and the measurement of time through the soul alone and not through cosmological movement. It is the soul that distends (*distentio animi*) and time then becomes an extension of the mind so that what remains is to conceptualize 'the threefold present as distension and distension as the distension of the threefold present'.[20] What is measured is the expectation of what is to come – the future which the mind expects and which 'passes through the present, to which it attends, into the past, which it remembers'.[21] It is the attention (the *praesens intentio*) of the mind that 'engages' memory and expectation in this act.

But this does not do away with aporias, as Ricoeur demonstrates, since each stage of the solution appears to create even further enigmas. For example, an even greater enigma arises from the question: how could the soul 'distend' itself while at the same time 'engaging' itself?[22] For Augustine, no matter where he turned for answers to his agonising questions on time he found discordance everywhere.

Aristotle, on the other hand, found in the creating of the tragic poem the triumph of concordance over discordance. Taking from Aristotle's *Poetics* two key themes, emplotment (*muthos*) and mimetic activity (*mimesis*) and allowing himself considerable latitude with these,[23] Ricoeur makes the bold move of deferring any judgement on how narrative is related to time until he has addressed the question of an 'interweaving reference'[24] of both fictional and historical narrative, based on our own lived temporal experience. This, he declares, will be a long journey; indeed he does not reach his destination until the end of Part IV, section 2. We will try to expedite this journey and reach its conclusion somewhat more concisely.

Poetics of course implies a productive, constructive, dynamic process of which muthos and mimesis are operations rather than structures.[25] For Aristotle, it is the art of composing plots (muthos) through the imitation or representation of action (mimesis). Ricoeur thus defines narrative as 'muthos' in the Aristotelian sense – as the organizing of events.[26] Crucially, though, Ricoeur does not break with Aristotle in the subordination of character to action:

> For tragedy is not the imitation of men but of actions and of life. It is in action that happiness and unhappiness are found, and the end we aim at is a kind of activity, not a quality . . . What is more, without action there could not be a tragedy, but there could be without characterization.[27]

The importance of this position ('first conceive the plot, then add the names'[28]) taken by Ricoeur cannot be overstressed because it represents a fundamental de-centering of the self in deference to action and a system of organization; if in the Aristotelian version of mimesis the representation or imitation is always of action and not of human beings, then for Ricoeur this is allowed because the emphasis has to be on this organization of the events. In response, we pose the following question: (Q1) Does this *suggest* that the 'character' emerges in the nexus of action, that he or she is formed at the juncture of events or between events, in the tensile interactions and forces that occupy the points of the over-arching plot; but that the character is not of itself known, in itself knowable, that the character has no generative or poetic power itself, that it is something like a 'spaghetti junction' of actions and forces only visible by what courses through it or by what happens around its name? We will need to follow Ricoeur carefully through the rest of *Time and Narrative*, to see whether this suggestion takes on the full force of a conviction regarding the nature of character and therefore of the self.

The play of discordance

For Aristotle, muthos provides a poetic solution to one of the paradoxes of time but only insofar as Aristotle ignores every temporal characteristic in the development of a plot. For Ricoeur, this Aristotelian theory not only underlines concordance but in a very subtle manner accentuates instead 'the play of discordance internal to concordance'.[29] We will return to this notion of 'discordance internal to concordance' later when we set it beside Deleuze's notion of 'difference-in-itself'; by doing so we raise the following and indeed somewhat central question: (Q2) are 'discordance internal to concordance' and 'difference-in-itself', *mutatis mutandis*, essentially the same?

A further question arises from Aristotle's definition of muthos as an organization of events that emphasizes concordance characterized by wholeness and completeness. If a complete narrative has a beginning, a middle and an end but only by way of the poetic composition itself does anything actually count as a beginning, a middle or an end, then we must ask is this also the case for the narrative self (Q3)? What is its beginning, and can it ever have an end or will it always finish, as Robert Zemeckis' film *Back to the Future* ends, with the words 'To be continued'? It is a question not disconnected from the earlier one – the subordination of character to plot – for if 'the universalizing of plot . . . universalizes the characters'[30] how then can this be achieved when the 'poet of the plot' writes himself or herself into the action as its hero? In other words, one question spawns another: (Q4) by obeying the rules of emplotment, does the self-narrative universalize or particularize the self, or produce something in-between? And is the story of the self, as Aristotle would see tragic emplotment, the story of one thing after another (episodic sequence) or one thing because of another (causal sequence)?

For Ricoeur, this universalization that springs forth from poetic composition is not an abolisher of discordance. On the contrary, discordance remains within what Ricoeur refers to as a model of 'discordant concordance'. In other words, in composing a plot 'the intelligible springs from the accidental, the universal from the singular, the necessary or probable from the episodic'[31] so that the art here is in making what is discordant appear concordant. It must be stressed at this point that Ricoeur is very clear in differentiating art from life: although the discordant overthrows the concordant in life, it does not do so in tragic art.[32]

Another important component of narrative (for Aristotle this is usually tragedy) is *catharsis* – the constructing of the spectator's emotional response (fear, pity) brought about by the plot. The fearful and pitiful incidents in the narrative represent its first discordances or threats to its coherence. Also, Aristotle adds to this discordant concordance the concepts of 'reversal'[33] (*peripeteia*) of fortune, recognition (*anagnōrisis*) and suffering (*pathos*), thus deepening the magnitude of emotional engagement of the spectator. This Aristotelian man that acts and suffers is a fundamental type explicated by Ricoeur.[34]

The Poetic Composition of the Self: Threefold Mimesis

Ricoeur extends and divides in three the Aristotelian term 'mimesis' in the context of the term 'narrative activity', beyond imitation and representation. This is in order to incorporate its relation to the real or to what comes before or prior to the poetic composition, that is, the pre-understanding of narrative composition (mimesis$_1$). Ricoeur distinguishes this from the creative composition itself (mimisis$_2$) and from the posterior element which is the requirement of a reader or spectator (mimesis$_3$). One consequence of this distension of mimesis is to gather in an ethical dimension, one that occurs as a connection – not a break – in the movement between mimesis$_1$ and mimisis$_2$.[35] Another is that it is only through the presence of the spectator or reader, who is presented with a persuasive if impossible story that 'the properly tragic emotions flower'.[36] For Ricoeur, this spectator/reader is implied in every tragic composition, required for the cathartic construction within the work to exit the text and enter the emotional world of the spectator/reader. However, central to the development of a threefold mimesis is 'to resolve the problem of the relation between time and narrative' by way of 'establishing the mediating role of emplotment' (con-figured time) between practical experience that precedes emplotment (prefig-ured time) and that which succeeds it (refigured time).

We must develop some of the elements key to each mimetic stage, insofar as they may have repercussions upon the narrative self. Ricoeur addresses three aspects of poetic composition: structural, symbolic and temporal – in this study we want to limit our analysis primarily to the structural and to a lesser extent the temporal aspects. We do this on the basis that our endeavour here is to clarify a foundational architecture to the self, an architecture that will provide the diagrammatics for a 'symbolic mediation' of the self or selves.

Structural elements

In our pre-understanding of narrative, we presuppose on the part of the narrator and listener a terminological understanding of 'agent, goal, means, circumstances, help, hostility, cooperation, conflict, success, failure' and an understanding of the rules pertaining to the diachronic order of a story whether you read the story forwards or backwards.[37] On the contrary, our practical understanding does not require such diachrony since the terms relative to our practical world (means, ends, agents, circumstance, etc.) are perfectly rever-sible, synchronic and part of a paradigmatic order. In going from praxis to nar-rative we move from a paradigmatic to a syntagmatic order, that is, from the order of action (paradigmatic) to the order of narrative (syntagmatic), thus providing 'actuality' and 'integration' to the terms of action. By 'actuality' Ricoeur means that the terms of action before narrative composition had but a 'virtual signification' in the paradigmatic order, 'a pure capacity to be used' but only through emplotment are they given an actual signification and this is by way of 'the sequential interconnections' that emplotment confers on the agents, their actions and their sufferings.[38] By integration he refers to the capacity of narrative composition to 'render compatible' the heterogeneous components of action in actual temporal wholes.

We have drawn out this Ricoeurian movement from mimesis$_1$ to mimesis$_2$ to underline one point: it is a movement from the virtual to the actual, from the heterogeneous and the different to the whole and the same. And with this vir-tual-to-actual movement in mind, let us formulate a further question regarding narrative identity: (Q5) if the self is delivered of itself as narrative, contingent upon Ricoeur's central precept that time becomes human time only insofar as it is organized 'after the manner of a narrative' and if narrative is only meaningful to us if it 'portrays the features of temporal experience',[39] then where is the movement from mimesis$_1$ to mimesis$_3$ in the narrative self? What is the nature of the pre-understanding, what are the rules of composition and are they contiguous with Aristotle's and Ricoeur's, and finally, who is the spectator/reader and who is implied by the poet of the self? In other words, can we map unto the self the activity of Ricoeur's threefold mimesis? Also, a further question arises from this: (Q6) is mimesis$_2$ the pivot of self narrative in the sense that it is so for Ricoeur in literary and historical narrative? Is it the self-as-narrative that draws from the virtual and the different the concordant and the same of itself, or is it the productive imagination at the heart of the virtual (Kant's autonomous imagination) that fires the self to narrate, that moves from mimesis$_1$ to mimesis$_2$ – is that the true fulcrum upon which narrative is supported?

With the advent of mimesis$_2$ the issue of truth and fiction emerges as we enter the realm of the *as if*. Narrative discourse is now divided into two large classes: fictional narrative and historical narrative. Much of *Time and Narrative* will be taken up with the difference between these two. It is timely to state unequivocally that the narrative self will have great difficulty being allocated to either of these great classes.

The configuring operation of mimesis$_2$ requires that emplotment has a mediating function between the pre-understanding of what human action is and the 'post-understanding of the order of action and its temporal features'.[40] It mediates in three ways: (1) it draws *from* a diversity of events, transforming these events *into* a story; (2) it permits all the components of the paradigmatic order that have been established by a semantics of action to appear in the syntagmatic order – put another way, it configures the actual from the virtual, 'grasping together' the actions and incidents of the story and drawing from '*the manifold of events* the unity of one temporal whole'[41] and (3) it synthesizes the heterogeneous by virtue of its mediating role in the plot's temporal characteristics. The key phrase here is 'grasping together'. This is the activity or operation of the configurational act of mimesis$_2$ *par excellence*. Indeed, Ricoeur is at pains to emphasize the kinship between this activity and how Kant describes the operation of judging.[42] This link to Kant becomes even more important when we realize how Ricoeur employs Kant's productive imagination to account for the 'grasping together' involved in the creation of narrative (mimesis$_2$) and for our very grasp of narrative itself (mimesis$_3$). (We should not miss the importance of the notion of 'drawing from the manifold of events' as this suggests an actualization of the virtual by means of the productive imagination. But for the narrative self where precisely is this productive imagination functioning? Is it within the realm of the actual or the virtual? We will address this later.)

From mimesis$_2$ to mimesis$_3$ (configuration to refiguration) 'schematization' becomes the key feature in this linkage and in the restoration of narrative 'to the time of action and of suffering in mimesis$_3$'.[43] According to Ricoeur, the production of the configurational act and by implication, the refigurational act, is akin to the work of the productive imagination. The productive imagination as a transcendental and not a psychological faculty has, fundamentally, a synthetic function, engendering syntheses that are both intellectual and intuitive. It is not only rule-governed but itself constitutes the very 'generative matrix of rules'.[44] Thus, in emplotment, the schematism of the productive imagination engenders a synthesis between our understanding of the point or theme of the story and the 'intuitive presentation of circumstances, characters, episodes, and changes of fortune that make up the denouement'.[45]

In this grasping together of the actions and incidents of a story, the configurational (and refigurational) act moves towards a sense of an ending. Endings play a crucial role in narrative – each episode and the composition of episodes lead inexorably towards the conclusion that permits the theme or point of the story to yield its meaning. It is only from the vantage point of the end of the story that the story can be seen as a whole. However, this raises another problematic question for the self as narrative: (Q7) as death has not yet occurred, does this make the narrative self always provisional or hypothetical, a narrative with a multiplicity of endings or rather a narrative that can only be configured and completed after death – and therefore not at all? Or must it be refigured by someone else, in one's absence? But is this not someone else's configuration and no longer a refiguration of one's own narrative? Moreover, does this problem not suggest that all self-narratives are sub-narratives whose subplots must be resolved before the major plot itself can be given a sense of an ending that will 'yield its meaning'? We will remember that the political subplot involving the fate of Victor Laszlo must be resolved before the central love story plot of Rick and Isla – in order for *Casablanca* to yield its full meaning. Does this mean that those 'little narratives' that are our subplots thus constitute mere fragments of a self or that they are occasional portraits or snapshots of an always becoming-self momentarily frozen or deferred, a self always about to yield its meaning but a self that never can? Or a self that can only yield its meaning when given up irrevocably to the Other?

Narrative tradition

It is also important to say something about tradition in the constitution of narrative composition. For Ricoeur, tradition develops through the interplay of innovation and sedimentation, but it is only by way of the latter that the paradigms that 'constitute the typology of emplotment' or the genre are laid down.[46] Ricoeur encompasses genre and form under paradigm, seeing paradigms as established products of the productive imagination. Paradigms constitute as such a sort of grammar that governs composition; a new work develops within this constraint, transcends it and becomes itself typical. There are constraints on the imagination brought upon it by the paradigms of tradition, but the range of solutions is endless; the imagination is deployed between two poles, one of 'servile application' and one of 'calculated deviation' but between these it may pass through every degree of 'rule-governed deformation'.[47] This interplay of sedimentation and innovation is one we have seen in the narrative-self of *Oneself as Another*. Indeed, the questions Ricoeur asks of innovation-within-tradition are just as pertinent to the narrative self as to fictional and historical narrative. For instance, one may innovatively challenge tradition in the following ways: (1) type through deviation: this would be constitutive of every individual work of fiction for no two are the same – and this would inscribe upon self-narrative the feature that no two people no matter whether they are genetically identical or not, will tell the same story; (2) genre through deviation: this is less frequent, though James Joyce in literature and Eisenstein in cinema would be examples of genre-challenge – for the self this would be to challenge or deviate from one's religious, cultural, sexual, gendered or racial narrative identity and (3) we can ultimately contest the formal principle or paradigm of discordant concordance itself. This is perhaps the most challenging area, and Ricoeur questions whether this would not in fact lead to the disintegration of the narrative form itself, if drawn to the point of schism[48] – and by extension, to the death of the narrative self were such tradition to be challenged by a human individual. We can formulate these propositions as further questions: (Q8) can we challenge the narrative type and narrative genre of the self through deviation? Can we ultimately contest the formal principle or paradigm of 'discordant concordance' itself without this leading to the death of the self?

Time and the past

Mimesis$_3$ identifies that specific chiasmic crossover between the world of the text and the world of the reader or listener 'where real action occurs and unfolds its specific temporality'.[49] This unfolding does not bring us back, viciously, to the same point where we began, though it is undeniably circular; according to Ricoeur, we trace an endless spiral returning to the same point but at ever different altitudes. In tracing this imposition of narrative consonance on temporal dissonance, Ricoeur refers to the 'violence of interpretation', as we resist the fascination of chaos in our nostalgia for order.[50] However, we should note – though he is confusing on this point – that Ricoeur acknowledges a play of 'concordant discordance' either within or against the flow of 'discordant concordance'.[51] Regrettably, he does not clarify what precise relationship can exist between these two movements (concordant discordance and discordant concordance); indeed, his most unusual recourse to psychological terminology in these pages – 'nostalgia for order', 'fascination for the unformed', 'horror of chaos'[52] – indicates the seriousness of the threat that a counter-flow to discordant concordance presents to narrative wholeness. In the light of this threat, the narrative self must answer to another problem: (Q9) in the face of a counter-flow of concordant discordance, how can the hermeneutic circle of mimesis$_1$ → mimesis$_2$ → mimesis$_3$ sustain its upward spiral? Will not concordant discordance reverse the flow or indeed catastrophically dismantle it altogether? Does not the aporia of disarray lie lurking at the heart of the mimetic circle that vouchsafes concordance? And might we find some solution to this aporia by considering this spiral that does not return to itself as a species of the 'eternal return of difference'?[53]

A final point in this discussion of the circle of narrative and temporality concerns narrated or refigured time. Ricoeur brings together in a threeway 'discussion of interweaving reference' history, literary criticism (applied to narrativity) and the phenomenology of time (from Augustine through Husserl to Heidegger). This is a 'long and difficult threeway conversation' with – at stake – the dialectic of time and narrative. We have already stated earlier that we would substantially restrict our discussion of the temporal aspects of poetic composition, drawing out only those points that may bear upon our later study of living self-narratives. Suffice it to say that we can never have a pure phenomenology of time, since we could not intuit its structure isolated or freed from the procedures of argumentation.[54] Indeed, every philosophical effort to resolve the aporias of earlier traditions, like the Augustinian ones, appears to bring with it only new aporias.

In other words, Ricoeur sets himself the task of establishing in *Time and Narrative, Vol. 2* the aporetic nature of any phenomenology of time as a preliminary to his thesis that 'the poetics of narrativity responds to the aporetics of temporality'.[55] Ricoeur underlines in Heidegger's hierarchization of the levels of temporality in *Being and Time* the middle position between within-time-ness and a radical temporality marked by an authentic being-towards-death. This middle position is termed historicality or *Geschichtlichkeit*. For Ricoeur, the question arises: in a hierarchy where the upper limit is characterized by a being-towards-death and not eternity, is it only through being constituted in history that art can oppose its eternity to the 'fugacity of things'?[56] For us, we may reformulate this question as follows: is it only by way of a personal history narrated to others that the living can counter their being-towards-death and the fugacity of their lives? Is the self as narrative a drive to guarantee eternity in the face of the inexorable ascent towards death? Do we sepulchre ourselves in story – against death?

Throughout this study of what has been primarily the *structure* of narrative, several questions have been posed where narrative and self interweave. When temporality is added to this dual lattice, we position ourselves within a developmental and genetic framework where the self is some-thing from no-thing, subject to fugacity and death, to eternity in remembrance and a debt to the dead.

The self in time is not just a being-towards-death but also a being-from-birth. As such, a new problematics of the narrative self arises, particularly with regard to its origins in the mimetic circle that diagrammatizes it: (Q10) do the rudimentary beginnings of the self reside in a pre-understanding of narrative configuration, or is there some-thing of the self prior to this mimesis$_1$? What are the originary configurations of the narrative self, configurations perhaps formed *in utero* and in infancy? Are these of a fundamentally narrative structure or is this narrative structure externally mediated, even imposed? If so, does it participate in what might be termed a discursive practice within a particular episteme of selfhood? Must we finally have recourse to positing a genetics of mimesis$_1$ which would inevitably present us with the unedifying Schellingian question: How does some-thing arise out of no-thing? How does a self develop from no-self through time; how does it bridge an abyss that appears to be an impossible aporia for selfhood? Does it in fact come from the abyss, the one that Kant backed away from?

The past raises a particular problem for us: how to talk about it within a theory of descriptions. Referring to Authur C. Danto's book, *Analytic Philosophy of History*, Ricoeur asks to what degree does our manner of thinking or speaking about the world necessarily involve sentences that both employ past tense verbs and take the form of 'irreducibly narrative statements'.[57] We must acknowledge that there is no history of the future or of the present, precisely because of the nature of narrative sentences which with regard to history describe past events; even if the story is fictional and set in the future, it must by necessity have happened in the past for the narrator to describe its events.[58] Therefore, narrative discourse is by nature incomplete, as its narrative is always open to revision by a subsequent historian (or by the individual or self-historian at a later point in his or her life); it is also incomplete, insofar as there are many elements of the past not amenable to narrative explication. Indeed, as we move increasingly and temporally away from an event and as we re-narrate it in the light of its consequences, whether foreseen or unforeseen, and as we judge that event alongside other similar events and with a developmentally changing perspective, we unremittingly alter the initial first descriptions of that event by subsequent narrative embellishment, and the intentional nature of action that our first descriptions bear is progressively diluted by what Danto calls this 'retroactive realignment of the Past'.[59]

These crucial problematics for describing the events of the past now add a whole new supplement of questions to our thesis: (Q11) can the narrative self be constructed in this sea of uncertainty? How much of the self has to be omitted in order to present a coherent account of itself within what we have noted to be the internal limits of narrative statements? Or if we orientate this problem somewhat differently, how much of the self can simply not be included when narrative discourse is by nature '*intrinsically incomplete*'?[60] We will discover in Chapter 10 a further problem: some people narrate their past or parts of it in the present tense. What is the nature of this present past for one's own personal history?

History and narrative

To apply caustic to an ever-increasing wound to the self, one that the dialogue between history and narrative seems intent upon developing, we return to a point mentioned earlier in the introductory remarks to this chapter. At one crucial point in *Time and Narrative, Vol. 1*, Ricoeur notes a triple epistemological break unfold between history and narrative at the level of procedures, entities and temporality. Through a method that stems from Husserl's 'genetic phenomenology',[61] Ricoeur attempts to locate a series of relay stations for his questioning back (*Rückfrage*) of the derivation of historical knowledge from the activity of narrative configuration. Essentially, he is intent on demonstrating that the procedures, entities and events of history as science indirectly refer back to the procedures, entities and events of narrative proper.[62] We can summarize Ricoeur's conclusions and note how these conclusions further problematize an already haemorrhaging narrative of the self.

We noted that the explanation of what happened and why it happened coincide, and any narrative that fails to explain is, according to Ricoeur, less than a narrative. Nevertheless, there remains a fundamental difference between narrative and history – above and beyond the mere fact that history alleges to relate to what really happened; the difference lies in emplotment in that the ordering of events in history is imposed, whereas in fiction they can be manipulated. Also, history is a form of enquiry that requires that the causal relations between events be explained explicitly rather than remaining implicit to the narrative configuration of fiction. These differences can however be reduced by the common requirement of both history and fiction that the story is *followable*. We need for the moment to simply hold these distinctions in mind when conceptualizing the narrative self. A theory of the narrative self needs to accommodate both the self as history and the self as fiction and the 'followability' of the self to both the self and to the other. Indeed, it will also require the unusual ability, having configured it-self and delivered it to the other for reconfiguration (mimesis$_3$), of following the followability of itself through the reconfiguration that the other has performed. It will become clearer later on how this can best be conceptualized, or if not simply conceptualized then perceptualized, through both a loosening of the definitional elements of narrative and by recourse to media at the blurred edges of narrative.

In summary, we will seek to demonstrate how history and fiction within the individual are woven into each other – again, somewhat like the two strands of the double helix. Indeed, we will find trace references within Ricoeur's texts to suggest that this is the defining characteristic of the narrative self. Now if we accept the view that the individual configures his narrative through the fictional resources of the productive imagination and that the historian is in the position of a judge intent on proving that one explanation is better that another[63] and if we acknowledge that this view describes more or less precisely the relationship between analysand and analyst in the psychoanalytic encounter, then we are faced with this intriguing problem: (Q12): is this also an accurate, even precise description of the infant–mother relationship? Is this the origin of the pre-understanding of narrative, of mimesis$_1$? Or are we mistaken in assuming that the infant or the analysand is the poet that produces and the mother or the analyst the historian that argues?

If the self is to survive as some hybrid of fiction and narrative then the problematic epistemological breaks and the 'gap'[64] (*écart*) that lies between narrative explanation and historical explanation will need to be sealed or, to use Ricoeur's term, sutured. He achieves this through the identification of specific relay stations or posting-houses[65] that situate history within the sphere of narrative. Through this process, Ricoeur successfully identifies the elements of emplotment in history as *quasi*-elements (in contrast to fictional narrative): *quasi*-characters, *quasi*-plots and *quasi*-events. The characters of history are no longer the individuals of fiction but society, peoples, civilizations and nations who behave in history as if they were characters ('participatory belonging' designates the relay station here); to these quasi-characters, historians impute causal explanations, as if the society, nation or civilization could be explained as one explains the behaviour of individuals (by the relay station of 'singular causal imputation'[66] rather than by recourse to nomothetic or law-based explanation), thus providing history with the appearance of quasi-plots; and from these quasi-characters who have collectively the capacity of agency arise events that unfold over time (the relay station here is the discordant rhythms of multiple temporalities) – these becomings of societies are the quasi-events set within quasi-plots that assure the narrative status of the quasi-events.[67] The merit of questioning back is ultimately to reveal what Ricoeur refers to as the 'tenuous and deeply hidden tie' that maintains history within the realm of narrative, thus preserving that very historical dimension itself.[68]

But with this in mind, the narrative self is confronted by even further problems, now arising from the epistemological breaks between history as science and narrative, and the relay stations that connect them. (Q13) To what extent is the '*ambition of truth*'[69] divorced or irreconcilably married to the narrative of the self? Is the self a whorl of the half-true, the half-false? If history contains imaginary structures that are inseparable from the singular causal imputation model, then is it not inevitable that in the configuration of the self as historian of the self an imaginary world of alternative stories is constructed on the hypothesis that 'every historian, to explain what did happen, asks himself what might have happened'?[70] Is not Ricoeur here opening up a breach in the enclosure of narrative identity, an enclosure that up until now has fiercely protected the actual narrative self from the virtual narrative self that both constitutes and delimits it? And finally, what ontological status has the self, if it can be constituted by both the false and the true?

Summary: Problems for Narrative Identity

Let us recall some of the central tenets of narrative identity. We first pose the question: *Who* says I? *Who* is the author, the agent of action? To answer the question is *to tell the story of a life*, so that 'the identity of this "who" therefore itself must be a narrative identity'.[71] To fulfil the telling of the story of that life, to be that 'Who', we must remain within the confines of narrative, and that entails submitting to the rules of emplotment. Under the mantle of narrative identity, we must ask to what degree it therefore matters whether that story contains inaccuracies or contradictions once it meets the requirements of narrative. How important to the self is truth? How debilitating is too much fiction, too much distortion, too little coherence? What is at stake extends beyond the constraints of narrative identity, insofar as the self remains immured within it.

Are we to presuppose that the self is confined to narrative and not borne also in the breath of the imagination that grasps it together or that it has no real being within the virtual narratives and potential narratives that are peremptorily excluded along a probability curve when the self is finally spoken? Our interest here – to state it somewhat differently from above – is to explore within the enclosure of narrative identity, to place cold hands before the imaginative warmth of the fireplace, to search for the tears in the wallpaper, to listen outside its walls for what is bidden and forbidden to narrative, to grasp the unseen, subterranean channels beneath the surface, by way of what Virginia Woolf called her 'tunnelling process',[72] and to accomplish, if possible, a wider grasp, a crazy reach, an imagination at the heart(h) of the narrative that reaches beyond the limits of emplotment. In other words, we must be certain that *narrative is not enough*.[73]

In this regard, we will postpone a more vigorous response to *Time and Narrative, Vol. 2* and the question of the limits of narrative with respect to the self until we have exhausted our investigation into the problems that have arisen since dragging narrative identity back to its philosophical origins. Ricoeur describes this limit very beautifully in reference to Virginia Woolf's *Mrs Dalloway*:

What now holds the centre of attention is the incompleteness of personality, the diversity of the levels of the conscious, the subconscious, and the unconscious, the stirring of unformulated desires, the inchoate, and evanescent character of feelings. The notion of plot here seems to be especially in trouble.[74]

This remark represents the true challenge to the survival of the self as narrative – for without a plot there can be no narrative identity. But what type of plot will nourish a self, what structure of plot will complete the personality? And what configures our so-called pre-narrative understanding if not something before, anterior, previous to narrative, something outside narrative drawing it to its plot-points? Indeed, do we need a non-plot for the 'inchoate' and the 'unformulated' or something entirely different from plot? It is here that we turn to Deleuze – across a Proustian bridge.

Chapter 6

Interlude

[We] have to find in the very functioning of poetic language the means to cross the abyss opened between these two worlds by the method of immanence characteristic of anti-poetics (la poétique anti-référentielle).[1]

Introduction

In moving from the region of hermeneutics to that of difference-in-itself we traverse a substantial barrier in the form of an abyss – as though the glass that separates Alice from the upside down, back-to-front Looking-Glass World beyond were a barrier that must be shattered by an antipoetics in order to traverse it. Thus, we have positioned an 'Interlude' in this transitional space, remembering Ricoeur's use of Antigone in *Oneself as Another* and Deleuze's strange interpellation of 'Notes on the Proustian Experiences' in the middle of *Difference and Repetition*. The purpose behind this interlude is not theatrical or magical, rather it inaugurates in this work a transversality between Deleuze and Ricoeur, an acknowledgement (as noted in the Preface) that some suturing of gaps may need to occur not just in a straight line (the traditional suture) but by cross-stitch. Indeed, it is the very definition of an 'interlude' that prescribes a form of play 'between'.

Transversals between Ricoeur and Deleuze

We mentioned earlier the importance of a transversal encounter between Deleuze and Ricoeur without providing any real explanation of what this means or how it is philosophically justifiable. We will do so now. In *A Thousand Plateaus*, Deleuze and Guattari are concerned with how things connect (multiplicities) rather than with what they are (essences), conceptualizing 'things in terms of unfolding forces – bodies and their powers to affect and be affected – rather than static essences'.[2] How do things change, take on new formations, form new conjunctions? They describe the process of 'deterritorialization' simply as 'a movement producing change [that] operates as a line of flight [and] indicates the creative potential' of a body.[3] This movement is one of transversality, classically described in *A Thousand Plateaus* in the connection between the wasp and the orchid:

> The pollinating transversal insect is not simply natural or organic, for that is a trope of the *logos*. Rather, it is a line of passage, a zig-zagging flight, or even the narration of involuntary memory, that productively transverses.[4]

This 'Interlude' presents a textual deterritorialization, acknowledging in the process that the straightforward path from the actual to the virtual presumes a homogeneous system in which the self is located and held suspended, awaiting its own revelation or that what is being discussed (the self) is always done so within the same system of discourse and under the same axioms that determine its intrinsic constancy, regardless of whether an empirical, phenomenological or rationalist approach is taken. It assumes that the selves from Rousseau to Merleau-Ponty and even the shattered self of Nietzsche, in spite of their differences, are all developmental variations of the same self (together or in pieces) but variations that have taken place over time and within an increasingly rigorous and refined philosophical system that has done no more that make manifest veil by veil what is presumed to await its own full self-exegesis.

But as we can see, we are often chained to metaphor when we seek to elucidate the self beyond what is immediately given to consciousness. Even Kant evoked the metaphor of the 'many-coloured' in this respect. Yet if we cannot know the self through observation and knowledge other than by way of the metaphorically concealed and partly revealed, then we have only partial knowledge of it – by way of its very heterogeneity. Is this not justification enough for us to also search for the self in its mutations alongside its metaphorizations? 'I am legion,' says Deleuze.[5]

If we think of the self as a multiplicity not an essence, then it becomes a movement across concepts, outside essences, a metamorphic and transversal movement. This is the self as an infinitive becoming, a verb 'with a consistency all its own', a self that does not 'reduce to, or lead back to, "appearing," "being" or "equalling."'[6] It is a self whose characteristics we are less interested in than its 'modes of expansion, propagation, occupation, contagion, peopling'.[7] We are legion in this sense.

In his understanding of the human as acting and suffering Ricoeur's narrative self performs a 'movement' away from Kant's categorical imperatives where moral worth is solely bound to duty and not to 'compassion, sympathy, pleasure, satisfaction, and happiness'[8] – and such contagious affects. In this new metamorphosis of the self, Ricoeur moves toward an ethics of action. For him the central questions are as follows: 'Who is speaking? Who is acting? Who is telling his or her story? Who is the moral subject of imputation?'[9]

Ricoeur proposes the following distinction between ethics and morals. He reserves the term 'ethics' for 'the *aim* of an accomplished life' and 'morality' for 'the articulation of this aim in *norms* characterized ... by the claim to universality and by an effect of constraint'.[10] It is the twin heritages here that are important and Ricoeur makes this very clear: the heritage of ethics is an Aristotelian one exemplified by 'a *teleological* perspective', a virtual that-for-the-safe-of-which, while the heritage of morality is a Kantian one characterized by 'the obligation to respect the norm' and therefore defined by a *deontological* perspective.[11] By performing such a division the teleological moment is placed as immanent to the action and therefore provides support for 'the reflexive moment of self-esteem', implying that in appraising our decisions and actions 'we appraise ourselves as being their author'.[12] For Ricoeur, this reflexive moment is embedded in several layers so that his ethics describes circles within circles yet immanent to the person. We echo the placing of the teleological as immanent to the deontological by situating Deleuze's larval selves as immanent to Ricoeur's narrative self. We are legion in this case too.

Estimations applied to our actions and evaluations correspond to what Ricoeur means by the narrative unity of life within which the subject is 'none other than the one whom the narrative assigns a narrative identity'.[13] If, however, this appears to be an enclosed and self-sufficient model, then it is not. And this is what needs to be emphasized – Ricoeur's model is dynamic and unstable, positing the self in constant movement from inner to outer circles of means-end assessments and back again, from action-estimations to self-evaluations to further action-evaluations appraised anew with a self altered through its last evaluation. Indeed, Ricoeur provides his most intriguing statement on the narrative unity of life and 'the fragility of the goodness of human action',[14] when he says that the good life is 'a plane of "time lost" and "time regained"'.[15] He does not clarify this remark, yet such a naked reference to Proust surely operates within the text as an opening or a metaphoric portal to a world that complicates, in the form of an intertextual conjunction, our understanding of the narrative self that Ricoeur develops. It suggests something more for us – something indeed lost to the text of narrative identity, something to be regained. It must be opened out, like the paper pieces Proust tells us the Japanese amuse themselves with, pieces that are 'without character or form, but, the moment they become wet, stretch and twist and take on colour and distinctive shape' and out of which whole worlds spring into being.[16] But in what way is this Proustian plane of time lost and regained to be understood in the sense of the narrative unity of life and the dominance of concordance? What 'unthought' in Ricoeur's phrase will spring into being when we play with it?

Ricoeur is very clear that poetic texts 'speak of the world' even if they do not do so descriptively and that by effacing a descriptive reference they set free what he calls 'a more radical power of reference to those aspects of our being-in-the-world that cannot be talked about directly'.[17] This is not just a call for an exegesis of the world and the horizon of the self (through metaphor and its interpretation) but a prescription that the self speak of that part of it that it cannot speak of itself. It is in this sense that antipoetics passes back through narrative.

The concepts of horizon and world are not limited to descriptive references but extend to poetic diction: the world is 'the whole set of references opened by every sort of descriptive or poetic text',[18] a world into which we interpret and beyond which we cannot but must speak of. Ricoeur notes that Eugene Fink compared Bild to a narrow 'window' that opened out upon a vast countryside.[19] This is what we mean by a 'metaphoric portal' – a window to the virtual and the unspeakable of the self through which we see darkly.

Now what are we to make of Ricoeur's allusion to Proust? Deleuze's book *Proust and Signs* is a work well regarded by Ricoeur. Deleuze's central theme is that *The Search* in question is a search for truth, 'a narrative of an apprenticeship' and not an exposition of involuntary memory.[20] It is a search oriented to the future not the past and a pedagogy concerned with *signs*. If we are to learn, then we must initially regard an object or a being 'as if it emitted signs to be deciphered or interpreted'.[21] For instance, to fall in love is to become sensitive to this particular world of signs (the signs of love), to individualize someone by the signs he or she bears or emits. Love is nourished on the silent interpretation of signs insofar as the one we love expresses 'a possible world unknown to us'; he or she does so with signs that imply and envelop this world 'that must be deciphered'.[22] To love is thus to explicate and develop 'these unknown worlds that remain enveloped within the beloved'.[23]

Is this not what the phrase about 'the plane of "time lost" and of "time regained"' is about? Is this phrase not an emitter of signs, a demand to 'become sensitive to this particular world' and to what it implies, envelops, imprisons?[24] In other words, are we not invited by Ricoeur to explore the implications of this phrase and what it says and does not say about the self? We therefore move from the phrase to its source and to Ricoeur's interpretation of Proust in *Time and Narrative*, one indebted to Deleuze.

Proust sits between Deleuze and Ricoeur. Embarking on his 'living totality' of self-narrative, Proust undertook a journey towards 'an invisible unity in the midst of dispersion' in a style described by Adorno as 'rank vegetal proliferation'.[25] This corresponds precisely with what Deleuze and Guattari term 'rhizomatic':

A rhizome has no beginning or end; it is always in the middle, between things, interbeing, intermezzo. The tree is filiation, but the rhizome is alliance, uniquely alliance. The tree imposes the verb 'to be,' but the fabric of the rhizome is the conjunction. 'and . . . and . . . and . . .'[26]

This use of the conjunction, the placing of 'everything in variation' as a form of stammering in writing is at its most exquisite in the works of Kafka and Proust.[27] Indeed Proust, in commencing his great work with the unavailability of the mother, begins with a break from constancy ('to be'), a rupture of the primary filiation of mother–child into mother-and-child. This 'and' will then proliferate wildly in the text. Indeed, the whole of the *Search* may be understood as a line of flight from unity, a 'drift, awaiting love's coming, vague and free, without precise attachment',[28] a deterritorialization from the moment when birth occasions the first separation and when the infant determines then and at every subsequent and more extended separation that he must always return to this – by whatever means at his disposal – but that he can never do so.

Is this something of what is unthought in Ricoeur: fracture in the heart of attachment, determination driving the self to contain the proliferating 'ands', reterritorialization as a giant 'plunged into the years,'[29] returned finally via that 'more radical power of reference to those aspects of our being-in-the-world that cannot be talked about directly',[30] in other words, to a form of feminine jouissance? Perhaps. Indeed he is very close to saying something like this, though with a voice from outside philosophy or from non-philosophy,[31] a voice external to what Derrida calls phallogocentrism.[32] In discussing the transformations of both a logocentric and phallogocentric philosophy brought upon it by deconstruction and the feminist movement, Derrida concludes:

> A return to the former logocentric philosophies of mastery, possession, totalization or certitude may soon be unthinkable. The philosophical and literary discoveries of the 'feminine' . . . are all symptoms of a deeper mutation in our search for meaning.[33]

We need 'another language', he says, 'to characterize the enormous deconstructive import of the feminine as an uprooting of our phallogocentric culture.'[34] But such mutation in Ricoeur?

We are reminded that the narrative unity of life confers upon the subject of ethics a narrative identity.[35] This suffering, acting subject unfolds upon a plane of 'time lost' but it is upon this plane that time is regained as follows:

> [The] irruption of involuntary memories [alongside] the apprenticeship to signs [that] represents the form of an interminable wandering, interrupted rather than consummated, by the sudden illumination that retrospectively transforms the entire narrative into the invisible history of a vocation.[36]

But what is this vocation? A 'lost unity' haunts the *Search,* and the irruptions of lost time are the bursting of scars where fragments of a shattered identity lie hidden but unified in a virtual plane. Ricoeur argues against the shifting of the stakes from lost time to lost unity; yet it seems that either reading has justification and indeed one is hardly substantial without the other, insofar as we understand time as constituted within human experience and human experience as determined within time.

The feminine interpretation here is the outside of the logocentric one – yet it too, like involuntary memories, irrupts. Thus, Ricoeur criticizes Anne Henry's *Proust romancier: le tombeau égyptien* for promoting the psychological and memorial aspects of a self in search of lost unity[37] rather than a metaphysical one in search of lost time, yet in his argument for time as the theoretical core of the novel he requires 'the challenge of death' and Marcel's 'anxiety on the subject of my death'.[38] Why has death been given such an elevated status over birth? Are not the irruptions of lost time part of the search for the fragments of a primary unity (of Marcel and mother) and a being-towards-birth? We should remember Ricoeur's warning that being-towards-death reflects the 'obsession' in metaphysics with the problem of death to the exclusion of 'the joy of the spark of life' and the theme of 'natality'.[39] Does not a being-towards-birth extend the soul to the past of our own birth and towards the future of our children's births? Ricoeur laments the 'absence of a reflection on the flesh' by Heidegger, one that would have prevented the designating of birth as simply a symmetrical event to death in between which being-towards-death provides the ontological anchor to life.[40] What meaning now might we attach to the 'irruptions' in Ricoeur's text?

Irruptions, as the return of what is lost or repressed or the rediscovery of what is missing, mark dramatic moments in texts when that which requires 'another language' but does not have one mutates the only language available (the logocentric one); they mark moments of difference, of a seeking to say the unsayable in another's discourse. One such 'irruption' occurs within the text of *Oneself as Another*, very soon after the phrase or portal we noted. Ricoeur argues for the restoration of a certain disavowed and unspecified conflict to the philosophy of practical wisdom, deeming it necessary and appropriate 'to make a voice heard other than the voice of philosophy'. This voice will perform an 'untimely irruption . . . capable of awakening our mistrust with respect not only to the illusions of the heart but also to the illusions born of the hubris of practical wisdom itself'.[41]

The voice is that of Antigone, who will speak for 'the family bond, so magnificently concentrated in [the term] "sisterhood"'.[42] But it is a sisterhood of *philia* without *eros* that she will bring, childless and in the company of the dead, to her 'marriage-chamber' and her 'tomb'. For Ricoeur, Antigone is not a person who suffers but she is 'Suffering itself'.[43] She is an affect, an infinitive. Placed outside philosophy, she is a bodiless other that irrupts in an untimely manner.[44] Ricoeur understands irruptions as unfashionable/untimely in that they confront our 'overwhelmingly historical culture', offering egress from this but only 'under the enigmatic sign of the nonhistorical'.[45] Since we are too much in the throes of history, beset by an overdose of historical culture, the irruption of Antigone represents the irruption of the non-historical, a voice outside the history of philosophy that represents not the men of the polis who define history but the women of family duties who beget the makers of history. If *Antigone,* as the 'agonistic ground of human experience where we witness the interminable confrontation of man and woman',[46] irrupts into *Oneself as Another,* ostensibly with the intention of instructing ethics,[47] then Antigone herself, as birth, natality and the maternal/feminine, irrupts in another sense, for she must 'digest the masculine'[48] and 'act as if she were a man'[49] in order to be herself. This is her only medium of presence in the phallogocentric world.

To act then, for Antigone, is to perform a mimesis of the male; in so doing she fragments her identity between public and private, between male and female, and in burying and grieving her dead brother she collapses the relationship between herself and her mother.[50] As Anderson puts it, Antigone encapsulates 'the dilemma of the postmodern woman who wants to assert her lack of a unified identity, yet has to wonder whether or not an acknowledgement of a fragmented self will only render her actions meaningless and her agency impotent'.[51]

Ricoeur's reading of Antigone conceals within it an invitation, demanded by a text on the self, to entertain this somewhat more disruptive and gendered reading. Ricoeur argues with Hegel that Antigone's fault is determined by 'the narrowness of the angle of commitment'[52] that ensures she reduce the unwritten laws of the gods down to funereal demands; but this can only be understood if Antigone is presented within the sisterhood of *philia,* immured in an identity that is constituted by way of the principles of binary opposition, that is, to Creon; she is neither entangled in the *polis* nor determined in history but exists as a dissolved self without a narrative of its own, miming the male but as a specular reversal of him. Only by being maintained as unitary and not fragmented, by existing as solid and not fluid, by being given a 'one-sidedness' of character and moral principles can Antigone's failings be seen to mirror those of Creon.[53] Yet it is a fact that what erupts in Ricoeur's text on the self, albeit disguised, is this untimely feminine, dissolved within the mimetically solid.

Does 'discordant concordance' then mean the subjugation of difference to identity, the fluid to the solid, rather than the synthesis of the heterogeneous? Ricoeur certainly demurs from permitting a philosophy of difference to stand alone; for him the sea that contains difference remains encased in a philosophy of identity, surviving only as 'single embellished facts [that] stand out as islands [above this flood]'.[54] As morality is the actualization of the ethical aim so also is identity the actualization of difference. In *Oneself as Another* and *Time and Narrative* Ricoeur's philosophy of difference, though present, repeatedly collapses into identity.[55] Indeed, there is always the Kantian presumption of 'one self' that draws difference together. In this sense, the self represents a cloth woven of difference but *one* cloth nevertheless. Yet if we are weavers of words and stories are woven together, is the narrative self of ipse and idem identities then unwoven as it is woven, or is it over-woven? Do tears appear, are ends frayed, are our stories of ourselves ripped down the middle or shredded by new weavings? It seems impossible to prevent this happening when we seek perpetually a discordant concordance, that is, when it is *presupposed that this is what is most germane to our human condition.*

If we return briefly to the good life that is 'the plane of time lost and of time regained' we will find a tear here also, a loose shard – a trace of difference. Here is what Ricoeur says after his Proustian portal when he discusses the encircling of means-ends in wider means-ends towards which our actions are directed:

> This finality within finality . . . does not destroy the self-sufficiency of practices as long as their end has been posited and continues to be so. This opening, which fractures practices otherwise held to be closed in upon themselves . . . maintains a tension . . . between the closed and the open within the global structure of praxis. What we are summoned to think here is the idea of a higher finality (*une finalité supérieure*) which would never cease to be internal to human action.[56]

Now what is this 'higher finality' that we are 'summoned' to think? Is it an immanent God or an eschatological God-to-come? Who or what summons us? And how could a summons be internal? Ricoeur fractures the surface of the concordant narrative self but nothing happens – unlike the tiny crack in the windscreen sustained by the violence of a loose pebble that begins to expand, diversify and spread like a contagion until the whole screen shatters into fragments. For Ricoeur, the unity of the narrative self must be protected, but it is done so only by recourse to a vague, even quasi-theological element deep to human action. Without this, the narrative becomes vegetal, feminine, proliferative, rhizomatic, metastatic, a flight of conjunctions – and the 'fragility of goodness' at the heart of the self and the self itself, are sundered. We are fallen from unity. Though we desire to return to it by whatever means at our disposal, we can never do so. We cannot put Humpty-Dumpty together again. Ricoeur has directed us to an opening into the virtual, to an unknown from which, like Kant, he withdrew. Yet it is precisely here that we will argue for the essence of unity in the narrative self.

Chapter 7

In the Land of the Larval Selves

Either we must posit a subject identical with itself through the diversity of its different states, or . . . we must hold that the identical subject is nothing more than a substantialist illusion, whose elimination merely brings to light a pure manifold of cognitions, emotions and volitions.[1]

Introduction

We have reached an impasse with the narrative self. There appear to be inordinate difficulties when it is interrogated through its own progenitors. The problem may well rest with its ontological status. Ricoeur accepts this when he refers to his Tenth study as an 'exploratory' investigation into the ontology of the narrative self that essentially asks, 'What mode of being . . . belongs to the self?'[2] In this chapter we will introduce the key ontological elements that underpin Deleuze's philosophy. This is by no means an easy task. Nevertheless, our goal is to lay out an ontological grounding for the self in difference so that we will be in a position later on to seek commonality between the larval selves that bubble away in a Deleuzian multiplicity and what is hidden, secret or implied in Ricoeur's narrative self.

The sequencing of the parts in this chapter will be as follows: (1) we will take up where we left off in our genealogical tree, tracing Deleuze's dissolved selves back to Schelling and (2) in the body of the chapter, we will engage in an explication of the ontological basis of Deleuze's selves by way of multiplicity, difference and his specifically 'new image of thought' that we will argue generates a virtual foundation for the actualization and individuation of the narrative self.

We must make a final introductory point regarding how we orientate ourselves towards the subject matter of philosophy when working with Deleuze's texts. Specifically, with Deleuze, we position ourselves differently towards the self than we did with Ricoeur. For the latter (and his forebears) we asked the question: 'What is the self?' This provides one specific way of reading the self where you see it 'as a box with something inside and start looking for what it signifies . . . and you annotate and interpret and question' the self in this regard.[3] But there is another approach and that is to see the self as a 'non-signifying machine' where the only questions to pose are 'Does it work, and how does it work?' This intensive manner of questioning the self begins from the position that there is 'nothing to explain, nothing to understand, nothing to interpret'.[4] It demands that we see the self as a flow among flows, as 'a little cog in much more complicated external machinery'.[5]

Origins in Schelling

We noted in Chapter 3 that Ricoeur considered the Kantian division of the self into transcendental/noumenal/empirical as a 'shattering of the problematic of the subject'[6] – but could such a shattered subject be repaired by Fichte and Schelling's Romanticism yet systematized under the same rules of determination and structure? If German Romanticism takes its departure from Kant's transcendental system, then it also relies heavily on his *3rd Critique*, where the notion of organic unity and beauty as 'the symbol of morality' is upheld. Romanticism was a rebellion against the 'established, oppressive order, against rigidity and feudal mediocrity', and it sought its sustenance in history and change, not in the stasis of eternal categories.[7] The romantic self's 'reigning metaphors . . . involved organic images of "fluidity" and growth (*Bildung*)',[8] and its functioning was achieved through deposing Reason from its seat of authority and placing the Passions upon the throne. The self in Deleuze begins life here.

In the age of Romanticism, the antinomies of Kant were no longer understood as obstacles to reason; instead, they heralded a path towards a radically new reason, propelled forward by the previously disparaged inclinations and emotions. For Kant, the convoluted transcendental deduction of the twelve categories was a limit point – there are no more and the constraint is to utilize this particular set of categories and no others. There are no *imaginative variations*. Fichte argued that this is precisely possible. The categories are not exclusive, and we are not limited to a single way of understanding the world. This freedom to submit to the 'play of the imagination' is a central presupposition for Romanticism and one that justifies the holding of such beliefs on practical rather than rigid and dogmatic grounds.[9] In other words – and as a forerunner to Deleuze's questioning – to what use will be put such knowledge, to what ends, to what advantages? This is an ethical concern rather than a moral one which places us as agents engaged in the world rather than observers and categorizers who act according to dogmatic imperatives that demand the empirical self be deposed or effaced in the moment of action.

Schelling, adopting Kant's *3rd Critique*, rejects the Newtonian mechanical universe for a view of 'the whole of nature as a living force, a purposeful teleological system'.[10] His emphasis is on 'the more radical, visionary, self-aggrandizing elements of the Critiques' that embraced 'a diversity, historicity and fluidity of forms of life and consciousness'[11]; thus he establishes the post-Kantian ground for Deleuze's later inversion of Platonism.[12] Indeed, if we can convincingly locate such an ancestral ground for the larval selves in relation to Schelling, we will have identified a proximity-point or perihelion in the dual trajectories of a self that leads, on the one hand, to Ricoeur and, on the other, to Deleuze.

Schelling's free play of forces

'The *sum* that is contained in the *cogito* is . . . only *sum qua cogitans*, I am as think-ing, i.e. in that specific way of being which is called thinking.'[13] It is by way of this move that Schelling becomes modern.[14] He takes his point of departure from Kant insofar as Kant's dualism, his split between our knowledge of things and 'things in themselves', was indefensible; Kant restricted 'the domain of our knowledge to the laws governing phenomena as they are given to conscious-ness, which excluded knowledge of what was not given in intuition'.[15] In Kant's own words, it is only because 'I can comprehend the variety of my represen-tations in one consciousness, do I call them my representations, for otherwise I would have as many-coloured and various a self as are the representations of which I am conscious'.[16] Kant considered this condition as a 'fact' but a fact that cannot appear in empirical consciousness. Fichte seized upon this and declared that before all positing in the 'I', the 'I' must itself previously be posited. Access to the 'I' is solely through the 'I' itself and it is so through an act of reflection upon itself that Fichte called 'intellectual intuition'.[17] The 'I' is therefore the condition of there *being* representations. Kant hinted at this in the first edition of the *1st Critique*, where 'the imagination had played a hybrid role by both pro-ducing and receiving intuitions'.[18] The problem for Kant is that the conditions set out in his system of reason 'are those posited by thought itself, and are thus conditioned by thought'.[19] Being cannot be an object of knowledge since it would therefore be conditioned and would no longer condition knowledge.

It is this that Schelling wants to overcome – to move beyond the problematic of Kantian critique, that is, the establishment of knowledge based on empirical experience or the necessity of synthetic propositions for the realm of experi-ence. Schelling undermines this position with the well-posed question, 'Why is there a realm of experience at all?' And he argues that this question cannot be answered as a 'theoretical question' about knowledge but 'demands the move into the practical realm', one not subject to the determinism of the theoretical realm. Only by achieving the unity of subject and object, Schelling claims, 'would we finally understand the division that leads to a realm of experience'.[20] And this requires an entirely different conceptualization of man and nature, one that now becomes a field of forces prior to a system of reason. Although Kant's theoretical philosophy presupposes the transcendental subject as the condition of possibility of anything that we can know, it cannot, as we argued earlier, explain the genesis of this transcendental subjectivity itself. It is this that Schelling attempts to achieve, and it augurs the investigation into the 'genitality of thought' that obsessed Deleuze. It is an insistence that all of nature be thought of in inherently dynamic terms, that is, as 'productivity'. It is best explicated in his *System of Transcendental Idealism*.

In the *System*, Fichte's intellectual intuition is the mode of being of the self, of the totality of the known and the knowing; indeed, the 'self is such an intuition'.[21] It is an *unconscious* principle of consciousness where our awareness is always an intuition directed back upon a production – *a production-intuition*. No totalization of intuition is possible in the transcendental system since intellectual intuition cannot be realized except as process, as 'the ongoing flux of our experiencings'.[22] This is because 'the opposition between conscious and unconscious activity is necessarily an unending one.'[23] The self is intellectual intuition subsistent; it exists by knowing itself in a non-objective manner insofar as intellectual intuition is not properly a cognitive state or an activity of or in the subject – it is the subject.[24] It is an archetypal knowing, separate from the intuition of empirical consciousness, and it fragments the self into productive and intuitive capabilities.[25] Schelling's 'dialectic of production' (*Erzeugungsdialektik*) must be contrasted with Hegel's 'dialectic of sublation' (*Aufhebung*). As Beach notes, 'the metaphor of procreation does not subordinate or transcend one element in favour of the other, even as it preserves the emphasis on volition and desire as the most original forces in the cosmos and the individual.'[26] By positing self-consciousness as grounded in this opaque activity which only produces and does not illuminate, Schelling abandons the old Cartesian ideal of consciousness as self-transparency and effectively 'invents' the unconscious. This opaque activity has long been our quarry in this book.

The replacement of negation with a productive desire is perhaps the most core driving force in Deleuze's work. Furthermore, Schelling's importance to Deleuze is also in the manner in which he proposes that the ultimate ascent to the Absolute is not cognitive or moral but aesthetic, based not on a transcendent value 'but on a symbolic and produced totality of subjective and objective elements' which reside in 'the unconsciously produced work of art, which fully reveals the nature of self-consciousness'.[27] Here perhaps marks the end of Idealism for Schelling, in the admittance of this enigmatic, unconscious, productive force into which the self loses itself in its productions – as the artist loses himself in his work.[28]

Deleuze reaches the same conclusion on the signs of art at the end of *Proust and Signs*. But there are many other similarities. For example, Deleuze's philosophy of the actual and the virtual in relation to the self parallels Schelling's description of the relationship between the actual, cognizing self and the virtual and purely productive unconscious. The self for Schelling contains the conflict of 'fundamental opposites, namely subject and object; they cancel one another out, and yet neither is possible without the other'. This conflict, according to him,

> [is] not so much a conflict between the two factors, as between the inability, on the one hand, to unite the infinite opposites, and the necessity of doing do, on the other, if the identity of self-consciousness is not to be blotted out. This very fact, that subject and object are absolute opposites, puts the self under the necessity of condensing an infinity of actions into a single absolute one. [29]

This multiplicitous self that 'comes to intuit itself as limited solution' does so through its 'mechanism of producing',[30] a mechanism that has, as Vater notes, 'a paradoxical and dark side, a hidden ground which is in fact an antitype'.[31] Later in this book we will see that Deleuze's 'dark precursor' or 'paradoxical element' (central to our thesis on the self) finds its natural origin in this dark side of Schellingian production.

Schelling's unconscious activity is not the guilt-ridden, repressive stuff of the Freudian unconscious; it is 'a conflict of absolutely opposed activities' where one, 'the real, objective, limitable activity', reaches out 'into infinity', while the other, 'the ideal, subjective, illimitable activity', tends 'to intuit oneself in that infinity'.[32] Deleuze will also develop an unconscious freed from the guilt-ridden family drama of Oedipus. And it will be a self without a centre, with a rhizomatic rather than arborescent structure. But had not Schelling already vouchsafed this? For him, the self never fully returns to itself, never fully knows itself.

> What we speak of as nature is a poem lying pent in a mysterious and wonderful script. Yet the riddle could reveal itself, were we to recognize in it the odyssey of the spirit [or self], which, marvellously deluded, seeks itself, and in seeking flies from itself.[33]

Indeed, Schelling even proposes to go beyond Kant's two forms of thinking, the synthetic and the analytic, by adding a third form derived from the following axiom:

> A form of conditionality determined by unconditionality (axiom of disjunction, connection of the analytic and the synthetic forms). Once the analytic and the synthetic forms were established, then, true enough, the third, which combines both, could not furnish a new form as such, but it could amount to a form no less important.[34]

It is by way of these axioms, particularly the third, that a theory of consciousness and imagination becomes possible for Schelling. It permits Schelling to conclude that 'what is commonly called theoretical reason is nothing else but imagination in the service of freedom'.[35] The third axiom prepares us for the disjunctive use of the faculties that will be central to Deleuze's argument for a new image of thought.[36]

Ontology of Productivity

Deleuze rejects the view that reality is made up of fully formed objects identified by their essence or 'core set of properties that defines what the objects are'[37] – for example, man as a rational animal. To argue this requires a transcendent position and the exclusion of elements that are not common among man. For Deleuze, something else is required to define what an object is – and following Schelling he turns to *dynamic processes* that are immanent to our world of matter and energy. Rather than depend upon timeless categories, Deleuze explicates a theory of morphogenetic processes where resemblance among members is 'explained by having undergone common processes of natural selection' or becoming.[38] In this way, he accounts for the abstract or virtual structure of these dynamic processes in developing his ontology, in sharp contrast to essentialism and transcendent factors. In short, he replaces the notion of essences (based on more or less perfect copies of ideal forms or models of the same) with a theory of morphogenesis based on the notion of difference not conceived upon negation 'or lack of resemblance, but positively or productively, as that which drives a dynamical process'.[39]

At a relatively simple level, these are the intensive differences we see 'in temperature, pressure, speed, chemical concentrations which are keys to the scientific explanation of the genesis of the . . . forms of organic plants and animals'.[40] It is in this space of intensive differences that Deleuze will situate his larval selves. To give these intensive processes a foundational status, Deleuze must reject the subordination of difference to identity or the rule of the negative and negation:

> There are four principal aspects to 'reason' insofar as it is the medium of representation: identity, in the form of the *undetermined* concept; analogy, in the relation between ultimate *determinable* concepts; opposition, in the relation between *determinations* within concepts; resemblance, in the *determined* object of the concept itself.[41]

Difference is mediated by being subjected to these four roots of representation and therefore, according to Deleuze, misconstrued throughout the history of philosophy. By creating a specific concept of difference, difference itself becomes no more than 'a predicate in the comprehension of a concept'.[42] Difference in this traditional sense submits to all the requirements of representation noted above, which allow for 'the cutting (*découper*) out of generic identities from the flux of a continuous perceptible series'.[43]

The view that difference is only negativity or that it must extend to the point of contradiction when taken to the limit must be challenged. It is true only if difference is 'already placed on the path . . . laid out by identity'.[44] And this identity is not just of the world but of the self too. But what does Deleuze find presupposed beneath the limitation or opposition that sets up self-identity but a veritable Schellingian world populated by a 'swarm of differences, a pluralism of free, wild or untamed differences; a properly differential and original space and time; all of which persist alongside the simplifications of limitation and opposition'.[45]

Beneath the world of representations lies presupposed this world of multiplicity; beneath the narrative self swarm the multiplicitous larvae. Furthermore, space and time, which display oppositions and limitations only on the surface, also presuppose in their real depths far more 'differences which cannot be reduced to the banality of the negative'.[46] He suggests it can be understood metaphorically 'as though we were in Lewis Carroll's mirror where everything is contrary and inverted on the surface but "different" in depth'.[47] The inversion for Deleuze – and this is in fact an inversion of Platonism ('*La tâche de la philosophie moderne a été définie: renversement du platonisme*'[48]) – is that instead of forcing difference into a previously established identity we should see difference as prior, deeper, more profound. In this position, difference no longer follows identities but 'remains attached in the depths of its own space, in the here-now of a differential reality always made up of singularities'[49] – that is, of memories, events and moments. Wherever there is mediation or representation, difference is left behind, and in establishing universals through representation the singular is not and cannot be represented. Difference is recalcitrant to representation, even allergic to it.

And difference must be affirmed in the becoming of things based on dynamic processes and intensities (i.e. Bergson).[50] Thus, I am different from you, but I do not negate you in the affirmation of who I am. My narrative self does not negate yours.

We noted Derrida's view of the feminine as 'movement' – in contrast to the stasis of representation where nothing moves. Affirmation-in-difference, for Deleuze, corresponds to movement since movement implies 'a plurality of centres . . . a tangle of points of view, a coexistence of moments which essentially distort representation'.[51] Making multiple representations does not achieve the same effect, since it simply ensures the convergence of multiple perspectives into 'properties of the same Self'.[52]

Which then is the narrative self: stories that converge to the same self or a 'tangled tale' (*une histoire embrouillée*)[53] of points of view? If stories converge on a uniquely centred state that 'gathers and represents' all the other representations (like the synthesis of the heterogeneous by a sole author/narrator), then this becomes 'indissociable from a law which renders it possible', and this law is the form of the concept 'as a form of identity'.[54] In other words, self-identity becomes either synonymous with or a by-product of the concept one has of the self or what psychologists call 'the self-concept'. For Deleuze, this law needs to be inverted. Difference needs to be 'the element, the ultimate unity . . . [that] refers to other differences which never identify it but rather differenciate it . . . Difference must be shown *differing*'.[55]

By rejecting representation as the only means of presenting a science of the sensible, Deleuze attempts to apprehend directly the very 'being *of* the sensible' – meaning that which can only be sensed but not represented, that is, difference, potential difference and difference in intensity. It is this 'strange reason'[56] of difference that becomes the object of his philosophy, the reason of the virtual, of the crowned anarchies (*les anarchies couronnées*) that become the medium of the larval selves.[57] Difference is behind everything, according to Deleuze, but 'behind difference there is nothing.'[58]

The Dogmatic Image of Thought

Difference is central to Deleuze's rejection of what he calls the dogmatic image of thought, an image that propounds the view that 'everybody knows' what it means to think or to be or indeed what the self is.[59] In fact, 'everybody knows men think rarely' and thought only occurs 'under the impulse of a shock than in the excitement of a taste for thinking'.[60]

In chapter 3 of *Difference and Repetition* ('The Image of Thought') Deleuze mounts his challenge against what he calls the prevalent and dogmatic image of thought.[61] But what is it? First, he notes the difference between objective pre-suppositions and subjective or implicit ones; the former may be exemplified by defining 'man' as a rational animal but in so doing presupposing the concepts of rationality and animality; the latter – far less addressed in philosophy – have the form of 'Everyone knows . . .'.[62] For example, 'everyone knows, independently of concepts, what is meant by the self, thinking, and being.'[63] Thus, when Descartes says, *Cogito, ergo sum*, everyone implicitly understands what it means to think and to be. For Deleuze, this is not a true beginning for philosophy because it is full of subjective and hidden premises – yet it claims to be presupposition-free. This is the thought of the Idiot 'endowed only with his natural capacity for thought'.[64] Deleuze prescribes a sort of Russian idiot instead, an 'underground' or 'untimely' man, who will reject this presupposition that man has 'a natural capacity for thought endowed with a talent for truth'.[65]

Deleuze attempts to undermine this image of the good will of the thinker, the good nature of thought and the postulates both imply. The dogmatic image presents three levels: (1) the image of a naturally upright thought that knows what it means to think; (2) the image of thought as the unity and harmony of all the other faculties (a *concordia facultatum*) where thought itself is not a faculty and (3) a transcendental model of recognition that aligns itself with the

form of the Same and presumes the same object for all faculties and the possibility of error if one faculty 'confuses one of its objects with a different object of
another faculty'.[66] Other postulates are implied in this dogmatic image, in particular, the postulate of the negative that 'recognizes only *error* as a possible
misadventure of thought'.[67] This implies that when the faculties have failed to
operate in collaboration they are presumed to have provided a false evaluation
of opposition, analogy, resemblance and identity. This failure is itself presumed
to be a failure of 'common sense' or of directing the beam of all the faculties
evenly upon what is supposed to be the same object.[68]

Deleuze's 'struggle' is to undermine those acts of recognition that presume
sameness in the object and to disrupt the structures that establish these acts; he
accepts their reality and utility but not their primacy and royalty. These acts
clearly exist and indeed 'occupy a large part of our daily life; this is a table . . .
this is a piece of wax', but who can believe, he asks, 'that the destiny of thought
is at stake in these acts, and that when we recognise, we are thinking?'[69] In contending that this dogmatic image prevents 'misadventures of thought' such as
stupidity, madness, the thoughts of a child, superstition, malevolence and illusion from 'richer determinations' than simply error and from being developed
on their own account,[70] Deleuze poses an interesting question to us about narrative identity. What happens when this so-called dogmatic image is placed
against the image we have of the self? If our narratives are from time to time
mad, stupid or childlike, then is the self somehow mistaken about itself, delivering an erroneous attestation or erroneously attesting for itself? How could
we argue for a poetics of the narrative self against the very dogma that turns it
to error?

A self without the dogmatic image

Deleuze contends, like Schelling, that we require first and foremost a 'genitality' of thought without dogmatic image.[71] But what then is left of the self, what
image without dogmatic image do we have of such a self denuded of representation, of the equal distribution of the faculties of good sense that have up to
now provided us with its comforting image?[72] What happens if we no longer
seek the self in recognition and the same, in *idem*, in what is banal in the person,
in what is recognized to have repeated itself in tedious habit? What are the consequences of debunking a self established upon a *terra cognita* (where nothing
new happens, where only the established is re-established) and summoning
instead 'forces in thought which are not the forces of recognition . . . but the
powers of a completely different model' to construct a self upon 'an unrecog-
nised and unrecognisable *terra incognita*'?[73]

To construct such a self(s) with the dogmatic image pulled from underneath
it, we must address three further areas: (1) the Kantian collaboration of the

faculties and Deleuze's problematizing of their common accord; (2) the link between thought and individuation in Deleuze and (3) the relationship between multiplicity and the virtual.

Deleuze's Kantian faculties: Uncommon discord

Deleuze regards Kant as the philosopher who introduced a self 'profoundly fractured by the line of time' but whose thought nevertheless continued 'to enjoy an upright nature' through the collaboration of all the faculties.[74] Thus, he argues that in the first two critiques, depending upon the situation, one of those faculties will take precedence and will be charged with the task of providing the model of recognition and subjecting the other faculties to it. One faculty chairs the tribunal: for example, in the case of knowledge of natural concepts and phenomena, the understanding is the 'legislative faculty' providing 'the speculative model' upon which reason and the imagination 'are summoned to collaborate'. But, Deleuze notes, there is also a model in Kant where the faculties attain a free accord with regard to a 'properly aesthetic common sense'.[75]

Central to Kant's critical philosophy is the prescription of limits to these faculties. Deleuze, on the other hand, emphasizes the *affect* in the Kantian system (characteristic of intuition) and places it in a position of primacy, disrupting the common accord and pushing the faculties beyond the limits imposed by Kant's critique. This involves a dismantling of that seat of facultative accord, the cogito, since it is the 'I think' that is the 'source' both of the elements of representation (identity, analogy, opposition, resemblance) and of the unity of all these faculties: I conceive, I judge, I imagine, I remember and I perceive. Upon these branches, he remarks, 'difference is crucified.'[76]

We should note here that Deleuze's attempt to intuit the realm of pre-representational thought is fraught with problems. He is in the domain of the abyss and the unspeakable and yet he attempts to speak it without of course being able to represent it. One could see his endeavour as paralleling that of Merleau-Ponty in *The Visible and the Invisible* in that what emerges in both texts is in places indistinguishable from poetics or a poetic philosophy. Its failure then is its all too obvious departure from reason; its success is the glimpse it provides of what is invisible, yet to be represented, abyssal.

Deleuze distinguishes what does not disturb thought (objects of recognition where thought 'has nothing to do with thinking') from what forces us to think (signs equipped with the 'claws of a strangeness or an enmity [which] awaken thought from its natural stupor').[77] This is 'involuntary thought', paralleled with Proust's involuntary memory. It heralds the assembly of what he sees as a new image of thought or what might be termed the invisible of the visible of thought. Only by agitating beneath the old image do we open ourselves to a sort of subterranean creative nature. This is not radically different from what Schelling and indeed Nietzsche prescribed.

What forces us to think, contends Deleuze, is not an object of conceptual recognition but the object of a 'fundamental encounter . . . grasped in a range of affective tones: wonder, love, hatred, suffering'.[78] We do not just encounter recognizable people – we engage in an event whose primary affective tone can only be sensed, like the work of art, the beautiful or intriguing person, the beatific scenery. This is in direct opposition to the object of recognition, which is sensed only insofar as it is absorbed by the categories of experience in an exercise of perception. The object of encounter is a sign to sensibility itself; no longer a 'sensible being but the being *of* the sensible' (the *sentiendum*).[79] Thus, in the presence of what can only be sensed and what is in effect imperceptible (*insensible*) by not being recognized, sensibility discovers itself before its own limit which is the imperceptible sign and thus elevates itself to the level of a transcendental exercise. Raised to its own limit, sensibility 'enters into a discordant play [where] its organs become metaphysical'.[80] In other words, Deleuze orchestrates a detached and virtual faculty (in this case, sensibility), unclasped of the elements of recognition – even if recognition continues to function for some of what is experienced.

In this encounter, something is going on behind the scenes, but where, in what region of the self or of subjectivity does this putative encounter occur? What exists in the depths beneath what is recognized that is specifically mine or yours – that is ignited by the *sentiendum* and transformed from insensate being to animated darkness? This region is the 'soul' (*l'âme*), according to Deleuze, a soul perplexed by the object of the encounter and forced to see it as the 'bearer of a problem'.[81] But the soul is not sensibility alone, for the other faculties must also, by the same argument, become subject to the violence of an encounter with the object. Sensibility, once forced to sense the *sentiendum*, now provokes memory to remember 'that which can only be recalled' rather than empirically remembered. And in the presence of that which can only be recalled the soul grasps 'the being of the past' (the *memorandum*) which is both 'unrememberable and immemorial.'[82] So too with thinking, which when provoked by transcendental memory grasps 'that which can only be thought, the *cogitandum*', not the intelligible but 'the being of the intelligible as though this were both the final power of thought and the unthinkable'.[83]

This highly abstract and unrecognizable triumvirate of shadows and elemental faculties forms the monstrous government of supreme powers of an interior soul (a crowned anarchy) that is – Deleuze seems to be claiming – made subject most of the time to the laws of representation and recognition or suppressed by them. How can they be untamed or 'unsexed', as Lady Macbeth desires? Indeed, they are like *Macbeth*'s three witches, the supreme conjunction of elemental forces that find expression in the real world, actualized in the war machine of Macbeth and Lady Macbeth.

It is worth looking at Macbeth as an example of what Deleuze seems to be arguing for. In *Macbeth*, evil is something separate from our own being, something that invades and ignites us; we are turned to evil as 'night's black agents to their preys do rouse.'[84] Hunter describes the evil in *Macbeth* as a plague that spreads among the characters with Macbeth as its first victim.[85] It is Macbeth's 'potentiality' to be the host of evil in his relationship with Lady Macbeth that generates the war machine. She is the 'unhinged faculties' that are brought to unrestrained destruction by cultivating the 'scorpions' in his mind[86] through her skilful blurring of the act with the desire and the deadly sting with the hunger.[87] The witches are the signs of evil (the object of the encounter), but 'the mode of evil they can create is potential only, not actual, till the human agent takes it inside his mind and makes it his own by a motion of the will.'[88] If one were to discern a character of supreme importance in *Macbeth* beneath the more obvious representational model that provides us with the recognizable *dramatis personae*, then it would be this war machine that comprises the following parts: the witches, Macbeth, Lady Macbeth and the relations between them. This is the organism that generates the 'miasma of undirected power'.[89]

Deleuze contends that such potential forces are at play within our selves, awaiting the 'violence' of an encounter (the witches), a violence that develops from the *sentiendum* to the *cogitandum* and in which 'each faculty is unhinged'. No longer do all the faculties converge and contribute 'to a common project of recognizing an object' but instead divergent projects develop, where each faculty has 'regard to what concerns it essentially . . . [and] . . . is in the presence of that which is its "own"'.[90] These divergent projects of the virtual indicate, for Deleuze, a creative and unlimited movement of thought by way of an intricate weave of elemental passion beneath the functioning of the Kantian faculties, a weave that delineates the 'free and untamed states of difference-in-itself'.[91] Thus, there is, for example, an element in the sensible (besides what is recognized and identified) that is itself difference and that when experienced is 'inseparable from a becoming or a relation which includes the opposite within it'[92] – in other words, the unlimited world of Alice where the unnatural torsions to thought can be endured in order to produce the new.[93] In this non-dogmatic image of thought forged on the *terra incognita* of the Looking-Glass world, the objects of Wonderland are no longer understood by Alice through representation but by way of 'explication, for the object is a sign, an internal difference pointing toward something other than itself'.[94]

The Narrative Self as Twin Multiplicities

If the faculties are to have their involuntary and virtual adventures, then this transcendental 'mad-becoming' (*le devenir-fou*)[95] that underwrites 'common sense' must also create real thought and novel ideas. But how is this becoming in the self of the novel and the new best demonstrated? For Deleuze, it is by way of Bergson's theory of multiplicities. While Bergson is remarkably lucid on this topic, Deleuze manages to obscure the ground considerably. We will thus attempt to clarify Deleuze by reference to Bergson's original work[96] whose importance to the narrative self is that it provides us with dual domains in which to place the self – a Ricoeurian half and a Deleuzian half.

For Bergson, there are two types of multiplicity: (1) exteriority or space which is actual, homogeneous and discontinuous, a multiplicity of 'order . . . quantitative differentiation, of *difference in degree* . . . a numerical multiplicity'[97] and (2) duration or memory which is virtual, heterogeneous and continuous, a multiplicity of 'succession, of fusion . . . of qualitative discrimination, or of *difference in kind*', a multiplicity that cannot be reduced to numbers.[98] The cube of sugar in exteriority differs by degree from other objects regarding its spatial dimensions, but in its 'rhythm of duration'[99] when it dissolves and in the time spent by us waiting for it to dissolve it reveals how it differs in kind from other things and from itself and how in our waiting other durations are caught up in it. Duration is a continuous multiplicity that divides 'only by changing in kind'.[100] There are no essences in such an intensive multiplicity because by dividing it up one changes its nature.

But where are we as embodied spirit in this multiplicity? For Bergson, we have a consciousness of the discrete multiplicity of space by retaining 'successive states of the external world . . . and then [setting] them side by side by externalizing them in relation to one another'.[101] These are states of consciousness 'which have first to be represented symbolically in space'.[102] Yet we also have states of consciousness that 'even when successive, permeate one another, and in the simplest of them the whole soul can be reflected'.[103] For example, the *enduring* of the notes of a musical piece: although the notes succeed one another 'yet we perceive them in one another, and . . . their totality may be compared to a living being whose parts, although distinct, permeate one another just because they are so closely connected.'[104] This is what Bergson argues we do with states of consciousness – we set them side by side 'so as to perceive them simultaneously, no longer in one another, but alongside one another', but this is effectively a projection of time into space and an expressing of duration in extensity 'as a chain, the parts of which touch without penetrating each other'.[105] Without this spatial projection we have 'pure succession', 'pure heterogeneity' in consciousness, a succession of 'qualitative changes, which melt into and permeate one another'[106] and constitute the gradual growth of the self. We exist both in a real space and in a real duration of heterogeneous moments, each of which can be 'brought into relation with a state of the external world which is contemporaneous with it'.[107] Thus, Bergson concludes that 'the past co-exists along with the present', the virtual along with the actual.[108]

Bergson identifies a problem for us in representing a multiplicity without reference to number or space (precisely the problem we have seen Deleuze attempt to overcome) – although we can do this 'for pure reflective thought, [it] cannot be translated into the language of common sense.'[109] And yet it operates behind the scenes nonetheless, so that we need the idea of a heterogeneous multiplicity in order to form the very idea of a discrete one. It is from Bergson's argument here that Deleuze contends that the trajectory from the *sentiendum* to the *cogitandum* is already presupposed in the dogmatic image of thought. Bergson puts this very simply:

> When we explicitly count units by stringing them along a spatial line, is it not the case that, alongside this addition of identical terms standing out from the homogeneous background, an organization of these units is going on in the depths of the soul, a wholly dynamic process, not unlike the purely qualitative way in which an anvil, if it could feel, would realize a series of blows from a hammer?[110]

Bergson deduces from these two multiplicities 'the two aspects of the self' – one virtual, one actual, one the site of the lightning flash (as we put it earlier), the other the site of narrative.

If we take Bergson's analysis further with respect to the self, then we will understand more clearly the complications Deleuze adds to it and its relationship with narrative. The self (which has the two aspects of multiplicity) 'comes in contact with the external world at the surface' so that our 'superficial psychic life comes to be pictured without any great effort as set out in a homogeneous medium'.[111] It is here that we are story and narrative, from here that we tell and are told as configurations and refigurations, as mimesis$_2$ and mimesis$_3$. It is where we 'betake [ourselves] to a symbolic substitute',[112] and if we delve deeper into consciousness, then we must perform even greater degrees of symbolic representation to alter the states of consciousness so that they may be represented or 'set out in space'.[113] Without such spatializing 'the deep-seated self which ponders and decides, which heats and blazes up' (*sentiendum* → *cogitandum*) would remain a self whose 'states and changes permeate one another' beyond symbolic representation.[114] Take away the 'incursion of space' into this region and we perceive homogeneous time – as in dreams where we do not 'measure duration but we feel it'.[115]

To summarize Bergson's theory: there is a fundamental self beneath the numerical multiplicity of conscious states that is 'the extensive symbol of true duration'.[116] This is a self whose states melt into each other as a fluid organic whole. Two faces of the self: 'the one clear and precise, but impersonal; the other confused, ever changing, and *inexpressible*, because language cannot get hold of it without arresting its mobility'.[117] Bergson places this inexpressible and fluid organic state in the soul.[118]

Thus, Deleuze is Bergsonian when he argues that representation arrests becoming into frozen being, while becoming dismantles the branches of representation and the faculties fall into a discordant chaosmos. Deleuze extends Bergson's position by attempting to determine the processes or immanent mechanisms of this inexpressible soul. And he is nothing but confusing on this point.

His argument, clarified by Manuel DeLanda, is that if the fundamental self is a continuous multiplicity then we can understand it as 'a state of possible states', the number of which being the dimensions of the manifold.[119] A simple example would be the pendulum which can change only with regard to its position and its momentum; thus, it has two degrees of freedom and each can be mapped onto a two-dimensional plane – this is all that its space of possibilities requires. A more complicated system has more degrees of freedom and requires a higher-dimensional mapping.[120] The state of the system at any particular point in time becomes a single point in this manifold, plotted from its respective coordinates. This is called a *state space*, and if we wish to plot change in this model, we must allow the single point to move through this 'abstract space' so that it describes a trajectory.[121] State space does not capture 'static properties but the way these properties change, that is, *it captures a process*'.[122] This remains within the world of Schelling. But Deleuze wants to place consciousness within this model, or at least that part that relates to process – the soul. But this is surely unsustainable given the innumerable parameters that would need to be accounted for; yet to be fair to Deleuze and Bergson, we see in this very sentence how quantity intrudes on our attempts to intuit this manifold.

Complex systems display recurrent behaviours or tendencies.[123] Is this the case for consciousness before we spatialize it? Deleuze believes so. There are recurrent tendencies of a system to converge on certain points in a manifold (so-called singularities) that appear to have a large influence on the behaviour of complex systems. A soup bubble is structured by a single point of attraction (a singularity) – its tendency towards the minimization of surface tension.[124] According to Deleuze's argument, in consciousness, the singularities towards which we tend are never themselves actualized, since they represent 'only the long-term tendencies of a system, never its actual states'. This does not make them less real, since their influence on consciousness is very real indeed, like Macbeth's tendency to evil, and they confer on consciousness 'a certain degree of stability'.[125]

We may now clarify what Deleuze means by the virtual in relation to the self. It is that aspect of our thinking being and consciousness that is not actualized but remains real (not just what is possible for that can always be actualized), that towards which the self tends within a heterogeneous and continuous multiplicity but which can never itself be actualized. *The virtual* is an ontological category that refers to multiplicities themselves – to that which is defined by differential relations and populated by 'points of attraction' that characterize its unfolding levels – singularities that are *real without being actual*.

But do such 'points of attraction' exist in the fundamental self, points representing 'the inherent or intrinsic long-term tendencies' of deeper consciousness that structure the possibilities of change? Again, Deleuze argues for this, contrasting the clear and distinct nature of essences with the 'obscure and distinct' nature of continuous multiplicities insofar as the singularities which define them 'come in sets . . . [which] are not all given at once but are structured in such a way that they *progressively specify the nature of a multiplicity* as they unfold'.[126] In other words, for the self, there is a processual unfolding that is not chaotic but drawn to points of attraction or driven by tendencies.[127]

This 'fundamental self' (Bergson's term) can be explicated by analogy. In embryogenesis we reject the notion of preformed tissues in embryo (the essentialist model) in favour of the view that 'differentiated structures emerge progressively as the egg develops' and that this egg is neither differentiated nor undifferentiated but 'possesses an obscure yet distinct structure defined by zones of biochemical concentration and by polarities' (points of attraction) that lead to the migration of cells.[128] Such progressive transformations characterize the worlds of physics and biology; they occur at the critical values of some parameter or other which switches the physical system from one state to another at points of bifurcation in the system.[129]

But is this what happens to consciousness and the self? Is our tendency to become angry under certain conditions just such a point of attraction? It has intuitive sense, yet it requires that one accept fundamentally that the self (in its depths) is processual, that the fundamental self (the becoming-self in the virtual) is a multiplicity. Thus, if we weave the self into a definition of multiplicity, we would be required to think or conceive of it in the following terms: as 'concrete sets of attractors (realized as tendencies) linked together by bifurcations (realized as abrupt transitions in the tendencies) . . . typically divergent [with] in principle no end to the set of potential divergent forms' that it may adopt.[130] If it is a multiplicity then, as such, it gives 'form to processes, not to the final product' so that the self 'must be thought of as *meshed together into a continuum*'. But since this 'further blurs the identity of multiplicities, creating zones of indiscernibility where they blend into each other, forming a continuous immanent space very different from a reservoir of eternal archetypes',[131] the self is also blurred and blended with zones of indiscernibility. This is Bergsonian through and through, and this conceptualization of 'the fundamental self' as a multiplicity is central to Deleuze's construction of movement from the virtual to the actual. It is the basis for how ideas form in this homogeneous multiplicity of consciousness, for how they move from being virtual and inexpressible to being actual and narratable.

Now if we read Deleuze productively and map his 'morphogenesis' onto the self, then the actual, narrative self (encased in its spatialized or metric properties) emerges from an intensive, non-metric multiplicity through a cascade of so-called phase transitions.[132] From an undifferentiated intensive space, the self progressively differentiates, moves to the surface (in Bergsonian terms) and eventually gives rise to extensive structures (discontinuous narratives with definite metric or spatialized properties *à la Bergson*).[133] It is in this transition zone, this interface of the virtual and the actual and between the continuous and the discontinuous multiplicity that the spatiotemporal dynamisms that define the embryogenesis of the narrative self occur. It is the space between mimesis$_1$ and mimesis$_2$ – the intensive. It is where Mad/King Sweeney lives in crowned anarchy.

The self is an egg

Individuation, Deleuze argues, means the unfolding of a multiplicity as an intensive process that embodies that multiplicity itself and therefore produces the different. For the self, the final product is the narrative or narratives that emerge from individuation, a process that spans 'three ontological dimensions which constitute the Deleuzian world: the virtual, the intensive and the actual'.[134]

The analogy of the fertilized egg returns to us here. The egg/embryo – mostly defined 'by chemical gradients and polarities' and 'neighbourhoods with fuzzy borders and ill-defined qualities' – is a topological space where precise metric lengths are unnecessary.[135] The space is filled with rigorous processes of adhesion and connectivity which are nevertheless inexact. However, as migration of cells begins to form anatomical structures, the *inexact yet rigorous* relations that specified non-metric space become 'progressively replaced by a less flexible set of metric ones'.[136] Larval selves become narrative self. The self is an egg with a story written on its shell.

But is this embryological analogy truly transposable to the self? Or is it a metaphor that attempts to draw out more than it says? Here we are at the limits of the representable, where the unsayable meets the 'impertinent attribution' of the metaphorical. Yet if we argue that an ontology of the narrative self descends to this embryological ineffable then we can ascribe coherence to the one by way of the other.

From larval selves to dead narrative

What implications does this threefold ontology have for the narrative self? If we are to adapt this model to narrative or construct an ontology of the narrative self in the stream of difference and multiplicity, do we not produce a narrative self with such fixed metrics that we cannot divert this self from unfolding into a rigid spatialization as a shell of narrative, one that falls away like dead stories in the gutter, forgotten or lost? Are we then what remains present to the individual, what adheres to the telling or are we all that has been and gone, all that has been remembered, forgotten and lost? As narrative selves are we all the stories ever told or are we also those virtual narratives never spoken, never declined or, indeed, declined in another sense? If the narrative self unfolds from an intensive process mired in a multiplicity, does anything then unfold from narrative itself – like other narratives or fragments of narrative? Indeed, is not each narrative no more than the actualization of a piece of the multiplicity from which it is delivered and into which it returns, as difference-in-kind? A thousand tiny narratives, each a crystal fragment, each a return to the virtual?

Chapter 8

Dis/solving the Narrative Self

Intuition is the jouissance *of difference.*[1]

Introduction

Having described the Deleuzian world around which the actual self appears to sit as though encrusted, we noted the possibility that this self is of a type that subordinates difference to identity, that for Deleuze the actualized self is a dead-end that appears to cancel out difference to an even greater degree than the ipse–idem narrative self in Ricoeur. It appears to be a self rigidified in its potential to tell itself and indeed in the very telling of itself. Is this not the problem that we have repeatedly attempted to avoid – difference subordinated to the same, the metamorphic to the unmalleable?

The problems at issue here are as follows: on the one hand, we do not want the narrative/actualized self to loose its anchorage in the intensive and the virtual; on the other hand, we do not want the individual to be divested of narrative – like a moulting snake divested of its dead skin. To obviate this dilemma, we must try to ensure that the anticipated 'rigidification' of the self in Deleuze is brought to an approximation with the ipse–idem self of Ricoeur in order to retain difference in the actualized or narrated self. Also, we must detect in some inchoate form in Ricoeur the ontology of the self proposed in the last chapter so that the rigidified self of Deleuze may be transformed to dynamic narrative and the narrative self of Ricoeur catabolized to non-narrative elements or larvae. In addition, we must respond to a crucial question: how can we establish a connection between the self that synthesizes the heterogeneous and the virtual world of multiplicities without meeting the impasse of a self of representation somehow entering a virtual world where everything is upside down and back to front – and inexpressible? If it is like Alice entering the world of the mirror, then can the self both become smaller as it gets larger without exploding, and can it survive the dogmatic madness of the Queen of Hearts without being beheaded? What is the becoming-Alice of the self?

This chapter will address two specific issues: the first, a summary and extension of a Deleuzian argument and the second, a counter argument to Deleuze.

We will summarize how Deleuze incorporates the Kantian notion of Ideas as problems into a virtual or differential system; to do so we must extend his central argument that individuation is an intensive dynamic that precedes 'differenciation' into organs and parts ('individuation always governs actualization'[2]) and then transcribe this argument to the actualization of the 'parts' of the self. Upon this argument hinges Deleuze's contention that the 'I' is fractured and the self no more than a differenciated psychic organ/ization after the event that cancels difference and suffocates the so-called creative larvae that populate an intensive space.

In our counter argument, we will locate in the interstices of this apparent dead-end process a crucial element, the so-called dark precursor, which we will contend *may* operate by both betrothing the Deleuzian virtual to Ricoeurian narrative and by 'vascularizing' those differenciated parts of the self without which narrative would effectuate a detachment and a falling away from the individual. But this 'crucial element' is not without critique. Indeed, we will raise not one but three arguments against Deleuze. First, we will contend that the actualized self cannot be construed as he proposes, detached from a virtual other half and left to rigidify without the life supports of this virtual. Secondly, we will argue against Deleuze that metaphor cannot be so easily dispatched from a philosophy of difference and that it is precisely metaphor that is demanded of this philosophy if it is to avoid the accusation of arbitrariness or disengage from a covert acquiescence to representation. Thirdly, and most fundamentally, we will raise serious and potentially ruinous questions over Deleuze's notion of the dark precursor that he alleges is at the base of thought and determines the laws of the virtual. Specifically, is the dark precursor nothing more than a fantastical dreamer within a dream, less a philosophical concept than a will-o-the-wisp glimpsed through the marsh lights of narrative that evaporates as soon as we try to grasp it? An atheist's Prime Mover, a religious vacuity? A nothing? Our conclusions will draw us close to this end-point before a rescue strategy of 'rehabilitation through metaphorization' intervenes, in the form of Ricoeur. In its nothingness, is this dark precursor not everything – the very being of becoming, the *Ursprung* at the heart of the productive imagination that produces the narrative self and leaves the traces of its having-being and its still-becoming in a particular style, a manner, a nuance in the narrative? It will be our contention that this dark precursor is a key element in forging an ontological connection between Deleuze and Ricoeur in the profundity of narrative or where narrative sheds it structure, and the capacity or potentiality to narrate is laid bare.

This will bring us to our abiding concern: is it only for the few or the many to achieve the self as an art form? We will ask whether such a thing is possible, whether the making of the self as a form of art does not in itself irrevocably destroy the self? Perhaps it is always an art form but far too often a very poor form of art? And if it is an art form can it be brought to being in the case of the narrative self, unleashed and emboldened?

Finally, we will return to our promised narrative persona of the self. We will argue that Sweeney, as our philosophical bathyscope, can narrate from the abyss of the unspeakable. Indeed, we need to explain why the legendary Sweeney meets the pathic, dynamic, relational, juridical and existential features that Deleuze and Guattari argue for when 'inventing' a conceptual persona to meet a particular philosophical task.[3]

From Multiplicity to the Narrative Self

For Bergson, the self is a hybrid of two multiplicities; Deleuze moves this self into the realm and language of systems theory. Now systems outside the laboratory are not closed but open, and if we accept with Bergson (and Deleuze) that the self is a multiplicity, then it too is an open system. Our vision of nature, as Prigogine and Stengers note, has undergone 'a radical change toward the multiple, the temporal, and the complex'.[4] We are no longer the objects of an ancient science, though we appear to remain trapped in the antiquated thought processes of that very science. Isaiah Berlin noted the contrast between the thinking of the humanities and that of sciences:

> The specific and unique versus the repetitive and the universal, the concrete versus the abstract, perpetual movement versus rest, the inner versus the outer, quality versus quantity . . . mental strife and self-transformation as a permanent condition of man versus the possibility . . . of peace, order, final harmony and the satisfaction of all rational human wishes – these are some of the aspects of the contrast.[5]

Berlin opposes the specific and unique to the repetitive and the universal, but with systems far from equilibrium 'we move away from the repetitive and the universal to the specific and the unique' where the universal laws of equilibrium are overthrown by 'a variety of mechanisms corresponding to the possibility of occurrence of various types of dissipative structures' and in which new dynamic states of matter may arise spontaneously as transformations from disorder or thermal chaos to order.[6] The self as multiplicity and open system, it can be argued, obeys not the universal laws of equilibrium (except when near equilibrium, that is, when not really thinking) but those of dissipative structures where 'chance' and 'necessity' are seen as essential aspects in 'the description of these non-linear systems far from equilibrium'.[7]

The parallels with Deleuze's theory of individuation and the self are clear. We point these out to place his project within the crucible of a contemporary science where a philosophy of thought and becoming is coterminous with a science of systems. That it is speculative in its formulation of the virtual and its mechanisms of immanence is undoubted; that it may turn out to be wrong in some or many of its parts is of course inevitable but that it represents a first and entirely rigorous engagement with complex phenomena culled from the increasingly chaotic seas of the sciences in the pursuit of new concepts for philosophy is surely a worthy enterprise in itself.

One consequence of placing the self in state space is that it changes the nature of the questions that have up to now accompanied it. We no longer ask is it one, is it many, is it fragmented, but rather, do we affirm a self near equilibrium behaving like the repetitive and the universal or a self that operates far from equilibrium (some, most or all of the time) behaving like the specific and unique from moment to moment? Has the narrative portrait that seemed to us to be the only portrait come to conceal in its depths the 'phase portrait'[8] in all its multiplicity? Is the concept of the narrative self worthy of disfigurement in order to embrace 'mental strife and self-transformation' in the truest sense of these terms?

By giving to the self a virtual other half in accordance with Bergson's theory of multiplicities,[9] we assume that the self is itself a hybrid multiplicity – continuous and discontinuous and functioning as a non-linear system at least at those times when it encounters the object as a violence to thought or when it is creative. It is worth noting that this construction of the self is quite contrary to Deleuze's since, for him, the self is a 'figure of differenciation' and falls outside the domain of individuation.[10] It is the end-stage, where lines of individuation cease, rather like Aristotelian entelechy, the end-stage of energeia or actuality. Against this, we will work towards the position that the self exists within the process of *narrative selving* (the product being inseparable from the production and the self being an infinitive verb). The soul encounters the violence of the object, the faculties are unhinged – this is the side of the self that is continuous multiplicity, the side of selving that, as we near the surface of consciousness, becomes spatialized to narrative.

However, before we can narrate we must generate ideas in the first place. How does this fit in with our process of narrative selving?

Ideas for portraits of the self

Deleuze situates Ideas in the virtual and argues that they have the nature of multiplicities, not essences. According to him, Ideas are 'constituted of structural elements which have no sense in themselves' but at the same time the Idea 'constitutes the sense of all that it produces'.[11] The real objects of Ideas are 'problems *qua* problems'[12] and these differ in kind from propositions. Fundamentally, he contends that we must address the genesis of the act of thought in the operation of the faculties and this genesis is in the art of problems and questions. How do Ideas arise from the violence of the encounter? Presumably, Deleuze's interest here is in new or created ideas rather than repetitious or rehashed ones – the ideas of habit.

Thus he defines 'problematic ideas' as multiplicities of differential relations and corresponding singularities – the hallmarks of the virtual, as we noted in the previous chapter.[13] This is a crucial move since it permits him to envelop Ideas in a differential network by first removing their specificity and representation and then situating them in the virtual, while at the same time retaining their Kantian structure, though founding it on difference.[14] Essentially, he constructs an ideational network of singular points where ideas appear in 'a system of differential relations between reciprocally determined genetic elements'.[15] It is in this sense that we plunge beneath what is represented and into the differential space of a continuous multiplicity where Ideas are conceived as the 'differentials of thought'.[16] Difference is now at the heart of thought.

If we think of the Idea as a problem then it 'can only ever be approximated through constructs that reveal aspects of its internal relations'.[17] We meet the inexpressible again. As virtual structures, problems are like Proustian reminiscences – 'real without being actual, ideal without being abstract'. They occupy a paradoxical place between existence and non-existence; *insisting* yet not existing they have, rather than being, a problematic being which Deleuze calls '?-being'.[18] (In the next chapter we will discuss the closeness between '?-being' and Aristotle's 'being-potentially'.)

From ideas, narrative evolves processually, emerging from an ideational space of differential relations as space is 'surreptitiously introduced', as Bergson so adroitly puts it.[19] This ideational space and its system of differential relations and singular points is what Deleuze refers to as 'the plane of immanence'. Since narrative begins with ideas then – if we agree with Deleuze – it is constituted fundamentally within this plane. And if the problem provokes an endless challenge to be viewed in new ways, to reveal its different singular points and conceive these singular points in different ways, then the possibilities to narrative are potentially endless.

Obscure Stammering for a New Narrative Self

We will now construct a defence against the most frequent and damaging accusation petitioned against Deleuze: is not all of this just obscurantism wearing the mask of differential calculus and chaos theory? Does Deleuze stretch credibility to the limit when he posits a virtual space criss-crossed with the longitudes and latitudes of differential relations through which thought travels? We may say 'yes' to this criticism – but with a cautionary reserve. Such a philosophy of difference unavoidably overturns our representational system, *un-representing* what inheres beneath the actualized, differenciated, spoken and declined – its underpresence as such. A hurricane whips up a coastal sandstorm that is the real being of the beach, a sandstorm whose differential chaosmos can barely be thought, imagined or grasped. Like the objects that Alice seeks on the shelves of the Sheep's shop, it is a sort of thought equivalent of peripheral vision, a field never seen but only seen through.

In the same way, Deleuze attempts to grasp the ungraspable that is the peripheral vision of thought, the between thought, a place that can only be thought through. When Deleuze says that 'we do not know how to go beyond experience toward the conditions of experience, toward the articulations of the real'[20] his destination is not different from the unknowable Real of Jacques Lacan. This is an admirable project, and even if Deleuze fails, it is the grasping of the ungraspable, the declining of the indeclinable, the turning over of the virtual and the differentiable that merits some admiration. And it is an attempt that is not without guidelines or systematicity.[21]

In essence, Deleuze attempts to think beneath the representations we have of thought and to intuit the faculties in their naked being, separated, pushed to their limits, before any representation we can have of them. In this sense, it cannot be said that his point of view is true or false – rather, the question is whether it is useful or not. He takes from Bergson the notion of intuition and gives to it the power of an archaeological investigator who finds beneath the sand the sarcophagus and within the sarcophagus the sandstorm.[22] How do we think? Across what plane does thought traverse to grasp ideas? With what propulsion does it appear to move? Under the steam of which faculty?

We can defy Deleuze and use a metaphor to explicate him. We think through the chaos of the sandstorm in an infinite and yet enclosed sarcophagus where all relations between each grain of sand are possible, even compossible insofar as the compossible is a property of the virtual. We can imagine the following: as we think, each grain employed in the differential relations that define that moment of thought lights up and flickers for an infinitesimal fraction of a second so that we glimpse what it looks like to think an idea before it is represented in language; have we not just glimpsed the peripheral of thought that is immediately lost in the saying of it? How do we think? With infinite speed and across an infinite space of points. The problem draws us to thought, the difference between points establishes a resonance that forces us to think. But not everyone thinks very often, and this is Deleuze's central point. We must be forced to think, or we simply repeat dead thoughts in the same way that a knee repeatedly kicks up to the hammer applied.

Only against the newly experienced do we learn – no swimmer learns to swim before getting into the sea. Similarly, it is only against the never-thought-before that we think anew. The swimmer against the unpredictable waves is one of Deleuze's few metaphors – but it is too good to ignore, for it is the embodiment of the thinker against the waves of his unhinged faculties, each differential of thought like a whirling molecule of water against the skin of the swimmer.[23] In a way, Deleuze maps out a sea of thought (the plane of immanence) against which we think but there are no landmarks to orientate this map. This is hardly the intention of an obscurantist. If there is a clear problem for the apprentice swimmer (the nature of the water at that particular point in time) then there is also one for the apprentice thinker who must navigate the intensive field that has been set in disharmony by the violence to thought of the sign. The sign forces us to interpret it, to enter its world. We are Egyptologists of the virtual in this sense.[24]

We can stretch this further if we expand on Liebniz's *Gedankenexperiment* (where we are shrunk to the size of a flea and enter the mechanics of the brain as one enters the interstices of a mill[25]) and imagine instead that it were possible to lay out the brain upon a flat surface. This would be like a frozen section in a laboratory but with every neuronal cell body and axon captured in two dimensions, every connection between axons, cell bodies and dendrites retained and every association between different nuclei and different cortical layers, between the cerebellum and the thalamic structures still in place. If we imagine further that this giant frozen section of the brain extends outwards in all directions (with centres of singular importance and others of relative unimportance), then we will see an impossibly complex neural tapestry made all the more so by perpetually forming novel dendritic connections and ever new encodings at the chromosomal level – and with everything bathed in electricity and neurotransmitter chemicals.

This is not impossible to imagine; in fact, we might one day see it visualized by computer graphics. But what would we see? Nothing less than the plane of immanence that Deleuze argues is inside thought. And if we were able to colour the electricity and stain the neurotransmitters we would see the movements of thought through this plane – we would see their points of departure, their points of arrival, their points of intersection and their points of resonance and amplification. We would see the Deleuzian world.[26] We should recall that this plane is 'always single, being itself pure variation',[27] but it is the infinite movements across it that constitute for Deleuze its 'variable curvature, its concavities and convexities, its fractal nature'.[28] Is this not the brain, described in the peculiar language of a philosopher of difference?

Why then did Deleuze not simply declare himself a neurophilosopher, or a philosopher of the neurosciences, a sort of Daniel Dennett or Antonio Damasio speaking in a foreign language? For this is precisely what he does – speaks as a foreigner in the language of neurophilosophy of which he speaks fluently. And it is no surprise that he is so easily accommodated within core aspects of Dennett (for example, the pan-demons of the multiple drafts model are largely indistinguishable from larval selves)[29] or Damasio (where the definition of the image is pure Bergsonism, particular the interpretation given it by the Deleuze of *Cinema 1, Cinema 2* and *What Is Philosophy?*).[30]

We must explain this aspect of 'being a foreigner, but in one's own tongue',[31] because the very methodology of Deleuze needs to be evoked if we are to sense narrative as a germinal event, or to apprehend beneath the language of the self an underpresence that speaks this language as a foreign language. Deleuze and Guattari describe style in writing as 'the procedure of a continuous variation . . .

an assemblage of enunciation' that produces a language within a language.[32] They cite Kafka and Beckett as examples of this rupturing of a language from within.[33] Style is the ability to produce different speeds and variations in the linguistic elements, to widen the chromatics of what is written or said, and to spread the language into non-linguistic elements like gestures, intonations and instruments. For Deleuze and Guattari, this is what makes language stammer from within by placing all linguistic and even non-linguistic elements in variation. Instead of the 'is' we have the 'AND . . . AND . . . AND . . .' of the rhizome – the in-between.[34] It is the struggle between the *est* and the *et*, the first term being a constant that 'forms the diatonic scale of language' and the second term placing everything in variation. We noted this earlier in Proust – the exquisite use of the conjunction that creates 'an affective and intensive language', where the stutter is 'no longer an affectation of the one who speaks'.[35] The style by which Deleuze creates concepts (the central task of philosophy, according to him[36]) is inseparable from the concepts themselves, so that if we understand Deleuze to be an occasional philosopher of the neurosciences, we do so by acknowledging his use of language not only as a system of constants but also as a sea of linguistic disequilibrium that makes or breaks these constants. Although not made explicit in his work, it is this use of language that is prescribed for a new narrative/non-narrative self.

The underpresence to narrative that introduces a continuous variation (an intensive stuttering without external marker) is now our interest. Is it possible ever to have a narrative without such an intensive stutterer in the system, without an underpresence that introduces 'the quiver, the murmur . . . the tremolo, or the vibrato' into the words spoken?[37] Can we have a narrative of the self without an underpresence of individual style, a *manner* in which we stutter and quiver the language from within and introduce 'vibrations, rotations, whirlings, gravitations, dances or leaps'[38] into it? Is this not our *manner*, our *way of being* narrative selves? In other words, in what manner does the 'I' of the 'I narrate' narrate?

Between Time and the Self: A Fractured 'I'

Why did your mind unhinge?[39]

It narrates from an unhinged mind, as Sweeney suggests. But what does this mean? One interpretation is offered by Deleuze with reference to Hamlet's remark that 'the time is out of joint.' By this, Deleuze means a form of time 'unhinged' from movement or from the ancient time when time was subordinated 'to the circular movement of the world'.[40] When time is out of joint or 'off its hinges . . . movement is . . . subordinated to time',[41] as Kant argues in his *Critique of Pure Reason*.[42] Hamlet needs time to act, unlike the heroes of Sophocles, where time is set in motion as the consequence of a prior 'aberrant action'.[43] Thus, movement is determined within time, and time determines the parts of movement as successive. Time itself does not 'change or move . . . but is the form of everything that changes and moves . . . the immutable form of change and movement'.[44] This is, for Deleuze, the totality of time in a moment, an 'empty form of time'.[45] But it also seems to be 'a profound mystery' that requires a new definition of time. What is interesting to our study here are the implications of this Kantian 'secularization or laïcization' of time to the self. We can only understand our existence 'in time, under the form of time'[46] so that the self (which for Deleuze is passive and receptive) is in time and constantly changing but punctuated by the act of the 'I' (I think) that actively determines one's existence as a passive, receptive self that, as we saw in our discussion of Kant's self, 'only represents to itself the activity of *its own* thought'.[47] This creates what for Deleuze is a *fêlure*, a crack or fracture in the I–Self:

> The I and the Self are separated by the line of time, which relates them to each other only under the condition of a fundamental difference. My exis-tence can never be determined as that of an active and spontaneous being, but as a passive 'self' that represents to itself the 'I' . . . as an Other that affects it ('the paradox of inner sense') . . . I am separated from myself by the form of time and yet I am one.[48]

Deleuze distinguishes the Self from the 'I' – the existential, passive self from the punctuating, active 'I', each separated by the 'therefore' of time that provides the form by which the passive self is determinable. The relationship between the Self and the 'I' is paradoxical in that the Self is separated from the 'I' by the form of time and yet it says 'I am one'. Deleuze's Cogito has therefore these three Kantian aspects: the indeterminate, passive 'I am'; the determining, active 'I think' and the 'therefore' of time as the 'form under which existence is determinable'.[49] Ideas as the differentials of thought, Deleuze asserts, repeat these three aspects of the Cogito. And if the Cogito refers to a fractured 'I', one 'split from end to end by the form of time which runs through it . . . [then] . . . ideas swarm in the fracture, constantly emerging on its edges, ceaselessly com-ing out and going back, being composed in a thousand different manners'.[50]

And Deleuze is fundamentally Kantian in developing this ideational triplet: 'Ideas are in themselves undetermined, they are determinable only in relation to objects of experience, and bear the ideal of determination only in relation to concepts of the understanding.'[51] The image of the 'antlike inhabitants'[52] at the fracture should not be dismissed as just a vibrant metaphor. These are the dif-ferential elements of the chaosmos that inhabit the fracture and must be con-tained in Ideas.[53] With such a differential swarm at the heart of thought, we can complete the Deleuzian Cogito, which has in its depth a specifically differential unconscious. It incorporates all 'the power of a differential unconscious, an unconscious of pure thought which internalizes the difference between the determinable Self and the determining I, and injects into thought . . . something unthought'.[54]

This 'something unthought' will return to us through Ricoeur; in fact, we may mark it now as the unthought of the productive imagination at the engine-heart of the narrative self but only insofar as we distinguish this narrative self from the Deleuzian self as a passive 'I am'. Our task is to understand whether the antlike inhabitants that swarm at the fracture are not considerably more active than Deleuze ever supposed.

The narrative self: Mad in craft

With Deleuze, we can no longer see the spontaneity of the self as an attribute of a Cartesian subject but instead we need to view it as an 'affection of a passive self that experiences its own thought'.[55] This is the I which is paradoxically a passive Other. It is within this paradoxical structure that Deleuze argues for unleashing the metamorphic nature of the will to power (as the differenciator of difference) in a 'theatrical world' of conceptual personae or larval selves deep to the self that will liberate individuation from the representative masks or the 'factitious limits of this or that individual, this or that Self'.[56] This rift or fracture in the 'I' is healed in Kant through his practical and speculative philosophy both by acting 'as if the I has a secure identity' and 'by drawing a distinction between synthetic activity and passive receptivity [so that] the rift is only implied in receptivity and is curtained off from the activity of the I'.[57] Without this security, the theatre of metamorphosis thrives and the self flies beyond its factitious limits.

The challenge here is against the presumption that the self ever has such a thing as a secure identity. How does this help the narrative self? The importance of this 'liberation' is crucial to Ricoeur's narrative self since it suggests the possibility of disengaging the *ipse* from the clasp of the *idem*, loosening it from the strictures of sameness, from brute repetition and a 'secure identity' that insists upon one author to narrative, even in the face of the impossibility of the narrative self having such cohesion or togetherness (as we argued in Chapter 5) or of the many fragments of self narratives (both told and untold) coming under the authoritarian chairmanship of an authorial board. We noted earlier that narrative becomes indissociable from a law which renders it possible, and this law is the form of the concept as a form of identity[58] – therefore, the laws of our putative board demand that all stories released follow the rules laid down for story delivery, in order to ensure that the series of narrative episodes conform to a transcendental pattern, a schema or genre with implicit values for narrative coherence. While such a schematization may be necessary for coherent practical and moral action (and that is itself debatable), it cannot be the case that the self is alone practical and moral, or that practical and moral action determines the self. In this sense, narrative is not enough because such a determining schematization would make the life of ipseity impossible and the synthesis of the heterogeneous would only be a mask underneath which is revealed the synthesis of the same – the same laws, the same values and the same constitution.

Liberating narrative through larval narrators

We have referred on several occasions to larval selves – but what are they and what is their relationship to the triplicate Cogito or the narrative self? For Deleuze, the world we live in is an actualization wrought from a continuous multiplicity that exists in the virtual:

> The virtual is opposed not to the real but to the actual. *The virtual is fully real in so far as it is virtual* . . . Indeed, the virtual must be defined as strictly a part of the real object – as though the object had one part of itself in the virtual into which it plunged.[59]

For Deleuze, the reality of the virtual is structure, since it consists of differential elements, their relations and the singularities towards which they converge or from which they diverge. He argues persuasively that we must desist from 'giving the elements and relations that form a structure an actuality which they do not have, and withdrawing from them a reality which they have'.[60]

According to his argument, the processes of thought that lead to narrative are twofold. On the one hand, we have a process of 'differentiation' that 'determines the virtual content of the Idea as problem' and therefore establishes the plane of immanence from which the synthesis of the heterogeneous will draw. On the other hand, we have a process of 'differenciation' that 'expresses the actualisation of this virtual and the constitution of solutions',[61] these solutions for our purposes being the many narratives that are the final products of this productive synthesis. 'Differentiation' here refers to the genetic process of narrative while the 'differenciation' refers to the actual world of narrative, the made and said story.[62] If Ideas exist in the virtual as continuous multiplicities, as a system of differential relations between genetic elements, then the formation of narrative fishes into this sea, so to speak, this sea of multiplicity.

But if ideas-as-multiplicities are the germ cells of narrative, then *can we not also conceive of narratives as multiplicities?* They have no prior identity, no deference to the same; in their genesis they are intrinsically defined and reciprocally determined, and they bear no similarity to essences but are 'made and unmade according to the conditions which determine their fluent synthesis'.[63] A true synthesis of the heterogeneous and the liberation of difference from sameness in a narrative that becomes a work of art would not be possible without larval narrators as inhabitants of a multiplicity. But why is this so? Because no circumscribed self could plunge into the virtual world of differential elements and singular points without divesting itself of its circumscription, without dissolving into larvae. That is because this world is specifically 'pre-individual'; it is a world where ideas include not only variety or multiplicity within themselves but also singularity.

If narratives constitute cases of solutions to problematic ideas based on differential relations, does the problem therefore not inevitably inhere in the narrative insofar as narrative points to 'the transcendence of the problem and its directive role (*rôle directeur*)' in relation to the organization of the narratives themselves?[64] Something of the virtual homogeneous multiplicity remains in the actualized narrative. This is rather like the *auteur* in film theory where the multiplicitous soul of a Welles, a Godard or a Wenders hovers over and within each film, over and within each *mise-en-scène*, despite the multifarious voices (cinematographer, screenwriter, actor, etc.) assembled in the making. And this 'over and within' is a transcendence immanent to the solution (in the form of the narrative). Deleuze is surely saying no more than that the self in its relation to the virtual must of necessity take on larval forms which can swim among these differential relations and seize their relatedness, intuit their strange determinations, grasp their anomalous reciprocations – the self must become unselved, unrepresentable, an elf in a sea dissolved into a multitude of larvae. These larval selves are cloaked by our propositional concepts, by what we say and what we think in language. Yet they remain immanent to our silent and vocal utterances, and reveal themselves in the narrative solutions by way of the *mise-en-scène*, the staging and the style. The 'adventure' of thought requires that we are dissolved into larvae from time to time. Otherwise, we would not think and rather than narrate the different we would be condemned to narrate the same.

Laws in the Germplasm of Narrative: The Dark Precursor

In this non-representational land of larval selves, this sea of chaos traversed by the plane of immanence across which course the differentials of thought and their singular points, what laws, if any, are there? If thought is simply chaotic in the chaos, then only madness is thought; only ideas that stab into each other, that eviscerate themselves and disappear in all directions could be considered thought. This would make thought impotent in the production of ideas or in the creation of the new. There must be some rules to this pre-individual thought, rules for thought thinking in a multiplicity. The rhetoric of metonymy and metaphor is insufficient for Deleuze – this would obviate the need to have difference as the bedrock of thought. Instead, he proposes a relatively obscure processor which he calls the 'dark precursor'. But what is it?

The problem with the virtual as it stands is that chaos would reign were there no mechanism to link the intensive processes that occur there and differentiate the heterogeneous series. The agent or 'force' that ensures such communication between these series is, according to Deleuze, 'an invisible, imperceptible *dark precursor*, which determines their path in advance'.[65] It is the differenciator of difference, an in-itself that generates second-order differences, 'relating the first-degree differences to one another'.[66] The dark precursor (close synonyms: the 'quasi-cause', the 'aleatory point', the 'conceptual persona') acts as an operator, performing transformations upon 'the ontological content of the virtual'[67]; it is defined by its capacity to affect multiplicities and the singular points within them. To put this as simply as possible: 'the task which the [dark precursor] must accomplish is to create among the infinite series springing from each singularity "resonances and echoes," that is, the most ethereal or least corporeal of relations.'[68] Thus, the series of childhood memories of close relationships and the series of present experiences of close relationships are set in resonance by this 'dark precursor', caused to relate, somewhat like two sound waves interacting to form increasing amplitudes, forced movements, interferences and diffractions. In our mental world, these forced movements cannot be sustained 'at the borders of the liveable, under conditions beyond which it would entail the death of any well-constituted subject endowed with independence and activity'.[69]

As an example of this, Deleuze notes the intensive foldings and torsions that the embryo must undergo and that only the embryo can sustain – 'an adult would be torn apart by them.' It is the same for Alice in Wonderland. In this way Deleuze understands the activities of thought as an acrobatics of contortion that neither the actualized self nor the putative self-narrator could itself sustain, an acrobatics that must therefore be performed by 'larval subjects and passive selves' (the near equivalents of conceptual personae for philosophical thought – 'even the philosopher is a larval subject of his own system'[70]). Deleuze takes James Joyce's work as an example in literature of the dark precursor in operation. In his use of portmanteau words and neologisms, Joyce draws together 'a maximum of disparate series' where there is no reliance on prior identity; these words then operate as linguistic dark precursors inducing 'a maximum of resemblance and identity into the system as a whole, as though this were the result of the process of differenciation of difference in itself' and not the cause. The result within the system is an 'epiphany'.[71]

Narrative events and quasi-causality

In *The Logic of Sense*, the dark precursor is renamed the 'quasi-cause' for the purpose of Deleuze's argument that events are incorporeal and virtual, the result of the actions and passions of bodies. Such events (the objects of narrative, as Ricoeur notes) could be swallowed up by their causes were it not for the 'heterogeneity of cause and effect, the connection of causes between themselves and the link of effects between themselves'.[72] Deleuze develops this from the Stoics who, as DeLanda notes, had been the first to split the causal link. Processes of individuation may be defined as sequences of causes (in that 'every effect will be the cause of another effect') and as singularities or events (in that these 'become pure incorporeal effects of those series of causes'); however, there is another side to this, another layer, since these pure effects themselves can be viewed 'as having a quasi-causal capacity to endow causal processes with coherent form'.[73] Thus, the incorporeal event preserves its difference from the corporeal cause, by linking up 'at the surface . . . to other events which are its quasi-cause'.[74]

One could regard history as a virtual multiplicity of incorporeal events linked by a quasi-cause. Indeed, Ricoeur's explication of the term 'quasi-plot' in *Time and Narrative, Vol. 1* bears resemblance to Deleuze's 'quasi-cause'. We noted earlier that Ricoeur identifies the elements of emplotment in history as *quasi*-characters, *quasi*-plots and *quasi*-events. To the quasi-characters, historians impute causal explanations, as if the society, nation or civilization could be explained as one explains the behaviour of individuals by 'singular causal imputation' rather than by recourse to nomothetic explanation. This provides history with the appearance of quasi-plots. It is from the quasi-characters that events arise and unfold over time so that these becomings of societies are the quasi-events set within quasi-plots that assure the narrative status of the quasi-events.[75] Single-causal imputation involves the imaginative construction of different courses of events, calculation of the probable consequences of these unreal courses and then the comparison of these consequences with the real course of events.[76] We only penetrate the real causal interrelationships by creating 'unreal past conditionals'.[77] In other words, every history as explanation is surrounded by the *unreal* (of alternative histories and outcomes) because it is upon this that we discern best what is necessary to the real. And this unreal occurs on the stage of the imagination.

Now clearly Ricoeur is referring to something different from Deleuze's virtual, a virtual marked as real and not as possible, the possible always being retrieved in reverse from the real. Nevertheless, we find beneath Ricoeur's singular causal imputation for emplotment a supportive structure in Georg von Wright's analysis of 'quasi-causal explanation'.[78] They are one and the same thing, although they refer to different domains – singular causal imputation to narrative causality and quasi-causal explanation to event, processes and states.[79] Indeed, von Wright's analysis of historical explanation is based on the same scientific basis that Deleuze employs – understanding the world as a dynamic system with 'state-spaces' (specifically 'states of affairs') which are the fundamental 'ontological building blocks'[80] of those worlds we inhabit and that inhabit us. If we construct chains of successive states which permit us to narrate fragments of the world's history, then we need to insert into our understanding of these chains not just causal and mechanistic explanations but also

teleological or finalistic ones, as pleaded by Aristotle.[81] Quasi-causal explanations give the appearance of causal ones but are far more complex, because
they take into account the ramifications of motivations involved, the practical
inferences that schematize these motivations and how these will constitute new
facts and new situations which have further implications for the premises of
new practical inferences.[82]

What is worth stressing here is that Ricoeur models emplotment on a model
drawn from the study of dynamic systems, refining it to meet the requirements
of a specifically representational structure. But if we remove the 'explanation'
from 'quasi-causal explanation' and simply regard the adjective as a noun, we
are in the domain of Deleuze's dark precursor; in other words, we remove the
intentionality to explain and we are left with the presumption of a process of
dynamic relatedness, of embroilment – specifically, of the quasi-cause. Quasi-
causal explanation becomes virtual when human intentionality is removed from
it; intentionality is what makes the possible by utilizing in a very limited sense
the resources of the imagination. In this sense the quasi-cause is the ultimate,
the first creator of (or the operator that creates) what comes before narrative,
not what comes after it, which is its explanation.

The quasi-causal operator or dark precursor gathers together the heterogeneous series of the virtual; where these series converge (in a pre-actualized multiplicity), an intensive individual develops (a larval subject). These larval
subjects are borne within the being of the sensible and are not psychological
phenomena. When differential elements are set in resonance, it is as though
the plane of immanence were illuminated like a night-time runway for a many
limbed alien spacecraft to set upon it, and when this bizarre grid of larval selves
has delivered itself to the synthetic powers of the imagination, then and only
then does the feeling and sensing subject become narrative. In other words, we
contend that inside the speaker that narrates the self, living intensively, resides
a larval narrator or narrators, alive to capturing the 'thought-events' of the
virtual, thought-events that can only be thought but at the same time indicate
the impossibility of thought 'from the point of view of a fully actualised
thinker'.[83] Our narratives may be born from different breeds and hybrids of
larval selves: the affective, the sensible, the conceptual – any constellation is
conceivable, potentially so, but it is a fact that the dominance of dead narrative
and the constraints of cultural and reactive forces has meant that very few variations are possible and that all too often the medium of the creative larvae is
polluted to the point of near extinction.[84]

Creative dark precursor

What then is required to make of our narrative selves something novel and
creative? The implication, though only tangentially made by Deleuze, is that

this quasi-causal operator has a specifically creative nature. It runs through his analysis of Proust and of the writings of Antonin Artaud and Louis Wolfson.[85] This creative nature is fashioned from his positioning of art within the differential elements of the virtual: to say that a work of art is 'immersed' in the virtual is not to summon up some confused determination but rather to evoke 'the completely determined structure formed by the genetic differential elements, its "virtual" or "embryonic" elements'.[86] Traces of the virtual and the dark precursor that operates upon the elements of the virtual should therefore be apprehended in works of art, if we suppose that the artist has dissolved himself or herself into larval selves that can withstand the life-threatening torsions of thinking pre-individually, of creating before representation.

We will provide here examples of the dark precursor or traces of the dark precursor in the creative arts (we will limit ourselves to four examples though its materialization or reification may be found in many popular cultural artefacts), acknowledging at the same time that we run the risk of actualizing this indeterminable differenciator of difference and thereby trivializing it. However, this is not the purpose of such an exemplification. Our examples are meant to function as part-allegory or allegory in peripheral vision, like what Alice glimpses but does not see on the shelves of the Sheep's shop. If she were to see what cannot be seen she might notice the inseparable conjunction between quasi-cause and plot, between the larval selves of Deleuze and the synthesis of the heterogeneous of Ricoeur. By exemplification, we divine what Deleuze abstractly and sometimes obscurely explicates regarding this dark precursor. But we exemplify also with a second purpose in mind – for if this putative dark precursor sets in resonance the heterogeneous series of the virtual then is it not precisely the necessary strategy, the necessary operator to be employed when setting the two heterogeneous series (the philosophy of Deleuze and that of Ricoeur) of our study in resonance? The dark precursor then becomes both the ontological meeting point of their respective philosophies of the self and the strategy by which we bring them to this point.

Example 1

In Tim Burton's 1990 film *Edward Scissorhands*, the eponymous hero is a young man created by an inventor who dies before he can complete him. Edward is left with scissors for hands. When the local Avon representative visits him at the historic mansion where he lives alone she sees his scissor hands and asks him what happened to him. 'I'm not finished', he replies. She lures him out of his home and takes him to live with her in the local community. Edward is both larval subject conceived of affects and conceptual persona of the self. He is coaxed out of one world and into the language of another but he is unfinished as a person – pre-individual, larval. He acts throughout the film as an aleatory point, moving through the pastel-shades of the houses and the gardens and generating connections between the heterogeneous elements of the community, in the process transforming everyone. He is non-sense, or less than sense, the differential and androgyne element from which the sense of the film derives. It is from 'the play of [this] aleatory point'[87] that is Edward that the domain of the film's events issue forth. In the end the aleatory point fizzles out and Edward returns to the laboratory where he was conceived and where his inventor and his enemy are buried. Birth and death demarcate the short and thrilling life of this larval subject's aleatory route through the community. He remains at the end of the film, like all true conceptual personae, unfinished.

Example 2

In Don DeLillo's *Underworld*, Bobby Thompson hits the home run that wins the World Series for the New York Giants and the baseball lands in the hands of young Cotter Martin in section 35 of the stands. Thus begins the prologue to a complex narrative that hurls itself backwards and forwards through time and across several continents, addressing on the way the Cold War, nuclear waste, human waste, recycled art, deprivation and anomie and finally the simulacra of modern worship, all under the leitmotif of Pieter Bruegel's *The Triumph of Death*. But the narrative or the plot that conditions the relationships between the elements of the narrative is configured by the history of the baseball as it passes from hand to hand over the next half century. It is the transversal or indeed rhizomatic path of this baseball that threads together the plot-points or the narrative elements. DeLillo determines the plot on the basis of a wandering and insubstantial baseball that in itself obeys none of the traditional laws of narrative structure – yet it creates this seam to narrative, this vein of a plot. And it is clear from the text that the nature of this baseball is not one of actuality, submitting to the laws of cause and effect. Instead, it is given a veritable virtual status, the status of a differenciator of difference. Like the Snark, the baseball is an aleatory point, the object Alice searches for in the sheep's shop, 'never where she looks, but always on the shelf above or below. It is an empty space lacking its own place, an unfixable element from which determinate elements arise.'[88] The baseball has a mythology with a history of simulacra and false trajectories; some claim to have it but there is never proof that the trajectory followed is the true one. The simulation of the baseball's journey is its truth:

> Nobody has the ball . . . The ball never turned up. Whoever once had the ball, it never surfaced. This is part of the whole – what? The mythology of the game. Nobody ever showed up and made a veritable claim to this is the ball. Or a dozen people showed up, each with the ball, which amounts to the same thing.[89]

Yet this virtual object that remains in the depths, moves through time and space to configure a modern classic. It is neither plot nor narrative, but the plotter of the plot-points of the plot, the skeleton of the narrative. Plotter and plot are inseparable, sealed in the plotting – like creator and creature sealed in the creating.

Example 3

W. G. Sebald's *Austerlitz*, tells the story of one man's search for identity. On the surface this appears to require a simple narrative; yet as Austerlitz's adventure of discovery proceeds and the narrative encroaches on the virtual past, it becomes progressively lost in a multiplicity of images (grainy photos litter the text), contiguous and indeed Proustian run-on sentences and a form that eschews paragraphing and chaptering. Austerlitz is a dark precursor of the self, a pre-individual identity 'finding his way around [the] strange jumble of countless unwritten rules, and the often almost carnivalesque lawlessness' that prevails in both his memory and in the world that his memory encounters.[90] The materials of the virtual for Austerlitz are never fully graspable but 'emerge out of nothing . . . as memories do in the middle of the night, darkening again if you try to cling to them'.[91] Like Proust, Sebald's *Austerlitz* is a paean to memory but its verse and metre are always uncertain, its form rigorous, its procedures inexact. Sebald's repeated use of architectural scenarios and diagrams underlines the 'sense of disjunction, of having no ground beneath' the actual.[92] But when representation begins to repeatedly fail him, diagrammatics and topology surface to overthrow it. Indeed, it is where Austerlitz's adventure of discovery is most formalized that the virtual intrudes to its greatest extent and Austerlitz himself is divested of identity and propelled along the trade-winds of a quasi-causal movement. For example, when he finds himself within the formalized structure of Liverpool Street train station, Austerlitz realizes that he is at 'the entrance to the underworld' where – not people as such – but 'great tides' of people board and disembark, 'coming together, moving apart',[93] like the divergent and convergent series of the Deleuzian virtual. To emphasize the point, Austerlitz notes that the station was built upon marshy meadows where time froze ('the so-called Little Ice Age'[94]) in a sort of Bergsonian pure past. In the station, Austerlitz recounts that he followed a porter to an entrance covered in a heavy curtain but 'to this day, I cannot explain what made me follow him.'[95] This is the dice-throw, the intervention of chance in necessity that propels Austerlitz beyond the curtain to a place where he 'completely and irrevocably' forgets 'the very part he has so often played' in life – in effect, his actual self.[96] In this room that he enters everything is uncertain, beams of light follow 'curious trajectories which violate the laws of physics, departing from the rectilinear and twisting in spirals and eddies before being swallowed up by the wavering shadows'.[97]

This pre-individual, larval self of Austerlitz has entered the virtual, a space felt to be 'expanding, going on for ever and ever in an improbably foreshortened perspective, at the same time turning back into itself in a way possible only in such a deranged universe'.[98] Here are the foldings of the plane of immanence Deleuze describes and the infinite speeds across which it is traversed; it is where all the hours of Austerlitz's past life are contained, a room that covers 'the entire plane of time' and where the laws are those of the curious trajectories of multiplicity. It is from this 'waiting-room' of 'labyrinthine vaults' that ideas emerge and Sebald is very clear regarding the spectral determinants that precede them: 'I observed the way his ideas, like the stars themselves, gradually emerged from the whirling nebulae of his astrophysical fantasies,'[99] ideas that appeared like 'constellations . . . almost lost in the shimmering dust of the myriads of nameless stars sprinkled over the sky'.[100] In support of our discussion above, Sebald places the virtual at the peripheral of vision, where the 'precarious structure' of the common accord of the faculties breaks apart and one is 'stricken with terror at the realization that . . . the edges of my field of vision were no longer my guiding lights . . . but malignant enticements to me to cast myself into the depths'.[101] We traverse the virtual as a 'crowd' of larval selves propelled by the dark precursor; we do so beneath 'the single living organism' that we are and into which the crowd merges, but it is a crowd 'racked by [the] strange, convulsive contractions' of an intensive field.[102]

Example 4

In one of the greatest of poetic autobiographies, William Wordsworth's *Prelude*, we can locate 'a narrative identity [that] never ceases to make and unmake itself' – as Ricoeur defines the self,[103] and a narrative difference where the '*either . . . or* itself becomes a pure affirmation' of the self – as Deleuze puts it.[104] Indeed Wordsworth rewrote his autobiographical *Prelude* three times, making up four texts (1798, 1799, 1805, 1850). In itself, this is testament to the necessity to re-edit the self in narrative and indeed to conceive of the narrative self as several or heterogeneous in series. Wordsworth's quarry was always that which 'interfused'[105] his being and he rejected the notion of a Platonic 'soul of our first sympathies' (present in the 1798 text, *Was It For This*) for something more inchoate, something that 'feeds upon infinity, that broods over the dark abyss, intent to hear its voices issuing forth in silent light, in one continuous stream'.[106] It is not a mind that broods over this abyss, but 'the emblem of a mind', a pre-individual figuration of mind, something like the empty space of an inlaid ornament, that feeds and broods and is 'exalted by an underpresence' which Wordsworth refers to as 'the sense of God, or whatsoe'er is dim or vast in its own being'.[107] This 'underpresence' is the dark precursor upon which the larval selves or emblems of selves feed. It is 'the power, which all acknowledge when thus moved'.[108]

Wordsworth sought to comprehend the nature of this 'underpresence' repeatedly, an underpresence that becomes for him an element of the faculty of the productive imagination. Throughout the *Prelude* he grapples with poetic adequacy and with the inadequacy of the spoken to summon this indeclinable underpresence to words.

> [F]or many days my brain
> Worked with a dim and undetermined sense
> Of unknown modes of being. In my thoughts
> There was a darkness – call it solitude
> Or blank desertion. No familiar shapes
> Of hourly objects, images of trees,
> Of sea or sky, no colours of green fields,
> But huge and mighty forms that do not live
> Like living men moved slowly through my mind
> By day, and were the trouble of my dreams.[109]

Like the impossible and intensive torsions of the embryo, this unknown mode of being that Wordsworth narrates is populated by what is impossible to the actual, by what cannot live like living men but only exist in the virtual and according to its laws. He is engaged, perpetually, in an 'unconscious intercourse',[110] but it is an intercourse with the lawlessness of the virtual which speaks to him.

> By chance collisions and quaint accidents
> (Like those ill-sorted unions, work supposed
> Of evil-minded fairies), yet not in vain
> Nor profitless if haply they impressed
> Collateral objects and appearances,
> Albeit lifeless then and doomed to sleep
> Until maturer seasons called them forth
> To impregnate and to elevate the mind.[111]

These are the procedures of the dark precursor, the elements of chance and necessity and the transversal movements that induce resonances in collateral objects and infuse new forms into the lifeless matter of the virtual. This dark precursor, this underpresence in the 'deranged universe' of the virtual is a direct descendant of Aristotle's prime mover (as we will argue in the next chapter).

The dark precursor's presence in literature and the arts is hard to conceal, since for Deleuze these creative endeavours are the quintessence of the virtual. However, Deleuze's own dark precursor in these matters may be more easily concealed.

Schelling: The dark precursor of Deleuze

Schelling notes that philosophy 'must present the course of the human mind itself, not only the march of the individual' but to do so we must begin with the presumption that 'only as we come forth from the absolute does opposition to it originate.'[112] If the philosopher wishes to draw something positive from opposition, he must begin from the precise point where 'the controversy of philosophy' issued forth or in what for Schelling amounts to the same thing, from the point from which the '*original* opposition in the human mind proceeds'. This precise point for Schelling is nothing other than the '*egress from the absolute*' or from the non-finite to the finite.[113] Of course the meaning of the terms 'absolute' or 'non-finite' is open to interpretation, and Schelling invites this in discussing Spinoza. He contends that Spinoza rejected

> [every] transition from the non-finite into the finite [and] all transitory causes whatsoever, and for the emanating principle he substituted an imma- nent principle, an indwelling cause of the world . . . a cause which would be one and the same as all its effects . . . I believe that the very transition from the non-finite to the finite is the problem of *all* philosophy, not only of one particular system. I even believe that Spinoza's solution is the only possible solution, though the interpretation it must have in his system can belong to that system alone and another system will offer another interpretation for the solution. I hear you say: 'This statement needs an interpretation itself.' I shall give it as well as I can.[114]

Were we, philosophically, to parse this sentence, we would isolate the key ele- ments of Spinoza, Nietzsche, Deleuze: the Absolute, the non-finite, the virtual, the interpretation of interpretations. Schelling's Absolute is Deleuze's virtual. And the indwelling cause is the dark precursor. The virtual is opposed to the actual (as Deleuze notes in Schellingian language) and the dissolved self is opposed to the narrative self. But if philosophy 'cannot make the transition from the non-finite to the finite . . . it can make one from the finite to the non- finite', and because of this, says Schelling, the finite itself (i.e. narrative) 'must have a tendency towards the non-finite, a perpetual striving to lose itself in the non-finite' – that is, in the virtual.[115] But this striving 'to become identical with the infinite and to merge in the infinity of the absolute object' is an impossibi- lity, since in order for the subject to annihilate itself 'it would have to survive its own annihilation'.[116]

Thus, the narrative self strives to dissolve (as we will see Ricoeur argue in Chapter 10) but cannot entirely lose itself. For Schelling it is inconceivable that one can think of being 'engulfed in the abyss of the deity' or the Absolute (or the virtual) without always retaining one's 'own self as the substratum of the annihilation'.[117] Now it is at this point between dissolution and narrative that we situate the dark precursor of the narrative self (the equivalent of the conceptual persona of the philosopher). There is a sort of narrative persona in the substratum of the narrative self's annihilation – where it meets what it is opposed to. It has two faces: one to the non-finite, the unlimited, one to the finite and the limited, one monoglossic, one heteroglossic, one bound, the other unbound. They oppose each other but one is not lost *in* the other (Ricoeur's error) or *to* the other (Deleuze's error).

Narrative Persona

Do we have a name for this narrative persona that prevents the self's annihilation, one that has these two faces and subsists outside the arts as an enduring myth? Did we not hypothesize earlier that it is in mythic time that the fragments of the self are provided with a grounding, a commonality that melts them together into a sense of oneness without unity? Mad Sweeney becomes the name of this narrative persona.

Sweeney, metamorphozed into a bird, wanders through nature's reserves like a nomad, filled with bird-like terror and mistrust of humans. One day, while perched on an old tree, his half-brother Lynchseachan finds him. Distraught at the news of the death of his family, Sweeney falls from the tree to the ground where Lynchseachan 'puts manacles on him.'[118] Then Lynchseachan tell him that he has deceived him and that all of his family are alive. Sweeney is taken home where he is put in 'locks and fetters'.[119] In this shackled state and with the wisdom of the nobles, Sweeney's 'sense and memory came to him', and he reverts to 'his own shape and guise'.[120] This is one of the earliest descriptions of psychotherapy in Irish literature, but it is preceded by a moment of homeopathic practice, where a dose of woe is prescribed. In other words, what begins the cure for Sweeney is the story of the other. Only through Lynchseachan's narrative can Sweeney be brought to care and the narrative self refigured from madness; indeed, only through the structure of narrative can Sweeney be lured out of nomadic madness, out of that which is outside formal language – *lalangue*, *délire*. However, it requires restraint to contain the centrifugal forces of *délire*, an opposing centripetal force symbolized by the manacles and fetters.

The story within a story of Sweeney's cure through Lynchseachan's narrative would be unremarkable on its own were it not followed within a few lines by another story within a story, one that involves further deception that is equally transforming, *but in the opposite direction* – for it engenders a metamorphic return to psychosis.[121] It is harvest time, and Sweeney is left in the care of 'the mill-hag' who has been 'enjoined not to attempt to speak to him'[122] for she may speak in a language that is outside language. Ignoring this warning, she asks Sweeney to tell her 'some of his adventures while he was in a state of madness'.[123] He tells her that such talk is dangerous and that he will not be narrated back into insanity. However, through her 'deceitful' behaviour she lures him into the conversation of délire, asking him to demonstrate 'one of the leaps you used to leap when you were mad'.[124]

Summoned to narrate (but in the opposite direction) he is seduced by the summons and drawn to délire. Soon he has 'bounded over the bed-rail' to the end of the bench.[125] Encouraged by the mill-hag's words, he continues to perform leaps (deterritorializations) that return him to the nature-world of madness and metamorphosis, accompanied on his journey by the mill-hag herself (who perhaps is an exemplar of feminine *jouissance*[126]). It is in words and stories, whether they be lies, curses or deception that Sweeney is moved across the boundaries that divide reason from unreason, or the poetic from the ethical imagination, the 'subject identical with itself' from the 'pure manifold', the self from the other and the despotic king from the nomad. Bidden by the other, he submits to the desire to recount his life story and to hear his life story recounted. But this 'other' may not always be the ethical other but the mill-hag poetic other of the abyss.[127]

Indeed, Sweeney's story is always entangled with the voice of the other, not just with one but many others, for his story is in itself not just one but many stories, each immersed in his intensive engagement with nature, each requiring for its true completion as a self-narrative a configurational act that moves towards a sense of an ending, inexorably towards a conclusion that permits the theme or point of Sweeney's life and his myriad stories to yield their collective meaning. Sweeney's self is an imbroglio through the other by way of nature; or rather, it is a becoming-imbroglio in the *musical* sense of the word, that is, an 'ordered confusion' in the end.

Does Sweeney not exemplify precisely what Schelling refers to when he argues that the self never fully returns to itself, never fully knows itself:

> What we speak of as nature is a poem lying pent in a mysterious and wonderful script. Yet the riddle could reveal itself, were we to recognize in it the odyssey of the spirit [or self], which, marvellously deluded, seeks itself, and in seeking flies from itself.[128]

Sweeney oscillates between a nomadic self lost in the poetic imagination of nature and a wonderful script that is the narrative self of the ethical imagination, between the centrifuge of nature and the centripetal force of narrative. Indeed, *Buile Suibhne* contains a multiplicity of narrative voices for the nomadic Sweeney (i.e. quotidian, rhetorical, artistic-prose, délire, artistic-poetic) that are 'the carriers of the decentralizing tendencies in the life of language'.[129] Acting against them is the centripetal force that reduces these soul voices (of larval and varied selves) to a 'unitary language'[130] whereby we meet the requirements of our community. As such, it is the sole voice of conscience. It is in the utterances of Sweeney (whether spoken aloud or silently to himself) that the dual forces, those of unification and disunification, intersect. It is a battleground of opposition. Although Bakhtin's heteroglossia is an event of the outside, of the medium into which one utters, this heteroglossia also flows from within the subject of Sweeney. Bakhtin's analysis of the controlling power of the unitary language resonates strongly with the 'voice of conscience' in the form of Lynchseachan that suppresses the creative, becoming-mad self of Sweeney and that acts as 'a force for overcoming this heteroglossia, imposing specific limits to it, guaranteeing a certain maximum of mutual understanding and crystallizing into . . . "correct language"'.[131] It is this that alters the epiphany of the imagination for Sweeney – it is this that draws him back from the abyss.

But what is this 'sense of an ending' towards which Sweeney oscillates? During one of his mad nomadisms he meets another 'madman' called the Man of the Woods. Sweeney asks him, 'Why did your mind unhinge?' The Man of the Woods tells him that for dressing his men in silk he invoked a curse from the kings and was now afraid to tell his story. With this revelation they each 'confided in the other', sharing their life stories.[132]

We may take from the 'unhinged mind' an interpretation similar to that of Deleuze with reference to Hamlet's remark that 'the time is out of joint' – for this is precisely what is at the heart of the story of *Buile Suibhne*. Sweeney and the Man in the Woods each transgresses the universal principles or laws of their communities (the Laws of the Fathers), each looks behind the curtain and sees a self 'cleft . . . in twain' and each is banished to a time out of joint, to another law, to a madness of the self that will insist, in time, on a narrative to tell and a metamorphosis to complete. And Sweeney achieves this in a remarkable end to *Buile Suibhne* when, having been viciously speared through the chest, he appears to stay around long after his death in what is clearly a virtual state to complete his story through the other and to conjoin the virtual self (the soul of Sweeney) with the actual self of Sweeney, as told by Moling, the good cleric. Only then, in a final *metaphoria-metamorphosia* (one that takes the form of an oscillating $mimesis_1 \rightarrow mimesis_2 \rightarrow mimesis_1$ cycle that had up until then eschewed handing victory to concordance) is Sweeney's poetic madness acknowledged and returned to him, specifically, through the valediction of Moling ($mimesis_3$). Only then are his animal habits honoured, his story and his name consecrated (actual) and his soul (virtual) allowed to fly to Heaven.[133] Only through metamorphosis and poetic narrative closure ('it is destined for you . . . to leave here your history and adventures', Moling tells him[134]) is redemption achieved and the fracture in the self salved.

It is only by virtue of this final narrative, the one which precedes and succeeds death, that the self achieves closure – unified, complete, the same as itself. Only at death does concordance triumph over discordance, does factitious unity overwhelm difference and the multiple. Only in death does the narrative self of the 'I' achieve rigidification.

Chapter 9

From Debt to Excess

I tried to put myself into her inner world, but . . . when I managed to hack my way through the thickets of fantasy and illusion inside which she was trapped I came only to an immemorial, childhood place, a region of accentless and unemphatic prose, exclusive haunt of the third person. She would not be known; there was not a unified, singular presence there to know. She was one of those creatures . . . who exist on a median plane between the inanimate and the super-animate, between clay and angels.[1]

Introduction

We are in the larval heart of the narrative self, beneath the super-animate soul that is home to the forms and the inanimate clay that is the prime matter of our flesh. Here the narrative self dissolves. But into what and by what means does it reconstitute itself? What narrative structure or form remains in the dissolution, if any? Indeed, when we say that the self dissolves, as it does in sleep, how can it come together again without not really having dissolved in the first place? Is this not the paradox of dissolution – that something of the self's ghostly angel must remain above or within the dissolve to prevent its annihilation? These and many questions raised in preceding chapters now require answers.

We have noted the opposing forces of a self towards a 'poetic imagination' where all is permitted and a self towards an 'ethical imagination' where it is 'answerable to the suffering and action of real human beings'.[2] We can argue that as selves we move forwards and backwards between the always excessive potential of clay and the always indebted angels fixed forever in their forms, eternally separate from their genitality. By way of this double movement we progress in two opposing directions and thus meet in places the same considerations (for example, Spinoza's *conatus*) but from radically different perspectives. Across this chapter and Chapter 11 we will keep in mind specific signpost terms that can act as guidelines and orientation points in our analysis. The key signpost terms in this chapter are *actuality, potentiality* and *conatus*.

Ricoeur's investigation of the ontology of the narrative self draws him down two *culs-de-sac*: Aristotle's actuality and potentiality and Spinoza's *conatus*. But were these in fact real or apparent *culs-de-sac*? Do they not only seem so from the hermeneutical position? We will revisit these routes taken by Ricoeur and attempt to step beyond hermeneutics and into a philosophy of difference. To do so we will need to show that at the fundament of Ricoeur's ontology of the narrative self lies an unacknowledged philosophy of difference and that this fundament occurs at the same decussation from which Deleuze's philosophy emerges, that is, from the cross-over of Spinoza and Bergson. In addition, we need to locate in Deleuze the virtual of this decussation, that is, the figure of Aristotle and the genotypic role of *dunamis* in Deleuzian thought. This is because it is here where Ricoeur ends his ontological explorations that we can, at the most profound level of being, forge a synthesis between Deleuze's dissolved and Ricoeur's narrative self.

If we cannot achieve this convincingly, then our project will falter and collapse. Specifically then, we will attempt to construct the 'unthought' in Ricoeur by drawing into cohesion several of the terms he comes to the cusp of in his Tenth Study of *Oneself as Another* with virtuality in Deleuze. In so doing, we will seek to interpret Aristotle's *dunamis–energeia* within the meaning of Deleuze's differentiation–differenciation dynamic – an adventure that will, if successful, translate these notoriously difficult metaphysical terms of Aristotle into genetic forerunners of which the Deleuzian terms are their avatars. In other words, Aristotle becomes a sort of second dark precursor to Deleuze – and we must force upon Deleuze this 'disavowed affinity'.[3] By so doing we can argue that the virtual that Deleuze explores contains within its interstices the seminal elements of Aristotle's *dunamis/energeia* and that the two principles of *energeia/dunamis* act as genetic ghosts to Deleuze's concepts of virtual differentiation/actualization. Only by doing this can the narrative self establish a foundation in an ontology of difference where being 'is said of difference itself'.[4] We cannot be sure at this stage whether the narrative self can survive this transition.

Ricoeur's Dilemma of the Self: Substance or Illusion?

The problem of an ontology for the narrative self is addressed in an exploratory manner in *Oneself as Another* through the question 'What sort of being is the self?'[5] We will first provide a summary of the procedures Ricoeur took in exploring this question and the obstacles he encountered before identifying where he believed there was hope for further negotiation. We must acknowledge at this point two important possibilities: (1) that the difficulties that arose for Ricoeur would have been surmounted had he conducted this study after *Memory, History, Forgetting*, given the movement in this latter work from a critical to an ontological hermeneutics conducted upon our historical condition and (2) that the questions addressed to the problem of the being of the self in *Oneself as Another* might have been differently posed had the question of memory in narrative identity been fully considered. This second possibility is related to a further problem or to an orientation towards the analysis of the concept of the self that Ricoeur employs. For him, the concept of the self is phenomenological[6] and therefore must be analysed from a phenomenological perspective. It is a self to be understood by virtue of 'the self-designation of a subject of discourse, action, narrative or ethical commitment'.[7] This cannot however be a limiting procedure in our investigation, given that the places we have visited (from Schelling to Deleuze) have not been populated by phenomenologists proper (even if they have from time to time been colonized by them) and have not conceptualized the self in such a manner.[8]

Ricoeur well understood the limitations of surface narrative and its reach or interpretation. No matter what form of hermeneutics we may employ or how well we set up our criteria for plausibility of interpretation, there always remains an 'impenetrable, opaque, inexhaustible ground of personal and cultural motivations', which the subject can never finally have exhausted.[9] It is in this sense that he acknowledges the presence of something beyond the signifiable. This is stated more clearly as a fundamental dilemma: the subject is either 'identical with itself through the diversity of its different states' or it is 'a substantialist illusion, whose elimination merely brings to light a pure manifold of cognitions, emotions and volitions'.[10] However, it need not be an *either/or* if we are to move beyond a phenomenological perspective; the *both/and* remains well within our comprehension. We may reach it through this pure manifold of cognitions, emotions and volitions (the being of the sensible and the intelligible) and into the impenetrable ground where Deleuze attempts to locate a will to power – that sundry creative force at the heart of narrative.

Ricoeur and Bergson: Memory and virtuality

Towards the end of *Memory, History, Forgetting*, Ricoeur turns to Bergson on the subject of forgetting. The importance of the distinction between surface and depth has been made repeatedly in this book with reference to Deleuze, where depth is synonymous with the virtual. It is no surprise that Ricoeur should employ the same distinctions when encountering memory and forgetting. Whereas the phenomenology of memory evokes the sense of distance and remoteness 'according to a horizontal formulation of depth', forgetting evokes something different, 'something like an endless abyss, which the metaphor of vertical depth attempts to express'.[11]

In invoking this depth to the intimacy of memory, Ricoeur enters the world of Bergson with a key presupposition: that it is 'a primordial attribute of affections to survive, to persist, to remain, to endure'.[12] Their image survives because without it there would be no recognition. This is Bergson's argument in *Matter and Memory*, and it is what places Ricoeur's entire analysis of forgetting within its compass and indeed within the virtual. Ricoeur supports Bergson's theory for the existence of a 'pure' memory as 'a virtual state of the representation of the past, prior to its becoming an image in the mixed form of memory-image'.[13] Bergson had argued that the body is fundamentally an organ of action and not an organ of representation so that the role of the brain in memory is not of the order of representation but of giving to the impression the power of surviving and enduring.[14]

The image is central to Bergson, the world being the 'totality of images' and the present moment being obtained 'by making an instantaneous section in the general stream of becoming'.[15] 'Pure' memory becomes an image and is then recollected, moving from a virtual to an actual state. But even in its actual state of recollection, Ricoeur notes, it must remain 'attached to the past by its deepest roots' and must retain 'something of its original virtuality'[16] for how else would we distinguish it as a memory distinct from the present? At this point, Ricoeur turns to Deleuze, acknowledging one of Deleuze's central interpretations of Bergson, that is, central to his own philosophy. This section on *Memory, History, Forgetting* is important in fully appreciating how closely we can approximate Ricoeur's narrative self to the dissolved self of Deleuze. Ricoeur notes that if images of the past survive in some latent state then any given present is already its own past – its past is constituted at the same time as its appearance in the present. And here he quotes directly and at some length from Deleuze's *Bergsonism*:

> There is here . . . a fundamental position of time, and also the most profound paradox of memory: The past is 'contemporaneous' with the present that it *has been*. If the past had to wait in order to be no longer, if it was not immediately and now that it had passed, 'past in general', it could never become what it is, it would never be *that* past . . . The past would never be constituted, if it did not coexist with the present whose past it is. . . . Not only does the past coexist with the present that has been, but . . . it is the whole, integral past; it is *all* our past, which coexists with each present. The famous metaphor of the cone represents this complete state of existence.[17]

The virtual is presupposed and the fact of recognition 'authorizes us to believe it', says Ricoeur.[18] Memories exist in the virtual, and this gives to memory and the virtual an ontological status, in spite of the latency of images and the powerlessness of pure memory. Ricoeur proposes a chain, survival–latency–powerlessness–unconsciousness–existence, whose elements are linked by 'the conviction that becoming, under the sign of memory, does not fundamentally signify passage but duration'.[19] A becoming that endures, Ricoeur concludes, is the central intuition of *Matter and Memory*.

Although Ricoeur moves towards a philosophy of virtual becoming,[20] it is in his discussions on the virtuality of memories and his evocation of the Bergsonian cone as a widening of the field of the virtual that he approaches a Bergsonian Deleuze. In moving down from the point-like episodes of recognition that lie at the summit of the cone to the depths of ever-widening concentric circles that line the conical interior, Ricoeur extemporizes on a range of experiences that give 'the dimension of a permanent existentiell structure to these points of recognition'.[21] Towards the base of this virtual field through which Ricoeur descends lies what he calls 'the immemorial: that which was never an event for me . . . which we have never even actually learned, and which is less formal than ontological'.[22] And at the very bottom he finds a 'forgetting of foundations' and, indeed, a 'life force, creative force of history, *Ursprung*'. Also, and in surprisingly Derridean language, he finds an origin 'irreducible to the beginning, an origin always already there'. It is in this most deep and immemorial place, Ricoeur concludes, that we 'leave behind all narrative linearities; or, if we can speak of narration, this would be a narrative that has broken with chronology'.[23]

Have we not entered here, by a route circuitous, the world of *Difference and Repetition*, the world of the intensive and the virtual deep to the world of representation, the very scenography of the Deleuzian soul? We remember that this was the soul perplexed by the object of the encounter, forced to see it as the 'bearer of a problem'. But the soul was not sensibility alone for the other faculties also became subject to the violence of an encounter with the object. Sensibility, forced to sense the *sentiendum*, provoked memory to remember 'that which can only be recalled' rather than empirically remembered. In the presence of that which can only be recalled, the soul grasped 'the being of the past' which is both 'unrememberable and immemorial'.[24] And in the heart of this 'immemorial' we find the disintegration of linear narrative, the replacement of Chronos with Aion and subtending it all, illuminating this 'perpetual ground',[25] we encounter life force and the creative force of history. In fact, we encounter Deleuze.

Ricoeur and Aristotle: *Dunamis/Energeia*

With this Bergsonian Ricoeur in mind, what sense can we now make of the obstacles Ricoeur met in his Tenth Study? Does his incursion into the virtual and into memory, when drawn retroactively back through his earlier work, reset the problematics he encountered or the procedures with which he addressed them? We will see. His question, 'what mode of being . . . belongs to the self?' is determined by 'the multiplicity of the meanings of being' concealed behind this very question, the polysemic meanings indebted to Plato and Aristotle.[26] Aristotle noted that 'there are many senses in which a thing may be said to "be"'[27] and he identified four kinds of being:

> 'Being' has several meanings, of which one was seen to be accidental, and another the true . . . while besides these there are the figures of predication

(e.g. the 'what', quality, quantity, place, time . . .), and again besides all these there is that which 'is' potentially or actually.[28]

Ricoeur attempts to explore the being of the self by way of one of Aristotle's four acceptations of being, that of being as *actuality* and *potentiality* (*act* and *power, energeia* and *dunamis*). This would certainly appear to complement the notion of a certain unity of human action and of the narrative self as the power to act, narrate, tell a story, to attest for oneself.

Yet Ricoeur discovers in his investigation that Aristotelian act and power are recalcitrant to analogical appropriation for an ontology of selfhood, principally because they appear to be terms that are interdependent for their meaning.[29] However, he finds in 'the extreme spread of the respective fields of application'[30] of these two notions and their definitional interdependence the argument for '*a ground of being, at once actuality and potentiality*' whose two features equally and together comprise an ontology of the self whose central character of action is one of actuality and potentiality.[31] From the more epistemological series of description, narration, prescription, through the more ontological 'power-to-act' or Aristotelian *praxis* to the ontological ground of actuality/potentiality, Ricoeur sees a 'decentring' of the central agent of action towards 'a *ground* of actuality and potentiality'.[32] Furthermore, Ricoeur insists on both the separation of these terms and their dynamic vibration together so that a tension – which he refers to as 'this very difference'[33] – exists between them that is essential in his view for an ontology of action. This is the unacknowledged philosophy of difference in Ricoeur. Its similarity to the specifically Deleuzian Nietzsche of *Nietzsche and Philosophy* is obvious.[34] The will to power, according to Deleuze, should be understood not as a force but as 'the differential element which simultaneously determines the relation of forces (quality) and the respective qualities of related forces. It is in the element of difference that affirmation manifests itself and develops itself as creative.[35] Thus, at the heart of creative action in Ricoeur is 'this very difference' between forces, this will to power between actuality and potentiality. The ontological ground of narrative is difference.

Ricoeur now turns to Spinoza to forge a relationship between 'the acting and suffering self' and the *ground* of actuality and potentiality 'against which selfhood stands out'.[36] The connection is *conatus*. Ricoeur notes that the issue of life is central to all of Spinoza's themes but that 'to say life is to say power . . . through and through.' And power, argues Ricoeur, means a productivity (not a potentiality) that ought not to be opposed to actuality or realization. Both realities are degrees of the power of existing. *Conatus,* according to Ricoeur, refers to 'the effort to persevere in being, which forms the unity of man as of every individual'.[37] Spinozist themes centre round the notion of life and that means power – power as productivity, as the interdependence of potentiality and actuality, and not just as potentiality alone.

There is a tension in Ricoeur's philosophy at this point, as it hovers beneath the ruin of representation, on the one hand, and over the abyss of a philosophy of difference, on the other, an abyss into which he does not wish to collapse his philosophy. However, there is another problem. Ricoeur seems to fall away not just from this cusp that separates Same and Other from Difference, but from Spinoza himself. He draws no significant conclusions regarding the being of the self in relation to *conatus* and yet clearly senses *the potentiality for conatus to act* within the sphere of the being of the self. This hesitation and disengagement seem to be because of his inability to appropriate Spinoza to his own ontology of the self via Aristotle's *dunamis/energeia*.

It is not clear in the end how one is to interpret Ricoeur's 'all too rapid over-view' of Spinoza. It is as if he senses the importance of Spinoza to an ontology of the narrative self as actuality and potentiality but has neither the connectors nor the procedures internal to his own discipline or through the work of others to perform this task. However, we are given a clue within his Tenth study as to how we might approach this 'almost' in his work. Ricoeur notes admiringly how Rémi Brague in *Aristote et la question du monde* takes not what Aristotle says as his theme but what 'remains unthought' and constructs this unthought through an interpretation of Aristotle's *energeia* with reference to Heidegger's being-in-the-world.[38] Our goal now is to construct what remains unthought in Ricoeur in terms of Deleuzian virtuality; in other words, the unthought in Ricoeur becomes the thought in Deleuze.

Deleuze and Aristotle: A Disavowed Affinity

It seems at first sight almost unconscionable to suggest interpenetration between Deleuze and Aristotle, specifically between Deleuze's differentiation/act-ualization and Aristotle's *energeia/dunamis* – and yet it is not at all clear how they can be entirely separated. In fact, that one is the somewhat malformed offspring of the other may find some support in the arguments that follow. In locating an Aristotelian philosophy at the heart of Deleuze, we must establish the following sequence of correspondences: (1) that there is a general similarity in terms of the functioning of their respective philosophies despite the all-too-obvious dif-ferences; (2) that Deleuzian essences are on a developmental trajectory from Aristotelian ones; (3) that the Deleuzian virtual and the Aristotelian potential have the same ontological status; (4) that *dunamis* can function in a Deleuzian virtual without collapsing it; (5) that a virtuality exists in embryo in Aristotle, even if as an 'unthought known'[39]; (6) that the virtual in Deleuze mirrors the Aristotelian soul even if they are explicated from radically different points of view and finally (7) that *energeia* can be placed in the virtual in Deleuze and will perform a similar function to that of the unmoved movers of Aristotle.

The importance of this conjunction between Deleuze and Aristotle is that only by excavating and unmasking Aristotelian *dunamis* and *energeia* in Deleuze can we establish the more immediate ontological connection between the narrative and the dissolved selves. We cannot take a short cut through this process (for example, simply arguing for a correspondence between *dunamis/energeia* and *differentiation/actualization* in isolation) since without the supports of the other parts the argument will seem spurious. We must work through each proposed conjunction in the series.

(1) *General similarities.* We should not be surprised to find the hand of the Stagirite on the shoulder of the Nietzschean Deleuze. Kaufmann notes the importance of some elements of Aristotle's ethics to Nietzsche, not least his 'beautiful soul' *(megalpsychia)*.[40] However, throughout his writings Deleuze is silent on Aristotle except in *Difference and Repetition* and here it is in connection with two related issues: difference and univocity. He criticizes Aristotelian categories for 'reconciling' difference to the concept, rather than liberating difference 'into simple diversity and otherness'.[41] Thus, being is not collective but distributive and hierarchical in Aristotle. For Deleuze, following Duns Scotus, being must be said 'in a single and same sense of everything of which it is said, but that of which it is said differs: it is said of difference itself'.[42]

Univocity is crucial for Deleuze, since it secures his philosophy of difference and expressive immanence. Only with univocity can there be real difference or can difference be fully real, for otherwise differences would be secondary to some grounding and more authentic being. Everything that is, *is* equally and possesses full reality. However, it is somewhat remarkable that he has little or nothing to say on other elements of Aristotelian ontology, like *ousia* or *dunamis*. And all the more remarkably so when one realizes that one of Deleuze's most fundamental considerations in approaching philosophy is inherited directly from Aristotle, although he does not acknowledge this. 'Badly stated questions' and 'false problems' are often at the heart of the philosophical impasse; they derive in part from assuming that the truth or falsity of a problem is conditional upon 'the possibility or impossibility of its being solved'.[43] Deleuze argues that the badly constructed problem 'always has the solution it deserves in proportion to its own truth or falsity – in other words – in proportion to its sense'.[44] He takes this from Bergson but it comes directly from the *Metaphysics*, where Aristotle addresses the problem of problems and sets up his philosophical approach as an aporia-focused one. He is clear that it is often the badly posed problem that is the problem, and he sets this out clearly with respect to Parmenides and the problem of motion and change: 'for those who wish to solve problems, it is helpful to state the problems well.'[45]

Deleuze does recognize indirectly a debt due Aristotle, by way of Spinoza, in the emphasis Aristotle placed on the genesis of knowledge:

> Consider an idea as the knowledge of some thing. It is only true knowledge to the extent that it bears on the thing's essence: it must 'explicate' that essence. But it explicates or explains the essence to the extent that it comprehends the thing through its proximate cause: it must 'express' this cause itself, must, that is, 'involve' a knowledge of the cause. This conception of knowledge is thoroughly Aristotelian . . . Knowledge should thus progress from cause to effect [and thus] must be understood as the law of Autonomous Thought, the expression of an absolute power on which all ideas depend.[46]

Here are three key elements of Deleuze's philosophy in miniature: (1) the enveloping of the virtual that is implicated in the actual or the explication of a world enveloped in a thing[47]; (2) the priority of the virtual over the actual in terms of cause, with its origins in the complex fourfold sense of cause in Aristotle – 'actualisation belongs to the virtual'[48] and (3) the emphasis on thought outside representation, that is, the '*genitality* of thinking'.[49] Thoroughly Aristotelian. Even if we acknowledge that Aristotle gives priority to the actual over the potential,[50] it is still the case that the teleological cause is more important than the material one in explanation and knowledge – and that teleological cause cannot be subtracted from what is in potentiality in matter.[51] Indeed, the status of the teleological cause ('that for the sake of which') must be itself virtual: real without being actual, ideal without being abstract.

(2) *Deleuzian essences as inheritors of Aristotelian ones.* We noted earlier that Deleuze frequently asks not just what something is but what does it do and what is it for?[52] These teleological questions are addressed to the virtual half of the actual thing and not just to the 'what' of representation. Aristotle asks *mutatis mutandis* precisely the same question though with a different accent: 'what is it for?' or 'what is it for the sake of?' This 'functional determinism' is not always easily distinguished from the 'what is it?' question that appeals to the form as material cause, but as Christopher Shields notes, in Aristotle 'that for the sake of which' places constraints on the other forms of causes and is therefore prior to the other causes.[53] In Aristotle's words:

> What a thing is is always determined by its function: a thing really is itself when it can perform its function; an eye, for instance, when it can see. When a thing cannot do so it is that thing only in name, like a dead eye or one made of stone, just as a wooden saw is no more a saw than one in a picture.[54]

It is the form posterior, meaning 'the essence of that which is coming to be . . . or "that for the sake of which"'[55] that will condition the form prior, meaning the formal cause.

Deleuze's essences, which are multiplicities sunk in the virtual, are hardly radically different in structure from Aristotelian essences, because both have their roots firmly embedded in function, the latter determined by a necessary future function, the former determined by a future function that is however unpredictable and less necessary. This is because essence as multiplicity is understood as part of a system, one with multiple attractors that 'break the link between necessity and determinism,' giving a thing at any particular point in time 'a "choice" between different destinies' so that whatever end state it has at another point in time will be the result of 'a combination of determinism and chance'.[56] It is almost inevitable, when Aristotle makes 'that for the sake of which' the 'cause of causes' or as prior to the other causes, that this exquisitely unstable form ('that for the sake of which') when placed within a complex system like the human being or nature, produces the nesting of 'that for the sake of whichs' within 'that for the sakes of which'.

Given Aristotle's own systemic understanding of man in society (i.e. 'the state is by nature clearly prior to the family and the individual, since the whole is of necessity prior to the part'[57]) we can hardly avoid placing, for example, the teleological form of an organ like the liver within that of the child within that of the man/woman within that of society – or indeed taking from the same first term some entirely different series of nestings. Deleuze's theory of essences is on a developmental trajectory that begins with Aristotle, that is, from where 'things are defined by their working and power'[58] and extends to where 'assemblages' are defined, even if only for the short periods of time that their parts interact, by their working and their productivity.[59]

The point we are making here is that, when we transcribe the teleological argument to dynamic systems far from equilibrium, Deleuze is not the contrary of Aristotle but his inheritor. If they look like radical contraries, then it is simply that these atavistic elements are well concealed. However, in investigating the being of the narrative self we need to do more than just demonstrate this ancestry in essence; we need to analyse what connection can be established between *dunamis/energeia* and Deleuze's parallel notions of virtuality/actuality or differentiation/actualization.

(3) *Deleuzian virtuality/Aristotelian potentiality and ontological status.* We do not need to argue for the correspondence between or equivalence of Aristotelian *energeia* (defined as actuality in the sense of 'the realization of a process'[60] or as activity 'characteristic of the ultimate cause of change'[61]) and Deleuzian actualization since Deleuze says so himself. In an interview in 1986, he talks about analysing the complex processes behind 'new things

being formed', referring to this as 'the emergence of . . . "actuality"'. This
actuality is, he says, 'perhaps *energeia*, almost Aristotelian, but closer to
Nietzsche (even though Nietzsche called it the untimely)'.[62]

It is with potentiality and virtuality that we have a more complicated and to
some degree deleted correspondence. Aristotle describes *dunamis* as 'the potentiality for being affected, which is a principle, in the subject of change itself,
or being changed by the action either of something else or by itself *qua* something else'.[63] The meeting point of this *dunamis* and the virtual begins however
in a confusion of terminology, specifically, the conflation of potentiality with
possibility which both Deleuze and Aristotle clarify. Indeed, it is this clarification in Aristotle, followed by Deleuze, which propels *dunamis* into a specifically
Bergsonian virtual. Aristotle comments:

> The possible, then, in one sense . . . means that which is not of necessity false;
> in one, that which is true; in one, that which may be true. . . . But the senses
> which involve a reference to potency all refer to the primary kind of potency;
> and this is a source of change in another thing or in the same thing qua
> other.[64]

What is possible is predicated on the actual, on what can be actualized. Potentiality is in the province of the virtual insofar as it implies power, capacity, potency.
The potency is not actualized but rather it actualizes. Brentano underlines the
importance of this very distinction when he notes that 'there is a great difference between what we here mean by the potential [the *dunaton* or *dunamei on*]
and what in more recent times is meant by calling something possible in contrast with real'.[65]

This distinction is developed by Deleuze in an Aristotelianizing of Bergson's
virtual multiplicity. The possible, as Bergson noted, is produced after the fact,
'retroactively fabricated in the image of what resembles it'.[66] For Deleuze, it is
opposed to the real, insofar as the process that the possible undergoes is itself a
realization. The virtual, on the other hand, is not opposed to the real because
'it possesses a full reality by itself . . . [and] . . . the process it undergoes is that
of actualisation'.[67] The possible would need to 'erupt' into existence; the potential already has being, or as Aristotle calls it, potential being (*on dunamei*). But
this potential being has a question mark attached to it, in the same way that the
being of the virtual has for Deleuze. For example, Proustian reminiscences as
elements of the virtual occupy a paradoxical place between existence and non-
existence – they have extra-being rather than being, or a problematic being
which Deleuze, as we have seen, calls '?-being'.[68] Thus, the nature of the virtual
as multiplicity admits the insertion of the Aristotelian description of being-in-
potentiality in spirit or soul, in memory or thought.

(4) *Can dunamis function in a Deleuzian virtual without collapsing it?* We must first propose a separation of Aristotle's *dunamis* and *energeia* from their problematic relationship with 'substance'. As kinds of being, it is not clear how *dunamis* and *energeia* could be part of the soul and still remain subsumed by primary substance. As Brentano notes, what has being-in-potentiality 'is actually a non-being'.[69] Do we not then deprive the virtual of its reality or dilute its ontological density if its contents have only being-in-potentiality?

This is the case only if we understand *dunamis* and *energeia* as *kinds* of being and not as *ways* of being. Indeed, Charlotte Witt makes this very distinction between Aristotle's being in *Book Zeta* (as substance) and in *Book Theta* (as potentiality and actuality) of the *Metaphysics*, the first being an analysis of being into its kinds or categories and the second being an analysis of being into its ways of being. The advantage to Aristotle is that it allows him to 'construct a developmental, hierarchical, and intrinsically normative conception of being'.[70] This is clearly of great benefit to our analysis of the being of the narrative self as continuous over time but changing, as ipseity, rather than as an analysis made in terms of fixed kinds or categories. It is in this sense that the separation of *dunamis* and *energeia* from primary substance is not at all illegitimate.

Ricoeur brought us down to where the fixed categories of narrative were denatured in the fluid substances of *Ursprung*: time unhinged, narrative cohesion disintegrated. Because of this we must utilize the Aristotelian ways of being in a more fluid environment or in a multiplicity where nothing is finally fixed. For example, when Aristotle says that we should understand the actualization of a potentiality by imagining 'a statue of Hermes existing in a block of wood',[71] we are forced to conceive of something static from which movement ensues, the movement being the element of change rather than to see movement as already in what is to change. We do not need to keep the tree's molecules in adherence with each other or stop the dead cells from falling away or ignore the perpetual change that ensues in the xylem and phloem of the tree itself, even as it is carved into Hermes. A sandstorm in the sky forms the face of Socrates by chance: did Socrates' face exist in potentiality in the sand? And in which grains of sand did that potentiality reside or inhere? If we are to conclude with Aristotle, that Socrates' face did exist in potentiality in the sand, then we can by no means be clear what constitutes the sand itself. There are no clear demarcations. Also, did the face of Plato also exist in potentiality even though it was not actualized? A statue of everyone exists in potentiality in that block of wood, even those not yet born. It is in this sense, that is, when we change the scenography to a fluid medium, to the 'poietic, rhythmic, melodic, more generally carnal requirements'[72] of matter that Irigaray entreaties us to consider, and add to this the time of duration, that the limit of potentiality is torn down and extended into the infinite and into the virtual. Potentiality is a limit case of the actual in Aristotle.

This extended understanding of potentiality is – potentially – already there in Aristotle. He presents a non-exhaustive list of pairs ('the thing carved from matter/the matter' and 'the processed/the unprocessed') and says that 'we simply require that the former element of these pairs be the actuality by definition, and the latter the potentiality'.[73] But the second term of a pair may be the first term of another pair. Thus, if one picks up a pen to write, it is the soul according to Aristotle that is in actuality, but what about the body? By being movable it has being-in-potentiality but to what – to pick up the pen or to write? And what of the pen; is it in-potentiality to being picked up or to delivering ink? Or is the body in actuality when moving to pick up the pen and the pen in actuality when writing or delivering ink? And what of the paper, does it have being-in-potentiality to receive the ink or being-in-actuality in containing it within its tissue? We can see that these two terms are themselves extremely vague in *Metaphysics Theta* 7 where Aristotle is equivocal about when precisely to designate being-in-potentiality to something. Indeed, the potentiality of one thing, earth, to be another thing, wood, can enter a series where now wood has being-in-potentiality to be a casket or indeed something else entirely.[74]

It seems that several divergent series can be formed through the crystalline interaction of *dunamis* and *energeia*. We only need to give to these series an ideality in thought and confer upon them a being-in-potentiality to resonate with each other and to amplify – and behold we have a Deleuzian virtuality in embryonic form. Would we not be better saying that the soul, the body, the pen and the paper (or the earth, the wood and the casket) operate together as a sort of indeterminate machine or an assemblage of parts or as a system where potentiality and actuality are in perpetual transmutation to each other and in such a complex matrix that it is no longer possible to determine where the one and the other begins and ends? That the terms are, as Ricoeur notes, interdependent? Have we not got this model established in nuclear physics, where the electron is both actual and potential, a particle and a waveform, not one nor the other and less one when sought as the other, and less the other when sought as the one?

We may briefly summarize what we have drawn together into a disavowed affinity. The being of the self has to do with its potentiality and capacity to narrate (the way of being) and attest to the truth of its narration (Aristotle's second kind of being, that is, being in the sense of being true); in its most primordial, deepest being, the narrative self is shorn of 'narrative linearities' and encounters 'life force, the creative force of history, *Ursprung*' within what we now call the being of the virtual or potential being (*on dunamei*). And this is a Nietzschean force or a difference between two forces, a creative efflorescence from the interpenetrations and transmutabilities of *dunamis* and *energeia*.

But if we accept both Deleuze and Ricoeur's ontological prioritization of the virtual over the actual in the sense of increasing 'ontological density', do we not now have the problem that the virtual appears, in spite of its ontological density, to have somehow less being, insofar as it is *on dunamei* (Aristotle) or *?-being* (Deleuze)? Although *on dunamei* adequately delivers upon the meaning of the being of the virtual, it is with one limb missing so to speak. And this is its second problem: the potential being of this virtual (insofar as it is a heterogeneous multiplicity with the power to act) does not itself appear to act. The virtual is impassive, powerless, a region of impotency rather than potency. But there must be being-in-actuality at the edge of the virtual or acting immanently within it, if it is to be harvested for narrative – if it is to be creative and if it is to have ontological density. These problems can only be remedied if it can be demonstrated that *energeia* is an integral part of the virtual, on the one hand, and bears an intimate relationship with it, on the other. To address this we will need to draw this virtual into an encounter with the Aristotelian soul. In so doing, we will follow our guiding principle: Ricoeur's argument for the interpenetration of Aristotelian *dunamis/energeia* and their inextricable enmeshment as demonstrated above.

There is, however, a final and perhaps irremediable problem. Although we have removed the limits on the Aristotelian world of being-in-potentiality and being-in-actuality, this world still differs substantially from the Deleuzian one in one fundamental aspect – the direction of its flow. Priority is given by Aristotle to actuality over potentiality (the chicken over the egg[75]), whereas in Bergson and Deleuze, the virtual holds ascendancy. We may have no answer to this; however, it need not radically undermine the fact that an Aristotelian ontology lies disguised more or less as itself in the virtual shadows of a Deleuzian one. One thinks of the replicant in Ridley Scott's *Blade Runner* disguised as a marionette to avoid detection.

(5) *The 'unthought known' of the virtual in Aristotle.* When Mad Sweeney laments his incessant collapse into the 'dark night' of mad flight and his inability to build upon the 'gleam of reason',[76] he notes that while 'the world [of representation] goes on, I return to haunt myself, I freeze and burn. I am the bare figure of pain.'[77] This return of the 'I' as a ghost of the narrative self to a dark night of contrary powers (heat, cold), a place where the self exists as a 'bare figure', echoes the movement we have described for the narrative self as it becomes unhinged of narrative cohesion and returns to clay as the ghost of its own narrative. In Deleuze, priority is given to this 'bare figure' of the Idea before it submits to the requirements of representation, a bare figure he calls a 'brute presence' whose being is virtual.[78]

But is there anything in Aristotle's writings that approximates to this profound bruteness and bareness in thought, this inchoate creativeness? Would it be a disfigurement to even find such a thing? Deleuze does locate it in Plato, without disfigurement, where 'the Heraclitan world still growls' suggesting 'its true secret'.[79] But there is no such growling in Aristotle, according to Deleuze, because here 'matter is already informed' and everything is 'under the protection of the categories'.[80] Nothing pokes its head out and nothing grumbles.

This does not mean that in Aristotle something else does not lie disguised or remain as an unthought known to be excavated at a later date. All systems retain somewhere within them the genitality of thought that went into their construction, the victims devoured and digested in the establishment of the system's own power to act, whether this genitality is placed as other to the system or is inscribed into the very heart of the system itself.[81] Heraclitus is everywhere in Aristotle, insofar as his philosophy of Form–Matter is one of change, process and motion, rather than one set in the frozen *glacés* of Platonic Forms. Indeed, it is to the 'aporetic Aristotle'[82] that we can most fruitfully turn, on the basis that where he struggles to retain cohesion we will discover what is not right with the system, but nevertheless what may well be right outside it or via alterations to the overall system itself. This is particularly so when *dunamis/energeia* are introduced into the soul.

Aristotle makes the clear distinction between matter as potentiality and form as actuality.[83] Now thinking and knowing are 'ways of being affected or moved'[84] and therefore have being-in-potentiality. They are set in motion by the objects of thought and knowledge, insofar as the objects of thought act upon thought; thought, when acted upon, acts to think. But if form is actuality then how can thinking be in potentiality (i.e. acted upon) unless it is in matter? In the case of knowledge, Aristotle distinguishes two ways in which we can speak of this actuality: as 'the possession of knowledge and the actual exercise of knowledge'[85] so that the soul is actuality as the possession of knowledge. It is the 'first grade of actuality' of the body to be distinguished from a second grade of actuality, which is the exercise of this knowledge.[86] But this exercising of knowledge, according to Aristotle's definition, does not occur within the soul but at the margins of or outside it. His example is sleeping and waking which 'both presuppose . . . a soul', but it is the waking that corresponds to actual knowing, while sleeping corresponds 'to knowledge possessed but not employed'.[87] Now this is strange as it suggests that knowing is not entirely within the soul, only the forms of what is known. However, since Aristotle is clear that knowing is a mode of appetition and belongs to the soul,[88] we cannot be sure how knowing is divided between the soul and the not-soul but also somehow belongs to it.

An additional problem is that the soul that possesses knowledge surely does so potentially before its exercise, that is, between the first and second grades of actuality, the first being in the soul and the second being, presumably, somewhere else. Aristotle says as much, likening the possession of knowledge to the 'power of sight' in the eye, while the exercise of knowledge is the 'seeing'.[89] Yet it cannot be ignored that the 'power' of sight is a capacity and a potentiality, just as the possession of knowledge is both the first grade of actuality and the first grade of potentiality to exercise that knowledge. Indeed, if we reject the chicken–egg orientation in *Metaphysics*, we have to assume that there is a first grade of potentiality that is before the first grade of actuality and that this potentiality is different from the matter 'that possesses a potentiality of being ensouled'.[90] Rejecting it is not without substance for we can argue that it is counterintuitive to think of the soul as without potentiality – how else would we come into the possession of sensations and knowledge without the potentiality to receive these in the first place?

It appears that the inseparability of *dunamis* and *energeia*, as Ricoeur suggests, extends even to the soul, where no sooner do we posit one than the other is immediately presupposed in a perpetual and mutually symbiotic coexistence. Indeed, as we move deeper into the soul with Aristotle, this 'inter-mutability' of *dunamis/energeia* escalates when Aristotle goes on to isolate the potential knower from the knower in actuality that realizes his respective potentiality,[91] in contradiction to [412a23] where Aristotle distinguished two ways in which we can speak of form as actuality in relation to knowledge: as 'the possession of knowledge and the actual exercise of knowledge'.

From [417a27] and [412a23] we could generate the following series: potentiality to know → actuality of learning → potentiality to exercise learning → actuality of using knowledge. Now, even if we substitute for the first term 'actuality of soul' our argument above tells us that the two terms are inseparable. For example, the soul as *actuality/energeia* is that 'by which primarily we live, perceive, and think'[92] and yet Aristotle refers to 'the potentiality of the soul'[93] or 'the power of the soul'.[94]

The confusion is hardly clarified if we move to the marginal areas of the soul, to those faculties like perception that appear to have one foot in the soul.[95] For example, Aristotle goes on to characterize the soul as having two 'distinctive peculiarities . . . (1) local movement and (2) thinking, discriminating, and perceiving'.[96] But again he characterizes 'that part of the soul with which the soul knows and thinks'[97] as potentiality: thinking is 'a process in which the soul is acted upon by what is capable of being thought'. If it is part of the soul, then the soul is clearly not pure actuality (like the Divine) but in many respects comprises several parts which are all fundamentally in the first grade of potentiality. To make matters more complicated, he declares that 'that in the soul which is called mind (by mind I mean that whereby the soul thinks and judges) is, before it thinks, not actually any real thing'.[98] In fact, the soul now becomes a 'place of forms' but forms in potentiality, not actuality.

How does Aristotle deal with this intrusion of potentiality again into the soul? He does so by declaring that this potentiality is in fact a kind of actuality insofar as the mind 'is able to think *itself*'.[99] But this entails an inevitable fracture in Aristotle's soul (or at least in the soul/mind/perception apparatus), because if mind becomes its own object it must of necessity divide into two: the mind that 'is in a sense potentially whatever is thinkable' and the mind that 'actually . . . is nothing until it has thought'.[100] This is not problematic in that most contemporary conceptualizations of the mind involve this split in some form or another (i.e. unconscious, conscious); however, this inseparability of *dunamis* and *energeia* in the soul/mind/perception apparatus in Aristotle demands a virtual aspect to his soul and the fracture at the heart of it invites the potential for inserting the Aristotelian soul into those formulations of the mind that postulate a virtual in parallel to an actual, or that re-conceptualize the unconscious as a positive virtuality. This argument is strengthened by another move which Aristotle makes when he introduces the notion of an Active and Passive Intellect (see below).

(6) *The Deleuzian virtual mirrors the Aristotelian soul.* We must remind ourselves of how Deleuze conceptualizes the mind from within the dichotomous terms of activity/passivity. An object of thought initiates thought through the nature of a fundamental encounter that proceeds through three 'passive syntheses' of time, the first involving the present, the second involving memory and the third involving the eternal return of difference.[101] We will concentrate on the first synthesis because it is this one that is foundational for Deleuze and where we can associate Aristotle's active/passive intellect with Deleuze's.

The first passive synthesis is a contraction of successive independent instances into one another to constitute the lived present, thus providing us with an internal qualitative impression which is the duration of Bergson.[102] Deleuze defines this synthesis further as the acquisition of habit and places it under the sign of 'Contemplation', contrasting it with the acquisition of habit understood as a product of activity.[103] In other words, we acquire habits through contemplating, through the drawing of something new, that is, difference, through repetition. Habits are contractions (we speak of contracting a habit), fusions of successive instances in a 'contemplative soul' – indeed, these passive syntheses constitute our habitual way of living and expecting that this living will continue.[104] But what is this contemplation at the level of the self? Psychology of course forbids the self from contemplating itself but is this not a response to a badly posed question? Should not the real question be: is the self in-itself a contemplation? 'Underneath the self which acts', says Deleuze, 'are little selves which contemplate and which render possible both the action and the active subject.' When we speak of our selves (ourselves) we do so 'only in virtue of these thousands of little witnesses which contemplate within us'.[105]

Aristotle frequently refers to the objects of thought that initiate thinking.[106] However, thinking is 'a process in which the soul is acted upon by what is capable of being thought'[107] and the thinking part of the soul receives the form or *eidos* of that object – or as we noted earlier – it is 'the intellective soul' that is 'the place of forms' that have being-in-potentiality, not actuality.[108]

The paradox returns to us, given that Aristotle has repeatedly informed us that forms are in actuality while matter is in potentiality. We have already noted one solution to this problem, whereby Aristotle declares that this type of potentiality is in fact a kind of actuality. But specifically, how are we to understand what it is to be a form-in-potentiality without species-alteration? We cannot understand a 'form' here to mean shape or *morphê* since it has no matter; it must instead refer to some essence of the meaning of a form as an 'essence-specifying definition'.[109] Given that the intellective soul is a place of forms-in-potentiality, we must then understand the form-in-potentiality in a limited, pre-semantic sense of *logos* – in the manner that *logos* is understood to capture the definition of something.[110] Thus it would be better to think of these forms in the mind in-potentiality as *accounts without narrative*, definitions without words or as 'the principle of organisation of a thing which leads it to have its particular existence'.[111] If this is what enters the mind, it clearly cannot be thought through the representative faculties. Indeed, for Aristotle, this form that cannot be thought resides in that part of the soul that is 'not actually any real thing'.[112] It is in this capacity (*dunamis*) or in this state of readiness that this part of the soul, this no-thing, can think itself.[113] This is *the soul* of the virtual, for Deleuze.

Aristotle distinguishes an active from a passive intellect in *De Anima*, III.5, a section regarded by Lawson-Tancred as otiose, relating neither to the chapter before nor the chapter after and having little function in the overall picture that Aristotle develops of the soul and mind.[114] Our purpose will be to relate the distinction active/passive with virtual/actual by utilizing the twin terms *dunamis/energeia*. Aristotle declares that there are two minds, one in potentiality and one in actuality; the first is that 'by virtue of becoming all things', while the second is that 'by virtue of making all things'.[115]

A problem arises here for Aristotle; if the chicken comes before the egg, then in the mind it appears otherwise, where what is potentially comes before what is actually. Actual knowledge, Aristotle says, 'is identical with its object: in the individual, potential knowledge is in time prior to actual knowledge, but in the universe as a whole it is not prior even in time'.[116] This division of Aristotle's is not at all redundant. The mind that is 'the becoming of all things' corresponds to the soul in Deleuze beneath the *concordia facultatum*, the soul that is perplexed by the object of the encounter and forced to see it as the bearer of a problem. Like Aristotle, it begins with sensibility but the soul is not sensibility alone and other faculties must also become subject to the violence of an encounter with the object. We move from sensibility sensing the *sentiendum* to our grasping that which can only be thought, the *cogitandum* or the essence; this is not however the intelligible but the being of the intelligible. Now is this not precisely the form-in-potentiality that has finally arrived from the original encounter with the object of thought, the being of the intelligible object? Does not Aristotle provide us with the first virtual, a passive, contemplative soul that receives the being of the sensible and intelligible and is the becoming of all things?[117]

If we take a different meaning to the phrase 'that in the soul which is called mind . . . is, before it thinks, not actually any real thing'[118] and read it instead as 'that part of the soul . . . called intellect . . . is before it thinks in actuality none of the things that exist',[119] then we can understand that Aristotle is implying that this part of the mind that is before thought is not actual though it is nevertheless real. This is the definition of the virtual: 'real without being actual, ideal without being abstract'. In fact, Deleuze employs the term 'potentially' to specifically characterize the elements of 'virtuality'.[120] It is within this structure that we can begin to make sense of Aristotle's enigmatic remark that 'in the individual, potential knowledge is in time prior to actual knowledge, but in the universe as a whole it is not prior even in time.'[121] This universe is the virtual as we understand it, that of memory and the pure past, or rather, the Bergsonian inverted cone that is at the heart of Ricoeur's narrative self.

(7) *Energeia in the virtual soul as an unmoved mover.* We have traced a parallel between the soul as the seat of 'passive affection'[122] in Aristotle and the contemplative soul as the seat of passive syntheses in Deleuze. But what of *energeia* and the active intellect? Can we return actuality to the soul that is 'by virtue of becoming all things' (the virtual) and give to it an inherent creativity?

The soul in Aristotle is somewhat metamorphic, especially when we try to find continuity between *De Anima* and *Metaphysics*.[123] But can the soul be moved, having as we have argued being-in-potentiality, or has it the definition of an unmoved mover, one of pure actuality? Aristotle is either equivocal on this or he adjusts his position from *Metaphysics* to *De Anima*. It is incorrect to say that the soul feels sadness or happiness, since there are no grounds for thinking that the soul is 'in motion'; rather, it is man who feels so 'in virtue of the soul', whose feelings are motions 'produced by the soul'[124] and of the nature of the body's *dunamis*. Intriguingly, Aristotle draws the soul's *energeia* into the domains of perception and memory: man's affectations are motions 'towards the soul and sometimes from it',[125] for example, perception moves from the sense organs towards the soul, while memory moves from the soul towards the body.

Memory is thus in the realm of the soul, therefore of actuality, and is a mover. Yet it does not itself move, even by its own doing.[126] The impassive pure past, the virtual cone of Bergson, is in the Aristotelian soul. And although man's feelings are in the world of representation, the being of what is felt, that is, the being of the sensible, is in the virtual. But is there not a contradiction here if the virtual is real but not actual yet memory is *energeia*? Not if we retain the distinction Aristotle makes between *energeia* as the process of actualization, the carving of the statue as such, and *entelecheia*, as the final goal of this actualization process, the teleological end-point, the statue of Hermes itself. Between the potential and the actual is the process of becoming (like the intensive between the virtual and the actual in Deleuze). This is the meaning of *energeia* when ascribed to memory – it is the acting of the potency to act.

In line with this distinction of two meanings of *energeia*, we need to differentiate between two meanings of *dunamis* in Aristotle – that of causal power and that of potentiality. 'Causal power' is the basic meaning of *dunamis* and 'all causal powers come in pairs; there is an agent or originating power to change another thing, and a passive receptivity or power to be changed.'[127] Aristotle argues that potentialities may be 'rational' or 'non-rational',[128] the rational ones being triggered by 'rational preference' or 'moved by desire'.[129] Desire decides which of two contrary effects will be achieved – otherwise both would occur.

This Aristotelian desire (as an appetition of the soul and therefore an actuality) that manoeuvres through the tapestry of potentialities is an image in miniature of the productive desiring-machines that populate the world of Deleuze and Guattari's *AntiOedipus* where desire 'remains in close touch with the conditions of . . . the objective being of man, for whom to desire is to produce, to produce within the realm of the real'.[130] Indeed, the notion of production is crucial to Aristotle: we do not simply mimic or habitually respond in the sense of a complex agglomeration of reflexes that can nonetheless be reduced to the patellar tap; instead, being is productive – or one of the ways of being produces: 'from the potentially existing the actually existing is always produced by an actually existing thing . . . we have said in our account of substance that everything that is produced is something produced from something and by something.'[131]

And that final something will be in the nature of an unmoved mover. But how did Aristotle get to this unmoved mover? On the basis that no series of movers and moved can go on to infinity but that it must begin somewhere.[132] This is the case with the mind that is at the beginning of the series that wrote with the pen. Mind can cause motion 'only by being itself unmoved, and have supreme control only by being unmixed' or separate from matter.[133] Thus, Aristotle works backwards from the given to that which must be inferred. However, the human may move the arm that moves the pen, but he certainly does not move the stars in the sky. They too must have a mover, the ultimate and supreme unmoved mover who sets the celestial firmament in motion though remains estranged to the world that has this eternal motion. For the universe, 'motion in space is the first of the kinds of change . . . and this the first mover *produces*.'[134] This prime mover 'exists of necessity', in actuality not potentiality and 'produces' movement but does not share in it.[135]

But if 'thought is moved by the object of thought'[136] and as Aristotle states, the 'primary objects of thought and desire are the same',[137] moving without being moved, then the prime mover is somehow affected by desire without being moved by it. How could this be so? Is this not a way of being-in-potentiality? Aristotle puts it this way: the prime mover 'produces motion as being loved, but all other things move by being moved'.[138] Lawson-Tancred offers this translation: the unmoved mover 'produces movement by dint of being the object of desire and it does so primarily in the heavens and, through them, in everything else'.

Now it is not at all clear whether the unmoved movers that are the souls of humans[139] are included in the 'everything else' or the 'all other things' or not. If they are, then they are not unmoved movers, and this is contradictory; if they are not, then they are either subservient to the prime mover or connected to it in some unspecified way. Clearly, they cannot be subservient or they will not be the end of the series and therefore will be moved. They must therefore be connected to the prime mover and it to them. This interpretation is supported by one central point. The prime mover possesses thought as the object of thought; it thinks itself in the purity of contemplation, and it is this possession which is its activity, not its own receptivity to itself.[140] This prime mover is the pure 'actuality of thought' – which is life also.[141] God is therefore, for Aristotle, both a living being and 'life and duration continuous'.[142] But what is the relationship between this thought thinking thought and the human soul, both of which are infused with life? Aristotle is very clear that the human soul at the zenith of its hierarchy is capable of just what the Divine soul is capable of, that is, thought thinking thought: 'the mind too is . . . able to think itself' or 'mind is itself thinkable'.[143] Is the connection then one of expression? If so, it is not an unimaginable leap from here to Spinoza.

Earlier in this chapter we noted Deleuze's argument that expressive immanence can only be sustained by 'a thoroughgoing affirmation' of the univocity of being and that this is what Spinoza provides.[144] It is Spinoza, Deleuze argues, who frees expressive immanence from one of two things: (1) the subordination of immanent causality to emanative cause, as in Plotinus and (2) the subordination of immanent causality to creation. In the latter case, Ideas are placed in God rather than lower forms so that whatever is created *ex nihilo* is done so through participation in God and thus is no more than a pale imitation of the exemplary.[145] Aristotle's prime mover, through the connectedness of souls, is in many respects close to the philosophy of Spinoza and therefore Deleuze, in spite of its position at the apex of a hierarchy of Being: 'Spinoza's God is a God who both is, and produces, all, like the One and All of the Platonists; but he is also a God who thinks both himself and everything, like Aristotle's Prime Mover.'[146]

Aristotle reaches the prime mover by necessity, working back from the given to what must begin the series that ends in brute behaviour, the picking up of the pen, the building of the house. There is no beyond the prime mover, no before. Deleuze reaches the dark precursor in a similar manner.[147] He must identify some operator that sets in resonance the differences of the various heterogeneous series that populate a virtual multiplicity or that ensure 'the communication of peripheral series'.[148] This is the dark precursor that operates as a 'differenciator of difference' or the 'in-itself of difference', an operator that exists of necessity.[149] The dark precursor is behind everything, but behind the dark precursor there is nothing.[150] It is the end of the series, as the prime mover is the end of the Aristotelian series. Behind both, there is nothing.

In the poetics of self-narrative we could name this dark precursor 'the under-presence' that Wordsworth struggled to articulate. In other words, there is a creative process within the created poem that is never separable from it; what lives in a Wordsworth poem is not the poem itself but the creator and the creating. 'The Prelude' is in this sense a creative event, barely cancelled out by the poem; the event of its creation both inheres in and protrudes through the poem as 'a creating liberated from its creature'.[151] Utilizing these terms, Peter Hallward argues that Deleuze's philosophy is broadly *theophanic* in conception, insofar as he contends that 'every individual process or thing is conceived as a manifestation or expression of God or a conceptual equivalent of God (pure creative potential, force, energy, life).'[152] Hallward places Deleuze on a developmental line through Bergson and Spinoza and back to John Scottus Eriugena. He notes Eriugena's fourfold division of nature as follows:

> [An] uncreated and consequently unknowable or unthinkable *creator*; the immediate and adequate expression of this creator in multiple self-revelations or *creatings* (which are both created and creative); the various *creatures* (created but not creative) that lend material weight to these creatings; and finally, a virtual state beyond creaturely perception and distinction, to which whatever is eternally creative about these creatures is destined to eventually return.[153]

In this theophanic position, God *is* only in these creatings which are expressive of a single, creative force, that is, the multiplication of singular creatings. It is in this sense that 'individuation does not itself depend on mediation through the categories of representation, objectivity, history or the world.'[154] If being is creation, as it is for Deleuze, and differentiates itself in an infinite number of ways, then the most basic element of being is not a flux but 'a distinct process or operation: *a* creating',[155] one implied or, to use Deleuze's term, implicated in its creator and explicated or unfolded in the creature. As expression, it is the 'unfolding of what expresses itself, the One manifesting itself in the Many (substance manifesting itself in its attributes, and these attributes manifesting themselves in their modes)'.[156] The creating is virtual; the creature, actual. In other words, the virtual is creative; the actual, created. Central to this creating is a limit point, a beginning beyond which is nothing. This is the 'élan of creativity itself, the affirmation of being conceived as a sort of primordial energy or constituent power, the inexhaustible source of pure potential and transformation'.[157] This is what Deleuze means by the dark precursor.

But does Aristotle's prime mover, in cohesion with the multiple souls of humans, offer to us something akin to this immanent and expressive God of

the dark precursor? Aristotle concluded that the prime mover is the pure 'actuality of thought' and that 'the actuality of thought is life.'[158] Bostock reads the
Aristotelian soul, that is, the soul across the animal and plant world as 'a kind
of life . . . not the *cause* of that life, but the life itself'.[159] Thus, it is the living as
the One and the Divine that is expressed in its attributes and modes in nature
or that part of nature that is living. But we cannot exclude what is inert from the
living or entirely divorce it from living systems; our bones are made of deposits
of calcium and other minerals which are not provided with nutrients; a snail
houses itself in an inert shell as we house ourselves in bricks and mortar, and we
live within ecosystems that depend upon the plants, animals, insects and inert
matter for their livingness, as we do our bones and teeth. Aristotle indirectly
acknowledges this when he says:

> [The] state is by nature clearly prior to the family and the individual, since
> the whole is of necessity prior to the part; for example, if the whole body is
> destroyed, there will be no foot or hand, except in an equivocal sense, so we
> might speak of a stone hand; for when destroyed the hand will be no better
> than that. But things are defined by their working and power . . . The proof
> that the state is a creation of nature and prior to the individual is that the
> individual, when isolated, is not self-sufficing; and therefore he is like a part
> in relation to the whole.[160]

Indeed, Aristotle makes no clear demarcation between the lifeless and the living: 'Nature proceeds little by little from things lifeless to animal life in such a
way that it is impossible to determine the exact line of demarcation, nor on
which side thereof an intermediate form should lie.'[161] He also acknowledges
the dependency of living creatures upon the inanimate, noting that many
would perish if detached from it.[162]

If we can really find, as Rémi Brague suggests, that which remains unthought
in Aristotle, it is not difficult to conclude that had Aristotle considered an eco-
system (whether it be a house, a neighbourhood, a mosquito-infested swamp,
the delta of a river or a rainforest) he would have determined it in precisely
the way he understood the individual and the family as a part of a wider system
'created by nature' and that he would have conferred upon it the determination of the living.[163] It is only in this sense, where parts are of wholes and wholes
themselves are the parts of greater wholes and indeed wholes overlap (a neighbourhood overlaps another neighbourhood or cuts across two ecosystems) in a
multiplicity of determinations that we can place the soul of man in the same
sentence as the soul of universe and that the many expresses the One in a
creative efflorescence that never has the goal of a final mimesis of the already
identical Divine. We can understand this life force that is the prime mover and
the essence of human souls (and by extension their living and inanimate environment) as *all* of a *one*, a precursor in part to Spinoza's expressionism. It is not

all of it, but it can be thought within the anthropological, cosmological and theological parts of Aristotle's system, and therewith reconstructed. Hallward suggests something of this when he writes of the dark precursor:

> There is first of all the pure impulse or élan of creativity itself, the affirmation of being conceived as a sort of primordial energy or constituent power, the inexhaustible source of pure potential and transformation. Considered on its own, isolated from what it constitutes, this constituent power can only be imagined as an unthinkable abstraction . . . It figures as an inconceivably compressed point of pure intensity . . . (the whole of time condensed to a single point) which at every moment passes through every other conceivable point, and generates every possible configuration of points. This would be a point travelling at infinite speed, never in any one place because it distributes every place. It is Deleuze's immanent alternative to Aristotle's prime mover.[164]

This description is not the alternative of the prime mover, if we draw the prime mover into coalescence with the souls of *De Anima*. In this fusion, the prime mover is immanent to the universe, a creative force of *energeia* expressing itself in and through the souls of man who are its authors and it their producer. If 'the actuality of thought is life', then this prime mover cannot be outside what is living and disconnected from what is alive. We author our selves and our souls and in so doing we author the Divine.

Chapter 10

Interzone

We wake remembering the events of which [dreams] are composed while often the narrative is fugitive and difficult to recall. Yet it is the narrative which is the life of the dream while the events themselves are often interchangeable. The events of the waking world on the other hand are forced upon us and the narrative is the unguessed axis along which they must be strung. It falls to us to weigh and sort and order these events. It is we who assemble them into the story which is us. Each man is the bard of his own existence.[1]

Introduction

In the previous chapter we reached the point of intersection between Deleuze and Ricoeur. Having located in the narrative self 'its own disavowed underside',[2] we now move in the opposite direction from Deleuze to Ricoeur or, more specifically, from the dark precursor to the narrative self. In Schelling's language, this is a move from the infinite to the finite. Earlier, we questioned the possible outcome of an approximation of the self of Ricoeur with the selves of Deleuze: that it might be additive, multiplicative, divisive or subtractive. But it is none of these things – for it is creative. Something new emerges through a metamorphic metaphorization of Deleuze's larval selves and a metaphoric metamorphosis of Ricoeur's narrative self. If their meeting point in the depths has been in the domain of Aristotle's *dunamis* and *energeia*, then on the surface we have shown it to be within Proust's 'unmatching puzzle-pieces' (*puzzle désaccordé*)[3] of *In Search of Lost Time*. We link these puzzle-pieces by what Proust calls transversal thinking, thinking without totality or only the 'illusion of unity'.[4] Therefore, as we move from excess to debt, from metamorphosis to metaphorization, we proceed by means of a transversal encounter between larval and narrative selves; through this we aim to enact a refiguration of the narrative self as just so many unmatched puzzle-pieces whose being in multiplicity is best conceptualized at the junction of Ricoeur's 'discordant concordance' and Deleuze's 'discordant harmony'.[5]

We want to show in this chapter that this point of intersection marks not just a point of return but an interzone between representation and the pre-representational, between narrative and non-narrative and between the spoken and the indeclinable. But we will argue in addition that this chapter marks this interzone as a point of meditation leading to what Heidegger calls *Gelassenheit*, a reassessment of position, a review of whether the procedures for argument that we have employed up until now need to be readjusted. It is *Gelassenheit* that will accompany our questions here. We will need to reflect in this chapter on what problems still inhere in spite of locating a common genetic point of intersection between Deleuze and Ricoeur; by specifying these problems, we may place them before us, as we construct a trajectory out from the realm of the dark precursor and into the narrative self. In other words, we will argue that this movement involves following a different Ariadne's thread for the ascent out of the *Ursprung* and into narrative than for the descent into it from narrative itself. Simply put, do we need to follow a less than linear argument or an argument that takes into consideration transversal or 'knight's-move thinking'?[6] The trajectory from narrative to *Ursprung* has necessitated the deconstructing of narrative; from *Ursprung* to narrative is one of constructing – but of what? Narrative is the end stage but what does one put together to get there, in what order and to what design? This is our task now.

Between Dark Precursor and Narrative Self: *Gelassenheit*

Identifying the difficulty of situating a study between dual trajectories (from Ricoeur to Deleuze and from Deleuze to Ricoeur) is not without precedent. Ricoeur argues that the circle of mimesis, the spiralling fight of concordance and discordance, involves two processes vying for superiority, either for discordant concordance (*discordance concordante*) or for concordant discordance (*concordance discordante*), a circle 'inevitable without being vicious'.[7] Indeed, it is Ricoeur's view that concordance wins in the world of literature, while discordance reigns in the world of life. But is the narrative self of the world of life or of literature or, indeed, of both? In Deleuze, we have what Alain Badiou describes as 'an athletic trajectory of thought . . . a narrative adventure' employing 'intuition (as a double movement . . . as writing, as style) [that] must simultaneously descend from a singular being toward its active dissolution in the One . . . and re-ascend from the One toward the singular being'.[8] In other words, once we embark on an ontogenetic study of the narrative self, we must do so with caution, given the potentially competing forces of discordance and dissolution (Deleuze), on the one hand, and concordance and narrative cohesion (Ricoeur), on the other. We noted the potential problems of this in Chapter 1 with our analogy of the mythological gryphon. Thus, this interzone defines an in-between point in our argumentation and a point of crossing-over, that is, between representation and what is pre-representational or indeclinable (in the sense both of what can neither be disowned nor represented). It is a place that demands reflection, a place where we move towards what Heidegger calls *Gelassenheit*.[9]

Heidegger contrasts meditative thinking with calculative thinking, the former alone leading to *Gelassenheit* or releasement, an 'openness to the mystery'[10] of the world that 'allows itself to be thought only by a thinking that is not representing, not a putting forward of concepts that one knows, in a structured thinking that already means something to me'.[11] That Heidegger's releasement occupies the same region as Deleuze's virtual (while not immediately apparent) is certainly implied. According to Heidegger, we are for the most part 'in flight from thinking'[12] (for Deleuze we seldom think), so that meditative thinking becomes a 'persistent, courageous thinking' much like what Deleuze suggests occurs in response to a form of violence to thought. Only when this occurs do we sense what is hidden in the virtual, or as Heidegger puts it, 'that which hides itself from us, and hides itself just in approaching us'.[13] It is meditative thinking that 'demands of us that we engage . . . with what at first sight does not go together at all'[14] that is, the unmatching puzzle-pieces of the virtual that are brought into correspondence through transversal engagement.

In the late Heidegger, Being takes on a more strongly spatial dimension, becoming that-which-regions or spatializes our lives:

Scientist: Now authentic releasement consists in this: that man in his very nature belongs to that-which-regions (*Gegnet*), i.e. he is released to it.

Scholar: Not occasionally, but . . . prior to everything.

Scientist: The prior, of which we really cannot think . . .

Scholar: . . . because the nature of thinking begins there.

Scientist: Thus man's nature is released to that-which-regions in what is prior to thought.

Scholar: [ ] . . . and, indeed, through that-which-regions itself.[15]

However, as we experience *Gegnet* and while the nature of *Gegnet* nears, 'that-which-regions itself seems . . . further away than ever before'.[16] In other words, as Dalle Pezze notes, 'it is the openness itself that here opens before us, but in its opening, the opening hides itself, and thus seems to be "further away" from us.'[17] For Heidegger, this is a thinking prior to representation, profound thinking that is 'an in-dwelling releasement to that-which-regions' and that-which-regions 'regions all, gathering everything together and letting everything return to itself . . . the nearness of distance and the distance of nearness'.[18] The world of *Gegnet* that Heidegger enters into is remarkably similar to the 'any-space-whatever' (*espace quelconque*) that Deleuze argues is the 'space of virtual conjunction, grasped as pure locus of the possible', a space that has lost 'the principle of its metric relations'.[19] The *espace quelconque*, like the space of that-which-regions, is a virtual or 'spiritual space',[20] a space that no longer expresses only 'the state of things' (or those objects of calculative thinking) but also 'the possibility, the virtuality, which goes beyond it'.[21] It is space before space is 'surreptitiously introduced' into it, as Bergson noted. By way of this, an ontological depth is given to space, or, rather, Being and Space express each other.

Thus, the importance of reflection in this interzone, in the space of that-which-regions or the *espace quelconque*, is that we bring to our work a determination to construct the narrative self by way of the virtual, by way of a partial releasement from calculative thinking. If the self has a virtual other half, then we must encourage that spirit of the self which resides in an *espace quelconque* to express itself or at the least to be part of the solution. From it, we draw the problems laid out below.

Inhering Problems for the Becoming-Narrative Self

(1) *Is there a faculty between nonsense and sense?* The term *délire* (formulated by Jean-Jacques Lecercle) denotes the borderline between madness and good sense or sense and nonsense. It refers to the emergence of sense from nonsense but with a specifically enfleshed formulation, 'where the material side of language, its origin in the human body and desire, are no longer eclipsed by its abstract aspect (as an instrument of communication or expression)'.[22] But if the narrative self can emerge from virtual or meditative thinking, then we must identify a faculty commensurate to the task of harvesting sense from nonsense, a faculty that traverses the virtual/actual divide and operates within 'that-which-regions'. In other words, just as Heidegger argues for two types of thinking (meditative and calculative), we contend that there are two sides to narrative – délire and sense; but, in addition, we argue for some means of transition between the two that does not sublate délire in the very formation of narrative (as both Ricoeur and Deleuze would argue happens).[23] Such a faculty would be analogous to a third organ for the gryphon, one that could alleviate the respiratory difficulties that beset the centaur.[24]

(2) *What is meant by a different Ariadne's thread in aiming towards an ontogenesis of the narrative self?* We have argued that beneath the narrative self are larval selves harvesting a potential story from the multifarious events of a life, but, as Ricoeur asks, what is an event when purged of every narrative connection? What can we know of this face of the self when turned to narrative, when translated into a form unrecognizable to itself? What is the face of the self seen from releasement, from the 'prior to everything', from the indwelling in that-which-regions? Put another way, we move from releasement by way of an itinerary that is transversal in nature and through which 'we engage ourselves with what at first sight does not go together at all',[25] in order that we neither fall back into the chaotic nor enter the rigidified.

What did Proust mean by 'transversal thinking'? In *In Search of Lost Time*, Marcel looks out the window of his carriage on a train journey to Balbec and sees on one side a nocturnal village and on the other 'the strip of pink sky' that only moments ago had occupied the view of the first window before the train had snaked its course through the countryside. Lamenting the loss of one or the other view Marcel spends his time 'running from one window to the other to reassemble, to collect on a single canvas the intermittent, antipodean fragments of my fine, scarlet, ever-changing morning, and to obtain a comprehensive view and a continuous picture of it'.[26] As Deleuze notes, Proust clearly invokes a totality and a continuity 'but the essential point is to know where these are elaborated – neither in the viewpoint nor in the thing seen, but in the transversal, from one window to the other'.[27] In other words, we link the fragments by what Proust calls transversal thinking, but no totality will be achieved, only 'an illusion of unity'.[28] Why? Because this Proustian world is made of 'unmatching puzzle-pieces',[29] fragments that when gathered together reveal themselves to be composed of still smaller fragments or indeed fractals. So also with the transversal connections – these too split into further transversals which force us:

> [To] leap . . . from one world to another, from one word to another, without ever reducing the many to the One, without ever gathering up the multitude into a whole, but affirming the original unity of precisely that multiplicity, affirming without uniting all these irreducible fragments.[30]

In *Time Regained*, Proust is very clear on the nature of this thinking when he reflects on the 'two great ways' that he has travelled – the Méséglise and the Guermantes – those 'high roads' that can never meet up, determined in part by others before him and representing a tradition of passage. But it is 'between these two high roads [that] a network of transversals was set up' by Marcel.[31] Difference is brought together, but it is not reduced to identity. The Méséglise and the Guermantes, the Deleuzian and the Ricoeurian ways – a transversal encounter does not merge or conflate them one to the other but 'affirms only their difference'.[32]

In other words, if we are to have a virtual, non-narrative or pre-narrative dimension to the self, then we cannot subject our analysis of this solely to a process that provides us with a representational derivative alone. We must retain the other side, the virtual half. And drawing from Proust, we contend that there are two important aspects to this other side (and therefore to the virtual half of the narrative self) that need to be considered in constructing a Deleuzian–Ricoeurian self(s): its fractal non-narrative or pre-narrative nature (that determines that it is composed of mismatched jigsaw pieces) and the transversal correspondence between these fractal elements or series of elements. Indeed, what other correspondence could there be when there is no transcendent image to dictate where each piece goes, when there is no picture on the cover of the jigsaw box?

(3) *Is the being of the narrative self not always a being-with?* Our narrative self
commences its outward journey (developmentally, that is) conjoined to
another and remains conjoined to others unto death and this being-with
begins in the womb – a fact that confers on its ontological status an irreducible being-with or *Mitsein*. There is no other starting point, no isolated
Dasein. Jean-Luc Nancy argues this point in his book *Being Singular Plural*.
In it, he places the '"singular plural" of Being' at the foundation of first
philosophy.[33] He displaces Being from its autistic position and authenti-
cates it in a being-with: 'Being cannot *be* anything but being-with-one-
another, circulating in the *with* and as the *with* of this singularly plural
coexistence'.[34] Such a being-with in its origins is not a being-alongside or a
being-against but a being-in-multiplicity where an origin is concealed; in
this sense our being is also a being-other, but again this is an alterity in
multiplicity (not a radical alterity but a being-many) in that this being-other
is 'a being-other *than* every being *for* and *crossing through* all being'.[35] In this
manner, Nancy raises the everyday to an authentic ontological status, in the
process decrying Heidegger for confusing the everyday with the undifferentiated and the statistical.[36] This being-with propels Being beyond its intimacy with time and into 'that-which-regions' or that-which-positions. In
other words, to posit something implies its being singular, that is, discrete
from and therefore *with*.[37] Nancy's argument effectively gives to the being of
the narrative self in its origins a fundamental plurality out of which, we
argue, larval narratives and narrative selves emerge – for it is 'the plurality
of beings [that] is at the foundation of Being'.[38] *Dunamis* and *energeia* are in
the heart of this being-with, since we have both the potentiality to narrate
with, to, for and *of* others and the actuality to do so. And this being-with is
one that forms the foundation of our transversal engagement between
Deleuze and Ricoeur. It is the crossing-through, this traversal *of* and *to* each
other in this 'alterity in multiplicity'.

In taking this being-with approach, we must remind ourselves of the twin
dangers which have defined the problematic field of the narrative self since the
start of this work: chaos, on the one hand, where anything goes (the Wonderland world of Alice) and organization, on the other, where rigidity imposes one
path to truth (the replicant world of Rachael). To some degree there is an
'unguessed axis' through these twin dangers, which neither eschews narrative
coherence nor ignores the benefits to the self of a productive unconscious.

An Unguessed Axis for Narrative Selves

What does McCarthy mean by the 'unguessed axis'? A film director can temporally rearrange the scenes or the sequences of scenes in a film, disrupting
our deductive and inductive reasoning (as Tarentino does in *Pulp Fiction*) but

without losing coherence; indeed, reasoning is returned to us but radically enhanced by altering what is newly expressed in this re-emplotment. The ineffable, the unthought known, the unsayable cannot be reasonably adduced; like many mythological creatures, it is always under the surface, its effects barely seen, barely felt. Jean-Luc Godard understood this when he said that 'cinema shows us that which we don't see – the incredible.'[39] If the ineffable is to be 'captured', then philosophy may need to adjust its procedures to do so.[40] In fact, this says no more than that we may need a cinematographic philosophy (not a philosophy of the cinema). If we related this to the stories of which we are, then the narrative self becomes the 'unguessed axis' upon which we string the events that make up our lives. We are poets in this endeavour, poets who harvest the events of our life for narrative. We cannot as philosophical selves stand above this, indifferently commenting. If the actualized stories we tell of ourselves are to be placed within their virtual otherness, then we must proceed in a manner that is most likely to augment this virtual or to draw the unsayable and the indeclinable into something that can be apprehended or intuited. Metaphor – as the atom of the *as if* of narrative – is one procedure we will employ.

So what is the argument for conjoining Deleuze and Ricoeur in a particular way, for guessing the axis and wrapping them together as two heterogeneous series that must be brought into resonance? Why not fastidiously connect them point by point? Because we are not left with a surgical choice of procedures; indeed, we do not have a recognized procedure for the anastomosis of larval selves to narrative. There are no guidelines. We must construct them – or rather, create the scenography into which we place Deleuze and Ricoeur, a scenography that permits both resonance and a differentiating between them. By way of this, we attest to the requirements of Deleuze to address subjective presuppositions in our arguments and we attest to the requirements of Ricoeur in acknowledging that any study of the self must of necessity be fragmentary and must include elements of the excessive and even the hyperbolic.[41]

It is with this in mind that we employ a metaphor (or clarify a presupposed metaphor employed up to this point) that serves to situate Ricoeur and Deleuze alongside each other, without at the same time provoking a misinterpretation of what we are attempting to achieve – the relation sought is that which holds true in a multiplicity, an in-between rather than a symbiosis or a conflation to an amorphous One. In so doing, we should not be put off by Deleuze's deploring of metaphor. In fact, there is a superfetation of metaphor in his writings; his argument that these are not metaphors but instantiations of the real or images or analogies is wholly unconvincing since they function as metaphors, and what a thing does rather than what it is has always been his principle concern. Without metaphorization, the dark precursor risks remaining eponymous, 'a hero invented to account for the name of a place or people',[42] an insubstantial and unknowable spectre of the inhabitants of the virtual. In so doing, it also remains outside any judgement of truth or falsehood – it is simply utilitarian. Metaphorization can be employed to give some reality to this eponymous element, to draw it out of the virtual, without at the same time actualizing it. Metaphorization senses the unsayable in this regard. It is the *as if* of the ineffable.

Deleuze used the 'image' (he will not call it a metaphor) of surface and depth extensively in *Logic of Sense* to delineate the actual (a contracted surface) from the virtual (an excessive depth), the conscious from the unconscious, the said from the sayable and the sayable from the indeclinable.[43] That he jettisoned this depth/surface construction in almost all his subsequent works for a radicalization of the surface as site of the event and of pure immanent production is unfortunate in many respects, but, in particular, by excising an undifferentiated depth to being and laying it instead upon the surface, he disguises his debt to Schelling and, indeed, to Nietzsche. By stitching the depth to the surface, there is only one plane and no imaged metaphor to negotiate. The rhizome rises to the surface; the depth collapses. But is not the rhizome, is not depth and surface, all metaphor – or, at the very least, image on the brink of metaphor? For it is at this brink that the Ricoeurian metaphor looks into the Deleuzian image: it is the brink of meaning and interpretation.

We will maintain the depth/surface construction (with its imaged and metaphoric potential) for two reasons: (1) in our investigation of the narrative self we are still bound to the unconscious of *Difference and Repetition* (the principal work of study in this book), an unconscious formulated by Deleuze on the basis of surface and depth (and not the extensively reformulated unconscious of *AntiOedipus*) and (2) the surface/depth construction returns, albeit with a somewhat altered mien, in Deleuze's two late works, *Cinema 1* and *Cinema 2*, where the abstractions of *Difference and Repetition* are actualized in the material of cinematography and, indeed, in the narrative elements of this media. The *Cinema* books represent Deleuze's most lucid statement on narrative – they are the lion's heart for the eagle's head that is the even later Ricoeur of *Memory, History, Forgetting*.

By way of maintaining this surface/depth metaphor (which has been everpresent in this study – larval selves deep to the narrative self), we do not trivially attach an unconscious depth to the narrative self but instead situate this narrative self in a determining virtual, placing it (perhaps precariously) within the creative or productive depths of being. Thus, the synthesis of the heterogeneous is no longer a barren statement of description but a fact of self-becoming. We do not remain brinkmen at the edge of narrative but plunge the narrative self into its virtual other half.

Yet we must still ask what organizes the form of correspondence between surface and depth – or to revert to our mythological position, what or who prescribes for a liveable gryphon, for the crowned anarchical living of Mad/King Sweeney? What principles determine how such an argument should unfold? The problem to be exposed here is that the position of the self in the exposition of the self is hardly irrelevant or separable from the argument itself, although one may wish it to be so. Indeed, such a detachment could only occur by one of those impossible torsions of thought that Deleuze argues are the province of the dissolved self. Even then, we are still left with our presuppositions and our unacknowledged prejudices. Furthermore, no matter how diligent we are in detaching 'our-selves' (a sumptuous paradox) from unconscious presupposition, we are never free from the accusation that something ineffable remains, that a disavowed still propels us to choose the Méséglise from the Guermantes, the analytic from the contemporary, the Greek from the Roman or the Medieval from the Enlightenment. Something ineffable of who we are in our narrative selves determines our choices in part and not reason alone. Yet if our analysis of the ontogenesis of the narrative self cannot be divorced or diverted by some means from the presuppositions of its author, then what is formulated of the self becomes imbued with a terrible problem: rather than oneself as another, we arrive at *oneself as all others.*

What then is possible? There is of course no guarantee of a presupposition-free work – but we may argue that if we fold the strategies of Deleuze and Ricoeur back upon themselves and into each other (within the narrative of this work) we may form a more or less sealed container, an inviolable molecule that leaves little room for a third party. Thus, Ricoeur's strategy throughout much of his work (but particularly in *Oneself as Another*) is to place opposites in correspondence; for example, the posited cogito of Descartes is set against the shattered self of Nietzsche so that a hermeneutics of the self is situated equidistant 'from the apology of the cogito and from its overthrow'.[44] We have taken this position in placing the narrative self of Ricoeur alongside the larval selves of Deleuze – however, we are not performing a hermeneutics in the space in-between. We remain in the space of that-which regions but introduce a dark precursor there, an 'intuiter' rather than an interpreter of meaning, a 'prior to thought'.[45] It is this 'priorness', we contend, which guesses the axis of narrative.

Here, an example will help us. Robert Schumann's piano piece *Humoresque* is written as a song but without a vocal line so that the piano accompaniment (for right and left hand) is to a silent voice. Nevertheless, between the staves of the music sheet for left and right hand is an in-between notation for the non-vocalized 'inner voice'. This is the prior, for Heidegger, music for a virtual hand around which the represented series resonate. It determines the guessing of the axis. As Žižek notes:

> This absent melody is to be reconstructed on the basis of the fact that . . . the right- and the left-hand piano lines . . . do not relate to each other directly . . . in order for their interconnection, we are compelled to (re)construct a third, 'virtual' intermediate level (melodic line) which, for structural reasons, cannot be played.[46]

And it is for similar structural reasons that the virtual cannot be thought. Heidegger notes that the prior is something 'of which we really cannot think'.[47] If this is correct, it should not deter us from approximating it, from being in its wake, from diagramming its traces. It is not outside philosophical enquiry to do so.

Chapter 11

From Excess to Debt: Evolving Constraints to Narrative Identity

[There] is little you can seek in this world . . . in the end all you can achieve are memories, hazy, intangible, dreamlike memories which are impossible to articulate. When you try to relate them, there are only sentences, the dregs left from the filter of linguistic structures.[1]

Introduction

In the interzone between descent and ascent, released to that-which-regions, we acknowledged that some subjective presuppositions for constructing an ontogenesis of the narrative self were inevitable. Nevertheless, we chose several themes that had surfaced throughout this book. We will construct this chapter and the next upon these. Both chapters seek to identify the constraints imposed on narrative identity in its ontogenesis. The chapters do not seek to be exhaustive, although the constraints identified will represent those considered most dramatic.

To some degree we step beneath representative thinking, beyond the logocentric, away from where meaning is given by what is possessed by a signifier and what is not possessed. (We may note now the need, potentially, to step beyond even the 'phallogocentric' if this means that a particular construction of narrative and desire needs to be subverted.[2]) Calculative thinking provides limited knowledge of the self, we argue, for why determine the self only within a representational economy of meaning when the self is not only an emanation of language but the very distributor of that emanation? There is an infant before the child that speaks and an unborn being before the infant that sees. Are these states of being to be disqualified from contributing meaning to the self, from bearing the non-linguistic meaning of the self into its future?

We can redistribute some of the elements of our presuppositions into the form of hypotheses. We have harboured a longstanding one about the self that it is a multiplicity and with some justification given the disclosed virtual in

Ricoeur's work. Yet if we are to demonstrate it with more than just 'some justification', then we must locate it between Ricoeur and Deleuze, between narrative and the virtual, between the spoken and the indeclinable, that is, within the relational network between objects and not in the objects themselves. This is the defining criterion for a multiplicity.[3]

In this chapter, then, we will begin a *speculative* ontogenesis of the narrative self by marking 'attachment theory' as this in-between at the level of narrative, that is, as the intersubjective substrate for an ontogenesis of the self that has as its parallel a Mitsein or *being-with* in ontology. Our purpose is to identify the historical or relational constraints to ipseity and the implications this brings to bear upon the synthesis of the heterogeneous. Attachment theory will reveal to us the mutual effacement of larval and narrative selves when the self is structured from the perspective of narrative alone or when it is cut from the virtual. This is the limit of story itself.

Where to Start? Three Stations: Natality, Personhood, Narrative Selfhood

Merleau-Ponty argues that a self formulated solely in discourse is only 'half the truth',[4] since this spoken cogito is anterior to the *tacit*, indeclinable one that holds an inarticulate grasp upon the world, like the infant at its first breath.[5] This is the cogito in the world of *Gelassenheit*, one made up of 'the spoken and the indeclinable' yet hovering in limbo between the two; it presents to us twin faces or the double-sided image of the self – one towards narrative and the actual, one towards the larval and the virtual. Thus, a Janus-faced or helical self in the medium of a linguistic multiplicity may be the more appropriate structure for the self than narrative proper. But what can we say of this tacit 'inarticulate grasp' of the self?

We noted that the self starts in the womb – for where else could it begin? The baby in the womb is not without ears to hear, flesh to feel and a developing brain to process experience. Yet we cannot start where we cannot be. Instead we must ask what distinguishes us as persons from our earliest moments, and how can this inform us of our subsequent narrative selves? Narrative identity, as we noted earlier for Ricoeur, is not a stable, seamless one but continues to make and unmake itself. By so doing, it becomes '*the name of a problem at least as much as it is that of a solution*'. Thus, he calls for a systematic investigation of self-portraiture to verify this instability in narrative identity.

But what is the nature of this problem? The foundations of a response to this may lie within the psychoanalytic attachment theories of John Bowlby, where we find the systematic investigation of self-portraiture that Ricoeur demands. This places us within the determining nature of what Hannah Arendt called natality, that is, where beginning and action are interpenetrative.[6] In other words, if ontogenesis is 'the history of the individual development of an organised being' then an ontogenesis of the narrative self demands a history of self-narrative. For this, we take as our point of departure the mother–infant relationship and we do so for three commonsensical reasons. One of these we have already argued for in the last chapter – that first philosophy be reconceptualized as a *being-with*. The other two are argued as follows.

(1) *What is the duty or task of memory?* Memory, for Ricoeur, is a movement among the materials of the past, a search and a weaving. It is 'the womb of history' but one that becomes a project, the aim of which is justice.[7] But we may argue that this is only a superficial, epistemological aim. At the level of being, its real imperative is that of survival and of self-protection so that even commemorative memory becomes the survivalist duty of the wider state – or what Ricoeur refers to as the 'quasi-character'. This ontogenetic positioning of the project can be revealed in our narrative identities by way of a systematic investigation of autobiography, not just to observe the form and structure of our self-narratives, their truth and fiction, the manner in which they are plotted and how they cohere, but more importantly, to understand their purpose, in other words, how do they function?

(2) *We can distinguish selfhood from personhood by placing the 'self' as an* infima species *of the genus 'person'*. Ricoeur argues that the concept of personhood fails to take into account a person's capacity 'to designate himself or herself in speaking; the person is one of the "things" about which we speak rather than itself a speaking subject'.[8] Only when we have recourse to self-designation do we break out of this objectification that covers over the speaker of self-designation – only then do we move from the 'what' of the person referred to, to the 'who' of the one speaking. And yet do we not find in this 'what' something of the nature of what is before the 'who' or that this objectification reveals an inchoate intersubjective 'in-betweenness' that must be in place prior to narrative – that is the site of oneself as another? What then might we consider to be an identifying criterion for 'personhood'? Personhood has been characterized by six conditions, according to Daniel Dennett, one of which is pivotal to the rest, particularly if argued through the notion of 'minimal personhood'.[9] The fourth condition (which follows from the third one: a person is a being towards which is adopted the *intentional stance*) states that a person is considered 'capable of *reciprocating*' the intentional stance.[10] Thus, reciprocity, prior to propositional language, is at the least one of the foundation-stones of a criteriology of personhood. This brings us closer to our ontological position for the narrative self. It is this reciprocity, the 'what' of our

personhood as distinct from the 'who' of our selfhood that binds us to attachment models of the narrative self, a reciprocity (or lack of it) best described by Proust.

First Constraint: Proustian Love and Lack

In drawing being-with and love towards the philosophical centre of our work, it is worth noting that when philosophy has engaged with psychoanalytic theory it has undoubtedly given far too much significance to the Oedipus complex to the neglect of pre-oedipal orality and maternality.[11] Bruno Bettelheim refers to this period of infancy as a time of 'belief in the unending supply of love and nutriment . . . where Mother has supplied all that was needed', a time of 'magic' that must be relinquished in order to face 'life's problems'.[12] But this psychoan-alytic–structuralist insistence on a relinquishment carries with it the error of an eclipse or a forgetting of being, of the feminine or what Wordsworth called 'the time of unrememberable being'.[13] It is this forgetting or erasure of Proustian love that we now endeavour to unveil.

> [T]he anguish that comes from knowing that the creature one adores is in some place of enjoyment where oneself is not . . . that anguish came through love . . . but when . . . it possesses one's soul before love has yet entered into one's life, then it must drift, awaiting love's coming, vague and free, without precise attachment.[14]

Proust provides the single greatest literary narrative of separation anxiety in the first 40 pages of *In Search of Lost Time*. Marcel cannot take his eyes off his mother at the dinner table[15] and cannot bear the fact that she will not give him 'that frail and precious kiss'[16] in his bedroom because she is too busy entertaining M. Swann. Alone with his throbbing anxiety[17] Marcel is overcome by 'a puberty of sorrow, a manumission of tears'[18] which does not abate until Mamma comes up the stairs and he throws himself upon her. But how does this adored and loving mother react? Not with affection but with the law of the father: 'her face assumed an expression of anger . . . "Do you want your father to see you waiting there like an idiot?"'[19] Proust describes the complex attachment of a child to a mother who is emotionally unavailable to him. It is the source of the problems that will continue to haunt the series of relationships he will have to endure for the rest of his life and his narrative of them. We earlier argued against Ricoeur's conclusion that Proust's epic is fundamentally a tale about time (Chapter 6). It is not. It is also fundamentally a story about love and therefore about lost love or the lack inscribed in love, a plenitude ridden with fissures that inaugurates a series of repetitious encounters haunted by the scraggy ghost of the lost parts of ideal love. 'Proustian love' refers to this turbulence in the repetitious series that finds its specific origins in the mother–child relationship. Yet it is Freud who heralds the repetition and the series.

Loss at the birth of the narrative self

In one of his most neglected texts, 'Inhibitions, Symptoms and Anxiety',[20] Freud recants on his long held belief that anxiety was transformed libido and presents instead a model of anxiety based on a reaction to situations of danger.[21] Here Freud regards our management of danger as *prior* to our defence against unwelcome libidinal impulses.[22] Our affective states are irrevocably connected to the events of the real world, laid down in the mind 'as precipitates of primaeval traumatic experiences' and resurrected 'like mnemic symbols' when a similar situation occurs.[23] It is a 'biological necessity' that demands that 'a situation of danger' is marked by an affective symbol.[24] Anxiety is a reaction of the ego to a situation of danger,[25] and this anxiety in children can, according to Freud, be reduced to a single condition, 'that of missing someone who is loved and longed for . . . anxiety appears as a reaction to the felt loss . . . [and] . . . a fear of being separated' from the mother.[26] If the infant then cries and she returns to soothe him then he has found out 'by experience that . . . [she] can put an end to the dangerous situation'. Freud regarded this as 'a first great step forward in the provision made by the infant for its self-preservation'.[27]

The relevance of Freud's article to the narrative self is this: might the infant's response to separation and loss, and the mother's capacity to comfort him inaugurate a fundamental narrative of the self upon which future stories will be constructed? This is what Bowlby takes from what he refers to as Freud's 'agonizing reappraisal of the theory of anxiety'.[28]

Bowlby argues that the infant is a sort of 'machine incorporating feedback' that is goal-directed.[29] He contends that there is a biologically based bond between the child and the caregiver that is the product of the activity of several behavioural systems that have 'proximity to the mother' as its set goal.[30] These systems are usually activated by the departure of the mother or by something frightening and are terminated by the 'sound, sight, or touch of the mother'.[31] Proximity is important because it provides the child with a 'secure base' from which to explore his environment with confidence. The function of the drive for attachment is clear: to protect the infant from predators and to learn from the mother the various activities necessary for survival.[32] This is the psychological equivalent of Spinoza's *conatus*.

But the caregiving behaviour of the mother is crucial in shaping the attachment systems of the infant. When a child finds that the clear communication of negative affect like fear or anger is effective in eliciting a caring response from the mother, he will develop a secure 'primary' strategy of attachment, secure to explore and to know that safety is proximate and quickly attained. Conversely, when he finds that this primary strategy of communicating negative affect leads instead to rejection or conflict, he learns to either inhibit or exaggerate negative affects (turning off the attachment system or over-activating it), thus producing different insecure strategies for dealing with the anxiety surrounding attachment. Whatever strategy he develops 'governs how present and future incoming interpersonal information is attended to, determines which affects are experienced, selects the memories that are evoked, and mediates behaviour with others in important relationships'.[33]

This management of information will *determine in part the future narrative self, how it will be written and storied*, because over time the child develops an 'internal working model'[34] of himself as 'acceptable or unacceptable in the eyes of his attachment figures',[35] as deserving or undeserving of attention and of others as trustworthy and responsive or as untrustworthy, unresponsive and rejecting. This represents a cognitive template for the narrative self in its relationships, one that is 'predictive'[36] and indeed potentially prophetic. Thus, an unwanted child may not only feel unwanted by his parents but 'believe that he is essentially unwantable, namely unwanted by anyone'.[37] His future self or selves may be haunted by the shadow of this unwantedness, by this theme immanent to the story or stories of the self he has yet to tell.

Procedural ancestors of the narrative self

The availability and responsivity of the mother in meeting the infant's need for protection has been critically analyzed by Mary Ainsworth using the 'Strange Situation' experiment.[38] This consists of a series of separations and reunions from the parent designed to arouse the infant's attachment system and elicit observable attachment-related behaviours.[39] Three discrete patterns of infant behaviour emerge: (1) 'secure' attachment in which the child, initially distressed by the mother's departure, settles and returns to the toys, a pattern associated with a history of responsive and nurturing parenting; (2) 'avoidant' attachment where the attachment system is deactivated and the child seems unconcerned by the mother's departure, a pattern associated with a history of rejection by the parent; and (3) 'resistant' attachment where the attachment system is over-activated and the child is markedly distressed by the mother's departure, a pattern associated with inconsistent and unpredictable parenting. What discriminates the categories is the availability and predictability of responsivity of the mother.[40] It is claimed that these behavioural paradigms are the *procedural ancestors of the narrative self before language*, heralding and predicting a manner of processing self-relevant information that will continue over time.

The true and the false in the narrative self

It is the acquisition of language that confers upon the person the unique opportunity to provide an account of himself and his relationships throughout the
years and to place this in the form of narrative. However, an honourable attestation of an account of oneself by no means guarantees an honourable account
in itself. The issue of truth and falsity in the narrative self emerges here. Bowlby
notes that the narratives that parents in clinical settings provide regarding
themselves and their families are often inaccurate, either through the omission, suppression or falsification of information.[41] This self-protective account
given by parents can determine the sort of story that the child will formulate as
part of his working model of himself.[42] Where neglect and abuse exist, a ripe
environment for the omission, suppression and falsification of information is
constituted and fostered from both ends: the child that does not wish to see his
parents as abusive and the parents that do not wish to see themselves as abusive
either. The child may give 'a misleading picture of the family because he hardly
knows where the truth lies', having been 'plied from childhood onwards with
systematically false information about family figures, their motives and relationships'.[43] Such distortions are then written into his own working models and
form part of both the process and content of his self-narratives.

This is the Ricoeurian face of Bowlby's work. In other words, Ricoeur's narrative self, that which responds to 'Who?', may be riddled with inconsistencies,
falsifications, omissions and distortions. There is no guarantee or necessity
of truth in the narrative self; indeed, it may only be the exceptional narrative
that is wholeheartedly true. This is because defensive phenomena (repression,
displacement) when reformulated within the model of human information
processing generate false account at the heart of self-narrative.[44] If sensory
information goes through 'many stages of selection, interpretation and appr-
aisal' before it influences behaviour and if this processing occurs at 'extraordinary speeds',[45] then we are largely unaware of the intensive procedures that
distort some of the elements of our stories.

Oneself as deceptive

Further to the distortions that determine in part the narrative-self, Bowlby
argues that our memory stores can be 'sectionalized' into a plurality of depart-
ments with 'barriers to communication set up between two or more major
sections of it'.[46] There are, according to Bowlby's reading of contemporary
studies of memory, more ways than one in which the same information 'can
coexist in storage, in several different forms and . . . also be accessible by any
of several different routes'.[47] Mental representations may be encoded 'in
analogue form, which mirrors certain selected properties of the world as in a
map . . . or . . . in propositional form, which comprises a set of interpreted

abstract statements about perceptual events as in a prose description'.[48] Thus, he connects the internal working models to different memory systems, in particular the semantic and episodic memory systems originally described by E. Tulving.[49] The storage of images of our parents and of the self, Bowlby argues, is of at least two distinct varieties. On the one hand, 'memories of behaviour engaged in or of words spoken on each particular occasion will be stored episodically'; on the other, generalizations about parents or the self will be enshrined in 'working models' and 'stored semantically (in either analogical, propositional or some combined format).[50] The bulk of information going into episodic storage will derive from 'what the person himself perceives and a subordinate part only from what he may be told about the episode',[51] whereas with semantic memory it derives from what he is told rather than what he thinks himself. And this information *may be about the self.* In other words, the self becomes composed of information the ingredients of which derive from multifarious sources that are not necessarily readily identifiable. It is across this divide that discrepancy and conflict may arise.

Discrepancies in self-narratives

In response to this hypothesized differentially composed narrative of the self, Mary Main interviewed parents of children assessed in the Strange Situation, asking them about their childhood memories of attachment figures. From studying the transcripts (interviews were transcribed verbatim, including place-holding responses like 'um . . . uh') of these speakers the Adult Attachment Interview developed. It consists of a protocol of questions engineered to probe and explore episodic and semantic memory systems.[52] In determining the 'overall coherence of the transcript' (that is, the coherence of the narrative), she refers to Paul Grice's four 'conversational maxims' for cooperative, rational discourse.[53] Where there is a lack of coherence, it is often noticed across memory systems. Two states of incoherence of mind are described: dismissing (of the importance of attachment relationships in childhood) and preoccupied (over-emphasis of attachment relationships from childhood to the point where they appear to intrude on the present).

In essence, Main establishes a continuity over time between, on the one hand, the different attachment behaviours of infancy (the procedural precursors of the narrative self) and, on the other, narrative coherence (or lack of it) and the presence of certain discourse markers (like run-on sentences, the use of impersonal pronouns) in the autobiographical stories adults provide about their childhood. What is seen in the Strange Situation in behaviour is recapitulated in the stories we tell about ourselves later in life and the manner in which we tell them. The avoidant infant grown up accounts for his past and current relationships in an incoherent manner; classified as 'dismissing', his semantic recall of early life is characterized by idealization of attachment figures but there is limited access to episode memory – in other words, the events did not happen as described in semantic idealization; the resistant infant grown up is also incoherent but with a different balance between memory systems; classified as 'preoccupied', he has vague and inaccurate access to semantic memory but profuse and disorganized access to episodic memory. The secure infant grown up and classified as 'autonomous', has good access to both semantic and episodic memory systems and agreement between both.

In conclusion, we may be limited in how we narrate our histories by the manner in which our parents were available and responsive to our distress; in addition, that which differentiates our experiences is not primarily the content of our stories of the past but the manner and style in which we tell them. Something of the virtual, of that before the story, is revealed in the style.

Narrative Constraints: Implications for the Synthesis of the Heterogeneous

Ricoeur's theory of the narrative self faces the problem that attachment theory places before it: there are severe limitations to self-narrative, particularly to those core elements that relate to love relationships. This limitation is not expressed in the content of the narrative but rather in the manner in which this content is described, that is, in the style and discourse used, perhaps even in the emplotment. This is what differentiates self-narratives and what structures them on a spectrum from chaotic disorganization to bland rigidification.

For the narrative self, the synthesis of the heterogeneous may lumber against the enduring habits of omission, falsification and idealization or ramble chaotically across the heterogeneous on the wave of anxious affect, pulling together elements whose only commonality is an ever-present danger to be managed. The adult's current state of mind regarding past attachment relationships is predictive of his or her ability to regulate affect and, thus, how he or she will narrate their story.[54] None of this of course disqualifies Ricoeur's narrative self of coherence – it simply withdraws from it the power of *ipse* and delivers it over to *idem*, to the habits and contractions, the passive syntheses that are performed by those larvae outside conscious awareness. Are we to conclude then that the synthesis of the heterogeneous becomes a passive synthesis of heterogeneous but habit-laden larvae? Has the productive imagination at the heart of the synthesis of the heterogeneous an infirmity deep to its harvesting? Is creativity (that the self will become a work of art) sundered here, drawn to a limit both in the ipse self of narrative and in the spawn of larvae that forms its pre-narration?

Chapter 12

The Poetic Imagination within the Evolving Constraints of Narrative Productivity

The Power, which all
Acknowledge when thus moved, which Nature thus
To bodily sense exhibits, in the express
Resemblance of that glorious faculty
That higher minds bear with them as their own.
This is the very spirit in which they deal
With the whole compass of the universe:
They from their native selves can send abroad
Kindred mutations; for themselves create
A like existence; and, whene'er it dawns
Created for them, catch it, or are caught
By its inevitable mastery.[1]

Introduction

Following from the constraints identified in the previous chapter, we will, finally, bring together the narrative and the dissolved selves within a structure determined by the work of the previous chapters. However, this is not a structure free of further constraints, and although we will place the poetic imagination within it, the degrees of freedom to determine narrative structure and even usurp narrative tradition will endure and indeed multiply. This is the legacy of the problems raised in Chapter 5. Narrative is constrained by its own being-narrative. In this chapter, we will argue against the seemingly intractable problems generated in Chapter 5 that narrative identity is a badly constituted solution to a badly posed problem. We do so, remembering that, for Ricoeur, personal history in the form of the narrative self stands for 'the name of a problem rather than that of a solution'. Following this, we will propose a three-part structure as a potential zone of solution to the limits of the narrative self – potential insofar as it retains rather than negates the constraints acknowledged up to now, indeed generates more, but offers an escape from identity placed within narrativity alone. It follows from our conclusion to Chapter 5: we must either assert that narrative is enough for the self or move beyond it.

This three-part structure will be placed under the following determinations: (1) to conceive of the narrative self as a salving debt for an original wound, a wound placed in the form of loss and a being-against-death; (2) to disclose the other face of this 'wound' as a poetic imagination always obscured by the requirements of a being-against-death but with a being-in-potentiality to rebel against the sepulchring of the self in stories and (3) finally, to contend that only by giving to the actualized narrative self a virtual status inseparable from non-narrative and developing a structure to contain this dual status (one borrowed from Lévi-Strauss), can we engender in the self a creative becoming that has thus far been deprived by the confines of narrativity alone.

Put more figuratively: if the lion's heart of *délire* is to be prevented from vaporizing the eagle's head of narrative, then we must propose a third organ, a productive imagination newly imagined at the heart of the narrative self that can withstand the restraints that being-against-death, being-with and love place on narrativity.

Where Deleuze Was, There Ricoeur Shall Be?

By the end of the previous chapter, we had brought upon ourselves a glaringly obvious problem in attempting to separate the larval from the narrative selves: once forced asunder in the domain of attachment theory, they replace each other. We noted two key differences in the narratives of the dismissing and the preoccupied speakers. For the former, *in extremis*, everything that is past is narrated and complete; the present is fixed and baked to a dried crisp, and what is to come is predictable, navigable and mapped with the greatest precision. The self is a story always already told, one that dismisses its own heterogeneous narrative, trading it in for the skeleton of a plot. Superficially, this appears to be an excess of the narrative self of Ricoeur (discordance subordinated to concordance, character to action and poetics to ethics) but in fact it behaves much more like Deleuze's rigidified self, with the individual no longer existing in the intensive but laid to rest or sepulchred in a controlled and dead-end configuration. For the preoccupied speaker, *in extremis*, the present of the past pervades the present of the present and the anticipation of safety or danger behaves as an ever-intruding future; time, persons and feelings are in perpetual flux and fragments of narrative are concatenated in conjunctions and gasps and borne along an affective tidal wave that has no meaning or direction, no *sens*. This is a self never told but always telling, an insubstantial self becoming but never arrived whose being can only be grasped in the telling and the hearing. It is the dissolved self of Deleuze but in an almost mad Ricoeurian threefold mimetic synthesis, prefigured in the intensive as an uncanny phenomenon of affect, grasped together in the Augustinian present of the future and restored to a semblance of narrative in the time of action and of suffering that is mimesis$_3$.

Should we conclude then that there is a spectrum along which the self comes told or telling and that there is an option from which we chose or are chosen between two species of self? But we have revealed two selves crossed between Deleuze and Ricoeur, one bearing within its narrative an intensive becoming that resists the closure of history and the stark emplotment of story, the other surrendering to the story its ownmost telling, to the chapter that arrives long before the end. Have we not somehow inverted ourselves with this spectrum that where we expected Deleuze we also found Ricoeur and where we expected Ricoeur we also found Deleuze?

The problem here is that this spectrum between two discourses (the one end laid to rest in the past yet bound to it, the other seething into the present from a past that can never be laid to rest) generates an invidious illusion of separability between the larval and the narrative – specifically that Deleuze's larval selves exist only in the intensive and Ricoeur's narrative self in the actual and in the told. Beyond this psychologizing illusion, the implication is clear: they interpenetrate. Unless we understand the larval and the ipse to be mutually metamorphic, we recede into the illusion of the two-dimensional perspective that places the self between opposing limits, with a shaded conjunctival area in the middle. We must retain the twin flows (the two faces of Janus) as different and inseparable rather than as one flowing into the other, a first flow from the virtual to the actual and *potentially* back again (a counter-actualization) through a second flow from the narrative self to the other by way of a synthesis of the heterogeneous. We require two series concatenated.

The Narrative Self: A Badly Posed Question

We can now clarify the importance of Deleuze and Ricoeur to each other. For Deleuze his differenciation of selves requires this narrative model of Ricoeur, indeed needs to be enchained to it, for otherwise we are most of us, according to him, doomed to repetition of the same in narrative. As selves we are simply narrative *habitus*. This is because Deleuze's model of differentiation/differenciation is fundamentally a unidirectional one, at least in practice; the evidence for this is that his ethical position is always to reverse this 'virtual → actual' flow by a counter-actualization, by a subtractive return into the virtual.[2] But this is not given to us, according to Deleuze, and it is only the few (Artaud, Joyce, the legion of schizophrenics) who reverse the flow, who counter-actualize. Most of us mortals are fated to be swept to our narrative deaths in a sea of insipidness.

But Ricoeur's ipse self also requires the dark precursor of Deleuze, if it is not to avoid submitting to the chaos of the virtual when divesting itself of the strictures of idem and of passive synthesis. The true limit here for Ricoeur is the limit of story itself. Our problem is that we presuppose that the narrative self functions like a story told by an author, that the accounts from attachment theory can be transposed from the encapsulated locus of the psychological to the rarified air of the metaphysical without remainder. But the self does not tell a story – it is told in the telling of the story. In fact, if Ricoeur's narrative self is vulnerable to the conclusions of attachment theory, then it is only so because of the question that he initially establishes: *Who* says I? *Who* is the author, the agent of action?

But this is a badly posed question, because it carries with it the presupposition that there is an extant narrator in the first place. And this is precisely what Hannah Arendt argues most convincingly against in *The Human Condition*. In our acting and speaking, we insert ourselves into 'the web of human relationships', weaving our own narrative into it, a narrative that reveals 'who' we are; but it is always into this pre-existing web that we insert our story so that our 'unique life story' affects 'uniquely the life stories of all those with whom [we] come into contact'.[3] Stories 'without intention' emerge in this web which have 'in their living reality . . . an altogether different nature than [their] reifications' in recorded documents or art works. Their status is virtual, in this respect. And because of this virtual/actual fracture in the web of narrative, 'nobody is the author or producer of his own life story'[4] – he may have initiated it, but now he is its actor and sufferer, not its author.

Ricoeur is not unaware of this problem that exists in self-narrative and which threatens coherence. Contradictions in history, he notes, are where we find 'dissension' and 'defects in discourse' and these must be described for themselves so that what emerges will be the theme of 'discontinuity, with ruptures, fault lines, gaps, sudden redistributions'. He concludes that if there is a paradox to an archaeological approach to history (and therefore to narrative) it is not that this approach 'multiplies differences, but that it refuses to reduce them'.[5] Furthermore, these gaps and defects, these fault lines and sudden redistributions that differentiate self-narratives are to be found within the manner, style and function of the discourse. This functionality needs to be inserted into Ricoeur's theory of narrative identity. Such elements, even if substantially overwhelmed by the representational requirements of story, are akin to the stutterings that Deleuze remarks upon, the speaking as a foreigner within your mother tongue; they are the traces of difference-in-itself, of the unsayable within narrative. In these stutterings and sudden redistributions are revealed the forgotten, the eclipsed and the events of the pure past that are perceptually debarred.

Ricoeur is close to this view when he asks if forgetting could be considered no longer an enemy of memory but something alongside which memory has to negotiate.[6] But is this a reactive forgetting, reacting against the threat of danger and death? Or is it a creative eclipsing, whereby through the *art and power* of forgetting, utilized strategically, we find the 'natural antidote' to what Nietzsche referred to as 'the stifling of life by history'[7] that besets many narrative selves? This is a better-posed problem that requires a better-posed question (How does the narrative self function?). Ricoeur notes the potential for forgetting to be more than just a selective procedure employed to persevere in life. Forgetting is bound up with memory, not the mortal enemy of it, and we can consider its strategies 'worthy of a genuine *ars oblivionis*' which places forgetting outside an effacement of memories that is part of the dysfunctions of memory. Indeed, forgetting is so closely allied to memory that it may be considered 'one of the conditions of it'.[8]

There is, as we can see, a potential art in memory and forgetting (a being-art-in-potentiality), immanent and virtual, but whether this is an art worthy of the title 'art for life' (a creative and active art) or 'art against death' (a reactive and contrived variety) remains in question. Either way, what is not told, what is forgotten or debarred is as much a part of our narratives as that which is included. The forgotten is a condition of the told.

Second Constraint: Imagination within Structure and Obligation

Can we rescue the narrative self from the constraints of attachment and from the badly posed problem of 'Who?' and find a way forward that does not collapse the dissolved self into narrative rigidity and the narrative self into preoccupied chaos? Can the self be structured in such a way that it neither implodes nor explodes, that it has the potential for narrative being an 'art for life' and not an 'art against death' – that it can be a creative and not a reactive stutterer? What else can constrain it from being this?

We return to a question that has haunted this text: what is the nature of the problem for which the narrative self is its solution? We hinted that it referred to survival or *conatus* – but why? What must survive and in what form? Is it the form of dead narrative or of vibrant art? And what is the spiral of narrative and larval lines; how do they interpenetrate so that an art may blossom or be diverted? The answer to this may lie in what has been the enemy of the creative, narratable self in the manner in which it confines superabundance to constrained meaning: the signifier, or more specifically, the signifier without signification. In other words, we need to address the narrative self as a form of solution from the perspective of structure; only then can we interrogate it from the perspective of artistic content or obligation, that is, from a *telos* to narrate in a prescribed way.

Deleuze refers to our linguistic system as a 'linguistic multiplicity . . . a virtual system of reciprocal connections between "phonemes" which are incarnated in the actual terms and relations of diverse languages'.[9] In other words, there are many articulable sounds which we do not punctuate or isolate from the multi-plicity of potential sounds, and, indeed, our occasional mispronunciations are testament to this virtual around that which is articulated and sanctioned as sayable within each language. This virtual multiplicity renders speech possi-ble; it circulates through it but cannot itself be spoken in the empirical use of language. Nevertheless, it is not unseen (or unheard) and can be spoken 'in the poetic usage of speech coextensive with virtuality'.[10] Thus, in the case of the narrative self, if we are to extend Deleuze's claim, only the poetic accom-plishments of the speaker will infuse the narrative self with a linguistic multi-plicity sufficient to transform it into a work of art. And this requires a poetic imagination, a structure to permit it and an obligation for or against which the imagination strives. We will address these final three aspects of our philo-sophical work now.

Poetic imagination in the narrative self

We are aware of the contribution made by the faculty of the imagination in the constitution of the narrative self in Ricoeur – as we noted in Chapter 4. How-ever, Ricoeur expands the role of the Kantian imagination so that the faculty, in action and movement, becomes the gatherer of narrative events. But is this the imagination of Kant's first edition of the *Critique of Pure Reason*, an imagination with such powers that, as Heidegger claims, Kant retreated from it, as though from the 'abyss', or is it the imagination of the second edition, a lesser power?[11] If it is for Ricoeur a poetic imagination, it is nevertheless always fettered to Aris-totelian storytelling and ethics, passing through the stage of storytelling in its obligation never to forget. Thus, there are three levels to the imagination in Ricoeur – a 'poetic imagination' from which he retreats like Kant,[12] a 'narrative imagination' which is the synthesizer of stories and an 'ethical imagination' which embarks upon different courses of action as part of 'the aim of a true life'.[13] Ricoeur is clear, however, that he will not go so far as R. G. Collingwood, who spoke somewhat like the Kant of the first edition of an 'a priori imagina-tion'[14] that is 'a self-dependent, self-determining, and self-justifying form of thought'.[15] However, Ricoeur does marginally acknowledge the role of such an unfettered imagination in the novelist even though he does not accept that the self is fictionalized in part by such an imagination.

The role of the imagination as a power and poetic act is developed by Gaston Bachelard, in whose work it is given an ontological status. The poetic act is now a 'flare-up of being in the imagination' and the poetic image is 'referable to a direct ontology'.[16] The being of this poetic image is not a matter of causality but of 'reverberation' and 'sonority'.[17] More recently, John Sallis has used the word 'hovering' (as a translation of *Schweben*) to signify the operation by which the imagination 'endeavours to unify what is not unifiable'. This hovering is also a 'gathering', a bringing together of 'the horizons around the upsurge of presence',[18] like the gathering involved in the synthesis of the heterogeneous for Ricoeur. (This gathering in Ricoeur, we must remember, is equivalent to the Kantian faculty of judgement, while the gatherer is the imagination proper.) Sallis even goes so far as to determine the imagination as 'a power of the soul'.[19] Bachelard already suggests as much, when he states that poetry is 'a phenomenology of the soul' or 'a soul inaugurating a form'.[20] For Bachelard, it is the soul that inaugurates. And it is in the soul, as we have repeatedly stated, that *dunamis* and *energeia* reside.

What is important to note in this gathering of investigations into the imagination is the recurrence of terms, metaphors and images of that which cannot be imagined (the imagination): states of flaring-up, flowing, wellspring and movements like hovering and gathering. If we take away from the imagination its products, what are we left with? It is like narrative devoid of its events. But if we perform this bracketing, we are left with the imagination as a movement, a metaphor, an image. In Chapter 2, we noted that Samuel Beckett, in *Imagination, Dead Imagine*, tries to strip the mind, including the imagination, of its contents only to find that geometric shapes immediately return; the being of the imagination is irrepressible, its becoming, indelible. This is no different in Eastern literature. When Gao Xingjian ventures into the deepest interior of the ancient forests, his journey into the heart of his narrative self, he too arrives at a plateau dominated by a basic geometry, a plateau where all the trees are 'of the same girth, equidistant from one another' and the 'pristine natural beauty . . . is irrepressible . . . derived neither from symbolism nor metaphor and needing neither analogies nor associations'.[21]

An image of the imagination arises before us – from Kant to Xingjian – surging, gathering, irrepressible. Can such an image be found in Deleuze? Among its roles in Deleuze, the imagination is the means by which we grasp the process of actualization from the virtual. It is the faculty that 'crosses domains, orders and levels, knocking down the partitions coextensive with the world . . . inspiring our souls, grasping the unity of mind and nature: a larval consciousness which moves endlessly from science to dream and back again'.[22]

The parallel with the synthesis of the heterogeneous is clear. In *What is Philosophy?* this role is further developed so that 'the invention of conceptual personae [is called] Imagination'. Conceptual personae occupy a position between narrative and the pre-narrative plane which Deleuze refers to as 'the plane of immanence'. Their function is to 'carry out the movements that describe' the author's thought, playing a part 'in the very creation of the author's concepts'.[23] He explains the difference between the plane and the concepts spread out across it in unusually metaphorical language: 'Concepts are like multiple waves, rising and falling, but the plane of immanence is a single

wave that rolls them up and unrolls them'.[24] Given that the conceptual personae
and the plane of immanence, according to Deleuze, presuppose each other,[25]
then the imagination (as the invention and functioning of conceptual personae)
appears to inhabit this plane. Like Bachelard's waves, it is the movements
across this plane. And for these movements Deleuze uses the term *survol*,
derived from *survoler* and meaning 'to fly over' but translated as 'survey' to
retain the sense of staying in one place, while at the same time having in one's
grasp the whole of the visual field. And this space of the movements of the
imagination is virtual – it is *Gegnet, espace quelconque*. If meditative thinking
'[gathers] everything together . . . the nearness of distance and the distance of
nearness'[26] in an *espace quelconque* that is a virtual or 'spiritual space'[27] that
expresses 'possibility . . . virtuality',[28] then meditative thinking is also inseparable, even if different, from the imagination.

Such metaphors permit us to interpret the antlike inhabitants that Deleuze
argues swarm at the fracture of the passive 'I am' as being considerably more
active than he supposes and that this swarming functions in an indistinguishable manner from the surveying in waves of the author's thought and from the
role played by Bachelard's imagination where the poetic act is a 'flare-up of
being in the imagination'.[29] The sense that Deleuze gives to the imagination
parallels the hovering and the gathering we noted in Ricoeur and Sallis. Indeed,
this imagination is inserted between the pre-narrative and the narrative, precisely in the same plane, as we will argue in the next section, Deleuze inserts the
dark precursor. The imagination is clearly this intensive movement of thought.
It synthesizes the heterogeneous, just as in Ricoeur, although immanently so.
It is movement across thought. It is the dark precursor of the synthesis of the
heterogeneous, the poetic behind the narrative imagination.

We can put this in our own terms. The imagination is the movement of
Sweeney, *survoler*, the 'flying over' in between the world of narrative and the
world of the virtual. Does not Nagy say precisely this when he argues that
Sweeney becomes poet at 'the moment he is robbed of his identity' in an 'adventure in the inner workings of the persona of the poet as he vacillates between
power and powerlessness',[30] that is, between the power of the virtual and the
powerlessness of our acquiescence to language. Sweeney is not a poet who peri-
odically retrieves truth from the unconscious, bringing it within the constraint
of his own identity; instead, he is poetic part and process of the unconscious.
Indeed, Sweeney operates (like the dark precursor) between the heathen world
(of the virtual) and the world of the Church (of scripture and narrative) or as
Nagy notes, 'within the peripheral vision . . . of clerics' – that is, within the
peripheral vision of representational thought as symbolized by the clerics in
Buile Suibhne.[31] Sweeney, by way of 'the poetic usage of speech coextensive with
virtuality'[32] that Deleuze prescribed, inaugurates for us an operative process
and structure between the two faces of the self, a process and structure which
we may now clarify.

Structure for the imaginative synthesis of the heterogeneous

We said earlier that only the poetic accomplishments of the speaker will infuse the narrative self with a linguistic multiplicity sufficient to transform it into a work of art. To do so structurally requires the dissolution of the narrative self. Now, if this seems a somewhat over-nuanced interpretation of Ricoeur's narrative self, then it is only so inasmuch as he prescribes it. Ricoeur argues that when the self is refigured (for instance through an encounter with fiction) it passes into a 'nothingness' that is not nothing but rather is the self 'deprived of the help of sameness'.[33] It is the self in pure difference or, better, *narrative difference*. He concludes that 'the most dramatic transformations of personal identity pass through the crucible of this nothingness of identity' without which narrative selfhood would be doomed to brute repetition.[34] And he equates this 'crucible' with the empty square that Lévi-Strauss proposes in his transformations and one that Deleuze borrows from repeatedly in *Logic of Sense*.[35] But what happens to the imagination (as synthesizer of the heterogeneous) in the space of this empty square? And can we populate this empty square with the movements of the imagination, with the leaps of Sweeney, so imagined in the previous section? We will approach this by way of the event (as object of narrative), although we must distinguish events from the stories that compose the narrative self and from the event of narrating itself.

When Ricoeur asks what one is talking about when one says that something happened, in the case of the narrative self, one is talking fundamentally of events, not facts. Events are 'the emblem of all past things', the very 'objects of narrative'.[36] Or as Deleuze puts it, an event is 'the opposite of . . . a story'.[37] Indeed, Deleuze attempts to trace a passage of thought between events and narrative or, more specifically, between the series of events that constitute an episode of life and the series of accounts in which these events are realized (two heterogeneous series, one largely signifying and the other largely signified).[38] He does so by trying to 'hollow out and to fill in the gap' between these two series rather than allowing them to remain inseparable or for one, the signifier, to dominate the other, the signified.[39] Yet it is in the signifying series that language bestows excess (everything of language is present to us) while in the signified series there is always the unknown, the yet to be discovered, the yet to be said and indeed the forgotten. The mobile element of thought, Deleuze argues, travels between these two unequal series like 'a mirror . . . a two-sided entity, equally present in the signifying and the signified series'.[40] It is the Janus-faced Snark of thought.

This mobile element is paradoxical, because it is 'never where we look for it, and conversely . . . we never find it where it is'[41]; its two Janus faces, while simultaneously synthesizing the heterogeneous, are absent from each other, one facing the signifying series where excess is always in the form of an empty square through which transformations can occur (as in a picture-puzzle of fifteen squares in a sixteen square frame), the other facing the signified, where there is 'a rapidly moving . . . occupant without a place'[42] (as in the game 'Musical Chairs'). These are the movements of thought as the events of the Sheep's shop or the third hand of Schumann's *Humoresque* that sets the other two hands in resonance but itself cannot be located. This 'paradoxical element' is of course another name for the dark precursor.

If we translate these two images (the picture-puzzle and 'Musical Chairs') to our construction of the self we can understand it this way: even if all the events that are the objects of the narrative self could constitute a plane of composition (one that equates to the plane of Nature insofar as we conquer it progressively, partially and step by step), the object that sets this series in resonance with the series of corresponding narrations will not itself be an occupant of it. It is in the virtual dance as the music plays but when it stops, that is, as we section the virtual for narrative gathering, there is no place for it. This *'floated signified'*[43] of the virtual dance is a sort of narrative self in perpetual *diaspora*, an occupant without a place. It is the always present lack, that which is forgotten (as part of the *ars oblivionis*) and that which has not yet been discovered (as part of the unknown). Its other side is the *floating signifier*, the empty square that permits the signifying chain to rearrange itself, to form new chains and potentially new meanings, new stories. It is this two-sided paradoxical element or dark precursor that causes the heterogeneous series of the events of the virtual to communicate and to bestow 'sense in both the signifying and the signified series', in the form of what Deleuze calls a 'tangled tale' (*une histoire embrouillée*).[44] This is the Self as process or as Snark.

We can consider these two series being comprised of different unfolding time lines that run parallel to one another: one, infantile and past, the other, adult and present. How do these two series interact to produce narrative, weave themselves into one another to give rise to something different from both series in isolation? A paradoxical element – as a signifier that appears in both series (each face of the mirror) – is required. In itself this signifier means nothing, but it is like the organizing principle around which all the other elements of both series are coordinated. In one series it appears as a lack, while in the other it appears as an excess. For example, the adult series may contain a certain lack characterized by something that is perpetually lost (the Lacanian *objet a*, cause of desire), while the infantile series might contain an excess to which one is always trying to return. By way of this signifier that appears in both series without itself signifying anything, the two series are able to interpenetrate each other.

For Deleuze and Ricoeur this mobile *case vide* or differentiator, 'at once word and object'[45] is the conduit for 'true creation'.[46] Structurally, it permits us to bring together the virtual and actual components of the larval/narrative selves and to generate resonances between them but with neither the one nor the other dethroned in the process. If we return to Ricoeur's earlier comments, then we see that the discontinuity, ruptures, fault lines, gaps and sudden redistributions refer to this dance of meaning around the empty square, and the paradox that refuses to reduce differences is the paradoxical element or two-sided movement of the empty square itself.

The risk to the self of others' interpretations

The importance to Ricoeur's narrative self of this double-faced asignifying-signifier, this paradoxical element in the heart of the dance, is that without it there is a danger that the apparent excess offered in the form of the empty square (whose slogan is 'dissolve in order to evolve') will become illusory when detached from an immanent and virtual other half; shorn of anchorage, it will perform the function of an emptying event instead. For example, even if we could narrate every event that comprised the compendium of our lives, we would still narrate into a language of excess where the multiple interpretations of others will send each narrative around the squares of another game in what would be a becoming-kaleidoscopic of the self. If we cannot limit the self to one internal narrator (as we have argued), then what of the Other – can we limit the self to one of a multitude of external narrators? Or is it always a case of *soi-même comme des autres*?

This is where the narrative self (as coherently my own, as belonging to me) is most in trouble. How can it have any coherence in this multitudinous community game of infinite interpretability for the floating signifier that is in this case a fragmentary narrative about oneself? Must we seek coherence elsewhere? How does the narrative self dissolve in order to evolve, while at the same time avoiding the rapacity of other people's desire to interpret it – and when it is at its most defenceless?

This problem may signal the potential for Deleuze's structure to enable Ricoeur's narrative self to dissolve and yet remain coherent. Only by postulating a paradoxical element in thought that moves immanently between two series, the lack that is filled with characters with nowhere to reside, the excess that is only so in the form of an empty square anchored to the *floated signified*, can the empty square of nothingness contain within itself the *potential for protection* against becoming itself an emptying event. The Deleuzian structure places this empty space in a complex but precarious relationship with the movement of thought and with the virtual, allowing for the prescribed dissolution without the *inevitable* rapacious absorption in the Other.

This is not to say that the empty square is thus gloriously salvaged from the social or that a Ricoeurian dissolution does not inevitably result in either the inanity that besets Derek Parfit's sci-fi humans or the craziness that inhabits Lewis Carroll's world. The structure itself prescribes a possibility – one of narrative rescue, so long as we place the imagination immanently in this empty square, as the dark precursor itself – or as the dark precursor of the synthesis of the heterogeneous.

Into the empty square

It is in the sense above that the narrative self must be understood as a problem and not a solution, existing as problematic or as differential; it is in this sense that the narrative self (as spoken) is only a provisional, evanescent and fleeting precipitate in a much more extensive solution that is itself problematic. This is the only solution to the problematic of the narrative self, if it is not to dissolve into a nothingness that is nothing or become devoured by the commonplace and the repetitious, or turn like Lot's wife to sedimentary salt. The narrative self in its natural state is in solution, dissolved; summoned to give an account of itself, it precipitates out. This is what Dennett means by the self as 'a centre of narrative gravity'.[47]

The narrative self is thus incarnated within a problematic field which conditions its actualization as narrative.[48] We can in theory counter-effectuate this actualization, turn back narrative upon itself and dissolve it into its problematic world. It is easily said, and in saying, it is as easily done. Yet it is not. Why? Because we are at liberty to refuse this problematic field and engage in bare repetition. We are at liberty to take the actualized parts of the self as the whole story, rather like one takes a film to be the two hours that we encounter in front of the screen and not the stories and events of scriptwriting, production, direction, cinematography and editing that go into its actualization. Indeed, the analogy between the narrative self and modern cinema is very strong. Ridley Scott reworked or 'counter-actualized' *Blade Runner* several times, removing from the original edition the voiceover of Harrison Ford. Frances Ford Coppola, having made several endings for the original *Apocalypse Now*, presented 'an all-new version' years later[49] with an additional 49 minutes of never-before-seen footage – a 'completely re-thought, re-mixed and re-edited interpretation'. Is this not sanctioned also for the narrative self? It is – but we are at liberty to refuse it, to refuse the new, the re-thought, to turn away from the making-of documentary, or the exploration of the original source.[50]

Yet what relationship do alternative endings, re-editions, re-thought plots, the multifarious source material, the making-of, even the rejected music scores and the deleted scenes (and whatever else) have to the first narrative and, indeed, each to each other? Although actualized, in some context they remain virtual elements to the world of the original – until actualized within it. Even then they are still virtual to something else. So too with self-narratives that we consciously or unconsciously think, mix, edit, add sound to and interpret. There are choices: precisely, in narrative we have the royal opportunity to counter-actualize, to steal behind the scenes and create new ones, to formulate alternative beginnings and endings (the work of psychoanalysis), to add special effects and concoct counter-histories so that we can question how we came to story ourselves in this way and not another. We could artify the self by transforming it into a musical, choreograph dance into our adolescence or weave in a multitude of additional features, without fear of the accusation of bathos.[51] Is not Wordsworth's *The Prelude* a poeticizing of the narrative self – its ultimate artification? Many of these artifying elements are intrinsically part of who we are even though we do not ordinarily turn them into stories and we do not – under the opprobrious ensign of the self as story – deem them to be intrinsic parts of the self. And we seldom dance or sing as we tell our stories.[52] To do so would be to become the heteroglossic self, with non-narrative attachments.

So what or who stops us? What duty or debt derails us from a sense of the self as play, as art, from a vision of the self as a 'factory' in Warhol's sense, which produces a series of short films rather than a series of short stories, where the self performs as it speaks? Is not *Beckett on Film* precisely what it says it is – the jigsaw-pieces of Beckett's narrative self? So, what binds us unnecessarily to the bare and the repetitious, the unctuous and the obtuse? What makes us narrative fodder for the commonplace and the predictable?

The historicity of the narrative self: A duty bound

The answer is that it is our being as historical. This historicity of the self marks an irrevocable engagement of the self with narrative, so much so that separating the two appears impossible to achieve, an impossibility brought to a limit where the narrative self is lost to its own historicizing. Since narrative 'stands for' the events that it recounts,[53] we may then ask for what does personal history in the form of the narrative self (articulated in its prefigurative, configurative and refigurative mimetic stages) stand? Ricoeur is clear on this: it stands for the name of a problem rather than that of a solution. In other words, the narrative self is never a fully actualized solution separable from the virtual – in contrast to Deleuze's position. Yet for Ricoeur, its debt to historicity (by which it follows the standards of historical praxis) is substantial.

Ricoeur privileges an acceptation of the being of the narrative self as fundamentally the power to narrate, remember and be accountable as author. Yet since being and power are inescapably related to time we must show how temporality (and thus historicality) becomes part to our ontogenesis of the narrative self. We can do this briefly by reference to both Augustine's threefold division of time and Ricoeur's critique of Heidegger's ontological prioritization of the future over the past. For Augustine there are three presents, 'the present of the past which is memory, the present of the future which is expectation, and the present of the present which is intuition (or attention)'.[54] But can we map this onto Heidegger's hierarchical ordering of the modes of temporalization, of our being-in-time? Ricoeur explains these as follows: *fundamental temporality* is our orientation towards the future characterized by 'being-towards-death'; *historicity* is the interval of our life that stretches between birth and death, one characterized by a privileging of the past by both history and memory and *intratemporality* is characterized by our being in the present alongside the manipulable things of the world.[55] Authenticity declines, according to Heidegger, from the first to the last of these.[56]

Where do we seek an ontogenesis of the narrative self in this ontological hierarchy of time? We would expect our ontogenesis to ally itself with an ontology of historical or narrative being at the second level; yet there is a conflict here, in that we also expect the most important alliance to be at the most authentic level, the level of fundamental temporality, of being-towards-death. And this poses an argument against our avowed freedom to narrate as we choose. We may claim, as we have done, that it is open to all of us to synthesize the heterogeneous in different ways and with varied meanings or to recount our lives in another way, as Ricoeur suggests, if we consider the rather 'selective nature of all emplotment'.[57] But do we not then deny to ourselves the density of our being when the emplotment that we employ fails to be attentive to the less vulgar modes of our temporality? Alternatively, do we imbue our narratives with more authentic being when we speak them from the position of a being-towards-death?

If we do not do so, then from this Heideggerian perspective the narrative self is largely inauthentic, doomed to the status of diluted ontology. Our hope for a narrative self as creative becomes truncated in its infancy by a remorseless being-towards-death towards which we must attend if we are to be authentic. Like the historian 'left speechless'[58] by Heidegger, we would be better off if we declined to speak or declined to decline ourselves. To be authentic, we should be reticent to speak. How do we resolve this problem?

By removing the very notion of authenticity – which is what Ricoeur does. With great rigour he argues against the vector of authenticity that crosses through the three modes in which we are in time. He does so from a dual perspective. First, he argues that the connection between narrative knowledge and truth cannot be dismissed on the basis that multiple interpretations are possible and therefore anything goes and no narrative is more or less authentic than another; indeed, for Ricoeur, history as interpretation should be placed 'under the sign of poetics'[59] or, more specifically, that in responding to the aporias of temporality our narrative knowledge engages us, sweeps us up in 'a poetics of narrative'[60] that continually grapples with the polysemy of words. We are historical; therefore, our narrative poetics when turned upon the self is indeed dense with Being. In other words, he returns by a route circuitous to Collingwood's *a priori* imagination.

Secondly, he engages in an intense dismantling of the Heideggerian hierarchy of temporal modes, in particular, our alleged 'being-towards-death' which prioritizes our futurity and places the seal of our authenticity in the shadow of our death. The priority claims of the past, the present or the future, Ricoeur argues, are undecidable in that the narrative self that embraces its temporal condition in its threefold structure is itself 'empowered to arbitrate the rival claims to hegemony in the closed space of introspection'.[61] It is the very nature or being of our historical condition that the undecidable haunts it. It is what Ricoeur calls the 'uncanniness' (*inquiétante étrangeté*) of our history.[62]

It would be better, according to Ricoeur, to remove the notion of authenticity entirely and have no sense of diminishing 'ontological density' in the modes of temporalization.[63] Instead, we should understand the historical condition as an existential one regarding a whole series of discourses related to 'the historical in general, in everyday life, in fiction, and in history'.[64] By doing so, we would be justified from an existential point of view in using the word 'history' in two senses: (1) as the 'set of events (facts), past, present, and to come' and (2) as the 'set of discourses on these events (these facts) in testimony, narrative, explanation'. Ricoeur succinctly concludes: 'we make history and we make histories because we are historical. This is the "because" of existential conditionality.'[65] Because we are historical we make narratives of the events of our lives. This is our existential condition, no more given to some than to others. By removing the notion of diminishing authenticity, a univocity of being emerges in its place and all narrative identities attain equal authenticity in being: from Churchill's memoirs to the ordinary man's diary.

But can we go further than this for the narrative self? Can we retain the ontological density of all speakers, ascribe to all 'an existential condition of the possibility of the entire series of discourses concerning the historical', but acknowledge that narrating one's life as an existential condition of our historicity may be well or poorly achieved, more or less accurate, and spiritually meaningful not just to the self but also to others? If we accept that a historical reality does not exist readymade and that this historical reality, since it is human, 'is *ambiguous* and *inexhaustible*',[66] then if one is to give a truer although not more ontologically authentic account of human reality as historical, one does so by being the more ambiguous, by being the more inexhaustible. It is only in this sense that narrative identities may be said to be the more authentic, as narrative being *qua* narrative being. Yet a difficulty remains in this act of prioritization of the historical because, in rejecting Heidegger's hierarchization of the various modes of our being-in-time, has not Ricoeur inadvertently placed the being of the narrative self into the past and into memory? Has he not entombed the self?

Narrating a self against death and for life

According to Ricoeur, being-towards-death seems to occult Heidegger's 'potentiality for being-a-whole'.[67] How could the latter project ever be achieved when written into it is the former which always impedes and prohibits it. The 'potentiality for being-a-whole' would never be achievable for the narrative self since no narrative of one's history can ever include its beginning and its end or provide a history of the present; we have only commentary on the present, not history. If our narrative self is to be authentic then it must necessarily be incomplete, as well as *ambiguous* and *inexhaustible*. Ricoeur suggests that we restore vigour to Heidegger's expression by removing the end tag that determines the completeness of the incomplete – our narrative closure. Instead, ours is a 'potentiality for being'. It is this minor amputation that for Ricoeur draws our ontology of the narrative self out from under the shadow of death and into 'the joy of the spark of life', into the theme of natality and the phenomenon of birth.[68] This is the openness of being in its potentiality, in its narrative poetics.

Will this remove our narrative constraints? Ricoeur reminds us of Spinoza's proposition: 'Free man thinks of nothing less than of death and his wisdom is a meditation not on death but on life.'[69] Ours is not a 'being-towards-death' but a 'being-against-death' or 'despite-death'.[70] And it is by way of biology and the flesh that we reach this point, since it is in one's body that our potentiality for being takes on the form of desire whether in the form of Spinoza's *conatus* or Freud's *libido*.[71] Death becomes inscribed in this desire to live in the form of a self-understanding of the mortality of the flesh – after 'a long work on oneself'.[72] Our desire to live (*conatus*) is primordial to a being-against-death, which only reaches our intimate sense of self when we are affronted by the death of others because it is this type of loss that is experienced. We learn from the deceased, who no longer answers, that a part of the self has been 'amputated', that the one who has disappeared forms 'an integral part of one's self-identity' and one's self-narrative. Also, we learn through mourning the terrible truth of our own mortality, of the loss of our own life through anticipation at the heart of mourning.[73]

This is the veracity of our being found in the depths of loss and mourning – that we are beings among other human beings, in plurality, or what Ricoeur reminds us of in Heidegger, in the *inter-esse* expressed in 'the vocabulary of the *Mitsein*'.[74] And this is still a constraint against narrative, this being-against-death.

The sepulchre of narrative: Why narrate a self?

We are left with a further peculiar difficulty. Why narrate a self even if one can? Why not remain silent and reticent to share? Indeed, why tell stories about ourselves and not about the indifferent 'they' or the anonymous 'one' or about the founding sagas of our culture and the people who populated them? Why does the 'I' of the 'I can' need to move beyond the 'I can narrate' to the 'I narrate myself'? We have understood up to now that we are historical in our very being and that this being is not a *Dasein* but a *Mitsein*, so much so that it is our nature to story and be storied. According to this understanding, and if we are interpreting Ricoeur correctly, the power to narrate finds behind it the motor of our historical being – that *we just must narrate*. To do otherwise would be to be less than human or to be inauthentic. But this does not satisfy *conatus* as 'the effort to persevere in being', unless we simply repeat the tautology: to persevere in being, we must narrate our being-in-this-world; this is because to be-in-this-world is to be historical, therefore we must narrate. And what if we cannot narrate? What if brain damage or a neuro-developmental disorder prevents us from doing so? Are we then only the narrative selves of others' stories, having no agency ourselves? There must be more to the self than narrative – even if we are historical in our mode of being and even if our selves appear on the surface to look like narrative.

This draws us back to the question posed earlier in this chapter ('What duty or debt derails us from a sense of the self as play, as art?'), one that we can now reformulate as follows: what precisely is it about our historical condition that enjoins us to narrate selves the way we do, in a genre that is acceptable and with themes that may be considered axiomatic? Why indeed gather up such particular vestiges of the past for storytelling? Can we not story the self in any old way, given the aporetic nature of history and temporality or are we trapped to a certain degree in a particular narrative of the narrative self, in a particular emplotment of it that elevates some ideals of selfhood to the exclusion or occultation of others?

With such constraints, we lose or diminish the 'spark of life', the paradoxical element that is the creative scribe at the heart of selfhood, in deference to either a being-towards-death (the future) or a being-against-death (the past).[75] Perhaps *conatus* needs a Heraclitean twist, so that we now define it as '*the effort to persevere in becoming, which forms the concordant discordance of man as of every individual*'. But even this implies that something is lost in all becoming, left behind, abandoned to the past so that loss is inscribed in the persevering in becoming from the very beginning, a loss to which we mourn in a particular manner, that is, in the way of a sepulchring of the past in story. Thus desire becomes lack and loss again, perhaps as part of an overarching phallogocentric economy of meaning, as we suggested at the start of this chapter. Would desire that is wholly positive, what Lacan called 'feminine jouissance' or 'jouissance of the body' call for a different way of persevering in narrative being that did not owe a debt?[76] We will return to this in the conclusion.

We cannot seem to avoid lack and loss in the heart of narrative. Indeed, Ricoeur firmly places it there. He notes that the ontological category of 'being-in-debt' acts as a bridging concept that assures the connectedness between futureness and pastness, where the past is a 'having-been' rather than the irrevocable 'being-no-longer of the elapsed past'.[77] It is through this 'having-been' that memory must take centre stage,[78] and this pushes Ricoeur towards a

Bergsonian memory (as we noted in Chapter 9) that is disconnected from the 'no-longer'. Memory must endure for Ricoeur, if it is to retain its ontological density and if it is to usurp our alleged 'being-towards-death'. Indeed, he displaces death from the future and buries it in our pastness. He notes history concerns itself 'with practically nothing but the dead of other times',[79] and this is not just of a few prominent individuals but also of quasi-characters like the Mediterranean.[80] Significantly, he draws this past 'kingdom of the dead' into the historiographical operation by noting that this operation may be considered to be 'the scriptural equivalent of the social ritual of entombment, of the act of sepulchre'.[81] In other words, if in this act of burying we transform the physical absence of the dead into an inner presence, then in the act of historiography we transform this act of sepulchre into writing.

The narrative self as act of sepulchre

But can we assign to personal history, in the form of self-narrative, a similar act of sepulchre? We had already raised this in Chapter 5, when we asked was it only by way of a personal history which we narrate to others that the living can counter their being-towards-death and the fugacity of their lives. Ricoeur turns to Michel de Certeau's *L'Absent de l'histoire* to offer a why to the sepulchring of the past. Writing is like a burial ritual in that it 'exorcizes death by inserting it into discourse'[82] – it makes of sepulchre-as-place sepulchre-as-act. In so doing it creates another place – the place of the reader. Thus, the narrativity that buries the dead is 'a way of establishing a place for the living'[83] and assigning a place to a reader, a place that must be filled. This is the why: that we sepulchre the past in discourse to another so that we can live our lives forward, against death, with a past alongside us.

Is this also the why of personal narrative? We noted earlier how our past is populated by former selves – infant, child, adolescent, young adult. These act like national identities that reduce contemporary and past difference to the identical. But if we prise open these high-level categories we will be surprised by the manifold that is hidden beneath: the me that started school, that first walked, the me in the photograph on the beach, the me that mother told me spoke its first word, the me that first loved, the bespectacled, the athletic, the obdurate, the coy, the crazy, the abstract, the animal, the idiotic me. And such selves can be re-formulated and renegotiated just like national identities. There is no end to the multiplicity of little selves that have inhabited these personal nations, each of which has lived a little life, sparkled briefly and had its light extinguished. Such is the Bakhtinian heteroglossia within the narrative self.[84] This multiplicity is also so with all those we have known and loved, and it is also true of all the quasi-characters and quasi-events that inhabit our history; the end of primary school is for us like the death of the Mediterranean that Braudel describes, time draws us forward and each day, each moment that passes is a 'having-been'. We are obsessional scribes sepulchring in story the characters and events that constitute our passing through the interval that stretches between birth and death.

Is this our debt to these events and characters that have been lost to us above and beyond, even before, our managing of death? A 'being-against-death' that for ourselves is a being against the death of our own multiplicity of selves? Is this the face of *conatus*, of the desire to live in the face of death? Perhaps. If it is said of the historiographical operation in general, then it can be said of it in particular – individual and collective memories are intimately and immanently interpenetrative, argues Ricoeur.[85] A being-against-death, a sepulchring haunts both operations. In so doing, it compels us to have our histories read or to have them listened to by another.[86]

We may now ask if we have satisfied our historicizing of ourselves – insofar as we understand this process as our perpetual debt to ourselves and those closest to us. That no moment should be forgotten (although it may be), that our obsession with the recollection of the past is as much a being-towards-birth as the already-born-to-lost-unity as it is a being-against-death as the gathering of the salvageable in the relentless erasure of being, and that we cannot disentangle the warp of death from the weave of the spark of life – is this not the quintessence of our aporetic being? Loss is inscribed in the very spark of natality. Excess in the burgeoning of our virtual lives as we age is at the same time a debt to the past because today's dead 'are yesterday's living',[87] even if these dead are our former selves, our being in yesterday and the day before, our unique passions that are no more but that are buried in memory and enlivened in story, former occupants of our world that we immure in story so that we may live forward with others.

A Self Entombed in a Debt to the Past

Yet in this heritage-debt to every moment of our lives, are we not fuelled by a form of *conatus* that is already sickly, effete, already reactive and debilitated? What has become of the poetic imagination or the poetics of narrative that Ricoeur announced? Has not our narrative 'effort to persevere in being' not already submitted to the so-called Law of the Father or to the symbolic – to the law of lack and loss? To persevere in being is not necessarily the same as being-against-death. The former can be understood to articulate an active force, to prescribe a creative becoming that is not against something, not preoccupied with the perceived and imagined threats that lurk in the shadows of a life, where the love of life's things is engulfed in the fear of what perfidious dangers lie beyond the mask of those things we love – this is life lived against the grain. The latter clearly inaugurates this very reactive state, an obligation to the community, to the generations that have gone before us and to the permissible psychic organizations of one's social world where to persevere in being is first and foremost to sepulchre the dead *so that we might live.* Here are the constraints, the reactive forces that attachment theory has so clearly demonstrated; here is where idem has overrun ipse, where ipse is just a narrative of enforced sepulchre, constrained by the negations of the 'Thou shalt nots' and the cliché-ridden habits of a storytelling that thwarts anything from rising from the sediment. The dust settles where death is 'calmed down'[88] in the language of our stories – everything becomes dust, sedimentation and ashes, and nothing can be created from this. Into tombs we narrate our selves. Or in Nietzsche's words: this is the problem of the past becoming 'the gravedigger of the present'.[89] There is no escape from this self stricken by the perverted desire to sepulchre in order to survive *against death.* Here are the discourses of those speakers in the Adult Attachment Interview where history overpowers memory, where the threat of annihilation forces upon the nascent self the foundations of a narrative of its future that has always already constrained it to remember and narrate according to laws that best guarantee remaining in life. But at what cost do we submit narration of the self to tradition and debt? At what cost to poetics? If we cannot recount what is beyond the sepulchre of the Law of the Father are we not doomed to produce narratives that are the extended equivalent of dead metaphors – dead narratives? Have we not run the dark precursor to ground, debilitated and incarcerated our Sweeney by placing him in an asylum where he is no longer free to roam Nature as both poet and poetry itself – have we not turned the poetic imagination back upon itself so that it describes only circles that return to the same point in a perpetual brutality of repetition?

If we are to extrapolate from Ricoeur's reading of the historiographic function (as a bearing of a debt to the past in the form of narrative) a similar debt at the heart of the narrative self, we might well wonder to what degree the 'spark of life' and the 'poetics of narrative' have been truly extinguished by this most fatalistic of interpretations, this most depressing of obligations that haunts human nature. For it heralds a return of Heidegger's being-towards-death to the throne in a coronation that sends natality back to the shadows of the Real, a coronation the currency of which is guilt, guilt that one might choose to leave the dead unburied (Creon) in order to live, that one might become supra-historical in order to defeat the debt that is written into narrative and that is the death of a narrative self (Antigone). Is this avoidance of guilt not the very watermark of *ressentiment* and the reactive nature of the forces that comprise a narrative self indebted to the past, a self of habit and rigid forms, a self of ceremony and oratory, a self of a sluggish and fading precursor? Is this not the triumph of the idem over the ipse, the true rigidified self? Narrative death comes the way of those who submit to a dogmatic image of the self which in contemporary culture has been the oedipalized and phallogocentric one, the one structured on hopeless desire that has pervaded the narratives available for subjective articulation. The alternatives for narrative: do we choose the Ricoeur of the historiographic analysis sepulchring the past for the sake of the dead or the Ricoeur at the door of the productive imagination, generating a poetics of history? The narrative self requires situating itself firmly in the latter's court, but to do this it will need to radically alter its fundamental structures of narrativity. For there are important 'remainders' that cannot be accounted for by the theory of the self as narrative. Outstanding among these in literature is Virginia Woolf's *The Waves*, a book we noted Ricoeur no longer considered a work of narrative fiction but an 'oratorio', a polyphonic work that has passed over the threshold and into a plotless presentation of consciousness. Should the structure of narrative identity not include rather than leave as a remainder something like *The Waves* as a model among many for the creative-narrative self – in this case a polyphonic one with the self as an oratorio, a story set to music and acting? Narrative is not enough; so we must move beyond it in the manner that Lacan, in moving 'beyond the phallus', finds a feminine jouissance. We must build *narrative difference* from here. Ultimately, it is neither Antigone nor Creon that determines the crossroads of the narrative self or lays out a new path. Creon resides within Antigone – in the heart of an obligation to the dead is the desire to live despite them.

Chapter 13

Conclusion

Between the past as pre-existence in general and the present as infinitely contracted past there are, therefore, all the circles of the past constituting so many stretched or shrunk regions, strata, and sheets (nappes).[1]

The term 'space' evokes the idea of different possible traversals following a multitude of itineraries, and above all the idea of a stratified structure assembled like a pile of sheets of paper (une structure feuilletée).[2]

Let us summarize what we have sought to do. We followed Ricoeur's narrative self to its *Ursprung*, to a virtual world of *Aion* where Aristotelian power and potency concocted a pre-narrative brew. For Ricoeur, the being of this narrative self, that which lies beneath the poetics of narrative, is here. Then we drew Aristotle and Deleuze into a disavowed affinity, demonstrating that in a virtual world, preserved in miniature, sit the same potency and act that Ricoeur sought, now genetic elements in a Bergsonian/Deleuzian multiplicity. Indeed, we found a prime mover, *a will to create*, a something in the *Ursprung* that is the dark precursor of the synthesis of the heterogeneous. *Dunamis* and *energeia* are the sutures between Deleuze and Ricoeur. We moved from debt to excess. In returning outwards (and sustaining this surface–depth metaphor) we noted that this athletic trajectory leaves behind remainder and loss, only for us to attend to this debt and, in so doing, reduce ourselves to the status of debit, of owing and of salvaging, of sepulchring and of mourning – so that we might live forwards. But another debit now remains – one of creativity, of squandered excess in the face of death. But this remainder is not inevitable.

We do not, as Deleuze suggests, collapse the pluripotentiality of the virtual to a flat narrative the moment we enunciate it. A poetics of narrative is optional but our desire-as-lack will always defeat us. We saw a glimmer of hope in the previous chapter, a heart of Creon in Antigone's debt. We also saw excess in the floating signifier, excess in the form of the empty square as well as excess in the uncanny and the unknown in the floated signified. And we placed Sweeney in this empty square with one face to roam the expanse of Nature and one face to tell his stories. The always present lack – that which is forgotten (as part of the *ars oblivionis*) and that which has not yet been discovered (as part of the unknown) – is a remainder to be recovered, but it is not all, or 'not-all'. There is an upsurge of being in the virtual that Bachelard argues is the being of the imagination and that is all positive, potentially all productive as in Aristotle, potentially all creative as in Nietzsche, potentially feminine jouissance as in Lacan. We have argued that we can live outside the economy of lack, we can narrate the self otherwise than what it has not. But how can we achieve this?

Central to the problem of the narrative self is that all models or formulations have been predicated upon some form of lack, so much so that we are perpetually trapped in explaining how we can recover the remainder, how we can occupy several empty squares without at the same time submitting the self to a thesis of debt – debt to a unity lost (Marcel-mother), debt to the loss of loved ones (the sepulchring of the dead in narrative) and debt to the loss of our own quasi-characters and quasi-continents (the sepulchring of our former selves and our former states in our narrative self). And this problem is further complicated by the illusion of there being just one narrator.

But we have identified and even constructed sutures that connect Deleuze and Ricoeur at the womb of invention, sutures which gather together otherwise 'concealed' and fulminant ways of being without lack. We bring them together without one having lacked the other in the first place. Concealed? We note the outcome of Lacan's attempts to think beyond the jouissance of the phallus (the despot of phallogocentrism), to glimpse the Real that cannot be spoken of. He finds there 'jouissance of the feminine', something only previously articulated by mystics, whether male (St. John of the Cross) or female (St. Teresa), and something of which we cannot speak.[3] Only from this region of the unnameable can a narrative self 'become' (a conatus of persevering in becoming) in a style fundamentally distinct from the phallogocentric variety, that is, different from a force of becoming betrothed to the symbolic. Narrative carried upon another force, the other jouissance, that is, in its wave so to speak, is narrative minus the symbolic, even if it uses the symbolic for some of its purposes or even if it combines with narrative in the symbolic, that is, narrative of metonymy and metaphor. Ricoeur divides the self in two: ipse and idem. Ipse self now further divides into two: phallic ipse and ipse of feminine jouissance. This is indeed a sexuation of narrative, but one not to be confused with a biological division.

It is a new scenography of the narrative self that is aimed at – or its own new scenography. Although we have constructed an argument for a creative-narrative self, it has always been against the grain of its own presuppositions – creative against the force of the symbolic upon which the narrative self is retroactively constructed and inserted into its own past. Unseen, fundamental brackets have not been removed, brackets on the inside of which is painted a particular scenography. A scenography inherent in Lacanian and Freudian constructions of the self. We look beyond it, as Lacan did, and we espy a different creative self, or a self differentially creative, one with two faces of which one is always in shadow and barely speakable (the stammering, ecstatic one), alongside but not opposed to the self of lack, loss and debt, the self that can never obtain the object of its desire, the self that sepulchres 'for the sake of'. Attachment theory reinforces this self of loss in the substance of love, even if it suggests an *ars obvilionis* to the power of this loss.

The narrative self is constructed on phallogocentric lines. It is to some extent patriarchally vouchsafed. Ricoeur's narrative self is founded upon presuppositions that inscribe a certain form of narrative, a certain Aristotelian emplotment to the exclusion of other narrative and non-narrative structures. They are the narrative self's remainder: polyphonic selves and others. Irigaray argues for a new scenography for thought, the conditions of which could be a new scenography of the creative-narrative self. She asks us to consider the following:

> [The] *scenography* that makes representation feasible . . . the architectonics of its theatre . . . its geometric organization, its props, its actors, their respective positions, their dialogues, indeed their tragic relations, without overlooking the mirror, most often hidden, that allows the logos, the subject, to reduplicate itself, to reflect itself by itself.[4]

A new scenography is called for in the place where Aristotle, Ricoeur and Deleuze are brought together, at the point of fracture where the self of Ricoeur is effaced in making itself available to the other, the other that is not the dissolved self (which is simply the being-available) but feminine jouissance and where the self of Deleuze dissolves into a multiplicity of virtual ideas that swarm through this fracture like ants – the termitary jouissance of difference-in-itself. Coterminous with each other, these selves are not the same. Two forces beneath them, as Nietzsche would have it, wrapped one around the other, but not in battle – one for a poetic yet sedentary narrative, the other for a whirling nomadic narrative. Reactive, these forces combine to produce a rigidified self. Creative, a metamorphosis (in the substance of *délire* and *lalangue*) stammers through the metaphor and metonymy of narrative structure and inserts the uncanny within the skilfully composed. A fenestrated self where narrative forms the interfenestration and love (in the form of feminine jouissance) the glass through which we see our virtual worlds emerge.

It may be argued against us that there is excessive sentiment in the claim that to narrate the self in any old fashion is just as worthy as narrating it according to a naïve inclination towards a truth never attainable. What value does our argument hold? What position does it occupy between the permissible and the preposterous, the ethical and the egregious? Questioning this is justified given that we have been brought face-to-face with the ultimate and excessive possibility of the self being precisely an exaggeration, a hyperbolic construction of fictions without discipline.

The potential consequences of such a scenario are dangerous indeed. Yet they arise when we succeed in overthrowing the dogmatic image of the self as a transcendental ground of the Cogito that abhors deception, legerdemain, contradiction and magic realism but permits the power of the true to guide events and even to intervene where necessary as the *deus ex machina* that solves the seemingly insoluble problems of the self. But is this not dangerous too, although in a less than interesting way? One always feels cheated by the entrance of the Tyrannosaurus Rex at the end of Spielberg's *Jurassic Park*. In betterment of this tame or tamed conclusion, do we have no choice but to do as the people of Tlön do in Borges' short story, construct the self by searching not for 'the truth or even for verisimilitude, but rather for the astounding'? In other words, by rebelling against the dogmatic image that fosters the phallogocentric self, we establish a metaphysics of the self that is now 'a branch of fantastic literature'.[5] We have a narrative self that is a creation-narration, one that is ludic without at the same time being ludicrous. No longer is the self the hero with a thousand faces but the face with a thousand heroes.[6] In Tlön there are no nouns, only verbs; there is no word 'corresponding to the word "moon," but there is a verb which in English would be "to moon" or "to moonate."'[7] This is the language of the virtual, identical to Deleuze's insistence on the verb 'to green' for the event of becoming-colour in trees. Can we infuse our own virtual language of Tlön, the stammers of jouissance through the traditional narrative of the self, distort it with obscure geometry, diffract its sentences with sudden escapes – but without ever usurping it? Can we introduce into our language the verb: 'to selve'? We have argued that this is more than possible – for it is a poetics not of the possible but of the potential, the not-yet.

We have asked what putative processes are subsumed within a greater power to story the self. Behind the narrative self there is a will to narrate, a desire that takes on the form of differential forces but is a pure productivity that declines lack.[8] The 'will to power' or to capacity manifests itself in the human as this will to narrate, to extract the self from a language of *délire*, the language of Tlön, but also from a language of gesture, movement and art and from an ensemble of anonymous authors and its entourage. But we need to go further than a will to narrate, to go beneath narrative to protect narrative from the loose rules of play that may be too easily substitutable for the more rigid rules of narrative.

If our ontological position is that 'I/we make histories because I/we am/are historical' then this 'I make/we make' (and their Heideggerian counterparts *Dasein/Mitsein*) requires a creative force deep to the will to narrate, one that holds narrative to account. Our debt is therefore to our being as creative rather than as historical. In other words, our duty is attenuated if our being-historical is performed in the manner of history rather than of art. It is no more than a poetics of self-narrative idealized. We located this creative force in an ontogenesis embedded in a field of differential forces, a field that has the capacity to generate a will to narrate alongside a will to play – or to quote Ricoeur, we have the will to '[escape] from the grid-work (*le quadrillage*) of narrativity'.[9] We have a sea for the self so that we may lose ourselves upon it and furlongs to map that sea so that we may also find our way upon it.

Attachment theory disassembled an ipse self, and we were left asking how narrative identity could survive when bled dry of invention, deprived of its archives or only offered the keys to a limited number of rooms of sometimes distorted and unreadable manuscripts. How could narrative identity claim any truth then? Would not *ipse* be *idem* in disguise, a pretentious clown of simulated habits? Indeed, how could narrative identity gather together a life, when there is nothing to tell, when what is most important cannot be seen or deciphered and where what is most true for the speaker is always what is most false? How could this be an answer to the question: 'Who?' If attachment theory is correct, then the answer to this question is indubitably, 'Not I.' Attachment theory certainly raises the spectre of the false at the heart of the true. In answer to 'Who says I?' a narrative unfolds that is woven of the exact and the distorted, the survived and the deleted, the trivialized and the exaggerated, and the true and the false. But what of this false and this true – are they not paradoxically the true determinants of a narrative self? What of the verifiable and the unverifiable in relation to self-narrative? Does not Ricoeur openly raise this point when he notes that 'the relation between reality and fiction will continue to torment us'?[10] When we ask that the narrative self be woven of the veritable and the fictitious, is there then a desired mixture of the two, an alchemical allotment, or does the self begin to disintegrate under the weight of suspicion when the factitious threatens to overwhelm the veritable? Ricoeur asks to what degree is testimony trustworthy, and he notes the precariousness of testimony in ordinary conversation where one does not know how to balance confidence and suspicion.[11] He attempts to ameliorate this problem through the notion of 'the self-designation of the testifying subject'[12] who makes 'the witness's triple declaration: (1) I was there; (2) believe me; (3) if you don't believe me, ask someone else'.[13] His advocacy of testimony, in this sense, heralds from his belief that 'we have nothing better than our memory to assure ourselves of the reality of our memories'.[14] But as we have demonstrated, 'I was there' may mean for the dismissing speaker, 'I was not there' or for the preoccupied speaker, 'We are here'. Ultimately, we can trust the 'I was there' when it comes from the mouth of what Ricoeur calls 'the capable human being'. But we are not all capable human beings and those designated so are not so all of the time. We exist in a 'betweenness'[15] that leads to individual and social *consensus* or *dissensus*. The reality of our memories must exist in both these spaces and the consensus or dissensus that crosses them; it is in this sense that what is brought from memory to the narrative self (that is both *Dasein* and *Mitsein*) is rendered artifice, if we understand artifice to be the ingenious, the feigned, the contrived, the skilful, the mechanical, the ingeniously expedient, the factitious and the creative. The self is an artificer in this sense, artificializing from the dissolved to the solved, from the problem to the solution, from *Ursprung* to the stories told.

Notes

Prelims

[1] MHF, pp. 82–83; *100–101*.

[2] This Deleuzian term will be explained later in the text.

[3] Fritz B. Simon, Helm Stierlin and Lyman C. Wynne, *The Language of Family Therapy: A Systemic Vocabulary and Sourcebook* (New York: Family Process, 1985), p. 38.

[4] David Grossman, *See Under: Love* (London: Jonathan Cape, 1990).

[5] TP, p. xx; *8*. 'A Thousand Plateaus is conceived as an open-system', translator's foreword, ibid., p. xiv.

[6] J. G. Ballard, *The Atrocity Exhibition* (London: Flamingo, 2001), p. vi (italics added).

[7] Jacques Lacan, *The Other Side of Psychoanalysis: The Seminar of Jacques Lacan, Book XVII*, trans. Russell Grigg (London: Norton, 2006), pp. 11–28. For an excellent summary of the four discourses, see Bruce Fink's 'The Master Signifier and the Four Discourses', in Dany Nobus (ed.), *Key Concepts of Lacanian Psychoanalysis* (London: Rebus, 1998), pp. 29–47. Essentially, discourse may begin from one of four positions: the master's discourse (based on nonsensical signifiers), the discourse of knowledge based on work (that of the university), the discourse based on the divided subject and uncertainty (that of the hysteric), and the discourse of desire (that of the analyst).

[8] MHF, p. 242; *312*.

Chapter 1

[1] Luce Irigaray, *The Way of Love,* trans. Heidi Bostic and Stephen Pluhček (London: Continuum, 2002), p. xx.

[2] Antonio Damasio, *The Feeling of What Happens: Body, Emotion and the Making of Consciousness* (London: Vintage, 2000). Damasio's neurological model of the self consists of three layers: the proto-self, the core self and the autobiographical self.

[3] OA, p. 297; *345*.

[4] Jean-Jacques Rousseau, *The Confessions*, trans. anonymous (London: Wordsworth, 1996). Despite Rousseau's 'depravity and even frenzy' his morality is repeatedly preserved (p. 14). Of course, this self of Rousseau ('I am not made like any of those I have seen; I venture to believe that I am not made like any of those in existence', p. 3) must remain fundamentally isolated in order to defy any sense of a self in relation to others that might be corruptible and not passionately self-referential or pristinely moral.

⁵ Slavoj Žižek, *Organs without Bodies: On Deleuze and Consequences* (London: Routledge, 2004), p. xi. Žižek is referring to the encounter he creates in this book between Deleuze and Lacan, although it could just as easily be read with respect to Deleuze and Ricoeur.

⁶ See Paul Ricoeur's *Freud and Philosophy: An Essay on Interpretation* (London: Yale University Press, 1970).

⁷ See George Kelly's *The Psychology of Personal Constructs*, Vol. 1 (New York: Norton, 1955) on constructivist psychotherapy; see Aaron Beck's *Cognitive Therapy and the Emotional Disorders* (New York: International Universities Press, 1976) and David Meichenbaum's *Cognitive-Behaviour Modification: An Integrative Approach* (New York: Plenum, 1977) on cognitive therapy.

⁸ See David White and David Epston's *Narrative Means to Therapeutic Ends* (New York: Norton, 1990).

⁹ Paul Ricoeur, '"La Conviction et la Critique," Entretien recueilli à l'occasion de ses 90 ans par Nathalie Crom, Bruno Frappat, Robert Migliorini', *L'Herne: Paul Ricoeur*, 81 (2004), pp. 15–18.

¹⁰ Indeed, other than a couple of articles, Dudley Andrews' 'Tracing Ricoeur', *Diacritics*, 30 No 2 (2000), pp. 43–69; and Olivier Mongin's 'L'excès et la dette: Gilles Deleuze and Paul Ricoeur ou l'impossible conversation?', *L'Herne: Paul Ricoeur*, 81 (2004), pp. 271–283, there are no works on either philosopher in which the other is meaningfully referenced or where important associations are drawn. None has attempted to forge a relationship between Ricoeur and Deleuze (other than Mongin), and certainly, none has done so in the manner that Žižek does in *Organs without Bodies*, where Deleuze is forced into a 'disavowed affinity' with his apparently mortal enemy, Hegel ('Deleuze equals Hegel: is this the ultimate infinite judgement?').

¹¹ MHF, p. 434; *562* (Deleuze on Bergson) and p. 603, n. 39; *633*, n. *39* (Deleuze on Nietzsche); and DR, p. 135; *146* (Ricoeur on the 'aborted cogito'). Also, see TN3, pp. 131; *236* (Deleuze on Proust) and LS, p. 97; *118* (Ricoeur on Husserl).

¹² OA, pp. 168–169; *141*.

¹³ See Leonard Lawlor's *Imagination and Chance: Difference between the Thought of Ricoeur and Derrida* (New York: State University of New York Press, 1993); and Jean-Luc Amalric's *Ricoeur, Derrida, l'enjeu de la métaphore* (Paris: Presses Universitaires de France, 2006).

¹⁴ OA, p. 169; *142*.

¹⁵ *Chambers Twentieth Century Dictionary* (Edinburgh: Pitman, 1977).

¹⁶ OA, p. 166; *196–197*. This term will be explained in detail in Chapter 12.

¹⁷ Luce Irigaray, *Way of Love*, p. xx.

¹⁸ TN3, p. 248; *446*.

¹⁹ For a distinction between the 'poetic imagination' and the 'ethical imagination' in Ricoeur, see Richard Kearney, 'Narrative Imagination: Between Ethics and Poetics', in Richard Kearney (ed.), *Paul Ricoeur: The Hermeneutics of Action* (London: Sage, 1996), p. 174.

²⁰ 'Dehiscence' is used here in its botanical sense of a pod that has burst open and scattered its seeds. It is irreversible.

²¹ We note in this regard Olivier Mongin's distinction in 'L'excès et la dette: Gilles Deleuze and Paul Ricoeur ou l'impossible conversation?' between Deleuze and

Ricoeur, the former as a philosopher of excess and the latter as a philosopher of debt.

[22] TN3, p. 249; *446–447*.

[23] Ibid., pp. 138–141; *246–251*.

[24] Ibid., p. 249; *448*.

Chapter 2

[1] J. G. O'Keeffe (ed. and trans.) *Buile Suibhne (The Frenzy of Sweeney) being The Adventures of Suibne Geilt* (London: Irish Texts Society, 1913), p. 15.

[2] OA, pp. 5–8; *15–18* and p. 14; *25*.

[3] See Deleuze's essay on Beckett, 'The Exhausted', in CC, pp. 152–174.

[4] René Descartes, *Discourse on Method and the Meditations*, trans. F. E. Sutcliffe (Middlesex: Penguin, 1968), p. 110.

[5] Immanuel Kant, *Critique of Pure Reason*, rev. and trans. J. M. D. Meiklejohn, ed. Vasilis Politis (London: Everyman, 1993), p. 100 [B133].

[6] See Plato's *Philebus* [23c–27c] for the fourfold classification of all existents: *apeiron* and *peras* (boundless/unlimited and bound/limit); a mixture of both and a fourth item – the *aitia* or cause of the mixture. Everything that exists is a mixture of Limit and Unlimitedness, definite and the indefinite, bound and the boundless [16c]. In this schema of mixture, 'one grasps a general character of being' – Hans-Georg Gadamer, *Plato's Dialectical Ethics: Phenomenological Interpretations Relating to the Philebus* (New Haven, CT: Yale University Press, 1991), p. 130.

[7] LS, p. 1; *9*.

[8] Ibid., p. 2; *10*.

[9] Jean-Jacques Lecercle, *Philosophy through the Looking Glass: Language, Nonsense, Desire* (La Salle, IL: Open Court, 1985), p. 6. We will return to this later in the book.

[10] LS, p. 2; *10*.

[11] Ibid.

[12] Ibid., p. 3; *11*.

[13] Jacques Lacan, *Book XX: On Feminine Sexuality, The Limits of Love and Knowledge, 1972–1973*, ed. Jacques-Alain Miller, trans. Bruce Fink (London: Norton, 1999). For Lacan, *lalangue* refers to the non-scientific aspects of language, those of the unconscious that are replete with shifting meanings and the polysemy of homonyms. Its purpose is not that of communication (p. 44 and p. 138).

[14] OA, p. 156; *130*.

[15] Ibid., p. 161; *134*. For the full discussion on the criteria and questionable nature of personal identity when subject to the imaginary Teletransporter, see Derek Parfit's *Reasons and Persons* (Oxford: Clarendon, 1984), pp. 199–217.

[16] It should be noted that Parfit addresses in some detail the issue of memory and personal identity in *Reasons and Persons*, in particular, the issue of one person's ability to experience another person's memories if these – by way of another imaginary scenario – have been surgically implanted (pp. 219–226).

[17] OA, p. 165; *137*.

[18] MHF, p. 85; *104*.

19   Ralph Waldo Emerson, 'Circles', in *Essays and Lectures* (New York: New American Library, 1983), p. 403.

20   David Levin, *The Philosopher's Gaze: Modernity in the Shadows of Enlightenment* (Berkeley: University of California Press, 1999), p. 36.

21   Descartes, *Meditations*, p. 96.

22   Michel Foucault, *Madness and Civilisation: A History of Insanity in the Age of Reason*, trans. Richard Howard (London: Tavistock, 1967), pp. 65–84.

23   Descartes, *Meditations*, p. 110.

24   Levin, *Philosopher's Gaze*, p. 37.

25   OA, p. 345; *297*.

26   MHF, p. 103; *124*.

27   TN1, p. 80; *150*.

28   We will look at this in much more detail in Chapter 10 when we attempt to prise open the space between the signifier and the signified of the narrative/dissolved self.

29   We might note Beckett's two short stories, 'All Strange Away' and its twin 'Imagine Dead Imagine' in which the faculty of the imagination is turned off – but only to reveal basic geometry beneath it. See *Samuel Beckett: The Complete Short Prose, 1929–1989*, ed. S. E. Gontarski (New York: Grove, 1995). For a fuller discussion of the 'failure of the imagination to escape itself' see Richard Kearney's *The Wake of Imagination* (London: Routledge, 1988), pp. 307–316.

30   WP, pp. 61–62; *60*.

31   Richard Kearney, *Wake of Imagination*, p. 310.

32   Samuel Beckett, 'Imagination Dead Imagine', in *Samuel Beckett*, p. 182.

33   WP, p. 62; *61*.

34   Authur Adamov, *L'Aveu*, (Paris: Editions du Sagittaire, 1946), p. 106.

35   LS, p. 52; *67*.

36   Ibid., p. 54; *69–70*.

37   WP, p. 70; *69*.

38   Ibid., p. 63; *62*.

39   TN3, p. 290; *160–161*.

40   Aeschylus, *The Orestes Plays of Aeschylus*, trans. Paul Roche, (New York: Mentor, 1962), p. 77.

41   For Deleuze, this conceptual persona that sets up the concepts of the absurd is never resigned to 'indubitable truths'.

42   See Vasilis Politis' *Aristotle and the Metaphysics* (London: Routledge, 2004), pp. 64–75.

43   Lewis Carroll, *Alice in Wonderland and Through the Looking Glass* (Hertsfordshire: Wordsworth Classics, 1993), pp. 211–213.

44   Ronald Bogue, *Deleuze on Literature* (London: Routledge, 2003), p. 25.

45   Lewis Carroll, *The Hunting of the Snark* (London: Penguin Classics, 1995), p. 73.

46   Bogue, *Deleuze on Literature*, p. 26.

47   Ibid., pp. 25–26.

48   An intriguing description of Woolf's self-prose is given by Deleuze and Guattari: 'When Virginia Woolf was questioned about a specifically women's writing, she was appalled at the idea of writing "as a woman." Rather, writing should produce a becoming-woman as atoms of womanhood, capable of crossing and impregnating an entire social field, and of contaminating men, of sweeping them up in that becoming' (MP, p. 276; *338*).

49 TN3, p. 241; *435*.

50 Although Alice fulfils the requirements of a narrative identity dissolving into a molecular or larval state or of an unlimited rising to meet narrative, her world is too embroiled with the imaginary to satisfy our criteria for a conceptual persona for the self, a persona who must in some sense be a poet.

51 Seamus Heaney based his translation of *Buile Suibhne* on J. G. O'Keeffe's bilingual edition. In Heaney's *Sweeney Astray* the cause of Sweeney's madness is the curse of Ronan; in O'Keeffe's translation it is both the horror of battle and the curse of Ronan. See Seamus Heaney's *Sweeney Astray* (London: Faber and Faber, 1983).

52 O'Keeffe, *Buile Suibhne*, p. 81.

53 Joseph Falaky Nagy notes that the damaging of the cleric's bell – 'as powerful an expression of a saint's authority as is his actual voice' – further concentrates Sweeney's violation of narrative and the spoken word. See Joseph Falaky Nagy's *A New Introduction to Buile Suibhne*, (London: Irish Texts Society, 1996), pp. 13–14.

54 Ibid., p. 2. Nagy quotes from a Middle Irish legal text that refers to 'becoming a *geilt*' – meaning, becoming one who goes mad – as a creative situation where 'the poetic and storytelling functions [are] turned inward upon themselves, with the poetic voice stripped of its illusion of impartial perspective' (p. 11).

55 O'Keeffe, *Buile Suibhne*, p. 77.

56 Ibid., p. 103.

57 Deleuze distinguishes between the colour 'green' in a tree as a quality and 'to green' as 'a noematic colour or attribute' (LS, p. 21; *33*). Thus: 'the tree greens' refers to the true event beneath the surface effect of the appearance of green. Events are verbs, not adjectives (ibid., p. 5; *13–14*).

58 We refer to Sweeney here as 'he', although it is clear in *Buile Suibhne* that Sweeney is ungendered when he is mad. 'They began describing aloud the madman; one man would say it was a woman, another that it was a man' (O'Keeffe, *Buile Suibhne*, p. 17).

Chapter 3

1 Immanuel Kant, *Critique of Pure Reason*, rev. and trans. J. M. D. Meiklejohn, ed. Vasilis Politis (London: Everyman, 1993), p. 100 [B133].

2 Robert C. Solomon, *Continental Philosophy since 1750: The Rise and Fall of the Self – A History of Western Philosophy: 7* (Oxford: Oxford University Press, 1988), p. 27.

3 It is worth noting that the therapies of the self most heavily sanctioned and empirically supported within modern health services are constructed upon a Kantian model, for instance, the cognitive therapies. Most foundational of all is Aaron Beck's cognitive model of depression which posits a chairmanship to the understanding over the affects and the imagination and which identifies the origins of depression as laid down in a maladaptive employment of the understanding; in other words, the categories have become disorganized or pathological and do not function to make proper sense of the empirical word but instead distort it. Beck also makes use of the concept of schemata, removing this from the province of the imagination and condensing it into a subterranean pattern of thinking, a sort of distorting triangle for thinking that sets up the categories to process the

empirical world in an aberrant manner and that prompts a depressive view of the self, the world and the future. See Aaron T. Beck, A. J. Rush, B. F. Shaw and G. Emery's *Cognitive Therapy of Depression* (New York: Guilford Press, 1997); also, see his daughter, Judith Beck's book, *Cognitive Therapy: Basics and Beyond* (New York: Guildford Press, 1995).

4   Solomon, *Continental Philosophy*, p. 5.

5   Ibid., p. 6.

6   Ibid. Solomon proceeds to expand his thesis to a socio-political framework, i.e., that this universalist framework for the self coincided with worldwide exploration and colonization and facilitated the global efficiency of this 'conquest of nature'; in other words, the transcendental pretence was 'no innocent philosophical thesis, but a political weapon of enormous power' (Solomon, *Continental Philosophy*, p. 6), one that allowed for unrestricted paternalism and self-righteous expertise on human nature. A related point not explicated by Solomon though strongly suggested is that the paternalism of the transcendental pretence of the self contains at its core a patriarchalism that defines its structure.

7   Ibid., p. 7. It is worth situating Kant within his times, that is, within the era of the Enlightenment and its core principles of humanism, rationality and universalism. The world had become a human world 'determined (and threatened) by human aspirations' (ibid., p. 9) and core to the human understanding of that world was man's reason and inherent rationality which could be understood in universalist terms – all men have reason and, if applied properly, all men will reach the same conclusions regarding moral and political virtues. Romanticism, in contrast to this arrogant apotheosis of rational man, extolled instead the passions, endorsing mysticism and elevating traditional religion and poetry over philosophy. Sentiment was seen as central to human nature and romanticists sought to usurp the rationalist self for a supra-personal one. Although Kant would be considered a central defender of the Enlightenment in Germany, he was for Solomon the man 'who set the stage for the most dramatic romantic themes, including the elevation of the self from mere personal identity to an Absolute Self of transcendental proportions' (ibid., p. 15).

8   Theodore Di Maria. 'Kant's View of the Self in the First Critique', *Idealistic Studies*, 32 No. 3 (2002), pp. 191–202.

9   Michael Kelly, 'Self-Awareness and Ontological Monism: Why Kant Is Not an Ontological Monist', *Idealistic Studies*, 32 No. 3 (2002), pp. 237–254. Kelly notes that Western philosophy assumes that there is only one form of awareness, that is, object-awareness and that therefore self-awareness is only possible through the mediation of an object other than the self as subject. However, Kelly argues that the meaning of self-awareness in Kant is one that occurs on a pre-thematic level 'where there is no distinction between that which appears, its appearing and that to whom it appears'. Yet this transcendental self remains 'in the unknowable realm of noumenality'.

10 Kant, *Critique of Pure Reason*, pp. 144–145 [A140/B179].

11 Ibid., p. 145 [A142/B181].

12 Ibid., p. 251 [A325/B382].

13 Ibid.

14 Ibid., p. 263 [A348/B406].

15 Ibid., p. 131 [A115].

16 Genevieve Lloyd, *Being in Time: Selves and Narrative in Philosophy and Literature* (London: Routledge, 1993), p. 79.

17 Ibid., p. 81.

18 Kant, *Critique of Pure Reason*, p. 263 [A348/B406].

19 Ibid.

20 Ibid.

21 Ibid., p. 261 [A344/B402].

22 As Körner puts it, 'In introspection I am at times aware of myself and perceive myself after the fashion of an object, that is to say under the form of time, though not of space, and under the unity of pure apperception. The experience of objects which must take place under the forms of perception and the understanding is not any experience of things in themselves. My empirical self must therefore be distinguished from myself in itself which is unknowable' (S. Körner, *Kant*, Middlesex: Penguin Books, 1955, p. 67). Körner also points out that the unknowability of the self was for Kant and many of his contemporaries a paradox that required resolution. See *Critique of Pure Reason* [B157].

23 Kant, *Critique of Pure Reason*, p. 262 [A346/B404].

24 Körner, *Kant*, p. 67.

25 Gilles Deleuze argues that Kant clearly induces the transcendental self from an empirical self: 'In the first edition of the *Critique of Pure Reason* [Kant] describes in detail three syntheses which measure the respective contributions of the thinking faculties, all culminating in the third, that of recognition, which is expressed in the form of the unspecified object as correlate of the "I think" to which all the faculties are related. It is clear that, in this manner, Kant traces the so-called transcendental structures from the empirical acts of a psychological consciousness: the transcendental synthesis of apprehension is directly induced from an empirical apprehension, and so on. In order to hide this all too obvious procedure, Kant suppressed this text in the second edition. Although it is better hidden, the tracing method, with all its "psychologism," nevertheless subsists' (DR, p. 171; *177*).

26 Henry Allison, *Kant's Transcendental Idealism* (New Haven, CT: Yale University Press, 1983), p. 289.

27 For an objection to this interpretation, see Theodore Di Maria's article, 'Kant's View of the Self', pp. 191–202. Di Maria argues that Allison has needlessly conflated the subject of apperception with the noumenal self and distinguished this from the phenomenal self, and by doing so thereby commits two metaphysical errors or unwarranted assumptions: (1) 'that Kant's view is that the noumenal and phenomenal self should be considered as two ontologically distinct objects' and (2) that 'noumena are ontologically prior to, i.e., are more real than, their appearances as phenomena.' However, as Di Maria notes, Kant does repeatedly identify the subject of apperception with the noumenal self – it is a matter of interpretation whether this subject of apperception is the noumenal self or is grounded in the noumenal self. But surely this only further complicates the Kantian self and adds new problems; instead of a divided self do we now have a tripartite self, one part in time, one part outside time and the subject of apperception both in and outside time?

28 Solomon, *Continental Philosophy*, p. 35.

29 Ibid.

30 Kant, *Critique of Pure Reason*, p. 277 [A350].

31 See Chapter 12. Ricoeur notes that, regarding the hierarchical ordering of the modes of temporalization in *Being and Time*, three headings are given: *Temporality*, characterized by our being-toward-death; *historicity*, characterized by our lived life between birth and death (with its references to the past and to memory); and *intratemporality*, characterized by our being in time alongside the manipulable things of the world (MHF, p. 348; *455*). The movement from temporality to intratemporality (to the so-called vulgar conception of time) is marked by decreasing authenticity and indeed primordiality (ibid., p. 349; *455*).

32 Ibid., p. 349; *456*.

33 KCP, p. 10; *17*.

34 Solomon, *Continental Philosophy*, p. 40.

35 Kant, *Critique of Pure Reason*, p. 134 [A121].

36 MHF, p. 97; *117*.

37 Kant, *Critique of Pure Reason*, p. 110 [B151].

38 Ibid.

39 Ibid., p. 135 [A123].

40 Richard Kearney, *The Wake of Imagination* (London: Routledge, 1988), p. 189.

41 Ibid., p. 191.

42 Ibid., p. 190.

43 Ibid., p. 194.

44 Kant, *Critique of Pure Reason*, p. 262 [A346/B404].

45 Martin Heidegger, *Kant and the Problem of Metaphysics*, trans. Richard Taft (Bloomington: Indiana University Press, 1990), p. 118.

Chapter 4

1 OA, p. 164; *194*.

2 FP, p. 45 (italics added).

3 See Jon Elster's 'Introduction', in Jon Elster (ed.), *The Multiple Self* (Cambridge: Cambridge University Press, 1987), pp. 1–34.

4 TN3, p. 105; *190*.

5 Ibid.

6 Deleuze discusses complicated time in *Proust and Signs*. An essence is, for Proust, always a birth of the world. Thus, essence is the birth of Time itself (PS, p. 45; *58*), before it is deployed or has distinct dimensions according to which it will unfold. Deleuze uses the notion of *complication* (a term used by Neoplatonists to designate the original state before the deployment and explication of time) to refer to the enveloping of the many in the One, thus affirming the unity of the multiple (ibid.).

7 OA, p. 179; *210*.

8 MHF, p. 102; *123*.

9 Ibid., p. 108; *129*.

10 Kant, *Critique of Pure Reason*, p. 110 [B151].

11 TN1, p. 68; *132*.

12 RM, p. 235; *253*.

13 TN3, p. 249; *447*.

[14] Ibid., p. 183; *334.*

[15] TN1, p. 66; *129.*

[16] Ibid., pp. 207–208; *364.*

[17] TN3, p. 241; *435.*

[18] Ibid., p. 245; *440.* This is so because 'world time remains the time of some Dasein, individual in every case, in virtue of the intimate tie between Care and Being-towards-death' (ibid.).

[19] Ibid., p. 246; *442.*

[20] Ibid.

[21] As we shall see, Deleuze will attempt a solution to this very problem.

[22] TN3, p. 246; *443.*

[23] Ibid.

[24] Ibid.

[25] Ibid.

[26] Ibid., p. 247; *443–444.*

[27] FP, p. 371. Discussing the Freudian unconscious, Ricoeur terms Freud's shift from an emphasis of the conscious to the unconscious as an 'antiphenomenology' that performs 'an epochê in reverse' (p. 118), inducing a reduction of consciousness 'since what is initially best known, the conscious, is suspended and becomes the least known', thus calling into question the central position of immediate consciousness as source and meaning. In so doing, Freud inflicts a 'wound' on the cogito and on man who is 'no longer master and lord within his own house, the mind' (p. 426). The triple 'humiliation' begun by Copernicus at the cosmological level and continued at the biological level by Darwin is now complete at the psychological level of the subject of reflection (pp. 426–427). This humiliation of the cogito is very important for Ricoeur because it becomes 'a necessary step if the philosopher is to move from the illusion of immediate consciousness to authentic self-reflection' – in other words, to move beyond Descartes. See Kathleen Blamey, 'From the Ego to the Self: A Philosophical Itinerary', in Lewis Edwin Hahn (ed.), *The Philosophy of Paul Ricoeur* (Chicago, IL: Open Court, 1995), p. 594.

[28] Ibid., pp. 590–591.

[29] Ibid., p. 591.

[30] Ibid., p. 595.

[31] Ibid., pp. 595–596.

[32] TN3, p. 247; *444.*

[33] Blamey, *From the Ego to the Self*, pp. 596–597.

[34] OA, p. 45; *61.* That the utterer is implied in the utterance is, for Ricoeur, clearly apparent in the substitutability of all illocutionary acts by explicit performatives such as 'I assert that' and 'I promise that'. Through this prefix the 'I' marks its presence in every utterance as 'an intentional prefix of extensional statements' (ibid., p. 45; *60*).

[35] Ibid., p. 45; *61.* The 'I' has a universality of application, indicating that person who designates himself or herself as the subject of utterance; it is the 'pivotal point' around which the other indicators, the deictic terms ('this,' 'here,' 'now') group themselves; but this is the making of its very strangeness (*étrangeté*) in that it fails the test of substitution since it cannot be replaced by what appears to be its own definition – 'any person who, in speaking, designates himself or herself'.

'I' cannot be identified by the path of reference; its universality of application empties it of any given content (ibid., pp. 46–47; *62–63*).

36 Ibid., p. 48; *65*.
37 Ibid., p. 49; *65*.
38 William Golding, *Lord of the Flies* (New York: Capricorn, 1959), pp. 28–42.
39 OA, p. 54; *71*. It is poignant to note that birth and death eluded the 'I can' of Merleau-Ponty: 'I am no more aware of being the true subject of my sensation than of my birth or my death.' See Maurice Merleau-Ponty's *Phenomenology of Perception,* trans. Colin Smith (London: Routledge, 2004), p. 250.
40 TN3, p. 246; *443*. Ricoeur consolidates this conclusion by reference back to Freud and the psychoanalytic experience. By 'working-through' the material of the case history the analysand moves towards his or her goal by substituting for those parts of stories that are 'unintelligible as well as unbearable, a coherent and acceptable story, in which the analysand can recognize his or her self-constancy' (ibid., p. 444; *247*).
41 Blamey, *From the Ego to the Self,* p. 598.
42 Ibid., pp. 577–578.
43 Ibid., p. 579.
44 Ibid., p. 574.
45 TN3, p. 247; *444*.
46 Blamey, *From the Ego to the Self,* p. 598.
47 OA, p. 124; *150*.
48 Ibid.
49 TN3, pp. 248–249; *446–447*, italics added.
50 OA, pp. 11–16; *22–27*. Ricoeur rejects Nietzsche's position as one of 'hyperbolic doubt', claiming that Nietzsche says nothing more than that '*I doubt better than Descartes*' (ibid., p. 15; *27*).

Chapter 5

1 Marcel Proust, *In Search of Lost Time, Volume VI: Time Regained,* trans. A. Mayor and Terence Kilmartin, rev. D. J. Enright (London: Vintage, 2000), p. 263.
2 OA, p. 297; *345*.
3 Ibid., p. 168; *198*.
4 Ibid., p. 172; *202*.
5 TN1, p. 177; *314–315*. The italics are in the original French edition but not in the English translation. The double emphasis is nonetheless important to retain.
6 Ibid., p. 179; *318*.
7 By way of a genetic phenomenology Husserl sought to understand the pre-scientific world before that of Galileo and Newton, a task impeded by the nature of scientific revolution which has as its corollary and precondition 'a concerted forgetfulness of its indirect derivation' (ibid., p. 181; *319*).
8 Ibid., p. 157; *297*.
9 TN2, pp. 97–98; *185*. Ricoeur borrows the term 'carnivalistic genre' from Mikhail Bakhtin.
10 Indeed, his conclusions on narrative identity followed a rereading undertaken a year after finishing his manuscript (TN3, p. 331; *435*).

[11] This last part is further divided into two sections: (1) the aporetics of temporality and (2) the poetics of narrative: history, fiction and time.

[12] Karl Simms, *Paul Ricoeur* (London: Routledge, 2003), p. 1.

[13] This is not at all an unfortunate or forced image – Ricoeur himself says of his threefold mimesis that mimesis$_1$ and mimesis$_3$ 'constitute the two sides [*l'amont et l'aval*] of mimesis$_2$.' (TN1, p. 53; *106*).

[14] Ibid., p. ix; *9*.

[15] Ibid.

[16] Ibid., p. ix; *10*.

[17] Ibid., p. xi; *13*.

[18] Ibid., p. 3; *17*.

[19] Ibid., p. 53; *107*. We will note here that Ricoeur engages in an unspoken and unquestioned hierarchization, which places concordance above discordance, the one as adjective, the other as noun.

[20] Ibid., p. 16; *40–41*. This is achieved by Augustine in the example of the recitation of a verse by heart, specifically, *Deus creator omnium*.

[21] Augustine, *The Confessions of St. Augustine*, trans. F. J. Sheed (London: Sheed and Ward, 1948), Book 11, 28:37.

[22] TN1, p. 21; *48*.

[23] See p. 32 (*68*) of TN1 for a full discussion on this point. In particular, Ricoeur removes some of the restrictions and prohibitions imposed by the *Poetics* on the applicability of the two terms to fields beyond the dramatic and the epic.

[24] Ibid.

[25] Ibid., p. 33; *69*.

[26] This is 'narrative' in a much broader sense than for Aristotle; for him, the term is confined to diegetic (*diēgēsis*) poetry. In modern cinema studies, diegesis refers to the content of the narrative, the fictional world described inside the story. See Susan Hayward's *Cinema Studies* (London: Routledge, 2000), pp. 84–86.

[27] Aristotle, *Poetics*, 50a16–24.

[28] TN1, p. 41; *84*.

[29] Ibid., p. 38; *79*.

[30] Ibid., p. 41; *84*.

[31] Ibid., p. 41; *85*.

[32] Ibid., p. 43; *88*.

[33] Reversal: 'a change from one state of affairs to its exact opposite:' (Aristotle, *Poetics*, 52a22).

[34] Ricoeur emphasizes the requirement to retain the elements of this model in theories of narrativity that address the non-tragic. We will continue to concentrate on the tragic model as a basis for human self-narrative for as long as we discuss narrative identity. This is a stated presupposition of Ricoeur, justified in two senses: first, we understand humans as acting and suffering individuals, as undergoing reversals of fortune, as prey to accident and misfortune as well as reversals of the opposite variety (the bad to the good), as empathic in the recognition of others' emotional worlds and others' good fortune and tragic misfortune – and we suffer with the ones we love and even with those we do not even know. This is our affective world, both within and outside us. Secondly, we are, for want of a better word, 'constructed' on a fault-line – rather like San Francisco – that predisposes us to err, to suffer, to cause others to suffer, to do evil. Ricoeur addresses

this in considerable detail in *Fallible Man,* trans. by Charles Kelbley (New York: Fordham University Press, 1986). That humans are prone, faulty, designed on a basic or existential error, is essentially Ricoeur's fundamental hypothesis in his earlier works, and it is the central precept of the tragic character that by way of some fault, through which he is subject to evil, he is prevented from achieving excellence (TN1, p. 91; *45*). This concept of the acting and suffering individual returns throughout *Oneself as Another* and is quite central to the series of studies contained within. This has of course the ring of common sense to it – in spite of those who will compose their self-narratives on the presupposition that 'Life is Beautiful'.

35 Ibid., p. 46; *93.*

36 Ibid., p. 50; *101.*

37 Ibid., p. 55; *111.*

38 Ibid., pp. 56–57; *112.*

39 Ibid., p. 3; *17.*

40 Ibid., p. 65; *127.*

41 Ibid., p. 66; *128–129* (italics added).

42 Ricoeur argues that this kinship is particularly so with what Kant called the reflective judgement (as opposed to the determining one) because the reflective judgement refers to the sort of thinking at work 'in the aesthetic judgement of taste and in the teleological judgement applied to organic wholes' (ibid., p. 66; *128*). This will be important in our later reflections on Schelling and Deleuze.

43 Ibid., p. 70; *135.*

44 Ibid., p. 68; *132.*

45 Ibid.

46 Ibid., p. 68; *133.*

47 Ibid., p. 69; *135.*

48 Ibid., p. 70; *135.*

49 Ibid., p. 71; *136.* This intersection of internal and external horizons carries with it a substantial ontological presupposition regarding the nature of linguistic and extra-linguistic reference. We will deal with this in Chapter 9 when we address the connectors between a Deleuzian and Ricoeurian ontology of the self(s).

50 We should note here that 'violence' is precisely the term used by Deleuze to refer to the initiation into thinking provoked by the sign (PS, p. 15; *24*).

51 TN1, p. 73; *140.* It is important to note a difficulty in McLaughlin and Pellauer's translation of the two terms 'concordance' and 'discordance'. In the French edition Ricoeur clearly distinguishes between the adjectival and substantive forms of discordance and concordance. For example: '*L'art de composer consiste à faire paraître concordante cette discordance*' and '*C'est dans la vie que le discordant ruine la concordance, non dans l'art tragique*' (*88*); or '*La modèle tragique n'est pas purement un modèle de concordance, mais de concordance discordante*' (*86*) and '*La concordance discordante est visée plus directement encore par l'analyse de l'effet de surprise*' (*87*). These are correctly translated by McLaughlin and Pellauer in their corresponding English adjectival and substantive versions ('concordance', 'concordant', 'discordance' and 'discordant'). However, later in the text, in the chapter 'Time and Narrative: Threefold Mimesis' the substantive is translated as an adjective; for example, Ricoeur writes that the deviation from the rule-governed traditional

narratives comes into play at every level even in relation to the '*principe formel même de la concordance-discordance*' (*Temps et Récit 1*, 135). This is translated in English into 'the formal principle of concordant discordance' (p. 70). This translation of the substantive for the adjectival is repeated throughout the text and has the effect of reducing discordance to concordance where Ricoeur either did not intend this or wanted the ambiguity to be retained. The hyphenated 'concordance-discordance' used by Ricoeur suggests strongly a hybridized term where neither element has priority or where one is a subsidiary of the other. We will proceed to use the hybridized term from now on wherever this was the original intention of Ricoeur in *Temps et Récit*. The importance of retaining the original meaning of Ricoeur's, indeed even his ambiguity, will become clearer later in this work.

[52] TN1, pp. 72–73; *139–140*.

[53] This Deleuzian notion is an interpretation of Nietzsche's twin concepts of the 'eternal return' and the 'will to power' and is explicated in Deleuze's *Nietzsche and Philosophy*.

[54] TN1, p. 83; *156*.

[55] Ibid., pp. 83–84; *157*.

[56] Ibid., p. 87; *162*.

[57] Ibid., p. 144; *256*.

[58] Thus there can be no 'substantive philosophies of history' that include the future since any narrative sentences about this future can only be given the form of a sentence about the past (ibid., p. 144; *257*). This point is made with reference to Hegel or any such philosophy that claims to encompass the whole of history.

[59] From Danto's *Analytic Philosophy of History*, quoted by Ricoeur (ibid., p. 147; *262*).

[60] Ibid., p. 144; *258*.

[61] As explained earlier in this chapter ('Methodology: Questioning Back').

[62] TN1, p. 207; *363*. The details of this crucial argument are in the pivotal chapter 6 of TN1.

[63] Ibid., p. 175; *311*.

[64] Ibid., p. 179; *318*.

[65] Ibid., p. 181; *320*.

[66] Ricoeur provides a definition of singular causal explanation (based on the work of Max Weber and Raymond Aron) as a process of logic whereby we construct in our imagination 'a different course of events'; then we calculate 'the probable consequences of the unreal course of events'; and finally we compare these with the real course of events (ibid., p. 183; *324*). See also Max Weber's *The Methodology of the Social Sciences*, trans. Edward Shils and Henry Finch (New York: Free Press, 1949) and Raymond Aron's *Introduction to the Philosophy of History: An Essay on the Limits of Historical Objectivity*, trans. George J. Irwin (Boston, MA: Beacon, 1961).

[67] TN1, p. 221; *391*.

[68] Ibid., p. 230; *404*.

[69] Ibid., p. 226; *397*.

[70] Aron, *Introduction to the Philosophy of History*, p. 160.

[71] TN3, p. 246; *443*.

[72] This refers to the manner in which Virginia Woolf links up the depth of the inner selves of her characters and their fits of memory with their everydayness and their

corresponding actions in the world (see TN2, p. 104; *195–196* and p. 189, n. 8; *195–196*, n. 2).

[73] For a variation on the argument that the self is not alone a narrative but also a non-narrative, see Galen Strawson's 'Against Narrative', in B. Gertler and L. Shapiro (eds), *Arguing About the Mind* (London: Routledge, 2007), pp. 248–261. Strawson argues for two different forms of self-experience, the episodic and the diachronic (closely paralleling the non-narrative and the narrative).

[74] TN2, p. 10; *22*.

Chapter 6

[1] TN1, p. 80; *150*.

[2] Adam Bryx and Gary Genosko, 'Transversality', in Adrian Parr (ed.), *The Deleuze Dictionary* (Edinburgh: Edinburgh University Press), pp. 285–286.

[3] Adrian Parr, 'Deterritorialisation/Reterritorialisation', in *The Deleuze Dictionary*, p. 67.

[4] Adam Bryx and Gary Genosko, *Deleuze Dictionary*, pp. 285–286.

[5] TP, p. 239; *293*.

[6] Ibid., p. 239; *292*.

[7] Ibid.

[8] Robert C. Solomon, *Continental Philosophy since 1750: The Rise and Fall of the Self – A History of Western Philosophy: 7* (Oxford: Oxford University Press, 1988), p. 39.

[9] OA, p. 169; *199*.

[10] Ibid., p. 170; *200*.

[11] Ibid.

[12] Ibid., p. 177; *208*.

[13] Ibid., p. 178; *209–210*.

[14] Ibid., p. 178; *210*. Ricoeur acknowledges his debt to Martha Nussbaum for the term 'fragility of goodness' taken from her book *The Fragility of Goodness: Luck and Ethics in Greek Tragedy and Philosophy* (Cambridge: Cambridge University Press, 1986).

[15] OA, p. 179; *210*.

[16] Marcel Proust, *In Search of Lost Time, Volume 1: Swann's Way*, trans. Scott Moncrieff and Terence Kilmartin, rev. D. J. Enright (Vintage: London, 2002), pp. 54–55.

[17] TN1, p. 80; *150*.

[18] Ibid., p. 80; *151*.

[19] Ibid., p. 81; *152*.

[20] PS, p. 3; *10*.

[21] Ibid., p. 4; *10*.

[22] PS, p. 7; *14*.

[23] Ibid.

[24] Ibid.

[25] Theodor Adorno, *Notes to Literature, Volume 1*, ed. Rolf Tiedermann, trans. Shierry Weber Nicholsen (New York: Columbia University Press, 1991), pp. 174–175.

[26] TP, p. 25; *36*.

27 Ibid., p. 98; *123*.

28 Proust, *Swann's Way*, p. 34.

29 Marcel Proust, *In Search of Lost Time, Volume VI: Time Regained*, trans. A Mayor and Terence Kilmartin, rev. D. J. Enright (London: Vintage, 2000), p. 451.

30 TN1, p. 80; *150*.

31 OA, p. 241; *281*.

32 Jacques Derrida, 'Le Facteur de la Vérité', in *The Post Card: From Socrates to Freud and Beyond*, trans. A. Bass (Chicago, IL and London: University of Chicago Press, 1987), pp. 413–496. Derrida criticizes Lacan for making the phallus a 'privileged signifier' that operates as a transcendental element, one that acts as an ideal guarantee of meaning; Lacan therefore reintroduces the notion of logocentrism, articulates this with phallocentrism and develops a new system of thought – 'phallogocentrism'.

33 See also Richard Kearney's dialogue with Derrida in *Dialogues with Contemporary Continental Thinkers* (Manchester: Manchester University Press, 1984), p. 121.

34 Ibid., p. 122.

35 OA, p. 178; *209–210*.

36 TN2, pp. 131–132; *247–248*.

37 Ibid., p. 133; *250*.

38 Ibid., p. 145; *273*.

39 Ricoeur argues that the *Angst* of death that hangs over the openness of 'the potentiality-for-being' ultimately conceals 'the joy of the spark of life'. And he refers to the silence in *Being and Time* about the fact of birth, contrasting this with Hannah Arendt's theme of 'natality', which she argues 'underlies the categories of the *vita activa*: labour, work, action'. Ricoeur concludes that this 'jubilation' should be 'opposed to what does indeed seem to be an obsession of metaphysics with the problem of death' (MHF, p. 357; *465*).

40 Ibid., pp. 374–375; *488–489*.

41 OA, p. 241; *281*.

42 Ibid., p. 244; *284*.

43 Ibid., p. 245; *285*.

44 We should note Ricoeur's use of this word 'untimely' and its reference to Nietzsche's *Untimely Meditations*, or as they are translated in *Memory, History, Forgetting, Unfashionable Observations*.

45 MHF, p. 287; *377*.

46 OA, p. 243; *283*.

47 Ibid., p. 245; *285*.

48 Luce Irigaray, *Speculum of the Other Woman*, trans. Gillian C. Gill (New York: Cornell University Press, 1992), pp. 220–221.

49 Tina Chanter, 'Antigone's Dilemma', in Robert Bernasconi and Simon Critchley (eds), *Re-reading Levinas* (Indianapolis: Indiana University Press, 1991), p. 140.

50 Pamela Anderson, 'Re-reading Myth in Philosophy: Hegel, Ricoeur and Irigaray Reading Antigone', in Morny Joy (ed.), *Paul Ricoeur and Narrative: Context and Contestation* (Calgary, AB: University of Calgary Press, 1997), p. 60.

51 Ibid., p. 61.

52 OA, p. 243; *284*.

53 Ibid., p. 249; *290*.

⁵⁴ Friedrich Nietzsche, *On the Advantage and Disadvantage of History for Life*, trans. Peter Preuss (Indianapolis, IN: Hackett, 1980), p. 17.

⁵⁵ See for example Henry Isaac Venema's central argument that *ipse* selfhood always collapses 'into a semantics of *idem* identity' in *Identifying Selfhood: Imagination, Narrative and Hermeneutics in the Thought of Paul Ricoeur* (New York: State University of New York Press, 2000), p. 136. This is because, for Venema, there is a fundamental fault in Ricoeur's construction. He asks, 'If the "what?" of selfhood is semantically expressed as sameness, how can the question "who?" give expression to a form of selfhood that is different from sameness when both questions are connected to each other through a common network of intersignification' (p. 136).

⁵⁶ OA, p. 179; *210*.

Chapter 7

¹ TN3, p. 246; *443*.

² OA, p. 297; *345*.

³ Deleuze is referring to a specific way of reading books in his 'Letter to a Harsh Critic' (N, pp. 3–12); however, it is symptomatic of a distinction he makes throughout his writings regarding the manner in which we ask or problematize what is before us.

⁴ Ibid., p. 8.

⁵ Ibid.

⁶ MHF, p. 97; *117*. It is of course arguable that the self in Kant is not indeed fragmented (or that only the empirical self is) but fully unified through the transcendental unity of apperception (see Kant's *Critique of Pure Reason*, rev. and trans. J. M. D. Meiklejohn, ed. Vasilis Politis (London: Everyman, 1993), [A107] and [B153–156]). However, the being both inside and outside time remains problematic (see Henry Allison's *Kant's Transcendental Idealism* (New Haven, CT: Yale University Press, 1983), p. 289).

⁷ Robert C. Solomon, *Continental Philosophy since 1750: The Rise and Fall of the Self – A History of Western Philosophy: 7* (Oxford: Oxford University Press, 1988), p. 48.

⁸ Ibid.

⁹ Ibid., p. 50. Fichte's freedom 'is not to be found only in the realm of action, but also, and even more importantly, in the realm of thought, in the play of the imagination – as Kant himself had argued'. We will see later that Deleuze, in the spirit of Fichte, will argue for the possibility of additional faculties.

¹⁰ Ibid., p. 53.

¹¹ Ibid., p. 55.

¹² Deleuze acknowledges what he considers to be Schelling's most important contribution to philosophy, that is, that he brought 'difference out of the night of the Identical, and with finer, more varied and more terrifying flashes of lightening than those of contradiction: with *progressivity*' (DR, p. 240; *246*). Deleuze's philosophical influences are well known – he wrote copiously on them as part of 'history of philosophy', but he did not write a book on Schelling. Perhaps one disguises or is unaware of that which influences one most. It has been suggested that Nietzsche had been significantly influenced by the writings of Max Stirner,

although he fails to mention him anywhere in his own work. See Rüdiger Safranski's *Nietzsche: A Philosophical Biography* (London: Granta Books, 2002), pp. 125–126.

[13] Andrew Bowie, *Schelling and Modern European Philosophy: An Introduction* (London: Routledge, 1993), p. 4.

[14] Bowie notes that 'a central interpretative problem' with Schelling is that many of his ideas 'begin as conceptions in grand Idealist philosophy, but seem most productive when they have been re-worked on the level of conceptions . . . that are concerned with the world of individual human consciousness. The key question underlying these preoccupations, though, is precisely the question of how consciousness is conceived in relation to the rest of nature, and it is here that Schelling arrives at some of his greatest insights' (ibid., pp. 8–9).

[15] Ibid., p. 16.

[16] Kant, *Critique of Pure Reason*, p. 100 [B133].

[17] Intuition as a method plays a central role in the philosophy of Schelling, as it does in that of Deleuze who takes it from Bergson. For a concise summary of the influence of Bergson on Deleuze, see Patrick Hayden's *Multiplicity and Becoming: The Pluralist Empiricism* (New York: Peter Lang, 1998), pp. 39–48.

[18] Bowie, *Schelling and Modern European Philosophy*, p. 18.

[19] Ibid., p. 21.

[20] Ibid., p. 27.

[21] F. W. J. Schelling, *System of Transcendental Idealism (1800)*, trans. Peter Heath (Charlottesville: University Press of Virginia, 1978), p. 27.

[22] Michael Vater, 'Introduction', in Schelling, *System of Transcendental Idealism*, p. xxiii.

[23] Schelling, *System of Transcendental Idealism*, p. 210.

[24] Ibid., p. 28.

[25] A Spinozistic inspiration to these characterizations of the self is argued for throughout Dale Snow's *Schelling and the End of Idealism* (Albany: State University of New York Press, 1996). See particularly, pp. 45–54.

[26] Edward Beach, *The Potencie(s) of the Gods* (Albany: State University of New York Press, 1994), p. 85.

[27] Schelling, *System of Transcendental Idealism*, p. 231.

[28] Ibid., pp. 74–75.

[29] Ibid., pp. 45–46, 50. Vater notes that the self in Schelling is 'an identity which is not an identity but a synthesis; a synthesis which is not one synthesis but many synthesis packed into one; not a timeless and immediate resolution of conflicts of its opposed modes of activity, but an indefinitely extended and ongoing partial solution' (Vater, 'Introduction', p. xxx).

[30] Schelling, *System of Transcendental Idealism*, pp. 51, 114.

[31] Vater, 'Introduction', p. xxx.

[32] Schelling, *System of Transcendental Idealism*, p. 49. Vater notes that the self for Schelling is 'an activity and a principle of activity . . . in conflict with itself, so that its life can be spoken of as the unfolding of the infinite contradictions implicit within it' (Vater, 'Introduction', p. xxxiii).

[33] Schelling, *System of Transcendental Idealism*, p. 232.

[34] The other two axioms are as follows: (1) 'A form which is absolutely unconditional, the form of the positing of an axiom, which is conditioned by nothing but

that axiom, and which therefore does not presuppose any other content of a superior axiom, in short, the form of unconditionality (axiom of contradiction, analytic form)' and (2) 'A form which is conditioned, which can be possible only through the content of a superior axiom – form of conditionality (axiom of sufficient reason, synthetic form)'. See F. W. J. Schelling, *The Unconditional in Human Knowledge: Four Early Essays (1794–1796)*, trans. Fritz Marti (Lewisburg, PA: Bucknell University Press, 1980), p. 50.

[35] Schelling, *System of Transcendental Idealism*, p. 176.

[36] For a further reading of the relationship between Deleuze and Schelling, see Alberto Gualandi's *Deleuze* (Paris: Les Belles Lettres, 2003), pp. 31–34. '*En se référent à tout ce qui dans la science est "nouveau et mineur" – les doctrines indéterministes de la matière, les théories des systèmes ouverts et du chaos . . . Deleuze définit les conditions pour une "nouvelle alliance" entre philosophie et science qui, dans la forme d'une ontology du Devenir et de la Différence, actualise et réactive les philosophies de la Nature de Schelling*' (p. 34). Also see Jason M. Wirth (ed.), *Schelling Now: Contemporary Readings* (Bloomington, IN: Indianapolis University Press, 2005) for a discussion on the importance of Schelling to several contemporary philosophical debates.

[37] Manuel DeLanda, *Intensive Science and Virtual Philosophy* (London: Continuum, 2002), p. 5.

[38] Ibid., p. 10.

[39] Ibid., p. 6.

[40] Ibid.

[41] DR, p. 37; *44–45*.

[42] Ibid., pp. 40–41; *48*.

[43] Ibid., p. 43; *51*.

[44] Ibid., p. 60; *70–71*. This point is reinforced again and again by Deleuze – 'difference remains subordinated to identity, reduced to the negative, incarcerated within similitude and analogy' (ibid., p. 61; *71*) and the problem is built on the error of 'confusing the concept of difference in itself with the inscription of difference in the identity of the concept in general' (ibid.).

[45] Ibid.

[46] Ibid., p. 62; *72*. For a fuller discussion on the problems of negating negation and opposing opposition see Judith Norman's article 'Nietzsche contra *Contra*: Difference and Opposition', *Continental Philosophy Review*, 33 (2000), pp. 189–206.

[47] DR, p. 62; *72*.

[48] Ibid., p. 71; *82*. This statement of Deleuze has been translated by Paul Patton as 'The task of modern philosophy has been defined: to overturn Platonism' but this misrepresents the 'task' at hand. James Williams argues that *renversement* would be better translated as 'reversal' or 'inversion'. He argues convincingly that 'if the line is read in terms of . . . positioning Deleuze as straightforwardly opposed to . . . Plato, then the consistency of the arguments of *Difference and Repetition* and . . . Deleuze's definition of difference will have been missed.' See James Williams, *Gilles Deleuze's 'Difference and Repetition': A Critical Introduction and Guide* (Edinburgh: Edinburgh University Press, 2003), p. 79. Deleuze's very next sentence only goes to reinforce this interpretation: '*Que ce renversement conserve beaucoup de caractères platoniciens n'est pas seulement inévitable, mais souhaitable*' (*Différence et répetition*, p. *82*). See also Heidegger on Nietzsche: 'Nietzsche himself

quite early characterizes his philosophy as inverted Platonism; yet the inversion does not eliminate the fundamentally Platonic position.' See Martin Heidegger, *Nietzsche, Vol. II: The Eternal Recurrence of the Same*, trans. David Farrell Krell (San Francisco: Harper Collins, 1991), p. 205.

49 DR, p. 63; *73.*

50 Ibid., pp. 63–64; *74.* The equation of difference with affirmation is surely a development of Schelling's '*I is I*'. Schelling addresses the requirement that 'philosophy – if it is to be a science – must be governed by a plainly absolute axiom that has to contain the condition of all content as well as of all form if it is really to condition it at all.' See Schelling, *The Unconditional in Human Knowledge*, p. 42. In so doing he argues for an 'axiom of all axioms' that 'furnishes the general form of the connection [of content and meaning], the form of the reciprocal determination of the content by the form, and of the form by the content' (pp. 43–44), such that they are 'mutually conditioned' (p. 44). This axiom, based on the 'criterion of absolute unconditionality' (ibid.) can only be, for Schelling, '*I is I*' (p. 45). Schelling explains this as follows: '*I* is the content of the axiom; *I is I* is the material and the formal form, which induce each other mutually' (ibid.). This is the original 'self-posited I' (ibid.).

51 DR, p. 67; *78.*

52 Ibid., p. 67; *79.*

53 LS, p. 51; *66.*

54 DR, p. 68; *79.* It is this law that constitutes 'the in-itself of the represented (A is A) and . . . the for-itself of the representant (Self = Self)'.

55 Ibid. Deleuze sees modern art as realizing these conditions insofar as it 'becomes a veritable *theatre* of metamorphoses and permutations . . . where nothing is fixed, a labyrinth without [Ariadne's] thread'. Modern art exits 'the domain of representation in order to become "experience" . . . or science of the sensible' (ibid.). The parallels with Schelling's aggrandisement of art are worth drawing. For Shelling, art, production and intuition fully coincide. Art 'ever and again continues to speak to us of what philosophy cannot depict . . . namely the unconscious element in acting and producing, and its original identity with the conscious' (Schelling, *System of Transcendental Idealism*, p. 231).

56 DR, p. 69. *80.*

57 Ibid. Such crowned anarchies mean no more than 'overturned hierarchies' where the identical is subordinated to the different (ibid., p. 51; *60.*)

58 Ibid., p. 69; *80.*

59 Ibid., p. 165; *170.*

60 Ibid., p. 168; *173.*

61 Questioning this so-called enslaving image of thought is first raised in *Nietzsche and Philosophy* where Deleuze notes that Nietzsche's aim was to free philosophy from nihilism by introducing 'a new way of thinking, an overthrow of the principle on which thought depends' so as to effect 'a transmutation' from being only able 'to think in terms of *ressentiment* and bad conscience' (NP, p. 35; *40*).

62 DR, p. 165; *170.*

63 Ibid., p. 164; *169.*

64 Ibid., p. 165; *170.*

65 Ibid., p. 166; *171.*

66 Ibid., p. 207; *216–217*.

67 Ibid., p. 185; *192–193*.

68 Ibid., p. xv (Preface to the English Edition).

69 Ibid., pp. 170–171; *176*.

70 Ibid., pp. 187–188; *194*.

71 See Deleuze on Antonin Artaud, ibid., p. 185; *192*.

72 For a concise reading of the implications of this 'thought without image' to pedagogy and a suggested convergence between Deleuze and Dewey's philosophy of education, see Inna Semetsky's 'Deleuze's New Image of Thought, or Dewey Revisited', *Educational Philosophy and Theory*, 35 No. 1 (2003), pp. 17–29.

73 DR, p. 172; *177*.

74 Ibid., p. 172; *178*. Deleuze regarded Kant as very close to reversing (*renverser*) the dogmatic image of thought (ibid.) and effectively achieving this in part in the *Critique of Judgement* where the harmony of the faculties is unclasped: 'Kant's *Critique of Judgement* is an unrestrained work of old age, which his successors have still not caught up with; all the minds faculties overcome the very limits that Kant had so carefully laid down in the work of his prime' (WP, p. 2; *8*). Also, for Deleuze, the doctrine of the faculties is 'an entirely necessary component of the system of philosophy' (DR, p. 180; *186*).

75 Ibid., p. 173; *178*. See also KCP, pp. 31–32; *36*. For a fuller discussion of the relationship between the imagination, understanding and reason in Kant's *Critique of Judgement*, see Rudolf Makkreel's 'Imagination and Temporality in Kant's Theory of the Sublime', *The Journal of Aesthetics and Art Criticism*, 42 No. 3 (Spring, 1984), pp. 303–315.

76 DR, p. 174; *180*.

77 Ibid., p. 175; *181*.

78 Ibid., p. 176; *182*.

79 That which can only be sensed, shorn of the common accord of the faculties is 'the being of the sensible' or what Deleuze calls the *sentiendum* (ibid.). Deleuze also describes it as designating 'the paradoxical existence of a "something" which simultaneously cannot be sensed (from the point of view of the empirical exercise) and can only be sensed (from the point of view of the transcendental exercise)' (ibid., p. 296; *304*). In going beyond our experience, 'an extraordinary broadening out forces us to think a pure perception identical to the whole of matter, a pure memory identical to the whole of the past. It is in this sense that Bergson . . . compares the approach of philosophy to the procedure of the infinitesimal calculus. When we have benefited in experience from a little light which shows us a line of articulation, all that remains is to extend it beyond experience – just as mathematicians reconstitute, with the infinitely small elements that they perceive of the real curve, "the curve itself stretching out into the darkness behind them"' (B, p. 27; *18*).

80 DR, p. 176; *182*.

81 Ibid. Deleuze uses the terms spirit (*esprit*) and soul (*âme*) and indeed 'the virtual' somewhat interchangeably to refer to which is outside or apart from the actual or material (C2, p. 80).

82 DR, p. 177; *183*.

83 Ibid., p. 177; *183–184*. Each faculty can be forced towards its limit – for the imagination, towards that which can only be imagined (the *imaginandum*) but is at the same time impossible to imagine; for language, towards that which can only be said (the *loquendum*) but which would be silence at the same time (ibid., p. 180; *186–187*). Deleuze suggests that there may well be faculties yet to be discovered whose existence is not even suspected or whose functioning has been repressed by the form of common sense.

84 William Shakespeare, *Macbeth* (Middlesex: New Penguin, 1967), III.2.52–53.

85 G. K. Hunter, 'Introduction', in *Macbeth* by William Shakespeare (Middlesex: New Penguin, 1967), p. 9.

86 Shakespeare, *Macbeth*, III.2.36.

87 Ibid., I.7.39–41. 'Art thou afeard/To be the same in thine own act and valour/As thou art in desire?'

88 Hunter, 'Introduction', p. 11.

89 Ibid.

90 DR, pp. 177–178; *184*.

91 Ibid., p. 181; *187*.

92 Ibid., p. 178; *184*.

93 Ibid., p. 181; *187–188*. Difference-in-itself (also referred to as authentic or internal difference) 'does not occur between self-contained entities . . . but between the tendencies of which each individual entity is the . . . expression within a finite segment of time' (Giovanni Borradori, 'The Temporalization of Difference: Reflections on Deleuze's Interpretation of Bergson', *Continental Philosophy Review*, 34 No. 1 (2001), pp. 1–20).

94 Ronald Bogue, 'Search, Swim and See: Deleuze's Apprenticeship to Signs and Pedagogy of Images', *Educational Philosophy and Theory*, 36 No. 3 (2004), pp. 327–342.

95 DR, p. 178; *184*. Deleuze also refers to this as 'an unlimited becoming' in reference to the Pythagorian terms *peras* and *apieron* (ibid., p. 296; *305*).

96 For the centrality of Bergson to Deleuze's philosophy, see Keith Ansell Pearson's *Philosophy and the Adventure of the Virtual: Bergson and the Time of Life* (London: Routledge, 2002).

97 B, p. 38; *30–31*. See also Henri Bergson's *Time and Free Will: An Essay on the Immediate Data of Consciousness*, trans. F. L. Pogson (New York: Dover, 2001), pp. 120–122.

98 B, p. 38; *31*.

99 Ibid., p. 32; *23*.

100 Ibid., p. 40; *32*.

101 Henri Bergson, *Time and Free Will*, pp. 120–121.

102 Ibid., p. 90.

103 Ibid., p. 98.

104 Ibid., p. 100.

105 Ibid., p. 101.

106 Ibid., p. 104.

107 Ibid., p. 110.

108 Ibid., p. 112.

[109] Ibid., p. 122. We remember Derrida's argument in favour of a new language for the non-phallogocentric.

[110] Ibid., p. 123.

[111] Ibid., p. 125.

[112] Ibid., p. 124.

[113] Ibid., p. 125.

[114] Ibid.

[115] Ibid., p. 126.

[116] Ibid., p. 128.

[117] Ibid., p. 129. Italics added.

[118] Ibid., p. 131. 'In the human soul there are only *processes.*'

[119] DeLanda, *Intensive Science and Virtual Philosophy*, p. 13.

[120] A bicycle has ten degrees of freedom and therefore requires a ten-dimensional space to represent the properties of its physical system. Given that it has the following moving parts: handlebars, front wheels, crank–chain–rear wheel assembly and two pedals, then each of these five parts can change its position and momentum, yielding ten degrees of freedom. The state of the bicycle at any particular point in time becomes a single point in this manifold, plotted from its ten coordinates (ibid.).

[121] Ibid.

[122] Ibid., p. 14.

[123] There is however a clear trade-off here in that we have exchanged 'the complexity of the object's changes of state for the complexity of the modelling space' (ibid.).

[124] Ibid. This contrasts with an essentialist view that describes the bubble as displaying the essence of sphericity.

[125] Ibid., p. 29.

[126] Ibid., p. 16.

[127] See Giovanna Borradori, 'On the Presence of Bergson in Deleuze's Nietzsche', *Philosophy Today*, 43 (1999), pp. 140–145. Deleuze's use of singularities or 'points of attraction' owes a substantial debt to Bergson's emphasis on tendencies.

[128] DeLanda, *Intensive Science and Virtual Philosophy*, p. 16.

[129] For example, temperature is the critical parameter that changes water from its single point of attraction that defines it as liquid to another single point of attraction which defines it as steam.

[130] Ibid., p. 21.

[131] Ibid.

[132] Extensive properties (length, area, volume and quantities) are intrinsically divisible while intensive properties (like temperature or pressure) are not. If a volume of water is divided into two equal volumes, each will be half the original volume; the temperature of each volume will not however be so divided without involving a qualitative change in kind, that is, by heating the container from underneath, introducing a temperature differential across it and throwing the system into disequilibrium. If we push the temperature differential further we can induce a phase transition to convection patterns of fluid motion where symmetry is lost.

[133] Ibid., p. 25.

[134] Ibid., p. 61.

[135] Ibid., p. 62. DeLanda gives a concise discussion of the two intensive processes in embryogenesis, 'one related to the production of extensies, the other to the production of qualities' (ibid., pp. 62–65).

[136] Ibid., p. 64.

Chapter 8

[1] Gilles Deleuze, 'Bergson's Conception of Difference', in John Mullarkey (ed.), *The New Bergson* (Manchester: Manchester University Press, 1999), pp. 42–65.

[2] DR, p. 313; *323*. The Deleuzian terms 'differentiation' and 'differenciation' will be explained in greater detail later. For the moment, 'differentiation' may be taken as a mathematical term and 'differenciation' as a biologic process.

[3] WP, pp. 70–73; *68–71*.

[4] Ilya Prigogine and Isabelle Stengers, *Order Out of Chaos: Man's New Dialogue with Nature* (London: Heinemann, 1984), p. xxvii.

[5] Quoted by Prigogine and Stengers, *Order Out of Chaos*, p. 11.

[6] Ibid., pp. 12–13.

[7] Ibid., p. 14.

[8] A state space filled with trajectories based on experiment and prediction is known as a system's 'phase portrait'.

[9] See chapter 2 titled 'The Multiplicity of Conscious States – the Idea of Duration' of Henri Bergson's *Time and Free Will: An Essay on the Immediate Data of Consciousness*, trans. F. L. Pogson (New York: Dover, 2001), pp. 75–139.

[10] DR, p. 319; *330*.

[11] Ibid., p. 193; *201*.

[12] Ibid., p. 215; *219*.

[13] Ibid., p. 203; *212*. In chapter 4 of *Difference and Repetition*, Deleuze lays out the principles for a general differential philosophy by making some subtle adjustments to a Kantian framework. Ideas present three objective moments – they are themselves undetermined but are determinable in relation to objects of experience and finally 'bear the ideal of determination' in relation to the concepts of the understanding (ibid., p. 216; *220*). Deleuze notes that these three moments are incarnated within the Kantian philosophy in distinct ideas: 'the Self is above all undetermined, the World determinable, and God is the ideal of determination' (ibid., p. 216; *221*).

[14] In retaining the Kantian threefold structure, Deleuze applies the symbol dx as a principle of the undetermined (dx, dy), as the reciprocally determined (dy/dx) and as a principle of complete determination (values for dy/dx). In short, 'dx is the Idea . . . the "problem" and its being' (ibid., p. 217; *222*). The analogy with differential calculus is straightforward. If the progressively actualized solution to a problem in the form of an equation is a curved line, then we can see that its problematic (for which it is a solution) is only determined by the relationship of a multiplicity of singular points – the curved line ultimately 'subsumes the distribution of distinctive singular points' (ibid., p. 223; *228*). Deleuze does not use differential calculus as a metaphor but rather sees it as corresponding to the

nature and genesis of Ideas, or more precisely to their specifically dialectical conditions; for him, this is the very foundation of our 'adventure of Ideas', the 'alphabet of what it means to think' (ibid., p. 229; *235*). It also allows him to conclude that Ideas are multiplicities and given the nature of multiplicities it follows, against Plato, that the Idea is not an abstract universal but a concrete one, a 'system of differential relations between genetic elements' (ibid., p. 227; *234*) This mathematization of thought draws Deleuze back to Plato, although in reverse, since the ideality is immanent to experience. For a full account of Deleuze's employment of mathematics see *Virtual Mathematics: The Logic of Difference*, ed. Simon Duffy (Bolton: Clinamen Press, 2006).

[15] DR, p. 220; *225*.

[16] Ibid., p. 229; *235*.

[17] James Williams, *Gilles Deleuze's 'Difference and Repetition': A Critical Introduction and Guide* (Edinburgh: Edinburgh University Press, 2003), p. 143.

[18] DR, pp. 76–77; *88–89*.

[19] Bergson, *Time and Free Will*, p. 104.

[20] B, p. 26; *17*.

[21] See Manuel DeLanda, *Intensive Science and Virtual Philosophy* (London: Continuum, 2002), p. 123. As DeLanda notes, it is not enough to replace transcendent entities with immanent natural states – what is crucial for Deleuze is to overthrow them with '*mechanisms of immanence* (however speculative) to explain the existence, relative autonomy and genetic power of the virtual'.

[22] The metaphor of the sarcophagus as a space for the virtual and the memorial is not idle; Augustine used a similar metaphor when developing the 'storehouse' of memory: 'forgetfulness obliterates [buries] all that we remember' (Augustine, *The Confessions of St. Augustine*, trans. F. J. Sheed (London: Sheed and Ward, 1948), 10.8, 214).

[23] See Ronald Bogue's 'Search, Swim and See: Deleuze's Apprenticeship to Signs and Pedagogy of Images', *Educational Philosophy and Theory*, 36 No. 3 (2004), pp. 327–342.

[24] PS, p. 4; *10*. We may argue that this Deleuzian map is hardly devoid of representation – and this is true; however, its principle domains of expression are those of topography and diagrammatics, both of which attempt to transgress representational systems.

[25] Gottfried Leibniz, 'The Monadology', in Anthony Savile, *Routledge Philosophy Guidebook on Leibniz and the Monadology* (London: Routledge, 2000), § 17. Leibniz's argument is that even if we could see the shapes and movements of the brain, perception, appetition and feeling could still not be explained on mechanical principles. We could not see consciousness or thought or the impulse of life.

[26] This is an extension of Paul Churchland's argument against Leibniz's *Gedankenexperiment* from *The Monadology*. Churchland argues that if we were able to see at the microscopic and cellular level we would indeed see the processes of changing mental states (memories being laid down in protein formation, the release of enzymes and neurotransmitters at moments of increased attention and so forth). See Paul Churchland's *The Engine of Reason: The Seat of the Soul* (Cambridge, MA: MIT Press, 1995), pp. 191–194.

[27] WP, p. 39; *41*.

[28] Ibid., p. 38; *41*.

[29] See Daniel Dennett's *Consciousness Explained* (London: Penguin, 1993). He suggests that beneath the self is a sort of amorphous arena where 'the larvae of other people's ideas renew themselves, before sending out copies of themselves in an informational Diaspora' (p. 202). In language and content very close to that of Deleuze, consciousness is realized in 'a more or less orderly, more or less effective, more or less well-designed virtual machine, the *Joycean machine*' (p. 228). There is no central conceptualizer but the mirage of conceptualization; instead, Dennett posits a 'pandemonium of word-demons' (p. 237) whose 'creative energies' (p. 238) are to some degree constrained by the process that leads to a unified speech act. These demons (like Deleuze's larval selves) are 'preverbal' (p. 240), exist in series and in parallel, and rather than the 'thought-thinker' beginning thinking, it is the passive nature of the word-demons that determines the 'thought to be expressed' (p. 241).

[30] See the appendix to Antonio Damasio's *The Feeling of What Happens: Body, Emotion and the Making of Consciousness* (London: Vintage, 2000), pp. 317–319, for his definition of images. 'The process we come to know as mind when mental images become ours as a result of consciousness is a continuous flow of images many of which turn out to be logically interrelated. The flow moves forward in time, speedily or slowly, orderly or jumpily, and on occasion it moves along not just one sequence but several. Sometimes the sequences are concurrent, sometimes convergent and divergent, sometimes they are superposed. *Thought* is an acceptable word to denote such a flow of images' (p. 318). For Damasio, as for Deleuze, everything begins with images.

[31] TP, p. 98; *124–125*.

[32] Ibid., p. 97; *123*.

[33] Ibid., pp. 97–98; *123–124*. Deleuze and Guattari note that Kafka was a Czechoslovakian Jew writing in German and Beckett was an Irishman writing in English and French (ibid., pp. 97–98; *123*).

[34] Ibid., p. 98; *124*.

[35] CC, p. 107.

[36] WP, p. 2; *8*. 'Philosophy is the art of forming, inventing, and fabricating concepts.'

[37] CC, p. 108.

[38] DR, p. 9; *16*.

[39] Seamus Heaney, *Sweeney Astray* (London: Faber and Faber, 1983), p. 48.

[40] CC, p. 27; *40*. In Bonnefoy's French translation of *Hamlet*, 'the time is out of joint' is translated as '*les temps est hors de ses gonds*' – literally, 'time is off its hinges.'

[41] Ibid.

[42] In other words, time no longer depends upon the intensive movement of the soul (that of Augustine) but itself determines the intensive production of consciousness. Time is the form of determinability given *a priori*, according to Kant, for without this how would the undetermined ('I am') be determinable by the 'I think'; put another way, time is the form in which the undetermined is determinable (see 'Analytic of Concepts' in Immanuel Kant's *Critique of Pure Reason*, rev. and trans. J. M. D. Meiklejohn, ed. Vasilis Politis (London: Everyman, 1993), [B157], footnote).

[43] CC, p. 28; *41*.

44 Ibid., p. 29; *42.*
45 DR, p. 111; *119.*
46 CC, p. 29; *42.*
47 Ibid.
48 Ibid., pp. 29–30; *43.*
49 DR, p. 216; *220.*
50 Ibid. What does Deleuze mean by 'the differentials of thought'? He gives the following example. The straight line may be the shortest path but this can be seen in two ways: either (1) as a schema whereby the imagination that defines the straight line as that which may be superimposed upon itself and therefore whose difference remains external to itself, encapsulated within a rule of construction or (2) from a genetic point of view, as that which is distinguished from a curve, as that which expresses an 'internal difference in the form of a reciprocal determination' between the straight and the crooked (ibid., p. 221; *226*). In this sense the straight line is but the shortest curve. This genetic point of view is what inhabits Deleuze's philosophy of difference.
51 Ibid., p. 216; *220–221.* Deleuze, however, does not incarnate this abstract ideational triplet in distinct Ideas or in the form of a Kantian representation. He rejects Kant's perspective that 'the Self is above all undetermined, the World is determinable, and God is the ideal of determination' (ibid., p. 216; *221*).
52 Ibid., p. 216; *220.*
53 Ibid. 'Ideas contain their dismembered moments.'
54 Ibid., pp. 220–221; *225.*
55 Keith Ansell Pearson, *Philosophy and the Adventure of the Virtual: Bergson and the Time of Life* (London: Routledge, 2002), pp. 102–103.
56 DR, p. 51; *60.*
57 James Williams, *Gilles Deleuze's 'Difference and Repetition': A Critical Introduction and Guide* (Edinburgh: Edinburgh University Press, 2003), p. 99.
58 DR, p. 68; *79.* It is this law that constitutes 'the in-itself of the represented (A is A) and . . . the for-itself of the representant (Self = Self)'.
59 Ibid., p. 260; *269–270.*
60 Ibid.
61 Ibid., p. 261; *270.*
62 'To be actualised is to be differenciated' as mentioned in ibid., p. 262; *272.*
63 Ibid., p. 235; *242.* Indeed, as objects of Ideas problems belong with events and affections in the virtual – their true correspondence is with the inessential. When Deleuze is thinking of Ideas as events, he is placing Ideas firmly in the domain of Charles Péguy's work. 'There are critical points of the event just as there are critical points of temperature: points of fusion, freezing and boiling points; points of coagulation and crystallization. There are even in the case of events states of superfusion which are precipitated, crystallized or determined only by the introduction of a fragment of some future event.' Charles Péguy, *Clio* (Paris: NRF, p. 269, quoted by Deleuze in DR, p. 238; *245*).
64 Ibid., p. 225; *230.*
65 Ibid., p. 145; *156.*
66 Ibid., p. 143; *154.*
67 DeLanda, *Intensive Science and Virtual Philosophy,* p. 84.

68 Ibid.
69 DR, pp. 144–145; *155*.
70 Ibid., p. 145; *156*.
71 Ibid., p. 148; *159*.
72 LS, p. 94; *115*.
73 DeLanda, *Intensive Science and Virtual Philosophy*, p. 101, n. 62.
74 LS, p. 94; *115*.
75 TN1, p. 221; *391*.
76 Ibid., p. 183; *324*.
77 Ibid., p. 184; *324*.
78 Georg von Wright, *Explanation and Understanding* (Ithaca, NY: Cornell University Press, 1971).
79 See TN1, p. 183; *324* where Ricoeur argues that quasi-causal explanation 'applies . . . to individual occurrences of genetic phenomena (events, processes, states) [and] ultimately refers back to . . . "singular causal imputation."'
80 Ibid., p. 133; *238* – in English in the original. Ricoeur's analysis of von Wright's work is more fully covered in chapter 5 of *Time and Narrative, Volume 1*.
81 Aristotle, '*Physics*', 194b23–25, in Richard McKeon (ed.), *The Basic Works of Aristotle* (New York: The Modern Library, 2001).
82 TN1, p. 141; *251*.
83 DeLanda, *Intensive Science and Virtual Philosophy*, pp. 219–220.
84 See Eric Alliez's *The Signature of the World: What Is Deleuze and Guattari's Philosophy?*, trans. E. R. Albert and A. Toscano (London: Continuum, 2004) for an elucidation of the role of conceptual personae in narrative. He argues that these 'strange personae' that inhabit the plane of immanence create 'so many enunciatory folds forcing a variation to the infinite . . . acting like sieves that restore operational narrativity' (pp. 9–10).
85 LS, pp. 82–93; *101–114*.
86 DR, p. 260; *270*.
87 Ronald Bogue, *Deleuze on Literature* (London: Routledge, 2003), p. 26.
88 Ibid., p. 25.
89 Don DeLillo, *Underworld* (London: Picador, 1997), p. 96.
90 W. G. Sebald, *Austerlitz*, trans. Anthea Bell (London: Penguin, 2001), p. 84.
91 Ibid., p. 109.
92 Ibid., p. 154.
93 Ibid., pp. 180–181.
94 Ibid., p. 182.
95 Ibid., p. 189.
96 Ibid.
97 Ibid., p. 190.
98 Ibid., p. 191.
99 Ibid., p. 164.
100 Ibid., p. 165.
101 Ibid., p. 173.
102 Ibid., p. 238.
103 TN3, p. 446; *249*, translation modified.
104 LS, p. 174; *204*.

[105] William Wordsworth. *The Prelude: The Four Texts: 1798, 1799, 1805, 1850* (London: Penguin, 1995), *Book II*, l. 292.

[106] Wordsworth, 1850, *Book XIV*, ll. 71–74.

[107] Wordsworth, 1805, *Book XIII*, ll. 70–74.

[108] Wordsworth, 1850, *Book XIV*, ll. 86–87.

[109] Wordsworth, 1805, *Book I*, ll. 418–427.

[110] Wordsworth, 1798, *Was It For This*, l. 127.

[111] Wordsworth, 1805, *Book I*, ll. 617–624.

[112] F. W. J. Schelling, 'Philosophical Letters on Dogmatism and Criticism', in *The Unconditional in Human Knowledge: Four Early Essays (1794–1796)*, trans. Fritz Marti (Lewisburg, PA: Bucknell University Press, 1980), p. 163.

[113] Ibid.

[114] Ibid.

[115] Ibid., p. 178.

[116] Ibid.

[117] Ibid., p. 181.

[118] O'Keeffe, *Buile Suibhne (The Frenzy of Sweeney) being The Adventures of Suibne Geilt* (London: Irish Texts Society, 1913), p. 59.

[119] Ibid., p. 59.

[120] Ibid., p. 61.

[121] The alteration in Sweeney's shape from man to bird and back again is not metaphorical; both Heaney and O'Keeffe's texts are clear on this. See Seamus Heaney, *Sweeney Astray* (London: Faber and Faber, 1983), p. 34.

[122] O'Keeffe, *Buile Suibhne*, p. 61.

[123] Ibid.

[124] Ibid., pp. 61, 63.

[125] Ibid., p. 63.

[126] Jacques Lacan, *Book XX: On Feminine Sexuality, The Limits of Love and Knowledge, 1972–1973*, ed. Jacques-Alain Miller, trans. Bruce Fink (London: Norton, 1999), pp. 61–77. Lacan argues that there is a pleasure beyond that of the phallus (pleasure based on lack), a pleasure that is the province of the Real, not the Imaginary or the Symbolic – but because of this it is quite unknowable.

[127] Richard Kearney refers to Ricoeur's 'reserve' at pushing fully open the door that marks the boundary between 'philosophical reflection' and the '"hidden art" of imagination'. See Richard Kearney's 'Narrative Imagination: Between Ethics and Poetics', in Richard Kearney (ed.), *Paul Ricoeur: The Hermeneutics of Action* (London: Sage, 1996), p. 174.

[128] F. W. J. Schelling, *System of Transcendental Idealism* (Charlottesville: University Press of Virginia, 1993), p. 232.

[129] M. M. Bakhtin, 'Discourse in the Novel' in *The Dialogic Imagination*, ed. Michael Holquist, trans. Caryl Emerson and Michael Holquist (Austin: University of Texas Press, 1981), p. 274.

[130] Ibid., p. 272.

[131] Ibid., p. 270.

[132] Ibid., p. 103.

[133] O'Keeffe, *Buile Suibhne*, p. 159.

[134] Ibid., p. 143.

Chapter 9

1 John Banville, *Shroud* (London: Picador, 2002), p. 332.
2 Richard Kearney, 'Narrative Imagination: Between Ethics and Poetics', in Richard Kearney (ed.), *Paul Ricoeur: The Hermeneutics of Action* (London: Sage, 1996), p. 174.
3 Slavoj Žižek claims a 'disavowed affinity' between Hegel and Deleuze (disavowed by the latter of course) in *Organs without Bodies: On Deleuze and Consequences* (London: Routledge, 2004), p. 49.
4 DR, p. 45; *53*.
5 OA, p. 297; *345*.
6 Ibid., p. 313; *363*.
7 Ibid., p. 335; *387*.
8 It is noteworthy that Ricoeur distinguishes his self opening to the world and concerned with everything in it (ibid., p. 314; *363*) from Lévinas' self within which 'a pretension dwells . . . more radical than that driving the Fichtean . . . ambition of universal constitution and radical self-grounding [which] expresses a will to closure, more precisely a state of separation that makes otherness the equivalent of radical exteriority' (ibid., pp. 335–336; *387*). Deleuze inherits something from Fichte (through Schelling) and shares an antipathy with Lévinas towards a phenomenology whose 'major theme of intentionality belong[s] to a philosophy of representation . . . that cannot help but be idealist and solipsistic' (ibid., p. 336; *387*). We must therefore be cautious of the point-of-view of the argumentation employed, with respect to both Deleuze and Ricoeur.
9 MHF, p. 337; *442*.
10 TN3, p. 246; *443*.
11 MHF, p. 414; *538*.
12 Ibid., p. 427; *554*.
13 Ibid., p. 431; *558*.
14 Ibid., p. 432; *559*.
15 Henri Bergson, *Matter and Memory*, trans. Nancy Margaret Paul and W. Scott Palmer (London: George Allen & Unwin, 1970), p. 86.
16 Ibid., p. 171.
17 B, pp. 58–59; *54*, quoted by Ricoeur in MHF, pp. 433–434; *562*. Deleuze's interpretations of the implications of Bergson's philosophy for temporality and for the status of our virtuality return in several of his later works, acting as fulcra to a whole series of different arguments. See for instance PS, pp. 58–59; *73–74*, regarding the parallels between Proust and Bergson; DR, p. 103; *111*, on repetition; ID, p. 29; *39*, specifically on Bergson.
18 MHF, p. 434; *563*.
19 Ibid., p. 435; *564*. For a concise analysis of the relationship between Ricoeur and Bergson and the importance of Aristotle to Bergson, see Peter Kemp's 'Mémoire et oubli: de Bergson à Ricoeur', *L'Herne: Paul Ricoeur*, 81 (2004), pp. 246–255.
20 Ricoeur's use of language supports this. For example, he repeatedly refers to depth in respect of memory, acknowledges the 'nonnumerical multiplicity of memories' or memory as a continuous multiplicity (MHF, p. 435; *564*) and comments that 'forgetting has a positive meaning insofar as having-been prevails

over being-no-longer in the meaning attached to the idea of the past' (ibid., p. 443; *574*).

[21] Ibid., p. 441; *571*. 'Existentiell' is a Heideggerian term, meaning 'the understanding of oneself' through existing itself. See Martin Heidegger, *Being and Time*, trans. J. Macquarrie and E. Robinson, (Oxford: Basil Blackwell, 1962), p. 33.

[22] MHF, p. 441; *571*.

[23] Ibid., pp. 441–442; *571–572*.

[24] DR, p. 177; *183*.

[25] MHF, p. 441; *571*.

[26] OA, pp. 297–298; *345*. Ricoeur's provisional thoughts on an ontology of selfhood have been responded to by Olav Bryant-Smith in *Myths of the Self: Narrative Identity and Postmodern Metaphysics* (Lanham, MD: Lexington Books, 2004). Bryant-Smith tries to marry Whitehead's pan-experientialist philosophy to Ricoeur's narrative self as its ontological solution. There are many parallels between Whitehead and Deleuze, and many differences. Deleuze referred to Whitehead's *Process and Reality* as 'one of the greatest books of modern philosophy'. Bryant-Smith provides an interesting depth to Ricoeur through Whitehead, but it is at the expense of some of the key principles that Ricoeur lays down in *Oneself as Another*, senior among these being the non-theologizing of the philosophy of the narrative-self. Bryant-Smith envelops the narrative-self in a world where God wants to hear our stories, where God replaces the Other. *Oneself as God* is the unfortunate outcome.

[27] Aristotle, *The Metaphysics*, trans. Hugh Lawson-Tancred (London: Penguin, 1998), 1003a33.

[28] Ibid., 1026a33. Although Aristotle identified other kinds and classifications of being, it is this fourfold classification that takes priority over the others as they can be subsumed within it. See Franz Brentano, *On the Several Senses of Being in Aristotle*, ed. and trans. Rolf George (Berkeley: University of California Press, 1975), pp. 3–4.

[29] OA, pp. 303; *352*.

[30] Ibid., p. 307; *357*.

[31] Ibid., p. 308; *357*. Ricoeur extends this argument, somewhat unsuccessfully he believes, through the guidance of Heidegger. Specifically he draws upon Care (*Sorge*) to give ontological density to the Aristotelian notion of *praxis*. The importance of this to Ricoeur is that *praxis* has held a pivotal position in his own hermeneutics of selfhood and by adding ontological weight to the term he hopes to secure 'the marker' he requires 'between selfhood and being as actuality/potentiality' (ibid., pp. 310–312; *358*).

[32] Ibid., p. 308; *357*.

[33] Ibid., p. 315; *364*.

[34] Ricoeur was clearly impressed by Deleuze's *Nietzsche and Philosophy*, a book he described as 'wonderful' (MHF, p. 603; *633*, n. 39).

[35] NP, p. 197; *225*.

[36] OA, p. 315; *365*.

[37] Ibid., p. 316; *365–366*. See also Baruch Spinoza, *Ethics and the Correction of the Understanding*, trans. Andrew Boyle (London: Dent, 1986), Part III, proposition VI which states that 'Everything in so far as it is in itself endeavours to persist in its own being.'

38 OA, p. 313; *363*.
39 This concept is central to Christopher Bollas' *The Shadow of the Object: Psychoanalysis of the Unthought Known* (London: Free Association Books, 1987).
40 Walter Kaufmann, *Nietzsche: Philosopher, Psychologist, Antichrist* (Princeton, NJ: Princeton University Press, 1968), pp. 382–384.
41 DR, pp. 40–43; *47–51*.
42 Ibid., pp. 44–45; *52–53*.
43 B, p. 17; *5*.
44 DR, p. 198; *206*.
45 Aristotle, *Metaphysics*, 995a27. This translation is provided by Christopher Shields in his book *Aristotle* (London: Routledge, 2007). W. D. Ross renders this translation as follows: 'For those who wish to get clear of difficulties it is advantageous to discuss the difficulties well.' For fuller discussions on the importance of a problem-centred philosophical approach, see Vasilis Politis's *Aristotle and the Metaphysics*, (London: Routledge, 2004), pp. 64–83; for further discussion on Aristotle's response to Parmenides, see Shields' *Aristotle*.
46 ES, p. 133; *118*.
47 This is detailed throughout *Proust and Signs*.
48 Gilles Deleuze, 'The Actual and the Virtual', trans. Elliot Ross Albert, in Gilles Deleuze with Claire Parnet, *Dialogues II*, trans. H. Tomlinson and B. Habberjam (London: Continuum, 2006). This essay is not included in the original French edition.
49 DR, p. 334; *342*. When difference is subordinated to representation in the concept, 'what disappears is that difference that thinking makes in thought, that *genitality* of thinking, that profound fracture of the I which leads it to think only in thinking its own passion, and even its own death, in the pure and empty form of time. To restore difference in thought is to untie this first knot which consists of representing difference through the identity of the concept and the thinking subject' (ibid., pp. 334–335; *342*).
50 Aristotle, *Metaphysics*, Theta 8.
51 Vasilis Politis, *Aristotle and the Metaphysics*, p. 55.
52 Deleuze's joint essay with Claire Parnet is entitled 'A Conversation: What is it? What is it for?' in DG, pp. 1–14; *7–26*.
53 See Shields, *Aristotle*, pp. 90–94.
54 Aristotle, '*Meteorology*', 390a10–15 in Jonathan Barnes (ed.), *The Complete Works of Aristotle, Vol. 1* (Guildford: Princeton Unversity Press, 1984). See also '*Politics*' 1253a19–20 in *The Basic Works of Aristotle*.
55 Aristotle, *Physics*, 198b4–5.
56 Manuel DeLanda, *Intensive Science and Virtual Philosophy* (London: Continuum, 2002), p. 35. See also DR, p. 105; *113*.
57 Aristotle, *Politics*, 1253a19–20.
58 Ibid., 1253a23.
59 AO, pp. 1–17; *7–22*. 'Everywhere it is machines' and 'everything is production' (pp. 1, 4; *7, 10*).
60 Hugh Lawson-Tancred, 'Introduction' (in Aristotle, *Metaphysics*), pp. lv–lvi.
61 Vasilis Politis, *Aristotle and the Metaphysics*, p. 281.
62 NG, p. 86. The 'untimely' being the '*inactuel*' in French.

63 Aristotle, *Metaphysics*, 1046a10–12 (Lawson-Tancred's translation).

64 Ibid., 1019b30–35.

65 Franz Brentano, *Several Senses of Being in Aristotle*, p. 28. Brentano argues that possibility is something 'which completely abstracts from the reality of that which is possible, and merely claims that something could exist if its existence did not involve a contradiction. It does not exist in things but in the objective concepts and combinations of concepts of the thinking mind; it is merely a rational thing' (p. 28).

66 DR, pp. 263–264; *273*.

67 Ibid., p. 263; *272–273*.

68 Ibid., pp. 76–77; *88–89*.

69 Franz Brentano, *Several Senses of Being in Aristotle*, p. 92.

70 Charlotte Witt, *Ways of Being: Potentiality and Actuality in Aristotle's Metaphysics*, (Ithaca, NY and London: Cornell University Press, 2003), p. 3.

71 Aristotle, *Metaphysics*, 1048a33.

72 Luce Irigaray, *The Way of Love*, trans. Heidi Bostic and Stephen Pluhček (London: Continuum, 2002), p. xx.

73 Aristotle, *Metaphysics*, 1048b4–5 (Lawson-Tancred translation).

74 Ibid., 1049a19–25.

75 See Aristotle, *Metaphysics*, Theta 8.

76 O'Keeffe, *Buile Suibhne*, p. 123.

77 Seamus Heaney, *Sweeney Astray* (London: Faber and Faber, 1983), p. 70.

78 DR, p. 71; *83*.

79 Ibid., pp. 71–72; *83–84*.

80 Ibid., p. 345; *353*.

81 See, for instance, Tzvetan Todorov's *Hope and Memory*, trans. David Bellos (London: Atlantic Books, 2003) for the inherence of mini-totalitarianisms in democracy after it had defeated both fascism and communism.

82 Lawson-Tancred, 'Introduction', p. 68.

83 'Now matter is potentiality, form actuality.' Aristotle, *De Anima (On the Soul)*, trans. Hugh Lawson-Tancred (London: Penguin), 1986, 412b10.

84 Ibid., 410a25.

85 Ibid., 412a23.

86 Ibid., 412a27.

87 Ibid., 412a24–25. See also 417a21–417b1 for a clarification of potential and actual knowers.

88 Ibid., 411a29. And see 429a10 where Aristotle refers to 'the part of the soul with which the soul knows and thinks.'

89 Ibid., 413a1.

90 Ibid., 414a27.

91 Ibid., 417a27.

92 Ibid., 414b13.

93 Ibid., 413b (Hugh Lawson-Tancred's translation).

94 Ibid., 413b7 (J. A. Smith's translation).

95 It is not at all clear whether perception is fully a part of the soul or not in Aristotle. That it is a 'distinctive peculiarity' of the soul is clear in 427a16: 'There are two distinctive peculiarities by reference to which we characterise the soul – (1) local movement and (2) thinking, discriminating, and perceiving'; that it

operates on the boundaries of the soul is clearly suggested in 417a7: 'the power of sense is parallel to what is combustible, for that never ignites itself spontaneously, but requires an agent which has the power of starting ignition; otherwise it could have set itself on fire, and would not have needed actual fire to set itself ablaze'. But, if the power of combustion requires the power of starting combustion, does not the power of starting combustion require the power of combustion that is within the combustible for it to actualize itself; in other words, are not these two powers potentialities? Thus, the power of sense or perception would be a potentiality and not of the soul.

[96] Aristotle, *De Anima*, 127a16.

[97] Ibid., 429a10.

[98] Ibid., 429a24.

[99] Ibid., 429b9.

[100] Ibid., 429b30.

[101] Although Deleuze clearly borrows the term 'passive synthesis' from Husserl, he does not acknowledge this. In fact, his declared debt is to Hume (DR, pp. 90–91). In repetition, (like AB, AB, AB, A . . .) it is the imagination that acts as a 'contractile power', anticipating the next B by retaining the A as if on a sensitive plate. We expect B when A appears 'with a force corresponding to the qualitative impression of all the ABs'. This is not memory or an operation of understanding, argues Deleuze, but a contraction that forms a synthesis of time, a synthesis to which Deleuze gives the name 'passive synthesis' (ibid., p. 91; *97*) – a name but not a debt to Husserl. For a brief analysis of the relationship of Deleuze to Husserl see Alberto Toscano's 'Phenomenology + Husserl, Edmund (1859–1939)', in Andrew Parr (ed.), *The Deleuze Dictionary* (Edinburgh: Edinburgh University Press, 2005), pp. 202–204.

[102] Ibid., p. 92; *98*. It is the imagination that contracts these instances and only afterwards does the intellect superimpose an active synthesis upon the passive synthesis of the imagination for the purposes of representation and reflection.

[103] Ibid., p. 94; *100–101*.

[104] Ibid., p. 94; *101*. By envisaging the living world as organically composed of a spectrum of habits or passive syntheses (like the contractions of water, earth, light and air that our bodies are made of, or the contractions inherent in plants that photosynthesize, or the contractions that form the experience of a sonata from a sequence of successive notes), Deleuze can conclude that we are able to attribute a soul to the heart and the liver, to the spleen, the nerves and the skin, but it is a contemplative soul that we thereby attribute, a soul 'whose entire function is to contract a habit' (ibid., p. 95; *101*). We can also say that a soul must also be attributed to the frog, the mollusc, the water-boatman and the primrose. Aristotle generously attributes souls in a similar fashion.

[105] Ibid., p. 96; *103*.

[106] 'Everything is a possible object of thought.' Aristotle, *De Anima*, 429a17.

[107] Ibid., 429a12.

[108] Ibid., 429a27–29.

[10] Shields, *Aristotle*, p. 411.

[110] Ibid., p. 405.

[111] Hugh Lawson-Tancred, 'Introduction', 'Glossary' and 'Commentary', in Aristotle *De Anima*, trans. Hugh Lawson-Tancred (London: Penguin, 1986).

[112] Aristotle, *De Anima*, 429a24.

[113] Ibid., 429b9.

[114] Lawson-Tancred, 'Introduction', 'Glossary' and 'Commentary', in Aristotle *De Anima*, pp. 90–101; p. 204; pp. 246–247, n. 110, n. 111. Some regard it as having been produced simply as 'a mere metaphysical ground for the operation of the intellect' (p. 204) with no functional role in thought-processes; others question its relationship with the first mover of *Metaphysics* Lambda.

[115] Aristotle, *De Anima*, 430a14.

[116] Ibid., 430a20–22.

[117] We must however be cautious as the terms and conditions do not map on to each other in their entirety. For example, when Deleuze uses the term 'essence' he means something quite different from Aristotle, even if both search for a particular quiddity or 'whatness' – although with radically different presuppositions. Ideas have no prior identity for Deleuze so that in their genesis they are intrinsically defined and reciprocally determined; bearing no similarity to forms or essences they are 'made and unmade according to the conditions which determine their fluent synthesis' (DR, p. 235; *242*).

[118] Aristotle, *De Anima*, 429a23–24.

[119] Lawson-Tancred's translation.

[120] ES, p. 93; *82*. See also DR, p. 234; *240* where the terms 'potentiality' and 'virtuality' are used interchangeably: 'the whole constitutes a virtuality, a potentiality.'

[121] Aristotle, *De Anima*, 430a20–22.

[122] Ibid., 429b23.

[123] David Bostock, *Aristotle: Metaphysics, Book Z and H* (Oxford: Clarendon Press, 1994), pp. 141–158.

[124] Aristotle, *De Anima*, 408b.

[125] Ibid., 408b.

[126] Ibid.

[127] Witt, *Ways of Being*, p. 72.

[128] However, he does not differentiate ontologically between 'the causal powers operating in nature like heat, and the causal powers, or abilities that originate purposive human actions, like the art of building, or practical reason' (ibid., p. 59).

[129] Aristotle, *Metaphysics*, 1048a.

[130] AO, pp. 28–29; *34–35*.

[131] Aristotle, *Metaphysics*, 1049b25.

[132] Aristotle, *Physics* in which he states that 'Everything that is moved is moved by the mover that is further back in the series' (257a11), but since it would be 'impossible that there should be an infinite series of movers' (256a18), the first mover 'must be unmoved' (256b20).

[133] Ibid., 256b27.

[134] Aristotle, *Metaphysics*, 1072b10.

[135] Ibid., 1072b10–11.

[136] Ibid., 1072a30.

[137] Ibid., 1072a27.

[138] Ibid., 1072b4.

[139] Aristotle, *Physics*, 256a9. 'In the man, however, we have reached a mover that is not so in virtue of being moved by something else.'

[140] Aristotle, *Metaphysics*, 1072b19–23.

[141] Ibid., 1072b26. 'The actuality of thought is life.'

[142] Ibid., 102b29.

[143] Ibid., 429b9 and 430a2.

[144] ES, p. 178; *162*. See also DR (pp. 44–50; *52–59*). But is Deleuze's reading of Spinoza faithful or not? Is it a correct or falsifying one, one that unearths the work of Duns Scotus or inserts him into Spinoza? For both sides of the argument see Simon Duffy's 'The Logic of Expression in Deleuze's *Expressionism in Philosophy: Spinoza*: A Strategy of Engagement', *International Journal of Philosophical Studies*, 12 No. 1 (2004), pp. 17 60.

[145] ES, pp. 169–186; *153–169*.

[146] Ibid., p. 117; *103*.

[147] The dark precursor is also referred to by Deleuze, in somewhat different manifestations depending on the context, as the aleatory point and the quasi-cause (see DeLanda, *Intensive Science and Virtual Philosophy*, p. 205).

[148] DR, p. 146; *156*.

[149] Ibid., p. 146; *157*.

[150] Ibid., p. 69; *80*.

[151] Peter Hallward, *Deleuze and the Philosophy of Creation: Out of this World* (London: Verso Press, 2006), p. 42.

[152] Ibid., p. 4.

[153] Ibid., p. 5.

[154] Ibid., p. 5

[155] Ibid., p. 27.

[156] ES, p. 16; *12*.

[157] Hallward, *Deleuze and the Philosophy of Creation*, p. 37.

[158] Aristotle, *Metaphysics*, 1072b26.

[159] Bostock, *Aristotle: Metaphysics, Book Z and H*, p. 141.

[160] Aristotle, *Politics*, 1253a19–27.

[161] Aristotle, '*History of Animals*', 588b4–5, in *The Basic Works of Aristotle*.

[162] Ibid., 588b114–16.

[163] For a fuller discussion of the relevance of Aristotle to contemporary theories of evolution, DNA and systems nested within systems, see Fran O'Rourke's 'Aristotle and the Metaphysics of Evolution', *The Review of Metaphysics*, 58 (Sept., 2004), pp. 3–59.

[164] Hallward, *Deleuze and the Philosophy of Creation*, p. 37.

Chapter 10

[1] Cormac McCarthy, *Cities of the Plain* (London: Picador, 1998), p. 283.

[2] Slavoj Žižek, *The Parallax View* (London: MIT Press, 2006), p. 365.

[3] PS, p. 125; *152*.

[4] Ibid., p. 126; *152*.

[5] DR, p. 183; *190*.

[6] 'Knight's move thinking' is used to describe the processes of thought displayed in some patients with schizophrenia where it is unclear how one sentence leads

to another (the diagonal of the knight's move) because the intermediate sentence has been omitted (the angle of the knight's move).

7 TN1, p. 73; *140*.

8 Alain Badiou, *Deleuze: The Clamour of Being*, trans. Louise Burchill (Minneapolis: University of Minnesota Press, 1999) p. 35.

9 Martin Heidegger, 'Memorial Address', in *Discourse on Thinking*, trans. John M. Anderson and E. Hans Feund (New York: Harper and Row, 1966).

10 Ibid., p. 55.

11 Barbara Dalle Pezze, 'Heidegger on Gelassenheit', *Minerva – An Internet Journal of Philosophy*, 10 (2006), pp. 94–122.

12 Heidegger, 'Conversation on a Country Path about Thinking', p. 45.

13 Ibid., p. 55.

14 Ibid.

15 Martin Heidegger, 'Conversation on a Country Path about Thinking', in *Discourse on Thinking*, trans. John M. Anderson and E. Hans Feund (New York: Harper and Row, 1966, pp. 82–83).

16 Ibid., p. 85.

17 Dalle Pezze, 'Heidegger on Gelassenheit', p. 117.

18 Heidegger, 'Conversation on a Country Path about Thinking', pp. 86–87.

19 C1, pp. 112–113; *154–155*.

20 Ibid., p. 120; *165*.

21 Ibid., p. 115; *158*.

22 Jean-Jacques Lecercle, *Philosophy through the Looking Glass: Language, Nonsense, Desire* (La Salle, IL: Open Court, 1985), p. 6.

23 As in the rigidified status of the actualized self in Deleuze and the triumph of concordance over discordance in Ricoeur.

24 See Primo Levi, *Other People's Trades*, trans. Raymond Rosenthal (London: Michael Joseph, 1989), pp. 27–32. Levi draws our attention to the science fiction writer Philip José Farmer's prescription for 'a supplementary organ similar to a set of bellows' for the centaur (Levi, p. 28).

25 Martin Heidegger, 'Memorial Address', p. 55.

26 Marcel Proust, *In Search of Lost Time Vol. II: Within a Budding Grove*, trans. S. Moncrieff and T. Kilmartin, rev. D. Enright (London: Vintage, 2002) p. 268.

27 PS, p. 185, n. 8; *153, n. 1*.

28 Ibid., p. 126; *152*.

29 Ibid., p. 125; *152*.

30 Ibid., p. 126; *152–153*.

31 Marcel Proust, *In Search of Lost Time Vol. VI: Time Regained*, trans. A. Mayor and T. Kilmartin, rev. D. J. Enright (London: Vintage, 2002) p. 427. The full quotation will clarify the fractal nature of Proustian transversals. 'And then between these two high roads a network of transversals was set up. Balbec, for example, the real Balbec where I had met Saint-Loup, was a place that I had longed to go to very largely because of what Swann had told me about the churches in its neighbourhood, and especially about its own church in the Persian style, and yet Robert de Saint-Loup was the nephew of the Duchesse de Guermantes, and through him I arrived at Combrey again, at the Guermantes way. And Mlle de Saint-Loup led to many other points in my life, to the lady in pink, for instance,

who was her grandmother and whom I had seen in the house of my great-uncle. And here there was a new transversal . . .' (p. 427). And so on.

32 PS, p. 127; *153*.

33 Jean-Luc Nancy, *Being Singular Plural*, trans. Robert Richardson and Anne O'Byrne (Stanford, CA: Stanford University Press), 2000, p. xv.

34 Ibid., p. 3.

35 Ibid., p. 11.

36 Ibid., p. 9.

37 Ibid., p. 12.

38 Ibid., p. 12.

39 *Room 666*, directed by Wim Wenders (1982). Available in *Wim Wenders Box Set (10 Discs)*, Anchor Bay Entertainment, 2007.

40 Is this not what modern physics has had to do to 'capture' some subatomic particles whose metastable status 'means that they live just long enough so that one can see their tracks in the hydrogen bubble chamber'? See Heinz Pagel's *The Cosmic Code: Quantum Physics as the Language of Nature* (Middlesex: Penguin, 1984), p. 185.

41 OA, p. 310; p. *343*.

42 *Chambers Twentieth Century Dictionary* (Edinburgh: Pitman Press, 1977).

43 This distinction is also present in *Difference and Repetition*. For example, extensity emerges from the depths 'only if depth is definable independently of extensity'. And the original depth is 'space as a whole, but space as an intensive quantity: the pure *spatium*' (DR, p. 289; *296*). Hallward notes the similarities between the Deleuzian excess of the virtual over the actual and Levinas' excess of pre-ontological *saying* (*dire*) over what can in fact be *said* (*dit*) as detailed in *Otherwise Than Being* (see Peter Hallward, *Deleuze and the Philosophy of Creation: Out of this World* (London: Verso, 2006), p. 173, n. 6).

44 OA, p. 4; *14–15*.

45 Heidegger, 'Conversation on a Country Path about Thinking', pp. 82–83.

46 Žižek, *Parallax View*, pp. 365–366.

47 Heidegger, 'Conversation on a Country Path about Thinking', pp. 82–83.

Chapter 11

1 Gao Xingjian, *Soul Mountain*, trans. Mabel Lee (London: Harper Perennial, 2004), p. 329.

2 Jacques Lacan, *Book XX: On Feminine Sexuality, The Limits of Love and Knowledge, 1972-1973*, ed. Jacques-Alain Miller, trans. Bruce Fink (London: Norton, 1999), pp. 61–77. As noted earlier, Lacan argues that there is a pleasure beyond that of the phallus (pleasure based on lack), a pleasure which he terms 'feminine jouissance', province of the body and not of the Imaginary or the Symbolic – yet because of this, quite unknowable.

3 See DG (pp. vi–viii) for the clearest account of what a multiplicity means to Deleuze. Also, see 'A Conversation: What is it? What is it for?' in the same volume (pp. 1–14; *7–26*). 'In a multiplicity what counts are not the terms or the elements,

but what there is "between," the between, a set of relations which are not separable from each other' (p. vii).

⁴ Maurice Merleau-Ponty, *Phenomenology of Perception*, trans. Colin Smith (London: Routledge, 2004), p. 268.

⁵ Ibid., p. 270.

⁶ Hannah Arendt, *The Human Condition* (London: University of Chicago Press, 1958), p. 247. 'The miracle that saves the world, the realm of human affairs, from its normal, "natural" ruin is ultimately the fact of natality, in which the faculty of action is ontologically rooted. It is, in other words, the birth of new men and the new beginning, the action they are capable of by virtue of being born.'

⁷ MHF, pp. 86–87; *105–106*.

⁸ OA, p. 31; *44*.

⁹ Giacomo Romano, 'Minimal Personhood' (University of Siena, unpublished manuscript, 2007).

¹⁰ Daniel Dennett, *Brainstorms* (Sussex: Harvester Press, 1978), p. 270.

¹¹ This point is well made by Luce Irigaray in *Speculum of the Other Woman*, trans. Gillian C. Gill (Ithaca, NY: Cornell University Press, 1992), especially the essays on Plato, Plotinus and Freud where what is specifically maternal is eclipsed by the Law of the Father, the phallus and the desire of the male for autogenesis. Freud is clear in his binary differentiation of 'masculine' and 'feminine': these terms are equated with activity and passivity respectively; therefore 'libido is invariably and necessarily of a masculine nature.' Upon this foundational differentiation boys will discover, following an initial 'disavowal', that girls do not have a penis, conclude that it has been removed and turn this conclusion upon themselves, thus inaugurating the castration complex (see 'The Infantile Genital Organization' (1923), 'The Dissolution of the Oedipus Complex' (1924) and 'Femininity' (1933), in *The Essentials of Psychoanalysis*, ed. Anna Freud, trans. James Strachey (Pelican Books, 1986), pp. 390–394, 395–401, 412–432.

¹² Bruno Bettelheim, *The Uses of Enchantment: The Meaning and Importance of Fairy Tales* (London: Penguin, 1978), pp. 187–188.

¹³ William Wordsworth, 'Was It For This', in *The Prelude: The Four Texts (1798, 1799, 1805, 1850)*, London: Penguin, 1995, p. 3.

¹⁴ Marcel Proust, *In Search of Lost Time, Volume 1: Swann's Way*, trans. S. Moncrieff and T. Kilmartin, rev. D. J. Enright (London: Vintage, 2002), p. 34.

¹⁵ Ibid., p. 30.

¹⁶ Ibid., p. 25.

¹⁷ Ibid., pp. 33, 40.

¹⁸ Ibid., p. 43.

¹⁹ Ibid., p. 40.

²⁰ Sigmund Freud, 'Inhibitions, Symptoms and Anxiety', in *The Complete Psychological Works of Sigmund Freud, Vol. XX (1925–1926)*, std edn, trans. James Strachey (London: Hogarth, 1959).

²¹ Ibid., p. 109. See also Strachey's introduction to the text, pp. 79–80.

²² Sigmund Freud, 'Inhibitions, Symptoms and Anxiety', p. 92. '[W]e may be assisted by the idea that a defence against an unwelcome *internal* process will be modelled upon the defence adopted against an *external* stimulus, that the ego

wards off internal and external dangers alike along identical lines.' This is in contrast to his original belief that separation as a problem for the child can be subsumed under the castration complex in the form of a loss of a part of the body regarded as important to the child. See Sigmund Freud, 'Analysis of a Phobia in a Five Year Old Boy', in *The Complete Psychological Works of Sigmund Freud, Vol. X (1909)*, std edn, trans. James Strachey (London: Hogarth, 1955), p. 8. An entirely different reading of Little Hans is provided by Bowlby where the horse phobia is understood as related to the anxiety of Hans regarding the availability of attachment figures and his mother's persistent threats to abandon him. See John Bowlby, *Attachment and Loss, Vol. 2. Separation, Anxiety and Anger* (London: Hogarth, 1973), henchforth referred to as AL2, pp. 284–287.

[23] Sigmund Freud, 'Inhibitions, Symptoms and Anxiety', p. 93.

[24] Ibid., pp. 93–94.

[25] Ibid., pp. 128–129.

[26] Ibid., pp. 136–137.

[27] Ibid., p. 138. In fact, Freud claimed there was more continuity between intrauterine life and the earliest days of infancy than the 'impressive caesura of the act of birth' would seem to suggest; indeed, anxiety 'conditioned by separation from the mother' can be explained biologically as part of this continuity and need not be explained on psychological grounds (p. 138). It is this biological factor, this helplessness and dependency that 'establishes the earliest situations of danger and creates the need to be loved which will accompany the child through the rest of its life' (p. 155).

[28] John Bowlby, *Attachment and Loss, Vol. 1: Attachment* (New York: Basic Books, 1969, 2nd edn, 1982), henceforth referred to as AL1, p. 12; and AL2, p. 26. Bowlby's model of the self is empirical insofar as it is based on the examination of 'actual situations in which fear or anxiety, or alternatively, a sense of security' is felt rather than by retrospective analysis, the chosen method of Freud (AL1, p. 87). Unlike Freud's theories which work 'from an end product backwards', Bowlby begins from 'an event or experience deemed to be potentially pathogenic to the developing personality' (AL1, p. 4).

[29] AL1, pp. 40–41: '[T]he actual effects of performance are continually reported back to a central regulating apparatus where they are compared with whatever initial instruction the machine was given, the machine's further action is then determined by the results of this comparison and the effects of its performance are thus brought ever closer to the initial instruction.' Bowlby gives the example of a falcon seizing its prey in flight as an instinctual behaviour that can easily be explained in terms of control systems (see ibid., pp. 44–45).

[30] Ibid., p. 179.

[31] Ibid.

[32] Ibid., pp. 224–225.

[33] C. H. Zeanah and P. D. Zeanah, 'Intergenerational Transmission of Maltreatment: Insights from Attachment Theory and Research', *Psychiatry*, 52 (1989), 177–196.

[34] AL1, p. 84. Attachment experiences are gradually internalized and organized into complex working models within goal-directed systems that regulate and guide later adult relationships and behaviour.

[35] AL2, p. 203.

[36] John Bowlby, *Attachment and Loss, Vol. 3, Loss: Sadness and Depression* (London: Hogarth, 1980), henchforth referred to as AL3, pp. 203–204.

[37] AL2, pp. 204–205. The key components of Bowlby's attachment theory have received substantial empirical support and are generally accepted. See Michael Rutter, 'Clinical Implications of Attachment Concepts: Retrospect and Prospect', in Margaret Hertzig and Ellen Farber (eds), *Annual Progress in Child Psychiatry and Child Development* (New York: Brunner/Mazel, 1996), pp. 127–156. Rutter also notes the need to 'reject the traditional psychoanalytic theories of development'.

[38] Mary Ainsworth and B. Wittig, 'Attachment and Exploratory Behaviour of One-year-olds in a Strange Situation', in B. M. Foss (ed.), *Determinants of Infant Behaviour*, Vol. 4 (London: Methuen, 1969); Mary Ainsworth and Silvia Bell, 'Attachment, Exploration, and Separation: Illustrated by the Behaviour of One-year-olds in a Strange Situation', *Child Development*, 41 No. 1 (1970), pp. 49–67. Bowlby's own comments on these studies are in AL1 (pp. 335–340).

[39] The sequence consists of the following stages: (1) a stranger introduces parent and child to a strange laboratory room and leaves them there; (2) the stranger comes back; (3) the parent leaves the child with the stranger; (4) the parent returns while the stranger leaves; (5) the parent leaves the child on his or her own, saying bye-bye and that she will be back; (6) the stranger returns; (7) the parent returns and the stranger leaves. Each episode lasts for three minutes.

[40] AL2, p. 225.

[41] Ibid., pp. 314–315.

[42] Ibid., p. 315. Children will vary enormously 'in the degree to which they accept their parents' definition of their situation'.

[43] Ibid., pp. 316–317. This falsehood in the narrative self must be distinguished from falsity based on the 'discrepancy between the story one lives and the story one tells' that is a form of self-deception (see Joseph Dunne, 'The Storied Self', in Richard Kearney (ed.), *Paul Ricoeur: The Hermeneutics of Action* (London: Sage, 1996), p. 153.

[44] AL2, p. 44. For Bowlby, it is both necessary and adaptive to exclude information – otherwise the human system would be either overloaded or entirely distracted and unable to function. For a most lucid account of this reformulation, see Emanuel Peterfreund's stimulating book, *Information, Systems, and Psychoanalysis: An Evolutionary Biological Approach to Psychoanalytic Theory*, Psychological Issues, Monograph 25/26, (New York: International Universities Press, 1971).

[45] AL2, pp. 44–45.

[46] AL3, pp. 59–60.

[47] Ibid., pp. 60–61.

[48] Ibid., p. 61.

[49] E. Tulving, 'Episodic and Semantic Memory', in E. Tulving and W. Donaldson (eds), *Organization of Memory* (New York: Academic, 1972), pp. 381–403. In semantic memory information exists 'as generalised propositions about the world, derived from a person's own experience or from what he has learned from others' (AL3, pp. 62). It includes 'knowledge of historical events and historical and literary figures . . . the ability to recognize family, friends and

acquaintances . . . [and] information learned in school, such as specialized vocabularies and reading, writing, and mathematics' – from Bryan Kolb and Ian Q. Whishaw, *Fundamentals of Human Neuropsychology* (New York: Worth, 2003), p. 460. Inflow to semantic memory always refers to some pre-existing cognitive structure. Episodic memory, on the other hand, consists of singular events that a person recalls. Also referred to as autobiographical memory, it is stored 'sequentially in terms of temporally dated episodes or events and of temporo-spatial relations between events' (AL3, p. 61).

[50] Ibid., p. 62.

[51] Ibid., p. 63.

[52] Main describes the AAI as follows: 'Speakers are asked to describe their attachment histories . . . [selecting] five adjectives that would . . . best describe the relationship with each parent . . . Speakers are then asked for memories . . . to support each adjectival choice. They are asked which parent they were closer to, what happened when they were hurt or ill, whether they experienced threat or abuse from parents' (Mary Main, Erik Hesse and Nancy Kaplan, 'Predictability of Attachment Behaviour and Representational Processes at 1, 6, and 19 Years of Age', in K. E. Grossmann, K. Grossmann and E. Waters (eds), *Attachment from Infancy to Adulthood* (London: Guilford Press, 2005), pp. 245–304. The interview is thought to provoke anxiety and to reactivate the attachment system since 'the central questions force attention toward early experience and require a rapid succession of speech acts, giving speakers little time to prepare a response' yet necessitating the performance of 'rapid action (speech) choices . . . [that] . . . encourage the kind of inflexible, relatively routinized responses' that were seen in previously insecure infants (ibid., p. 291).

[53] Herbert Paul Grice, 'Logic and conversation', in P. Cole and J. L. Moran (eds), *Syntax and Semantics III: Speech Acts* (New York: Academic Press, 1975), pp. 41–58; and Paul Grice, *Studies in the Way of Words* (Cambridge, MA: Harvard University Press, 1989). Coherent transcripts were both '"consistent" (in keeping with Grice's maxim of "quality" – i.e. being internally consistent and thus most probably "truthful") and "collaborative" (adhering to Grice's maxims of "quantity," . . . and "relevance")', in other words, the speaker did not provide too much or too little information and the answers given were by and large relevant to the questions asked and did not wander off topic.

[54] Here is an example Main gives from a dismissing state of mind: 'In most texts judged dismissing, the speakers described their early relationships to their parents as good or normal, and themselves as strong and/or independent. Thus, just as their infants behaved in the Strange Situation as though nothing untoward was happening, and showed little or no overt distress in the face of what . . . for an infant are highly stressful circumstances, their parents spoke as though their childhoods had included little or no real difficulty, tending to use positive . . . adjectives for one or both parents. However . . . these texts were considered incoherent in that the speakers usually failed to support their adjectival choices ("I said she was loving because she was caring"), or . . . actively contradicted them (a "very loving" mother may, later in the text, have been described as having been so frequently angry with the speaker for hurting himself that he once had hidden

a broken arm) . . . later in the interview . . . In sum, then, like an infant who "ignores" the natural clues to danger implicit within the Strange Situation procedure, the dismissing interviewee has attempted to act as though all is/was well, despite weak or even contradictory evidence' (Main et al., 'Predictability of Attachment Behaviour', p. 276).

Chapter 12

[1] William Wordsworth, *The Prelude*: 1850, *Book XIV*, pp. 86–97.
[2] Peter Hallward makes this point repeatedly in *Deleuze and the Philosophy of Creation: Out of this World* (London: Verso, 2006). To become, for Deleuze, is 'not at all to attain a distinctive form or identity' but to be indiscernible and indeterminate, to extract 'the indefinite virtual event or force' that determines a situation or a state of being; in this sense, 'Deleuze's project is . . . austere or *subtractive*' (p. 81), meaning, with respect to the self, that we must subtract the actual in order to liberate ourselves of its hardened and suffocating crust.
[3] Hannah Arendt, *The Human Condition* (London: University of Chicago Press, 1958), p. 184.
[4] Ibid.
[5] MHF, pp. 201–202; *255*.
[6] Ibid., p. 413; *537*.
[7] Ibid., p. 292; *384*. Ricoeur here references Nietzsche's second *Untimely Meditation* where Nietzsche exhorts us to counter the excess of memory at the base of a culture that demands that history become a science.
[8] MHF, p. 426; *553*.
[9] DR, p. 242; *250*.
[10] Ibid., p. 243; *250*.
[11] Martin Heidegger, *Kant and the Problem of Metaphysics*, trans. R. Taft (Bloomington: Indiana University Press, 1990), p. 118.
[12] As Kearney notes, the 'hidden art' of the imagination that Kant referred to represented perhaps a threshold for Ricoeur across which philosophizing ended and poetics began. See Richard Kearney, 'Narrative Imagination: Between Ethics and Poetics', in *Paul Ricoeur: The Hermeneutics of Action*, ed. Richard Kearney (London: Sage, 1996) p. 174.
[13] OA, p. 164, n. 31; *194, n. 1*.
[14] Robin George Collingwood, *The Idea of History* (London: Oxford University Press, 1961) (quoted by Ricoeur, TN3, p. 145; *257–258*).
[15] Ibid., (quoted by Ricoeur, TN3, p. 307, n. 13; *257, n. 2*).
[16] Gaston Bachelard, *The Poetics of Space*, trans. by Maria Jolas (Boston, MA: Beacon, 1994), pp. xvi and xviii.
[17] Ibid., p. xvi. Bachelard references Eugène Minkowski who writes of the essence of life as a 'wellspring' existing 'in a sealed vase' whose waves, 'repeatedly echoing against the sides of this vase' fill it 'with their sonority'. See Minkowski's *Vers une cosmologie* (Paris: Aubier-Montaigne, 1967) (quoted in *Poetics of Space* as Editor's Note, p. xvi). This expansion of the faculty, to the point of it functioning as a power of being that the imagination harnesses, appears in the late eighteenth century in the work of the Scottish philosopher Dugald Stewart. In *Philosophy of*

the Human Mind (Toronto and Buffalo, NY: University of Toronto Press, 1977), Stewart describes the imagination as a 'complex' and 'unlimited' power that presupposes abstraction, judgement and taste (pp. 477–478 and 134). It is 'the great spring of human activity and the principal source of human improvement' (p. 521). The imagination operates by 'multiplying . . . beyond' what a limited scene affords us and when there is no object upon which we can rest our hopes, the imagination invites us 'beyond the dark and troubled horizon which terminates all out earthly prospects to wander unconfined in the regions of futurity' (pp. 524–526).

[18] John Sallis, *Force of Imagination: The Sense of the Elemental* (Bloomington: Indiana University Press, 2000), p. 127.

[19] Ibid., p. 129.

[20] Bachelard, *The Poetics of Space*, p. xx. He quotes this from Pierre-Jean Jouve.

[21] Gao Xingjian, *Soul Mountain*, trans. Mabel Lee (London: Harper Perennial, 2004), pp. 60–61.

[22] DR, p. 273; *284*.

[23] WP, p. 63; *62*.

[24] Ibid., p. 36; *38*.

[25] Ibid., p. 78; *75*.

[26] Martin Heidegger, 'Conversation on a Country Path about Thinking', in *Discourse on Thinking*, trans. J. M. Anderson and E. Hans Feund (New York: Harper & Row, 1966), pp. 86–87.

[27] C1, p. 120; *165*.

[28] Ibid., p. 115; *158*.

[29] Bachelard, *The Poetics of Space*, p. xviii.

[30] Joseph Falaky Nagy, *A New Introduction to Buile Suibhne* (London: Irish Texts Society, 1996), p. 2.

[31] Ibid., p. 15.

[32] DR, p. 243; *250*.

[33] OA, p. 166; *196*.

[34] Ibid., p. 166; *196–197*.

[35] Deleuze develops his understanding of the 'empty-space' from a synthesis of the work of both Lévi-Strauss and Jacques Lacan, particularly the latter's reading of Edgar Allen Poe's *The Purloined Letter* – see Lacan's *Écrits: The First Complete Edition in English*, trans. Bruce Fink (New York: Norton, 2007), pp. 6–50. Deleuze is certainly a structuralist in some sense, although he never gives priority to the signifier over the signified, as Lacan does.

[36] MHF, p. 180; *239*.

[37] DG, p. 49; *80–81*.

[38] LS, pp. 36–41; *50–56*.

[39] ID, p. 187; *262*.

[40] LS, p. 40; *55*. Indeed, more series may be involved, diachronically or synchronically, and what is signifying and what is signified may change places. A multiplicity of heterogeneous series is drawn into resonance.

[41] Ibid., p. 41; *55*.

[42] Ibid., p. 41; *55* and p. 50; *65*.

[43] Ibid., p. 49; *64*.

[44] Ibid., p. 51; *66*.

[45] ID, p. 187; *262.*

[46] Ibid., p. 183; *256.*

[47] Daniel Dennett, 'The Self as a Centre of Narrative Gravity', in B. Gertler and L. Shapiro (ed.), *Arguing About the Mind* (London: Routledge, 2007), pp. 237–247. In fact, Dennett suggests that there may be several centres of gravity towards which selves as largely fictional narratives cohere (p. 246).

[48] DR, p. 258; *267.*

[49] *Apocalypse Now Redux*, directed by Francis Ford Coppola (1979). Available in DVD, Buena Vista, 2002.

[50] 'Making-of' documentaries are available on *Apocalypse Now* in film format (*Heart of Darkness: A Filmmaker's Apocalypse,* directed by Fax Bahr and George Hicken-looper [2007, Paramount]. Available in DVD) and *Blade Runner* in narrative format (Paul M. Sammon's *Future Noir: The Making of Blade Runner,* London: Orion Media, 1996). The original source for Coppola's film is Joseph Conrad's *Heart of Darkness* (London: Penguin, 2007) while that for Ridley Scott's is Philip K. Dick's *Do Androids Dream of Electric Sheep* (London: Millennium, 1999).

[51] Robyn Brothers raises similar questions regarding the maintenance of the narrative self within traditional plot and the problematic of retaining Ricoeur's 'narrative identity' in the wake of 'the nonlinear matrix of cyberspace', hypertext and infomania. See Robyn Brothers' 'Cyborg Identities and the Relational Web: Recasting "Narrative Identity" in Moral and Political Theory', *Metaphilosophy*, 28 No. 3 (July, 1997), pp. 249–258.

[52] Adriana Cavarero familiarizes us with the story of Ulysses in his quest to find his life narrated by another. It is only when he hears his story narrated by the blind rhapsode in the court of the Phaecians that he weeps as never before. It is his epiphany, the coming together of a life. See Adriano Cavarero, *Relating Narratives: Storytelling and Selfhood,* trans. Paul Kottman (London: Routledge, 2002).

[53] MHF, p. 279; *365–366* notes that 'Narrative does not resemble the events that it recounts'.

[54] Ibid., p. 347; *454.*

[55] Ibid., p. 348; *455.*

[56] See Martin Heidegger's *Being and Time*, trans. J. Macquarrie and E. Robinson (Oxford: Basil Blackwell, 1962) which notes that, 'What is characteristic of the "time" which is accessible to the ordinary understanding' is that it is in conformity with a temporality which 'temporalizes as inauthentic the kind of "time" we have just mentioned' (p. 377). Also, 'the future has priority in the ecstatical unity of primordial and authentic temporality' (p. 378).

[57] MHF, p. 339; *445.*

[58] Ibid., p. 350; *457.*

[59] Ibid., p. 340; *445.*

[60] Ibid., p. 578, n. 62; *445, n. 65.*

[61] Ibid., p. 351; *458.*

[62] Ibid., p. 303; *398.*

[63] Ibid., p. 349; *456.*

[64] Ibid.

[65] Ibid. See also Richard Kearney's *On Stories* (London, Routledge, 2002) – Kearney notes that 'the retelling of the past is an interweaving of past events with present

readings of those events in the light of our continuing existential story' (p. 46) and that in recounting these life stories we find ourselves 'wavering between . . . an anti-narrativist and neo-narrativist stance' (p. 156).

[66] Raymond Aron, *Introduction to the Philosophy of History: An Essay on the Limits of Historical Objectivity*, trans. George J. Irwin (Boston, MA: Beacon Press, 1961; quoted by Ricoeur in MHF, p. 334; *438*).

[67] MHF, p. 356; *464*.

[68] Ibid., p. 357; *465*.

[69] Baruch Spinoza, *Ethics and the Correction of the Understanding*, trans. Andrew Boyle (London: Dent, 1986), part 4, proposition 67.

[70] MHF, pp. 360–361; *469–470*.

[71] Ibid., pp. 357–358. Ricoeur argues for the equivalence of these in 'the broadest sense' of the term 'desire'. They are two forms of desire, differentially construed. He adds to this list Leibniz's 'appetite' and 'the desire to be and the effort to exist' in Jean Nabert.

[72] Ibid., p. 358; *467*.

[73] Ibid., p. 359; *468*.

[74] Ibid., p. 359; *467*.

[75] Is not the character of Samuel Beckett's trilogy (*Molloy, Malone Dies, The Unnamable*) precisely the self that fragments into larval subjects but whose life sentence is the Heideggerian being-towards-death? See Sarah Gendron's argument in '"A Cogito for the Dissolved Self:" Writing, Presence, and the Subject in the Work of Samuel Beckett, Jacques Derrida, and Gilles Deleuze', *Journal of Modern Literature*, 28 No. 1 (Fall, 2004), pp. 47–64.

[76] Jacques Lacan, *Book XX: On Feminine Sexuality, The Limits of Love and Knowledge, 1972–1973*, ed. Jacques-Alain Miller, trans. Bruce Fink (London: Norton, 1999), pp. 61–77.

[77] MHF, p. 363; *473–474*.

[78] Ricoeur notes that '*Being and Time* ignores the problem of memory' (ibid., p. 364; *474*).

[79] Ibid., p. 364; *475*.

[80] Ibid., p. 365; *475*. Ricoeur argues that the Mediterranean plays the role of a quasi-character in Fernand Braudel, *The Mediterranean and the Mediterranean World in the Age of Philip II*, 2 vols., trans. Sián Reynolds (New York: Harper and Row, 1972–1973).

[81] MHF, p. 365; *476*.

[82] Michel de Certeau, *L'Absent de l'histoire* (Paris: Mame, 1973) (cited by Ricoeur in MHF, p. 367; *478*).

[83] Ibid., (cited by Ricoeur in ibid., pp. 581–582, n. 26; *478, n. 29*).

[84] M. M. Bakhtin, 'Discourse in the Novel', in *The Dialogic Imagination*, pp. 272–274. For a summary on heteroglossia see Sue Vice's *Introducing Bakhtin* (Manchester: Manchester University Press, 1997), pp. 18–44.

[85] MHF, p. 393; *512*.

[86] The issue of the voice in the listening and telling of narrative identity has not been addressed in this work. However, Adriana Cavarero has dealt with this in some detail in *A Più Voci: Filosphia dell'Espressione Vocale* (Milan: Feltrinelli, 2003). In particular, she stresses the uniqueness of the voice against all others even when the narrative is the same (p. 10).

[87] MHF, p. 380; *495*.

[88] Jacques Rancière, *The Names of History* (quoted by Ricoeur in ibid., p. 369; *480*).

[89] Friedrich Nietzsche. *On the Advantage and Disadvantage of History for Life*, p. 10.

Chapter 13

[1] C2, p. 96; *130*.

[2] TN3, p. 208; *376*. Ricoeur is referring to the past as a space of experience.

[3] Jacques Lacan, *Book XX: On Feminine Sexuality, The Limits of Love and Knowledge, 1972–1973*, ed. Jacques-Alain Miller, trans. Bruce Fink (London: Norton, 1999), pp. 64–77.

[4] Luce Irigaray, 'The Power of Discourse', in *This Sex Which Is Not One*, trans. C. Porter and C. Burke (Ithaca, NY: Cornell University Press, 1985), pp. 74–75.

[5] Jorge Luis Borges, 'Tlön, Uqbar, Orbis Tertius', in *Labyrinths* (London: Penguin Classics, 2000), p. 34.

[6] See Joseph Campbell's *The Hero with a Thousand Faces* (New York: Pantheon, 1949).

[7] Ibid., pp. 32–33.

[8] Adriano Cavarero, *Relating Narratives: Storytelling and Selfhood*, trans. Paul Kottman (London: Routledge, 2002).

[9] TN3, p. 438; *243*.

[10] MHF, p. 163; *204*.

[11] 'Suspicion unfolds itself along all the chain of operations that begin at the level of the perception of an experienced scene, continuing on from that of the retention of its memory, to come to focus in the declarative and narrative phase of the restitution of the features of the event' (ibid., p. 162; *202*).

[12] Ibid., p. 163; *204*.

[13] Ibid., p. 278; *364*.

[14] Ibid.

[15] Ibid., p. 166; *207*.

Bibliography

Adamov, Authur. *L'Aveu*, Paris: Editions du Sagittaire, 1946.

Adorno, Theodor. *Negative Dialectics*, trans. E. B. Ashton, New York: Continuum, 1987.

Adorno, Theodor. *Notes to Literature, Volume 1*, ed. Rolf Tiedermann, trans. Shierry Weber Nicholsen, New York: Columbia University Press, 1991.

Adorno, Theodor. *The Jargon of Authenticity*, trans. Knut Tarnowski and Frederic Will, London: Routledge, 2003.

Aeschylus, *The Orestes Plays of Aeschylus*, trans. Paul Roche, New York: Mentor, 1962.

Ainsworth, Mary and Bell, Silvia. 'Attachment, Exploration, and Separation: Illustrated by the Behaviour of One-year olds in a Strange Situation', *Child Development*, 41 No. 1 (March, 1970), pp. 49–67.

Ainsworth, M. and Wittig, B. 'Attachment and Explanatory Behavior of One-year-olds in a Strange Situation', in B. M. Foss (ed.), *Determinants of Infant Behaviour*, London: Methuen, 1969, pp. 111–136.

Ainsworth, M., Blehar, M., Waters, E. and Wall, S. *Patterns of Attachment: A Psychological Study of the Strange Situation*, Hillsdale, NJ: Erlbaum, 1978.

Alliez, Eric. *The Signature of the World: What Is Deleuze and Guattari's Philosophy?* trans. E. R. Albert and A. Toscano, London: Continuum, 2004.

Allison, Henry. *Kant's Transcendental Idealism.* New Haven, CT: Yale University Press, 1983.

Amalric, Jean-Luc. *Ricoeur, Derrida, l'enjeu de la métaphore*, Paris: Presses Universitaires de France, 2006.

Anderson, Pamela. 'Re-reading Myth in Philosophy: Hegel, Ricoeur and Irigaray Reading Antigone', in M. Joy (ed.), *Paul Ricoeur and Narrative: Context and Contestation*, Calgary: University of Calgary Press, 1997, pp. 51–68.

Andrews, Dudley. 'Tracing Ricoeur', *Diacritics*, 30 No. 2 (Summer, 2000), pp. 43–69.

Arendt, Hannah. *The Human Condition*, London: University of Chicago Press, 1958.

Aristotle. *The Complete Works of Aristotle, Vol. 1*, ed. Jonathan Barnes, Guildford: Princeton University Press, 1984.

Aristotle. *De Anima (On the Soul)*, trans. Hugh Lawson-Tancred, London: Penguin, 1986.

Aristotle. *Poetics*, trans. Malcolm Heath, London: Penguin, 1996.

Aristotle. *The Metaphysics*, trans. Hugh Lawson-Tancred, London: Penguin, 1998.

Aristotle. *The Basic Works of Aristotle,* ed. Richard McKeon, New York: The Modern Library, 2001.

Aron, Raymond. *Introduction to the Philosophy of History: An Essay on the Limits of Historical Objectivity*, trans. George J. Irwin, Boston, MA: Beacon, 1961.

Augustine, *The Confessions of St. Augustine*, trans. F. J. Sheed, London: Sheed and Ward, 1948.

Bachelard, Gaston. *The Poetics of Space*, trans. Maria Jolas, Boston, MA: Beacon, 1994.

Badiou, Alain. *Deleuze: The Clamour of Being*, trans. Louise Burchill, Minneapolis: University of Minnesota Press, 1999.

Bahr, Fax and Hickenlooper, George, dirs. *Heart of Darkness – A Filmmaker's Apocalypse*, DVD, Paramount, 2007.

Bakhtin, M. M. 'Discourse in the Novel', in Michael Holquist (ed.), *The Dialogic Imagination*, trans. Caryl Emerson and Michael Holquist, Austin: University of Texas Press, 1981.

Ballard, J. G. *The Atrocity Exhibition*, London: Flamingo, 2001.

Banville, John. *Shroud*, London: Picador, 2002.

Bateson, Gregory. *Mind and Matter: A Necessary Unity*, London: Flamingo, 1985.

Beach, Edward. *The Potencie(s) of the Gods*, Albany: State University of New York Press, 1994.

Beck, Aaron. *Cognitive Therapy and the Emotional Disorders*, New York: International Universities Press, 1976.

Beck, A. T., Rush, A. J., Shaw, B. F. and Emery, G. *Cognitive Therapy of Depression*, New York: Guilford Press, 1997.

Beck, Judith. *Cognitive Therapy: Basics and Beyond*, New York: Guildford Press, 1995.

Beckett, Samuel. *Samuel Beckett: The Complete Short Prose, 1929–1989*, ed. S. E. Gontarski, New York: Grove Press, 1995.

Bell, Jeffrey. 'Philosophizing the Double-bind: Deleuze reads Nietzsche', *Philosophy Today*, 39 No. 4 (1995), pp. 371–390.

Bergson, Henri. *Matter and Memory*, trans. N. M. Paul and W. S. Palmer, London: George Allen & Unwin, 1970.

Bergson, Henri. *Time and Free Will: An Essay on the Immediate Data of Consciousness*, trans. F. L. Pogson, New York: Dover, 2001.

Bettelheim, Bruno. *The Uses of Enchantment: The Meaning and Importance of Fairy Tales*, London: Penguin, 1978.

Blamey, Kathleen. 'From the Ego to the Self: A Philosophical Itinerary', in Lewis Edwin Hahn (ed.), *The Philosophy of Paul Ricoeur*, Chicago, IL: Open Court, 1995, pp. 571–604.

Bogue, Ronald. *Deleuze and Guattari*, London: Routledge, 1989.

Bogue, Ronald. *Deleuze on Literature*, London: Routledge, 2003.

Bogue, Ronald. 'Search, Swim and See: Deleuze's Apprenticeship to Signs and Pedagogy of Images', *Educational Philosophy and Theory*, 36 No. 3 (2004), pp. 327–342.

Bollas, Christopher. *The Shadow of the Object: Psychoanalysis of the Unthought Known*, London: Free Association Books, 1987.

Borges, Jorge Luis. *Labyrinths*, London: Penguin Classics, 2000.

Borradori, Giovanna. 'On the Presence of Bergson in Deleuze's Nietzsche', *Philosophy Today*, 43 (1999), pp. 140–145.

Borradori, Giovanna. 'The Temporalization of Difference: Reflections on Deleuze's Interpretation of Bergson', *Continental Philosophy Review*, 34 No. 1 (March, 2001), pp. 1–20.

Bostock, David. *Aristotle: Metaphysics, Book Z and H*, Oxford: Clarendon, 1994.

Bowie, Andrew. *Schelling and Modern European Philosophy: An Introduction*, London: Routledge, 1993.

Bowie, Malcolm. *Lacan*, London: Fontana, 1991.

Bowlby, John. *Attachment and Loss, Vol. 2, Separation, Anxiety and Anger*, London: Hogarth, 1973.

Bowlby, John. *Attachment and Loss, Vol. 3, Loss: Sadness and Depression*, London: Hogarth, 1980.

Bowlby, John. *Attachment and Loss, Vol. 1, Attachment* (1969), 2nd edn, New York: Basic Books, 1982.

Braudel, Fernand. *The Mediterranean and the Mediterranean World in the Age of Philip II*, 2 vols., trans. Sián Reynolds, New York: Harper & Row, 1972–1973.

Brentano, Franz. *On the Several Senses of Being in Aristotle*, ed. and trans. Rolf George, Berkeley: University of California Press, 1975.

Brothers, Robyn. 'Cyborg Identities and the Relational Web: Recasting "Narrative Identity" in Moral and Political Theory', *Metaphilosophy*, 28 No. 3 (July, 1997), pp. 249–258.

Bryant-Smith, Olav. *Myths of the Self: Narrative Identity and Postmodern Metaphysics*, Lanham, MD: Lexington Books, 2004.

Bryx, Adam and Genosko, Gary. 'Transversality', in Adrian Parr (ed.), *The Deleuze Dictionary*, Edinburgh: Edinburgh University Press, 2005, pp. 285–286.

Burton. Tim, dir. *Edward Scissorhands*, DVD, 20th Century Fox, 2000.

Bury, Robert Gregg. *The Philebus of Plato*, Cambridge: Cambridge University Press, 1897.

Campbell, Joseph. *The Hero with a Thousand Faces*, New York: Pantheon, 1949.

Carroll, Lewis. *Alice in Wonderland and Through the Looking Glass*, Hertsfordshire: Wordsworth Classics, 1993.

Carroll, Lewis. *The Hunting of the Snark*, London: Penguin Classics, 1995.

Cavarero, Adriana. *Relating Narratives: Storytelling and Selfhood*, trans. Paul Kottman, London: Routledge, 2000.

Cavarero, Adriana. *A Più Voci: Filosphia dell'Espressione Vocale*, Milan: Feltrinelli, 2003.

Certeau, Michel de, *L'Absent de l'histoire*, Paris: Mame, 1973.

Chanter, Tina. 'Antigone's Dilemma', in R. Bernasconi and S. Critchley (eds), *Re-reading Levinas*, Indianapolis: Indiana University Press, 1991, pp. 130–146.

Churchland, Paul. *The Engine of Reason: The Seat of the Soul*, Cambridge, MA: MIT Press, 1995.

Collingwood, Robin George, *The Idea of History*, London: Oxford University Press, 1961.

Conrad, Joseph. *Heart of Darkness*, London: Penguin, 2007.

Coppola, Francis Ford, dir. *Apocalypse Now Redux* (1979), DVD, Buena Vista, 2002.

Dalle Pezze, Barbara. 'Heidegger on Gelassenheit', *Minerva – An Internet Journal of Philosophy*, 10 (2006), pp. 94–122, available at www.mic.ul.ie/stephen/vol10/Heidegger.pdf, accessed 29 January, 2008.

Damasio, Antonio. *The Feeling of What Happens: Body, Emotion and the Making of Consciousness*, London: Vintage, 2000.

DeLanda, Manuel. *Intensive Science and Virtual Philosophy*, London: Continuum, 2002.

Deleuze, Gilles. *Nietzsche et la philosophie*, Paris: Presses Universitaires de France, 1962.

Deleuze, Gilles. *La philosophie critique de Kant*, 3rd edn, Paris: Presses Universitaires de France, 1963.

Deleuze, Gilles. *Le Bergsonisme*, Paris: Presses Universitaires de France, 1966.

Deleuze, Gilles. *Différence et repetition*, Paris: Presses Universitaires de France, 1968a.

Deleuze, Gilles. *Spinoza et le problème de l'expression*, Paris: Minuit, 1968b.

Deleuze, Gilles. *Logique du sens*, Paris: Minuit, 1969.

Deleuze, Gilles. *Proust et les signes*, 3rd edition, Paris: Presses Universitaires de France, 1976.

Deleuze, Gilles. *Cinema 1, L'image-mouvement*, Paris: Minuit, 1983a.

Deleuze, Gilles. *Nietzsche and Philosophy*, trans. H. Tomlinson, New York: Columbia University Press, 1983b.

Deleuze, Gilles. *Kant's Critical Philosophy: The Doctrine of the Faculties,* trans. H. Tomlinson and B. Habberjam, London: Athlone, 1984.

Deleuze, Gilles. *Cinema 2, L'image-temps*, Paris: Minuit, 1985.

Deleuze, Gilles. *Pourparlers*, Paris: Minuit, 1990.

Deleuze, Gilles. *Bergsonism*, trans. H. Tomlinson and B. Habberjam, New York: Zone Books, 1991.

Deleuze, Gilles. *Expressionism in Philosophy: Spinoza*, trans. M. Joughin, New York: Zone Books, 1992.

Deleuze, Gilles. *Critique et clinique*, Paris: Minuit, 1993.

Deleuze, Gilles. *Negotiations*, trans. M. Joughin, New York: Columbia University Press, 1995.

Deleuze, Gilles. *Essays Critical and Clinical*, trans. D. Smith and M. Greco, London: Verso, 1998.

Deleuze, Gilles. 'Bergson's Conception of Difference', in John Mullarkey (ed.), *The New Bergson*, Manchester: Manchester University Press, 1999, pp. 42–65.

Deleuze, Gilles. *Proust and Signs*, trans. R. Howard, London: Athlone, 2000.

Deleuze, Gilles. *The Logic of Sense*, ed. C. Boundas, trans. M. Lester and C. Stivale, London: Continuum, 2001.

Deleuze, Gilles. *L'île déserte et autres texts: Textes et entretiens 1953–1974*, Paris: Minuit, 2002.

Deleuze, Gilles. *Desert Islands and Other Texts (1953–1974)*, ed. D. Lapoujade, trans. M. Taormina, Los Angeles: Semiotext(e), 2004a.

Deleuze, Gilles. *Difference and Repetition*, trans. P. Patton, London: Continuum, 2004b.

Deleuze, Gilles. *Cinema 1: The Movement Image*, trans. H. Tomlinson and B. Habberjam, London: Continuum, 2005a.

Deleuze, Gilles. *Cinema 2: The Time Image,* trans. H. Tomlinson and R. Galeta, London: Continuum, 2005b.

Deleuze, Gilles and Guattari, Félix. *Anti-oedipe*, Paris: Minuit, 1972.

Deleuze, Gilles and Guattari, Félix. *Capitalisme et schizophrenie Tome 2: Mille plateaux*, Paris: Éditions de Minuit, 1980.

Deleuze, Gilles and Guattari, Félix. *Qu'est-ce que la philosophie?*, Paris: Minuit, 1991.

Deleuze, Gilles and Guattari, Félix. *What is Philosophy?*, trans. G. Burchell and H. Tomlinson, London: Verso, 1994.

Deleuze, Gilles and Guattari, Félix. *A Thousand Plateaus: Capitalism and Schizophrenia*, trans. B. Massumi, London: Continuum, 2003.

Deleuze, Gilles and Guattari, Félix. *Anti-Oedipus*, trans. R. Hurley, M. Seem and H. Lane, London: Continuum, 2004.

Deleuze, Gilles and Parnet, Claire. *Dialogues*, Paris: Flammarion, 1977.

Deleuze, Gilles and Parnet, Claire. *Dialogues II*, trans. H. Tomlinson and B. Habberjam, London: Continuum, 2006.

DeLillo, Don. *Underworld*, London: Picador, 1997.

Dennett, Daniel. *Brainstorms*, Sussex: Harvester, 1978.

Dennett, Daniel. *Consciousness Explained*, London: Penguin, 1993.

Dennett, Daniel. 'The Self as a Centre of Narrative Gravity', in B. Gertler and L. Shapiro (eds), *Arguing about the Mind*. London: Routledge, 2007, pp. 237–247.

Derrida, Jacques. 'Le Facteur de la Vérité', in *The Post Card: From Socrates to Freud and Beyond*, trans. A. Bass, Chicago and London: University of Chicago Press, 1987, pp. 413–496.

Descartes, René. *Discourse on Method and the Meditations*, trans. F. Sutcliffe, Middlesex: Penguin, 1968.

Dick, Philip K. *Do Androids Dream of Electric Sheep?* London: Millennium, 1999.

Di Maria, Theodore. 'Kant's View of the Self in the First Critique', *Idealistic Studies*, 32 No. 3 (2002), pp. 191–202.

Duffy, Simon. 'The Logic of Expression in Deleuze's *Expressionism in Philosophy: Spinoza*: A Strategy of Engagement', *International Journal of Philosophical Studies*, 12 No. 1 (2004), pp. 47–60.

Duffy, Simon (ed). *Virtual Mathematics: The Logic of Difference*, Bolton: Clinamen, 2006.

Dunne, Joseph. 'The Storied Self', in Richard Kearney (ed.), *Paul Ricoeur: The Hermeneutics of Action*, London: Sage, 1996, pp. 137–157.

Elster, Jon. 'Introduction', in Jon Elster (ed.), *The Multiple Self*, Cambridge: Cambridge University Press, 1987, pp. 1–34.

Emerson, Ralph Waldo. 'Circles', in *Essays and Lectures*, New York: New American Library, 1983.

Erdelyi, M. H. 'A New Look at the New Look: Perceptual Defence and Vigilance', *Psychological Review*, 81 No. (1974), pp. 1–25.

Fink, Bruce. 'The Master Signifier and the Four Discourses', in Dany Nobus (ed.), *Key Concepts of Lacanian Psychoanalysis*, London: Rebus, 1998, pp. 29–47.

Foucault, Michel. *Madness and Civilisation: A History of Insanity in the Age of Reason*, trans. Richard Howard, London: Tavistock, 1967.

Freud, Sigmund. 'Analysis of a Phobia in a Five Year Old Boy', in *The Complete Psychological Works of Sigmund Freud, Vol. X (1909)*, std edn, trans. James Strachey, London: Hogarth, 1955, pp. 1–149.

Freud, Sigmund. 'On Narcissism: An Introduction', in *The Complete Psychological Works of Sigmund Freud, Vol. XIV (1914)*, std edn, trans. James Strachey, London: Hogarth, 1957, pp. 67–102.

Freud, Sigmund. 'Inhibitions, Symptoms and Anxiety', in *The Complete Psychological Works of Sigmund Freud, Vol. XX (1925–1926)*, std edn, trans. James Strachey, London: Hogarth, 1959, pp. 77–175.

Freud, Sigmund. 'The Ego and the Id', *The Complete Psychological Works of Sigmund Freud, Vol. XIX (1923)*, std edn, trans. James Strachey, London: Hogarth, 1961, pp. 1–66.

Freud, Sigmund. 'The Dissolution of the Oedipus Complex' (1924), in *The Essentials of Psychoanalysis*, ed. Anna Freud, trans. James Strachey, Middlesex: Pelican Books, 1986a, pp. 395–401.

Freud, Sigmund. 'Femininity' (1933), in *The Essentials of Psychoanalysis*, ed. Anna Freud, trans. James Strachey, Middlesex: Pelican Books, 1986b, pp. 412–432.

Freud, Sigmund. 'The Infantile Genital Organization' (1923), in *The Essentials of Psychoanalysis*, ed. Anna Freud, trans. James Strachey, Middlesex: Pelican Books, 1986c, pp. 390–394.

Freud, Sigmund. 'Three Essays on the Theory of Sexuality' (1905), in *The Essentials of Psychoanalysis*, ed. Anna Freud, trans. James Strachey, Middlesex: Pelican Books, 1986d, pp. 277–375.

Gadamer, Hans-Georg, *Plato's Dialectical Ethics: Phenomenological Interpretations Relating to the Philebus*, New Haven, CT: Yale University Press, 1991.

Gendron, Sarah. '"A Cogito for the Dissolved Self:" Writing, Presence, and the Subject in the Work of Samuel Beckett, Jacques Derrida, and Gilles Deleuze', *Journal of Modern Literature*, 28 No. 1 (Fall, 2004), pp. 47–64.

George, C., Kaplan, N. and Main, M. *An Adult Attachment Interview*, unpublished manuscript, University of California at Berkeley, Department of Psychology, 1985.

Golding, William. *Lord of the Flies*, New York: Capricorn, 1959.

Grice, Herbert Paul. 'Logic and Conversation', in P. Cole and J. L. Moran (eds), *Syntax and Semantics III: Speech Acts* (New York: Academic Press, 1975), pp. 41–58.

Grice, Herbert Paul. *Studies in the Way of Words*, Cambridge, MA: Harvard University Press, 1989.

Grossman, David. *See Under: Love*, London: Jonathan Cape, 1990.

Gualandi, Alberto. *Deleuze*, Paris: Les Belles Lettres, 2003.

Hallward, Peter. *Deleuze and the Philosophy of Creation: Out of This World*, London: Verso, 2006.

Hayden, Patrick. *Multiplicity and Becoming: The Pluralist Empiricism*, New York: Peter Lang, 1998.

Hayward, Susan. *Cinema Studies*, London: Routledge, 2000.

Heaney, Seamus. *Sweeney Astray*, London: Faber and Faber, 1983.

Heidegger, Martin. *Being and Time*, trans. J. Macquarrie and E. Robinson, Oxford: Basil Blackwell, 1962.

Heidegger, Martin. 'Conversation on a Country Path about Thinking', in *Discourse on Thinking*, trans. J. M. Anderson and E. Hans Feund, New York: Harper & Row, 1966a.

Heidegger, Martin. 'Memorial Address', in *Discourse on Thinking*, trans. J. M. Anderson and E. Hans Feund, New York: Harper & Row, 1966b.

Heidegger, Martin. *Kant and the Problem of Metaphysics*, trans. R. Taft, Bloomington: Indiana University Press, 1990.

Heidegger, Martin. *Nietzsche, Vol. II: The Eternal Recurrence of the Same*, trans. D. F. Krell, San Francisco: Harper Collins, 1991.

Hunter, G. K. 'Introduction', in William Shakespeare. *Macbeth*, ed. G. K. Hunter, Middlesex: New Penguin, 1967, pp. 7–45.

Husserl, Edmund. *Cartesian Meditations: An Introduction to Phenomenology*, trans. by Dorian Cairns, Dordrecht: Kluwer, 1973.

Ionescu, Eugene, 'Rhinoceros', in *Rhinoceros, The Chairs, The Lesson*, trans. by Derek Prouse, London: Penguin, 1962, pp. 9–124.

Irigaray, Luce. *This Sex Which Is Not One*, trans. C. Porter and C. Burke, Ithaca, NY: Cornell University Press, 1985.

Irigaray, Luce. *Speculum of the Other Woman*, trans. G. C. Gill, Ithaca, NY: Cornell University Press, 1992.

Irigaray, Luce. *The Way of Love*, trans. H. Bostic and S. Pluhček, London: Continuum Press, 2002.

Kant, Immanuel. *Critique of Pure Reason*, rev. and trans. J. M. D. Meiklejohn, ed. Vasilis Politis, London: Everyman, 1993.

Kaufmann, Walter. *Nietzsche: Philosopher, Psychologist, Antichrist*, Princeton: Princeton University Press, 1968.

Kearney, Richard. *Dialogues with Contemporary Continental Thinkers*, Manchester: Manchester University Press, 1984.

Kearney, Richard. *The Wake of Imagination*, London: Routledge, 1988.

Kearney, Richard. 'Narrative Imagination: Between Ethics and Poetics', in *Paul Ricoeur: The Hermeneutics of Action*, ed. Richard Kearney, London: Sage, 1996, pp. 173–190.

Kearney, Richard. *On Stories*, London, Routledge, 2002.

Kelly, George. *The Psychology of Personal Constructs*, Vol. 1, New York: Norton, 1955.

Kelly, Michael. 'Self-Awareness and Ontological Monism: Why Kant Is Not an Ontological Monist', *Idealistic Studies*, 32 No. 3 (2002), pp. 237–254.

Kemp, Peter. 'Mémoire et oubli: de Bergson à Ricoeur', *L'Herne: Paul Ricoeur*, 81 (2004), pp. 246–255.

Kolb, Brian and Whishaw, Ian Q. *Fundamentals of Human Neuropsychology*, 5th edn, New York: Worth, 2003.

Körner, S. *Kant*, Middlesex: Penguin, 1955.

Lacan, Jacques. *Book XX: On Feminine Sexuality, The Limits of Love and Knowledge, 1972–1973*, ed. Jacques-Alain Miller, trans. Bruce Fink, London: Norton, 1999.

Lacan, Jacques. *The Other Side of Psychoanalysis: The Seminar of Jacques Lacan, Book XVII*, trans. Russell Grigg, London: Norton, 2006.

Lacan, Jacques. *Écrits: The First Complete Edition in English*, trans. Bruce Fink, New York: Norton, 2007.

Laplanche, Jean and Pontalis, J-B. *The Language of Psychoanalysis*, London: Hogarth, 1973.

Lawlor, Leonard. *Imagination and Chance: Difference between the Thought of Ricoeur and Derrida*, New York: State University of New York Press, 1993.

Lawson-Tancred, Hugh. 'Introduction', in *The Metaphysics*, trans. Hugh Lawson-Tancred, London: Penguin, 1998, pp. lv–lvi.

Lawson-Tancred, Hugh. 'Introduction' and 'Glossary', in *De Anima (On the Soul)*, trans. Hugh Lawson-Tancred, London: Penguin, 1986, pp. 11–122.

Lecercle, Jean-Jacques. *Philosophy through the Looking Glass: Language, Nonsense, Desire*, La Salle, IL: Open Court, 1985.

Leibniz, Gottfried. 'The Monadology', in Anthony Savile, *Routledge Philosophy Guidebook to Leibniz and the Monadology*, London: Routledge, 2000.

Levi, Primo. *Other People's Trades*, trans. Raymond Rosenthal, London: Michael Joseph, 1989.

Levin, David. *The Philosopher's Gaze: Modernity in the Shadows of Enlightenment*, Berkeley: University of California Press, 1999.

Lingis, Alfonso. 'The Last Form of the Will to Power', *Philosophy Today*, 22 No. 3 (1978), pp. 193–205.

Lloyd, Genevieve. *Being in Time: Selves and Narrative in Philosophy and Literature*, London: Routledge, 1993.

McCarthy, Cormac. *Cities of the Plain*, London: Picador, 1998.

Main, Mary, Hesse, Erik and Kaplan, Nancy. 'Predictability of Attachment Behaviour and Representational Processes at 1, 6, and 19 Years of Age', in K. E. Grossmann, and E. Waters (eds), *Attachment from Infancy to Adulthood*, London: Guilford Press, 2005, pp. 245–304.

Makkreel, Rudolf. 'Imagination and Temporality in Kant's Theory of the Sublime', *The Journal of Aesthetics and Art Criticism*, 42 No. 3 (Spring, 1984), pp. 303–315.

Mark, John. 'W. G. Sebald: Invisible and Intangible Forces', *New Formations*, 55 (Spring, 2005), pp. 89–103.

Meichenbaum, David. *Cognitive-Behaviour Modification: An Integrative Approach*, New York: Plenum, 1977.

Merleau-Ponty, Maurice. *The Visible and the Invisible*, trans. Alphonso Lingis, Evanston, IL: Northwestern University Press, 1968.

Merleau-Ponty, Maurice. *Phenomenology of Perception*, trans. Colin Smith, London: Routledge, 2004.

Minkowski, Eugène, *Vers une cosmologie*, Paris: Aubier-Montaigne, 1967.

Mongin, Olivier. 'L'excès et la dette: Gilles Deleuze and Paul Ricoeur ou l'impossible conversation?', *L'Herne: Paul Ricoeur*, 81 (2004), pp. 271–283.

Muldoon, Mark. 'Ricoeur and Merleau-Ponty on Narrative Identity', *American Catholic Philosophical Quarterly*, 71 No. 1 (1997), pp. 35–52.

Nagy, Joseph Falaky. *A New Introduction to Buile Suibhne*, London: Irish Texts Society, 1996.

Nancy, Jean-Luc. *Being Singular Plural*, trans. Robert Richardson and Anne O'Byrne, Stanford, CA: Stanford University Press, 2000.

Nietzsche, Friedrich. *On the Advantage and Disadvantage of History for Life*, trans. Peter Preuss, Indianapolis, IN: Hackett, 1980.

Norman, Judith. 'Nietzsche contra *Contra*: Difference and Opposition', *Continental Philosophy Review*, 33 (2000), pp. 189–206.

Nussbaum, Martha. *The Fragility of Goodness: Luck and Ethics in Greek Tragedy and Philosophy*, Cambridge: Cambridge University Press, 1986.

O'Keeffe, J. G. (ed. and trans.) *Buile Suibhne (The Frenzy of Sweeney) being The Adventures of Suibne Geilt*, London: Irish Texts Society, 1913.

Olkowski, Dorothea. 'Nietzsche–Deleuze: The Aesthetics and Ethics of Chance', *Journal of the British Society of Phenomenology*, 26 No. 1 (1995), pp. 27–42.

O'Rourke, Fran. 'Aristotle and the Metaphysics of Evolution', *The Review of Metaphysics*, 58 (Sept., 2004), pp. 3–59.

Pagel, Heinz. *The Cosmic Code: Quantum Physics as the Language of Nature*, Middlesex: Penguin, 1984.

Parfit, Derek. *Reasons and Persons*, Oxford: Clarendon, 1986.

Parr, Adrian. 'Deterritorialisation/Reterritorialisation', in Adrian Parr (ed.), *The Deleuze Dictionary*, Edinburgh: Edinburgh University Press, 2005, pp. 66–69.

Pearson, Keith Ansell. *Germinal Life: The Difference and Repetition of Deleuze*, London: Routledge, 1999.

Pearson, Keith Ansell. *Philosophy and the Adventure of the Virtual: Bergson and the Time of Life*, London: Routledge, 2002.

Peterfreund, Emanuel. *Information, Systems, and Psychoanalysis: An Evolutionary Biological Approach to Psychoanalytic Theory* (Psychological Issues, Monograph 25/26), New York: International Universities Press, 1971.

Politis, Vasilis. *Aristotle and the Metaphysics*, London: Routledge, 2004.

Prigogine, Ilya and Stengers, Isabelle. *Order out of Chaos: Man's New Dialogue with Nature*, London: Heinemann, 1984.

Proust, Marcel. *In Search of Lost Time, Volume VI: Time Regained*, trans. A. Mayor and T. Kilmartin, rev. D. J. Enright. London: Vintage, 2000.

Proust, Marcel. *In Search of Lost Time, Volume 1: Swann's Way*, trans. S. Moncrieff and T. Kilmartin, rev. D. J. Enright. London: Vintage, 2002a.

Proust, Marcel. *In Search of Lost Time Vol. II: Within a Budding Grove*, trans. S. Moncrieff and T. Kilmartin, rev. D. J. Enright. London: Vintage, 2002b.

Ricoeur, Paul. *L'Homme faillible*, Paris: Aubier, 1960.

Ricoeur, Paul. *De l'interprétation. Essai sur Freud*, Paris: Seuil, 1965.

Ricoeur, Paul. *Freud and Philosophy: An Essay on Interpretation*, trans. Denis Savage, New Haven, CT and London: Yale University Press, 1970.

Ricoeur, Paul. *La métaphore vive*, Paris: Seuil, 1975.

Ricoeur, Paul. *The Rule of Metaphor*, trans. R. Czerny with K. McLaughlin and J. Costello, Toronto and Buffalo, NY: University of Toronto Press, 1977.

Ricoeur, Paul. *Temps et récit. Tome 1*, Paris: Seuil, 1983.

Ricoeur, Paul. *Temps et récit. Tome 2*, Paris: Seuil, 1984a.

Ricoeur, Paul. *Time and Narrative Vol. 1*, trans. K. McLaughlin and D. Pellauer, Chicago: University of Chicago, 1984b.

Ricoeur, Paul. *Temps et récit. Tome 3*, Paris: Seuil, 1985a.

Ricoeur, Paul. *Time and Narrative Vol. 2*, trans. K. McLaughlin and D. Pellauer, Chicago: University of Chicago Press, 1985b.

Ricoeur, Paul. *Fallible Man*, trans. Charles Kelbley, New York: Fordham University Press, 1986.

Ricoeur, Paul. *Time and Narrative Vol. 3*, trans. K. Blamey and D. Pellauer, Chicago: University of Chicago Press, 1988.

Ricoeur, Paul. *Soi-même comme un autre*, Paris: Seuil, 1990.

Ricoeur, Paul. *Oneself as Another*, trans. K. Blamey, Chicago and London: University of Chicago Press, 1992.

Ricoeur, Paul. *La mémoire, l'histoire, l'oubli*, Paris: Seuil, 2000.

Ricoeur, Paul. '"La Conviction et la Critique." Entretien recueilli à l'occasion de ses 90 ans par Nathalie Crom, Bruno Frappat, Robert Migliorini', *L'Herne: Paul Ricoeur*, 81 (2004a), pp. 15–18.

Ricoeur, Paul. *Memory, History, Forgetting*, trans. K. Blamey and D. Pellauer, London: University of Chicago Press, 2004b.

Romano, Giacomo. 'Minimal Personhood', unpublished article, University of Siena, 2007.

Rousseau, Jean-Jacques. *The Confessions*, trans. anonymous, London: Wordsworth, 1996.

Rutter, Michael. 'Clinical Implications of Attachment Concepts: Retrospect and Prospect', in M. Hertzig and E. Farber (eds), *Annual Progress in Child Psychiatry and Child Development*, New York: Brunner/Mazel, 1996, pp. 127–156.

Rycroft, Charles. *A Critical Dictionary of Psychoanalysis*, Middlesex: Penguin, 1972.

Safranski, Rüdiger. *Nietzsche: A Philosophical Biography*, London: Granta Books, 2002.

Sallis, John. *Force of Imagination: The Sense of the Elemental*, Bloomington: Indiana University Press, 2000.

Sammon, Paul, M. *Future Noir: The Making of Blade Runner*, London: Orion Media, 1996.

Schelling, F. W. J. *System of Transcendental Idealism (1800)*, trans. Peter Heath, University Press of Virginia: Charlottesville, 1978.

Schelling, F. W. J. *The Unconditional in Human Knowledge: Four Early Essays (1794–1796)*, trans. Fritz Marti, Lewisburg, PA: Bucknell University Press, 1980.

Schelling, F. W. J. *Philosophical Investigations into the Nature of Human Freedom*, ed. E. D'Araille, trans. J. Gutman, London: Living Time Press, 2002.

Scott, Ridley, dir. *Blade Runner - the Final Cut*, DVD, Warner Bros., 2007.

Sebald, W. G. *Austerlitz*, trans. Anthea Bell, London: Penguin, 2001.

Semetsky, Inna. 'Deleuze's New Image of Thought, or Dewey Revisited', *Educational Philosophy and Theory*, 35 No. 1 (2003), pp. 17–29.

Shakespeare, William. *Macbeth*, Middlesex: New Penguin, 1967.

Shields, Christopher. *Aristotle*, London: Routledge, 2007.

Simms, Karl. *Paul Ricoeur*, London: Routledge, 2003.

Simon, Fritz, Stierlin, Helm and Wynne, Lyman. *The Language of Family Therapy: A Systemic Vocabulary and Sourcebook*, New York: Family Process Press, 1985.

Snow, Dale. *Schelling and the End of Idealism*, Albany: State University of New York Press, 1996.

Solomon, Robert C. *Continental Philosophy Since 1750: The Rise and Fall of the Self – A History of Western Philosophy: 7*, Oxford: Oxford University Press, 1988.

Sophocles. *Antigone, Oedipus the King, Electra*, ed. E. Hall, trans. H. Kitto, Oxford: Oxford University Press, 1998.

Spinoza, Baruch. *Ethics and the Correction of the Understanding*, trans. Andrew Boyle, London: Dent, 1986.

Stewart, Dugald. *Philosophy of the Human Mind*, Toronto and Buffalo, NY: University of Toronto Press, 1977.

Strawson, Galen. 'Against Narrative', in B. Gertler and L. Shapiro (eds), *Arguing about the Mind* (London: Routledge, 2007), pp. 248–261.

Tarantino, Quentin, dir. *Pulp Fiction* (1994), in *The Quentin Tarantino Collection* (8 Disc Set), Buena Vista, 2007.

Todorov, Tzvetan. *Hope and Memory*, trans. David Bellos, London: Atlantic Books, 2003.

Toscano, Alberto. 'Phenomenology + Husserl, Edmund (1859–1939)', in Andrew Parr (ed.), *The Deleuze Dictionary*, Edinburgh: Edinburgh University Press, 2005, pp. 202–204.

Tulving, E. 'Episodic and Semantic Memory', in E. Tulving and W. Donaldson (eds), *Organization of Memory*, New York: Academic Press, 1972, pp. 381–403.

Vater, Michael. 'Introduction', in F. W. J. Schelling's *System of Transcendental Idealism*, Charlottesville: University Press of Virginia, 1993, pp. xi–xxxvi.

Venema, Henry Isaac. *Identifying Selfhood: Imagination, Narrative and Hermeneutics in the Thought of Paul Ricoeur*, New York: State University of New York Press, 2000.

Vice, Sue. *Introducing Bhaktin*, Manchester: Manchester University Press, 1997, pp. 18–44.

von Wright, Georg. *Explanation and Understanding*, Ithaca, NY: Cornell University Press, 1971.

Weber, Max. *The Methodology of the Social Sciences*, trans. Edward Shils and Henry Finch, New York: Free Press, 1949.

Wenders, Wim, dir. *Room 666* (1982), in *Wim Wenders Box Set* (10 Discs), Anchor Bay Entertainment, 2007.

White, David and Epston, David. *Narrative Means to Therapeutic Ends*, New York: Norton, 1990.

Williams, James. *Gilles Deleuze's 'Difference and Repetition': A Critical Introduction and Guide*, Edinburgh: Edinburgh University Press, 2003.

Wirth, Jason M. (ed). *Schelling Now: Contemporary Readings*, Bloomington, IN: Indianapolis University Press, 2005.

Witt, Charlotte. *Ways of Being: Potentiality and Actuality in Aristotle's Metaphysics*, Ithaca, NY and London: Cornell University Press, 2003.

Woolf, Virginia. *The Waves*, London: Grafton, 1977.

Wordsworth, William. *The Prelude: The Four Texts (1798, 1799, 1805, 1850)*, ed. Jonathan Wordsworth. London: Penguin, 1995.

Xingjian, Gao. *Soul Mountain*, trans. Mabel Lee, London: Harper Perennial, 2004.

Zeanah, C. H. and Zeanah P. D. 'Intergenerational Transmission of Maltreatment: Insights from Attachment Theory and Research', *Psychiatry*, 52 (1989), pp. 177–196.

Žižek, Slavoj. *Organs without Bodies: On Deleuze and Consequences*, New York and London: Routledge, 2004.

Žižek, Slavoj. *The Parallax View*, London: MIT Press, 2006.

Index

Printed in Great Britain
by Amazon

47535653R00149